HARDPRESS.NET
HOME OF HARD-TO-FIND BOOKS

The Travels and Adventures of Edward Brown ...
by John Campbell

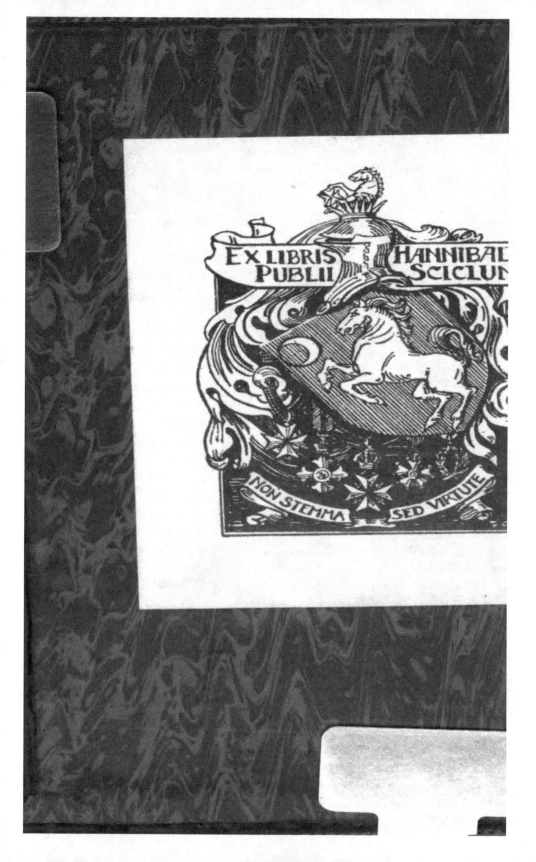

THE
TRAVELS
AND
ADVENTURES
OF
EDWARD BROWN, *Esq*;

Formerly a MERCHANT in *London*.

CONTAINING

His OBSERVATIONS on *France* and *Italy*; his Voyage to the *Levant*; his Account of the *Isle* of *Malta*; his REMARKS in his Journies thro' the lower and upper *Egypt*; together with a brief DESCRIPTION of the *Abyssinian* Empire.

Intersperded throughout

With several curious Historical PASSAGES relating to our own as well as Foreign Nations; as also with Critical Disquisitions as to the present State of the Sciences in *Egypt*, particularly Physic and Chemistry.

LONDON: Printed by J. APPLEBEE,

For A. BETTESWORTH, and C. HITCH, at the *Red-Lyon* in *Pater-noster-Row*; WILLIAM HINCHLIFFE, at *Dryden's-Head*, under the *Piazza* of the *Royal-Exchange*; and STEPHEN AUSTEN, at the *Angel* and *Bible* in St. *Paul's* *Church-Yard*. M DCC XXXIX.

THE

PREFACE.

I T is neither out of a Desire to prepossess the Reader in Favour of the following Sheets, nor yet meerly to comply with a Ceremony which Custom hath long confirm'd, a Point of good Breeding between an Author and his Readers, that I prefix a Preface to these Travels. Two Reasons determined me thereto, First, that the candid Peruser might receive all the Satisfaction in my Power, as to the Gentleman who wrote this Book; and Secondly, that I might clear myself from any

Charge

Charge of Impertinence or want of Circumspection, in giving to the World the private Papers of a Person long since deceased, who as he chose to live unknown, might well be supposed to have wished after Death, that he might be forgotten.

THE first Scenes of this Gentleman's Life are so accurately described by his own Pen, that it would be not only needless, but impertinent in me to say any Thing of them here. After his Return to England he settled as a Merchant, not so much with a View to Profit, as to keep his Thoughts employ'd, being equally an Enemy to, and incapable of bearing Idleness. His great Abilities and his Experience, drawn both from Reading and Travel, gained him not only the Acquaintance, but an Intimacy with several Persons of Distinction, which he the more easily maintained, because his own Circumstances were easy, and so he had no Occasion, as in himself he had no Will to trouble them for Favours. Besides these Friends at Home, our Author kept up a constant and general Correspondence with Persons of Learning, as well as Business abroad, of which he preserved an exact Journal, and caused all their Letters to be fair copied. This Manner of employing his Time the Reader will perceive he took up early, and he continued it (as I believe most Men do whatever pleases plaçes them in their Youth) the beſt Part of his Life. His Writings were therefore always held valuable by his Relations, to whom I am indebted for the Acceſs I have had to them, and would willingly make them more ample Acknowledgments, if I were not reſtrained by their expreſs Commands. The Leave they have given me to transcribe his Memoirs, being founded only in a generous Deſire of rendering Service to the Publick, and not out of any Vanity whatſoever.

WHEN Mr. Brown grew pretty far in Years, he retired into the Country for his Health, and lived ſome where in the Vicinity of Buxton-Wells, whence many of his laſt Letters are dated, and where it appears that he reviewed all his Papers. He came afterwards up to London on ſome particular Buſineſs, and being ſurprized by a Pleuretick Fever, died in the Winter of 1704. He left a conſiderable Sum of Money behind him to ſome diſtant Relations of his own, and his Wife's, having had no Children. He was always eſteemed a Man of great Modeſty in his Diſpoſition, extremely moderate in his Sentiments, a Friend to Learning, without affecting to be learned, ſincerely pious, without any Tincture of Bigotry, and ſo little inclined to Party, that I am not able to learn to which Side he leaned ; even in thoſe Times when

when almoſt every Man ranged himſelf with the Whigs, *or with the* Tories.

AS *to the Publication of theſe Travels, it will appear from the firſt Pages of them, that the Author had it not abſolutely in View to hinder their ſeeing the Light. On the contrary, he either had ſome Thoughts of publiſhing them himſelf, tho' perhaps in another Dreſs, or he had Foreſight enough to apprehend that they would one Day find a Reader, who would think it unjuſt to delight himſelf with the peruſal of them, without deſiring to communicate that Delight to his Countrymen. It is plain therefore, that in committing this Volume to the Preſs, I have not violated the Will of the Dead. As to the Merit of the Work itſelf, I apprehend it will ſpeak for itſelf. It is full of very entertaining Relations, curious Reſearches into Hiſtory, as well private as publick, and abounds with Diſcoveries in thoſe Places where they are leaſt expected. As to the Language it is very natural and intelligible, tho' altogether artleſs and unaffected. Mr.* Brown *meant to draw the Pictures of himſelf and of other Men, as like as he could, and not with thoſe fine Strokes and agreeable Touches which delight us ſo much in* French *Memoirs, and in Courtly Panegyrics.*

THE

THE several Passages in this Book relating to English *Affairs, may not only be depended on as* Facts, *but with respect to their Circumstances also, may be safely regarded as impartial Narrations, falling from the Pen of a Man altogether void of Party. The Author as he left his Country young, and without having addicted himself to any Faction, so from those with whom he conversed abroad, it is very evident he acquired full Satisfaction, that the Bigots of all Parties were either Slaves to their Passions or their Interests ; and therefore as Men visibly misled, were least of all fit to lead others. Hence without Doubt it came to pass, that he contracted that coolness and moderation which distinguishes all his Accounts of Things, from those we have already had, and sets them in such a Light, as leaves the Reader no just Ground to doubt, that it is the true one.*

ALL the concise Memoirs of Persons of Distinction which are inserted in his Work, are penn'd with much Impartiality, and exhibit nothing to the Reader's View, but what tends to his Information and Instruction. They are not indeed very regular or conformable to those Rules which of late Years have been established in Biography, but they are pleasant and natural ; they come in pertinently, are
told

told with Spirit, and are generally concluded with useful Reflections. This was a fashionable Method of writing in the last Age, and a Method which needs no Excuse to be made for it in this, wherein, if we have learned to compose with greater Accuracy and neatness, we have perhaps lost something of that masculine Vigour which is discernable in the Characters drawn by former Writers. While I am on this Subject, I cannot forbear observing, that the Account he has given us of the Italian Duke of Northumberland, is alone sufficient to make the Book valuable. I remember that in the Year 1718, when it was said that an unfortunate Italian Marquiss was lineally descended from that famous Duke who made such a Figure in the Courts of Henry VIII. and Edward VI. and from the no less famous Earl of Leicester, the first of Queen Elizabeth's Favourites; I say, I remember when this was talked of, it was looked on as a Fable, and many believ'd it a Story invented to do Honour to a certain Family. From this Author it appears not only that the Fact was true, but there are also a multitude of other Facts assembled, relating to the same Family, which I believe are not to be met with any where else. The collecting all these scatter'd Memoirs, was certainly an Act of virtuous Compassion, since the House of Dudley was

then

then in no Condition to repay him, or any other Man for Civilities of this sort; neither does it appear, that he compiled this Account with any other View than to satisfy his intimate Friends as to the State of this once illustrious Family, and to wipe away that Aspersion which the ignorant had thrown on the unhappy, by intimating that these Dukes were of their own making.

THE Descriptions he has given us of France, Italy, Malta, Egypt, &c. are such as shew that the Genius and Disposition of the People made as strong an Impression on him, as the natural or artificial Wonders of their respective Countries. He is equally an Admirer of Men and Things, examines both candidly, and wherever he can be suspected of erring, it is on the right Side. He had it seems, a great Delight in collecting scattered Pieces of History of all sorts, and was as well pleased to contemplate the Steadiness and solid Prudence of a Dutch Skipper, as the wonderful variety of Adventures which have happened to Princes, publick Ministers or Favourites, of which however we find Instances in his Writings. I know it may be objected, that we have already many particular Accounts of Egypt, but this has so little to do with the present Affair, that I am positive if we did not know from their Titles that the Accounts tents we already have, relate to the same Country of which Mr. Brown speaks, we should scarce discern it from the Comparison of their Contents, as I could easily shew, if it were not for anticipating the Reader's Pleasure.

THE intelligent Reader may possibly wonder, after turning over these Sheets, that he finds in them no particular Account of the Antiquities in the Upper Egypt, which our Author had such an Opportunity of describing, and delivering his Opinion upon. To obviate this, I must inform him, that our Author wrote a distinct Treatise on this Subject, addressed to a Person of Distinction in France, and that after his Return into Europe, he illustrated it with very curious Notes, and many Quotations from the Ancients; and that he disjoined it from his Travels, because its Length would too much have interrupted them, and on Account of its relating to a learned Subject; and was therefore intended to be made a Part of a Volume of Miscellanies, which he had actually made ready for the Press. So much of this Subject however as was necessary to explain the several Topics on which he treats in this Book, is interspersed in proper Places; for tho' he made it his Practice to write distinct Treatises on important Heads, yet he very seldom refers hither and thither,

being

being such a Friend to Method, that he never thought any Time lost which was employ'd in making a Thing perspicuous. I have Reason to believe, that besides what will be found in this Book relating to the Art of Medicine as practised by the Egyptians, he wrote also a more large and distinct Treatise of Chyrurgical Operations, which in all Probability is lost; but there is still remaining among his Papers a sort of Egyptian Dispensatory, whether written by himself, or transcribed from the Works of any Author, I am not Judge enough of the Matter to determine. More I could say as to other Things of a like Nature, but as they have no very strict Connection with the Points I propose to explain in this Preface, I shall not swell it by expatiating on them here.

SUCH Pieces of Natural History as are here and there interspersed in this Work, as they come in pertinently, so they are penn'd with great Circumspection, our Author always affecting the middle Track, and being alike afraid of deviating into Credulity on the one hand, or into a supercilious Infidelity on the other. It does not appear that he has relied much on Authority in what he delivers of this sort, and that whenever he does do so, he gives fair Warning to the Reader to prevent the placing of other Men's Mistakes to his Account. A necessary Precaution this,

this, since not only unlearned Travellers, but even Men of deep Reading, and tolerable Understanding, have erred grosly in this Particular, the former thinking they had travelled to no Purpose, if thereby they had not acquired a Licence to relate all they heard, as confidently as all they saw; the latter so intoxicated with the Love of the Antients, that to support a Passage in Herodotus, to justify a Fact related by Diodorus, or to make good somewhat in Pliny's Natural History, take a great deal of unnecessary Pains, and not only give a wrong Biass to their Thoughts, but which is still more extraordinary to their Eye Sight; so strongly are they possessed with a Desire of beholding Things not as they are, but as they were in the Times of those ancient Writers, or rather as they were represented to them, and on that Account by them to their Readers. But tho' our Author had read, and very much esteemed the Ancients, yet he did not idolize them, for which he certainly deserves Commendation. I might say somewhat in Favour of that Accuracy and Perspicuity with which all his Accounts of Natural Things are written; but that I think would be prejudging the Reader, and might possibly prejudice the Author, rather than do him good; I shall therefore pass this by, and proceed to another remarkable Head.

THE

THE *Paffages relating to Chemiftry, or rather to Alchimy in the following Book, deferve particular Notice. It was the darling Folly of the laft Age, and of many Ages preceding it, there was fcarce a Monaftery in* England *which had not its Chemift; and in* Germany *the Humour was ftill ftronger, infomuch that there were not only many Pretenders to the Philofopher's Stone, I mean Men who pretended to have the Poffeffion of it, but they alfo devifed fo many Methods for fecuring their own Reputation, that there are very Numbers, and thofe not unintelligent People, who ftill believe that the grand Secret was known to and practifed by feveral of thefe* German Monks. *Every Body knows, that this Enthufiaftic Notion prevailed fo ftrongly here, that it was found neceffary to make a Law to prevent fuch pernicious Practices as Men were found to run into under Pretence of the Multiplication of Gold. In* France, Spain, *and* Italy, *the fame Notions turned the Heads of many, and that they were not confined within the Bounds of* Europe, *the Reader will find abundant Proofs in the following Sheets. As to our Author himfelf, he appears in this Work to have been quite an Infidel with Refpect to the Doctrine of Transmutation; for though on Account of certain Reafons which he mentions,*

be

be delivers his Sentiments cautiously, and in soft Terms, yet nothing can be more apparent, than that be look'd upon all the pompous Pretences of the Alchymist, either as unmeaning Rapfodies, or down right Delusions. This he did not from any Prejudice, but from the Knowledge he had had both of the Theory and Practice of this Art, in Favour of which he has inserted a short Account of the Reasons why Transmutation may be accounted probable, which as some intelligent Persons have informed me is an excellent Piece. His want of Belief therefore proceeded from Defect in the Evidence, and from nothing else; and consequently though the Friends of this Science may believe him in the wrong, yet they must impute the Error not to his Will, but to his Judgment.

ABOUT the Year 1692, he wrote a pretty large Treatise expresly on this Subject, at the Request as it should seem, of some Person of very great Distinction, who had his Head turned this Way, and who was mightily pleased with our Author's Conversation on the Subject. In this Treatise he does not seem to have alter'd his Opinion, or at least very materially, for having first explained the Nature of Metals, and the Reasons for and against Transmutation, he then proceeds to a most copious History of all the

the Poffeffors and reputed Poffeffors of the Philofopher's Stone in all Ages, and in all Parts of the World, including an Account of the Roficrucians, or illuminated Brethren. He likewife mentions, where they occur, the Objections which had been made to the Credibility of any of thefe Hiftories. This is the moft finifhed Piece which remains in my Power, and as far as I am able to judge, is not the original Treatife, but a fair Copy from it, there being no Amendments or Interlineations, whence it is poffible there may be other Copies of it. Our Author concludes nothing therein, he contents himfelf with ftating the Facts and Reafons on both Sides, leaving the Judgment to the Perfon to whom the Treatife is addreffed. It is however my private Sentiment, that by this Time he inclined to believe that Tranfmutation was poffible and practicable, but that there was little hopes of being able to render it profitable. I confefs I have gone a little out of my Road, but the Sight of fo curious a Building may poffibly excufe me, and even oblige my Reader, efpecially fince I have not detained him long; but having juft fhewn him a Profpect of the Edifice, returned again into the beaten Track.

I have now difcharged my Duty as an Editor, and if the following Piece is fo happy as to meet with a

good

good Reception (as I doubt not it will) I shall consider it as an Obligation laid upon me, to publish the Treatises which made up the rest of the Volume I copied. At present they are Curiosities, and they will be always so, unless by this Means I should gain an Opportunity of making them of general Use. But this depends upon the Publick, and to the Publick I therefore leave it.

THE

THE
TRAVELS
OF
Edward Brown, &c.

 **W**HEN Men write the Hiſtory of their own Lives, Vanity, whatever Colour may be pretended, is generally at the Bottom the real Motive. The Tenderneſs we have for our ſelves, unſatisfied with extending as far as the Grave, often preſſes thoſe who have the Capacity of Writing, to transfer it alſo to their Memory ; and like *Horace*, to erect Monuments to themſelves beyond the reach of Rage or Time. Perhaps I may my ſelf be governed by that fooliſh Self-fondneſs in what I am now writing, or at leaſt it may paſs for ſuch, amongſt critical Judges, if theſe Sheets ſhould ever tranſgreſs the boundaries of a Cloſet, and thruſt themſelves amongſt the numerous Lives, Hiſtories and Travels, which are daily ſent from the Preſs, into the World.

B

BUT

BUT if I am in any Degree acquainted with the Secrets of my own Breast, this Work is compofed from very different Inducements. The Heart of Man, is hardly open to himfelf, and perhaps moft People will find it as hard to account for the true Motives of their own Actions, as fome Hiftorians make it, to judge of thofe of Princes. My Cuftom throughout my Life has been, to preferve in a *Diary*, not only my Actions, and the Occurences which have happened to me, but even the Thoughts and Reflections they occafioned, at the Time when they befell me. Thefe Papers, which compofed for the moft Part the bulk of my Library, through all my Travels, are now fwollen to a large Compafs, and as I am happily arrived at laft at that Haven of Reft, which through fo many Climates I have been purfuing, I judged it proper to put them in Order for my own Ufe ; not I confefs without fome View to their advantaging Others, if the impartial and candid Picture I draw of human Nature be capable of doing Service. As it is, I fhall leave it behind me, to perifh or to be preferved, as the Order of Things fhall happen, and without farther Preface, proceed to it's Materials.

ON the 29th of *April*, 1641, the fame Day the *Houfe* of *Lords* voted the *Earl* of *Strafford* guilty of *High-Treafon*, I was born at a Village call'd *Cottenham*, in *Cambridgefhire*. My Father was a Gentleman of about 300 Pounds *per Ann.* fome of which lay in the *Ifle* of *Ely*, and the reft in *Lincolnfhire*. As my Parents had no other Children but my felf, they were exceedingly careful of my Education, and efpecially took care to inftill in me while Young, the Principles of the *Chriftian Religion* ; but with Refpect to particular Opinions, I was, by the Confent of

them

them both, left at greater Liberty, becaufe my Father was much in thofe Sentiments, called the Puritanical, and my Mother on the Contrary, who was the Daughter of a *Knight*, whofe Name was *Brown*, a great admirer of Archbifhop *Laud*.

My Father being himfelf well skill'd in the *Greek* and *Latin* Tongues, as having been for fome Years bred up in the Family of the Lord *Leapington*, kept me under his own Tuition, 'till I was between twelve and thirteen Years old, when he fent me to *London* to Mr. *Wm. Taylor*, a Minifter of great Learning, then much followed and admired. I came to Town the fame Day that the famous *John Lilburn* was tried and acquitted: And though then a Boy, yet being never put out of the Room when my Tutor received Company, or left at Home when he went to make a Vifit, I obferved a great many Things which made Impreffions fo ftrong upon me, as were not for many Years after to be worn out. Being upwards of Seventeen at the Deceafe of the Protector *Oliver*, with whom my Father had ftood in high Favour, and under whom he had held Offices of confiderable Profit, I took Notice of the great Concern he expreffed thereat, being fenfible alfo that it much haftened his own yeilding to Fate, which was in the *October* following of a hafty Confumption.

My Mother breathed her laft about fix Months before, and having no Relation of any Nearnefs left, except my Mother's Brother, who was a Trader of confiderable Reputation at *Hull* in *Yorkfhire*. Things too taking a furprizing Revolution, and making me, through the Share my Father had had in certain publick Tranfactions, obnoxious to the Perfons then coming into Power, all

together

together concurred firſt to throwing me into a deep Melancholly, and next bringing me into a ſettled Reſolution
of quitting my native Country, in hopes that Time and
Travel might wear out moſt of thoſe Grievances which
then oppreſſed me. My Tutor, Mr. *Taylor*, who ſur-
vived but a very little Space after, at firſt oppoſed my
Deſign, but finding me fixed, gave me, in Writing, a
moſt excellent ſet of Inſtructions for the Regulation of
my future Conduct.

THIS Determination of mine to quit *England*, was
about the latter End of the Year 1660; but Things
being then in ſo much Confuſion, that a Licence was
neceſſary for every Perſon who would go out of the
Kingdom, and there being ſome Difficulty for me to obtain one, I retir'd, 'till the Intereſt of my Friends could
procure it, to a Gentleman's Houſe near *Spalding*, in
Lincolnſhire, to which I was recommended by my good
Friend and Tutor Mr. *Taylor*.

THE Gentleman himſelf was a Man of the moſt
agreeable Diſpoſition, had all the Experience of a Life of
threeſcore Years, without the leaſt Taint of thoſe troubleſome Humours which generally attend old Age. His
Family conſiſted of two Daughters, who lived at Home
with him; his only Son, after having been under the
Tuition of Mr. *Taylor*, ſtudying then at the Univerſity
of *Aberdeen*, in *Scotland*, whither his Father had ſent him
to preſerve the Purity of his Morals. When I firſt came
down to his Seat, I promiſed myſelf much Satisfaction,
as well from the Temper of the old Man himſelf, as
from the modeſt and ſweet Behaviour of the Daughters.
But as all Things here are uncertain, and nothing more
ſo than the Conjectures of human Underſtanding, ſo
the

the Accidents which befell me here, added, to the general Difguft I had taken, a particular Source of Uneafinefs which neceffarily required the Cure of Abfence.

THE Seat wherein we dwelt, was one of the old-fafhioned Structures, which appeared to be built without any other Rule, than the Inclination of its Founder. It had abundance of good Rooms, large Clofets, feveral Galleries, and three or four different Gardens round it, as irregularly laid out as the Houfe was built. In it's Front there was a *Rookery*, and another very large one behind it beyond the Gardens, near which were feveral Fifh-Ponds, and on one Side of them a Warren, and on the other a thick Grove. All together it was confufed, and yet agreeable; its Apartments not magnificent, but convenient; and the rural Ornaments about it, though rude in their Difpofition, did not want their Beauties.

THE melancholy Temper which at that Time I was in, and to which I have always had a natural Tendency, inclined me perhaps to like this Place better than I fhould have done the neateft and moft regular Building. There was about half a quarter of a Mile from the Houfe, a long, ftrait, walk of Trees, which terminated at the Church-yard; hither I ufed frequently to refort, and either divert myfelf with fome Book or other, or elfe entertained my Thoughts in the undifturbed Solitude of that Retirement. About three Weeks after my coming into the Country, when that civil ftrangenefs which is paid to a New-Comer was pretty well worn off, and the Family treated me with almoft the fame Intimacy they did each other, I began to perceive that Mrs. *Lucy*, the old Gentleman's younger Daughter, behaved towards me with a peculiar Air. Abundance of Circumftances forc'd

me

me to take Notice of it, as well as confirmed me in my Conjecture, and a short interval of Time very fully revealed it.

AFTER Dinner one Day, while the old Gentleman went to his Nap, I had taken in my Pocket, *Barclay's Euphormion*, and stroled down the solitary Walk before mention'd. As I was amusing myself there with the Author I spoke of, I perceived the young Lady sitting on a little Bench, which was under three old spreading Trees, on a rising Ground, about a Stone's cast from the Path in which I was. Immediately, and almost without knowing what I did, I went up to her, and with an Air of Freedom, which I very rarely assumed, took out of her Hand a Book which she was reading : She parted with it very readily, though she would never receive it afterwards, and it proved to be the Poems of *Michael Drayton*, in which she was reading the Letter of King *John* to *Matilda*. This Interview, notwithstanding its suddenness, seemed not to have occasioned much surprize on either Side ; the Lady managed her Share of Conversation so agreeably, that though my Bosom neither before nor since for any other Woman, ever felt any Emotions of an amorous Kind, yet I retired, after walking with her about two Hours, with a Heart full of Love.

THE *elder* Sister whose Name was *Martha*, and who was about 22 Years of Age, was a young Woman of an open, merry and generous Disposition, one who was always doing something which might delight or do good to others. This Sister *Lucy*, who was about *four* Years younger, seemed to be of a more reserved Temper, she spoke very little, but when she did, it was with a

Sweetnefs

Sweetnefs which I at leaſt never obferved in any other Woman; fhe affected to read much, was often in her Clofet, and though her Behaviour in Company was always eafy, yet fomething in her Countenance plainly fhewed fhe was better pleafed when alone.

THE old Gentleman, when I had been about *fix Weeks* in his Houfe, informed me with great Joy, that his Son was fafely arrived at *York*, and that the *Thurfday* following he expected him Home. He is (faid the good old Man) about three Years older than you, and as I fee there is a great Likenefs in your Tempers, I promife myfelf much fatisfaction from that Friendfhip which I fhall recommend to you both. As you think it will be improper to make much ftir about your Licence 'till the beginning of the Spring, I hope we fhall all be Happy together 'till that Time. I am defirous that my Son *Philip* fhould alfo fee the World; and if it be convenient to you, would have him be the Companion of your Travels. I expreffed the greateft refpect and fatisfaction at what the old Gentleman had been pleafed to fay, and affured him that nothing could give me greater Pleafure, than the being able to do any Thing which might be acceptable to him or his Family.

THINGS ftood thus when the young Gentleman arrived, he appeared to have made the beft ufe of his Time and of his Studies, having acquired all the Advantages that could be drawn from an *Academical Education*, without receiving from it the leaft Stain of Pedantry, or feeming to have leaned in any Degree to the other extream in order to avoid it. His own Virtues were fufficient to have recommended him to my Efteem and Friendfhip, had he not had an additional Title of being Son to a

Father

Father, to whom I stood so much obliged. *Lucia's* Amour and mine was now so far advanced, that I was in some doubt, whether to propose a Marriage between Us, before, or after my return with her Brother from our Travels. For Love had so far altered my Intentions, that I, who before had resolved never to return Home after I had once left the *English* Shore, now with reluctance suffered the very Thought of my Departure to enter my Mind.

During this Space, I received by a special Messenger an Account from *London*, that the Earl of *Clarendon*, instead of yeilding to my Friends request for a *Licence* for me to depart the Kingdom, had declared that the Government stood in great need of certain Papers which were in the Hands of my Father at the Time of his Decease, and for which he was resolved to question me, where ever I could be found. This News augmented that embarrasment which from a Multitude of concurring unlucky Circumstances I was at that Time in ; and of all, none perplexed me so much as this Affair of Love.

LUCIA, I observed from the Time of her Brother's return, was exceedingly careful of speaking to me in his Presence. I saw her however almost every Night when the Moon shone, at our Walk by the *Church-Yard*, and when the Nights were dark sometimes in the Hall, near to which there were back Stairs that came both from her's and also my Apartment. The Lady did not indeed press me directly upon the Score of Matrimony, but I fancied at least that I saw in her a secret uneasiness which I judged must arise from that Cause. My Principles sufficiently restrained me from attempting any Thing beyond the Bounds of Decency and Honour ; and the
Lady's

Lady's Behaviour was always such as gave me not the least Suspicion of their not having been treated with a just Indignation if I had. However, there had so much passed between us, that I could not myself but think it reasonable, that some way or other should be proposed to put an End to this Affair; and the Consideration of this way almost continually took up my Thoughts; for on the one Hand, I could not bear to part entirely from *Lucia*, and on the other Hand, Matrimony was a Thing very inconvenient for me at this Time.

My Intimacy with her Brother encreasing daily, and the likeness of our Manners seeming to have created a very strong Affection, I resolved to make him my Confident in this Affair, in which my Passion had engaged me against the dictates of my Reason. I proposed to my self both to ask him his sincere Advice as a Friend, and at the same Time to engage his Interest as a Brother in speaking to his Father. Accordingly one Morning as he came into my Chamber while I was reading, I begged him to sit down and permit me to inform him of an Affair in which he himself was concerned, and on which my Quiet very strongly depended. The young Gentleman seemed very much surprized, and replied that there could be nothing which affected my Peace in which he was not Interested, begging me to go on, and depend on this, that nothing I could ask of him should be omitted.

When in as few Words as I was able, I had acquainted him with the Sources of my Uneasiness, I perceived the Story affected him with almost as much Concern as it did me; I imputed it wholly to the sincerity of his Friendship, and expected with Impatience what Expedient he would propose. As soon as he had recovered
himself

himself from that Surprize into which the Story that I had told him had put him ; my Friend (said the young Man at laft) there could not poffibly have happened a Thing in which I would more ftudioufly have avoided giving my Advice, than where a Perfon, for whom I have fo deep an Affection as for you, fhould have indulged himfelf in an amorous Inclination ; I know very well, though I cannot fay by Experience, how little regard is had to Reafon, by him who hath once fuffered his Breaft to be taken up by that enfnaring Paffion ; but when to thefe Difficulties there is added, the near Relation I have to the Lady with whom you are in Love, I fee myfelf furrounded with fo many difficulties, that nothing but the tender Friendfhip I have for you, fhould engage me to fpeak a Syllable more on this Head.   As it therefore fo nearly concerns you, I will comply entirely with your Requeft, and without any Regard to Family, or that Affection we naturally have for fo near Relations, give you my fincere Sentiments on the Subject as you have propofed it.

I thanked him for fo extraordinary a Proof of his Efteem, and begged he would go on: He hefitated a little, and then faid, I am perfuaded (my Friend) you will not infift on my defcending to particulars, when out of regard to your Peace, I tell you that you would do well to banifh from this Hour all Thoughts of my Sifter.   I know her, Sir, and her Difpofition, it would make you uneafy in Marriage.   I am convinced you have more good Senfe than to afk me more Queftions, and I expect it from our Friendfhip that you afk them no where elfe. As foon as he had faid this, he went out of the Room, and left me more difquieted and more confounded than

fince

fince that Time I ever was from all the Accidents that have befallen me in Life. That Evening being to meet *Lucia* in the Church-yard Walk, I had a thoufand Thoughts crouded into my Head, which occafioned as many different Refolutions of going, and not going, as Love or Reafon, or rather Sufpicion prevailed.

AT laft, when the Hour of Appointment drew nigh, I went without determining with myfelf whether or no I fhould mention to her any Thing that had paffed between me and her Brother. I walked to and fro a long Time, fo much taken up with the hurry of my Cogitations, that the Moon declined almoft before I perceived it, and being difappointed in my defigned Interview, I had much ado to blunder Home in the Dark. As foon as I entered my Chamber, looking on my Watch, I found it was Four o'Clock in the Morning, I did not go to Bed but paffed the Remainder of the Time 'till the Family were up, in a Multitude of uneafy Reflections.

The next Day at Dinner, *Lucia* was miffing, upon which I could not forbear asking her Father whether fhe was gone ; the old Gentleman faid, he had a younger Sifter dangeroufly ill at *London*, and that he thought it proper that her Neice fhould be near her in cafe of Death. I looked very fteadily on her Brother, when his Father was making me this Anfwer, and obferved that he heard the Difcourfe with a great deal of Pain. After Dinner we walked a good while in the Garden, where the young Gentleman repeated the fame Story his Father had told me, but without taking the leaft Notice of that uneafinefs, which he might naturally fuppofe her abrupt Departure might give me. As foon as conveniently I could, I difengaged myfelf from his Converfation, and

retiring

retiring to my own Chamber, began to think more cooly of what had hitherto paffed.

My Temper which at that Time was very unpractifed in bearing Uneafinefs, made me incapable of hiding it ; to prevent therefore any Notice being taken of my Diforder, I declined going down to Supper, under pretence of my having a Fit of the Gravel : I pretended to be worfe toward Night, that I might not be plagued with Company ; and indeed it fucceeded fo well, that I had all the Evening to myfelf, which I fpent in very ferious Confultation. The Refult of which was, that in order to make myfelf eafy, I would quit the Houfe. About fix the next Morning, I ordered my Servant to get the Horfes ready, and fet out for my Uncle's Houfe at *Hull*; leaving a Letter with the old Gentleman's Groom for his Mafter, in which I informed him, that my Affairs had taken a very ill turn at *London*, and that I found it neceffary to retire farther *North*, in order the better to conceal myfelf. I knew very well that *Lucia* was fent away on my Account, and as they had not thought fit to acquaint me with the Reafons of her Journey, I did not think myfelf obliged to be very particular, as to the Motives of mine.

I travelled with great Speed, 'till I arrived at my Uncle's Houfe, where without fuffering the late Accident which had happened to me, to make too great Impreffion upon my Mind, I began to fettle my Affairs in earneft for my Journey, in which the Affiftance of my Uncle forwarded me a great deal. I foon converted my Eftate, which my Father before his Death had difpofed of to this Uncle in truft for me into ready Money, which with what my Father had left me in Cafh, amounted to

about

about feven thoufand Pounds, befides fome Jewels of confiderable Value, which I always referved, and carried privately about me.

THE only Thing that remained was, to confult my Uncle as to the Method I fhould take, of getting out of the Kingdom fafely, and the Route I was to follow after my landing in *France*, thorough which Kingdom it was agreed I fhould Travel. My Uncle advifed me to affume my Mother's Name of *Brown*, and having bought an old Chariot privately, we had it with like fecrecy painted in a fpare Warehoufe, and my Mother's Arms blazoned thereon: This effectually anfwered our Defign, for the Officers at the Port took the Chariot to belong to fome of the *Mountacute* Family, and fuffered me to go on board the Veffel I had hired to tranfport me, with hardly a Queftion afked or examining any Part of my Baggage. I carried over with me a Servant whofe Name was *Johnfon*, and another Perfon very fkillful in the *French* Language and the Manners of that Nation, all whofe Expences I had agreed to furnifh to *Paris*, whether he was going to fome Relations.

THIS Perfon I mentioned laft, I found to be a Man very well verfed, not only in the *French*, but in the *Italian* and *Spanifh* Tongues, having paffed almoft *ten* Years, as he told me, in travelling through moft Parts of *Europe*. I had the Curiofity, both to inform myfelf, and to divert the Paffage, to enquire fomewhat more particularly into his Adventures than otherwife I fhould have done. The Man who had already been very much obliged to me, and who was to depend on me at leaft as far as *Paris*, made no great Scruple of talking very freely of the Reafons which engaged him to pafs through fo many Places heretofore,

tofore, and which had now driven him, though much unprovided, upon travelling again.

He said that his Father being a Tenant under the Marquefs of *Newcaftle*, he himfelf, while a Boy, was taken into the Service of that noble Lord, that he was in his Family when he became General in the *North* for the King againft the *Parliament* Forces, that he ferved him and under him his Majefty with the utmoft Fidelity, 'till every Thing was loft, and the Royal Party quite vanquifh-ed, when he was under a Neceffity of fubmitting on the beft Terms he could to thofe then in Power. Having been raifed to a Lieutenant of Horfe, under the afore-mentioned Marquefs of *Newcaftle*, and having been much entrufted in Expreffes, and private Meffages to and from the King at *Oxford*, and on his Affairs alfo in *France* and *Holland*; one of his Relations mentioned him to *Thurloe*, the Protectors Secretary, as a Man who might be of Ufe, if he could be brought over.

He was then at *London*, and his Friend having obtained Leave, fpoke to him of the Affair. At firft, his old Principles of Loyalty made him abfolutely refufe having any Thing to do with the Secretary or his Mafter; but after fome Time, his Friend's perfuafions, and much more his own Neceffities, forced him to think better of it, and to confent to making a Vifit to *Thurloe*, in order to hear his Propofitions. His Friend was very well pleafed at this, knowing that nothing could be more ac-ceptable to *Oliver*, than the gaining fuch Perfons to his Party. He fignified it therefore immediately to the Secre-tary, and begged he might have a Day appointed him to bring his Friend.

THURLOE

THURLOE ordered that he fhould come the next Evening, when having converfed with the *Lieutenant* about an Hour, he defired him to retire into an Anti-Chamber, and in about half an Hour after, the Secretary returned and introduced him to the *Protector*, who fat in a little Room behind that in which they had been firft entertained, where he could hear every Word that paffed. The Man, who appeared to me upon other Occafions to have wanted no Courage, acknowledged that he had never in his Life felt fo great an Emotion of his Spirits, as at this Interview. The *Protector* perceived it, and bid him fit down and compofe himfelf, that he might be affured Nothing fhould hurt him as to what had paffed, and that he had fomething to propofe to him, which might make him very eafy for the future. The *Lieutenant* at this began to take Heart, and when he had recollected himfelf a little, after thanking his Highnefs for that Favour, affured him that he would ferve him as faithfully in whatfoever he entrufted him, as ever he had done his Royal Mafter. *Oliver* fmiled at that Expreffion, and faid, he knew his Principles too well to put him upon any Thing that had any Relation to the Affairs of *Charles Steward*. For (added *Cromwell*) I have fmall Regard for any new Servant who would recommend himfelf to me, by betraying the Secrets of him whom he had pretended to ferve from a Principle of Religion and Duty. I will pay you very well, for what ever I employ you in, and expect nothing more from you than Secrecy and Refolution. I am going to Council upon a Matter which will keep me late, but *Thurloe* will acquaint you with what I expect of you.

AFTER

AFTER the *Protector* was gone, the Secretary paid him one *hundred* Pounds before he fpoke a Word to him of the Bufinefs, and then giving him two Letters of Credit, each to the Extent of *five hundred* Pounds, one on a *Swifs* Banker at *Paris*, and the other on a *Merchant* at *Marfeilles*; he then gave him his Inftructions in very few Words, which were, that he fhould travel from *Calais*, through the Heart of *France* to *Marfeilles*, according to a Route which fhould be delivered unto him by the Banker on whom he had his Credit at *Paris*. He was commanded to obferve very diligently the State of that Kingdom in every Refpect, which he was ordered to put into Writing, and to digeft in the beft Method he could ; it was more particularly recommended to him to have a ftrict Eye to the Condition of the *Huguenots* in that Kingdom ; to difcover as well as he was able, the general Characters of the Perfons then of greateft Rank in *France* ; and he was finally enjoined to pay a ftrict Obedience to whatever Order he received, fealed with a particular Seal which was fhewn him, and a fair Impreffion thereof in Wax, put up in a little Cafe like a Medal delivered to him.

THUS furnifhed, he fet out in confequence of the Orders he had received, and performed his Commiffion with fo great Exactnefs, that at *Marfeilles* he received new Letters of Credit, and frefh Commands to pafs with the utmoft privacy through *Spain*. When he had fo done, to embark for *Leghorn*, and after vifiting fuch and fuch States of *Italy*, to return by the Way of *Swizerland*, *Burgundy* and *Lorain*, into the *united Provinces*, and fo Home. He performed this Journey fo as to return into *England* the very Year that *Oliver* died, and about two

Months

Months after it. By this he loſt that Reward he might reaſonably have expected, for the great Services he performed and Intelligence he gave; ſome Inſtances of which, I ſhall have Occaſion hereafter to mention.

THIS Diſapointment was the Cauſe of his falling into low Circumſtances, and at the ſtrange Change in the Year 1660, great Endeavours being uſed to take him, on a falſe Accuſation of his having been a Spy on the Court of King *Charles* the *Second*, in his Exile, he privately fled into *Yorkſhire*, and lived there in a very low State, 'till he happened to be recommended by a near Relation of his to my Uncle, who ſent him with me in order to his getting to *Paris*, where he had an Uncle in the Service of the Duke of *Orleans*, by whoſe Intereſt he was in hopes of getting ſomething, which might gain him Bread.

FINDING by this Relation, that Mr. *Fetherſtone* was in much the ſame Condition with myſelf, I adviſed with him as to the propereſt Place for my landing in *France*; we agreed at laſt that it ſhould be at *Diepe*, and I gave the Maſter Inſtructions accordingly, who promiſed to comply with them, and to recommend us at our Arrival in Port, to a Perſon of his Acquaintance, at whoſe Houſe we might be well accomodated ſo long as we ſhould incline to ſtay there. This was very acceptable to a young Traveller, whoſe Apprehenſions had driven him from Home, and who had as yet ſettled no Reſolution as to his Conduct abroad. In ſeven Days we arrived at *Diepe*, and were carried by the Maſter to the Houſe of one Mr. *Villeneufe*, who had been formerly Maſter of a Veſſel, trading to *England*; but growing in Years, and having acquired a ſufficiency, choſe to paſs the remnant of his

C

Life

Life in quiet. He was a little Man, well made, and though near *threescore*, very lively and full of Spirit. He received us very kindly, and treated us with as much familiarity, as if he had been as long acquainted with us as the Master of the Vessel, who recommended us. The latter who was to remain at *Diepe*, 'till he could take in a Freight on my Relation's Account, lodged with Mr. *Fetherstone* and myself, at this Gentleman's House, which was of great Service to me. The very Day after my arrival, I took care to be provided with a *French* Master, who proved a very sensible Man, and taught me to distinguish between the true *French*, and the *Dialect* of *Normandy*, as well in regard to the turn of Expression, as to the Words and Pronounciation peculiar to the Inhabitants of this Province.

I soon found that Mr. *Fetherstone*, though he often talk'd of it, was in no great hurry to go to *Paris*, and I readily guessed the Reason, which was his fear of not meeting there with a supply of Money. When I had considered this Matter attentively, I began to look upon it as a very great good Fortune to myself; never were *two* Travellers better suited, he had Years, Experience, and Integrity: I had just Sense enough to discover my own Wants, and to know that as Things stood, I should be more benefited by his Instructions, than he could be by any Services I could do him. The former were Treasures whence I drew great Advantages during my whole Life, the latter temporary Things no way answerable to his Merit. The first Thing I did, was to remove all scruples between us, I informed him thoroughly of my Condition, and having received *fifty* Pistoles on a Letter of Credit, I made him a Present of *Twenty*, intreat-

intreating him to give me his Advice freely, as to my Conduct, and the necessary means to make my Residence easy in *France*, 'till either Necessity or Choice induced me to remove.

HE told me that he was well acquainted with a Gentleman at *Roan*, a Man of great Honour, and very extensive Knowledge, one who had formerly made a great Figure in the World, but had for many Years lived in privacy, on account of his having incurr'd the displeasure of *Cardinal Richelieu*. To this Gentleman he assured me, he would recommend me in the strongest Terms, adding, that after a Residence of *five* or *six* Months under such a Tutor, I should have Knowledge enough of the *French* Language and Nation to regulate my future Behaviour without farther help. This Point once resolved on, I addressed myself to the Provision of our Master's Freight, according to the Instructions given me by my Relation, and while this was doing, diverted myself very agreeably with Mr. *Villeneuf*, and the rest of my Friends, not caring as yet to mix much with Strangers.

ONE of the first Discoveries I made was, that our *Protector* had rendered himself strangely formidable in *France* ; they believed in this Country, that he could draw together *forty* or *fifty* thousand Men when he pleased; they thought him wise enough to foresee all Things, and bold enough to undertake any Thing. This was chiefly owing to the great Deference paid him by the *Cardinal Mazarin*, of whom it was commonly said, that he did not fear the *Devil* so much as *Oliver Cromwell*. As far as I could afterwards learn, he feared both of them enough, and suffered his fears to have a strong Influence on his Actions. It happened that as we were

C 2

con-

conversing one Evening on the Subject of *Oliver*'s Power and Grandeur, Mr. *Villeneufe* asked me if I knew what became of the young *Lady* who attempted to assassinate the *Protector.* I told him very freely that I had never heard of any such Thing; but that living as I did, at a great Distance from *London*, it might for all that have happened, and therefore I desired he would tell me what he had heard of it, which he readily did. The Sum of his Relation was this.

THE famous *Duke* of *Buckingham*, who was assassinated at *Portsmouth*, left behind him *two* Sons. *George*, who succeeded him in his Honour, and the Lord *Francis Villiers*, who was kill'd at *St. Neots* in *Huntingtonshire*, by *Cromwell* himself. This young Nobleman was passionately fond of Mrs. *Letitia Greenville*, who was as much in Love with him. From the Day of his Death, she conceived in her Mind a strong Resolution to revenge it. In order to this, she procured a Picture of General *Cromwell*, which she set up in a Barn adjoining to her Father's House, whether she went frequently to fire at it with a Pistol, 'till by Degrees she had attained a Facility in hitting it, which she judg'd sufficient for her purpose. Coming then up to *London*, with her Father, Mother, and other Relations, she for some Time watched an Opportunity to perpetrate the Murder she had premeditated. At length, in the Year 1654, an Occasion offered: The *Protector* was invited to Dinner in the *City*, and was to pass in Pomp by the House in which herself and the Family lodged. Mrs. *Greenville* dress'd herself with all imaginable Care, a Thing she had never done since the Death of her Lover, and having placed herself in the Balcony, fired at the *Protector* as he passed, and lodged

lodged a brace of Balls in the Shoulder of his Son *Henry's* Horfe, who rode next him. This put a Stop to the Proceffion; the *Ladies* in the Balcony threw themfelves on their Knees, while Mrs. *Greenville* extending the Piftol, cried out, that it was fhe who had fired it, and that fhe was forry fhe had not kill'd the *Tyrant*. The *Protector* defired the Company to go on, faying the Woman was mad, leaving Colonel *Holmes* and a fmall Party of the *Guards* to protect the Houfe, and to fecure her Perfon. When the *Colonel* came to execute his Commiffion, the Parents of the young Lady affured him fhe had been melancholly for fome Years, and that fhe was certainly *out* of her *Senfes*; upon which the Colonel withdrew to carry this News to the *Protector*. When *Cromwell* was acquainted therewith, he ordered the Guard to be withdrawn; but the next Day fent Orders to the Lady's Father to take Care to confine his Daughter, that fhe might not attempt any Thing of the like Nature againft another. After this, Mrs. *Greenville* was never heard of, and the Enemies of *Cromwell* fay, he caufed her to be *poifoned*.

W H E N Mr. *Fetherftone* and I were alone, I asked him if he had ever heard any Thing of this Story before. He anfwered in the *Negative*, and affured me it was a pure Fiction. Lord *Francis Villiers* faid he, was kill'd the fame Year the King was murder'd. He was a very handfome Gentleman, and very amorous. I have heard it faid, that when the Soldiers ftripp'd him, they found a Lock of a Lady's Hair faftened to a Ribban which hung upon his Breaft under his Shirt. But this Lady's Name was Mrs. *Kirk*. Befides, he was neither kill'd by *Cromwell*, nor at *St. Neots*. His Party was routed on *Banftead*

Downs,

Downs, by Sir *Michael Livefay*, whofe Soldiers killed *Lord Francis* becaufe he obftinately refufed Quarter. I was mightily furprized at this Tale, out of which our Landlord would never be perfuaded; but before I left *France*, I heard fo many of the fame Sort, that I began to doubt almoft every Thing I heard. Hence I took a Refolution never to be over Confident as to the Circumftances of Facts happening out of the Sphere of my own Obfervation, which proved of great Ufe to me afterwards, by eradicating that Tenacioufnefs almoft inherent to Youth, and by opening the Door to all Inftructions that were offered me.

WHEN all Things were ready, and we expected every Day a fair Wind to carry the *Veffel*, we came in, back to *England*, the *Mafter* fell Sick of a kind of malignant Fever, which detained him and us three Weeks at *Diepa* longer than we defigned. During his Illnefs, he was attended by an *Irifh* Phyfician, and a *Scotch* Minifter. The former was of the *Romifh* Perfuafion, but a Man of good Senfe and great Moderation, who had quitted his Country a little after the breaking out of the Rebellion. He complained heavily of the Adminiftration of publick Affairs in that Ifland. He faid, that the *Englifh* Governors were too ready to drive the Natives to extremities; that they might enrich themfelves and their dependants by Forfeitures. He fpoke with great abhorrence of the *Maffacre*, but alledged, that the Punifhment thereof fell heavieft upon thofe who had nothing to do with it. That at firft, no Diftinction was made between the Rebels and the well affected of the Catholicks; but that on the contrary, all the Papifts in general were treated as Perfons profcribed, which compelled Numbers to take Arms in their own Defence,

Defence, who otherwife abhorred Rebellion. That by degrees the King and his Minifters were perfuaded of this which induced them to enter into a Correfpondence with the loyal *Catholicks*, and this gave a Handle to the Earl of *Holland*, when he deferted the King, and returned to the Parliament to report that the Rebels in *Ireland* were countenanced by the King. He fpake with mighty Concern of the Mifery of his Country, which in the Space of *thirty* Years, he affirmed had loft a third Part of its Inhabitants, and defcribed, whenever our Difcourfes led him to it, the fad Condition of the native *Irifh* in very moving Terms.

THE *Scotchman* was defcended of a *Popifh* Family, and had been fent while a Youth to *Paris*, for Education. The Murder of *Henry* IV. and the Books publifhed on that Occafion, gave him a high Difguft of the *Religion* he had been bred in, and a moft bitter Averfion to the *Jefuits*. He was, in other refpects, a humane and pious Man ; he recommended to the fick Perfon folid and rational Penitence, and advifed him to be rather afraid of continuing in a finful World, than of Death. He told him that to a Man who firmly believ'd the fundamental Doctrines of the *Chriftian Faith*, the latter could not be very terrible ; and he faid, that it was a ftrong Tefti-mony of the Truth of the *Chriftian* Religion, that it difarmed Death of its Sting, and taught a rational Creature to expect Diffolution without horror. By the Care of thefe Men, our Mafter and ourfelves were much better'd, and as foon as he recovered, he embarked, and with a fair Wind, failed for the Port of *London*, where he arrived in *three* Days ; and on Advice thereof, we immediately prepared for our Journey to *Roan*.

DIEPE,

DIEPE, one of the safeft Ports in *Normandy*, is feated on an Arm of the Sea, between *two* Hills, which by their fhooting into the Sea, form a *Bay* ; the entrance of the Haven is narrow, but once entered is very commodious. The Town itfelf is handfomely built, its Streets broad and well paved, the Houfes fair but not high ; it was at this Time well fortified, but hath been fince much improved. It was the firft Town which acknowledged the Authority of *Henry* IV. and in its Neighbourhood he firft fought for his Crown, and that too not much for his Advantage. During the whole War, he was very careful of it, being the Port where the *Englifh* Succours generally debarqued. There are in it a great Number of Ivory Turners, and the Inhabitants in general feem to be active and induftrious, and one Thing is efpecially remarked for their Honour, that they have always produced from amongft them, the beft *Seamen* in *France.* To fay the Truth, they are, generally fpeaking, well qualified for maritime Employment, as they are more active, daring, and inquifitive than their Neighbours. In the Broils which happened in the laft Reign, the *Duke* of *Longueville*, who declared *againft* the *King*, or rather *for* his *Mother* againft his *Minifter*, fortified *Diepe*, and the Works he then caft up have been ever fince maintain'd, and new ones added as Occafion offered.

THE firft of *June* 1662, we fet out for *Roan*, where we arrived next Day, having travelled *thirteen* Leagues, *nine* the firft Day, and *four* the fecond. Mr. *Fetherftone* having by way of Precaution written to his Friend M. *de St. Dennis*, he met us at *Toftes*, where we lay, with a Coach, in which we came fafe to his Houfe before

Noon

Noon next Day. The Country through which we travelled was extremely pleafant, or at leaft it feem'd fo to me. The Accommodations in the *Inn*, were not fuch as could be boafted of ; but the Complacency of the People, and the earneft Defire they fhewed to oblige us, amply fupply'd all deficiences, and left us no room to complain. As we travelled the laft four Leagues, Mr. *Fetherftone* acquainted his Friend that fome difappoint-ments in my expectations had engaged me to vifit *France*, and that he had recommended me to him as to a Perfon who would be fure to prevent my repenting the beginning my Travels with the Sight of *Normandy*. Mr. *St. Dennis* faid, it happened very luckily, for that a Friend who had lived with him for about *Seven* Years being lately dead, he had fome Thoughts of leaving *Roan*, moft of the Inhabitants being of fo litigious a Temper, that he found it no eafy Matter to live at quiet, though he ufed all the Precaution imaginable, and was content to fuffer fmall Inconveniences, rather than attempt to remedy them by Law-Suits. He affured me that I fhould be as much at Home as if the Houfe was my own, and that he would do all in his Power to make the Time of my ftay agree-able to me. Mr. *Fetherftone* faid, that in lefs than a Month he fhould be obliged to go to *Paris*, and that it would give him the higheft Satisfaction to fee me fo well fettled. Thus by the Time we reached our Journey's End, all our Affairs were as well adjufted, as if we had lived together many Years ; nor do I know that during my ftay at *Roan*, there happened the flighteft Caufe of diffatisfaction to any of us.

THE Houfe of Mr. *de St. Dennis* ftood near the City Wall. It was compofed of a Body and two fmall

Wings, the former had three, the latter, one Room each on a Floor, there was a Garden behind, which by the Gales from the River was render'd very cool and pleasant; at the Bottom of it there was a small Apartment, consisting of a kind of Hall, and two Closets, over which was a Library, twice as long as the lower Building, the Ends of it being supported by Pillars, forming two little Porticoes, one on each Side of the Hall. In this Hall we used to sup of an Evening, during the Heat of the Summer, and to entertain ourselves with Discourses, either of a Serious or Comic Nature as Occasion serv'd. Mr. *de St. Dennis* had an excellent Memory, a Blessing which I have observ'd to be more common in *France* than elsewhere; he had spent his Youth at Court, or in the Army; he had been always a great Lover of Books; and having enjoy'd a long Season of Rest and Recollection, there was hardly any Subject of which he could not speak with great Propriety, and illustrate it with Stories equally pleasant and to the Purpose.

It happen'd once, that speaking of doubtful Events, Mr. *de St. Dennis* asked me, whether the Death of *Perkin Warbeck* as an Impostor, was not held to be of this Nature in *England?* To which I answer'd in the Negative, and that most People were satisfied he was what he was executed for, a *downright Impostor:* That may be; said he, but at the Time of his Death, the general Opinion was otherwise, and many of your Countrymen of great Quality, took it upon their *Deaths*, that he was the Son of *Edward* IV; how the general Opinion comes to be now otherwise, continued he, I find it not difficult to assign the Cause. *Henry* VII. a wise

and

and artful Prince, as he put him to Death for an *Impoſtor*, ſo he took all the Care he could to eſtabliſh the Opinion of his being guilty after his Demiſe; as he likewiſe took Care to extinguiſh the Pretenſions of the *Houſe of York*, and to depreſs its Adherents during his whole Reign. His Son *Henry* VIII. followed the ſame *Maxims*; and in the Courſe of near 50 Years, that the Throne was afterwards fill'd by his Poſterity, whoſe Intereſt it was that this Story, true or falſe, ſhould be believ'd, we need not wonder that it became at laſt a kind of Article in your political Faith; and eſpecially ſeeing the *Houſe* of *Stuart* derived their *Rights*, not from the *Houſe* of *York*, but from that of *Lancaſter*.

FROM this Subject, by a Tranſition natural enough, we fell upon that of the Death of *Don Sebaſtian* King of *Portugal*, which we all agreed was a moſt myſterious Point. As myſterious as it is, ſaid Mr. *de St. Dennis*, I have in my Library above Stairs, a little Tract concerning it, which belonged to Father *Gayet*, and which may be taken for as certain and impartial a Relation thereof, as any that the World hath hitherto met with; this was a Curioſity not to be paſſed by, I intreated the Favour of peruſing and making an Extract from it, which was readily granted. I have enquir'd concerning its principal Circumſtances with great Circumſpection, and have never met with any Reaſon to doubt the Credit of my Author, the Subſtance of whoſe Relation follows.

" *SEBASTIAN* King of *Portugal* was born in
" the Year 1554. Sometime after the Demiſe of his Fa-
" ther, Brother to the reigning King, and was carefully
" educated by his Mother, who was Daughter to the
" famous

" famous Emperor *Charles* V. In 1557, he succeeded
" his Uncle *John* III. In 1574, he conceiv'd a De-
" sign of making War on the *Moors*, and having made
" mighty Preparations for putting his Design in Execu-
" tion, on the 9th of *July*, 1578, he landed at *Tan-*
" *gier* with a great Army; on the 4th of *August*, the
" same Year, he fought the unfortunate Battle of *Al-*
" *cacar*, in which the *Moors* were victorious; tho' they
" lost their King, who died of a Fever, of which he
" had been long sick, in his Litter.

" AFTER the Battle, the *Portugueze* missing their
" King, sent to those who were taken Prisoners, who
" thereupon sought carefully for his Body, which, as
" many supposed, was found. It had seven large
" Wounds, and by Reason of the excessive Heat of
" the Climate, was already in a State of Corruption.
" However, it was laid in a Tent, and the Nobility
" went to see it, but receiv'd no kind of Satisfaction,
" that it was the Body of their King; on the contrary,
" it was generally thought that it was not. Notwith-
" standing which, King *Philip* of *Spain*, having de-
" manded it, and as some report, having given a vast Sum
" for it; at length it was sent him, and he caused it to be
" interr'd, with all Royal Honours at *Bethlehem*, which
" stands a Mile from *Lisbon*, and is the usual Burying
" Place of the *Portugueze* Kings.

" 'TIS certain, that the *Portugueze* Nation in gene-
" ral, did never credit the Story of his Death; but were
" so firmly persuaded that he was alive, that they readi-
" ly countenanc'd *two* Impostors, who were hardy
" enough to assume his Name. The *first* of these was
" the Son of a *Tile-Maker*, who was put upon it by

" a

" a Prieft, who gave himfelf out to be the Bifhop of
" *Garda*; and who took a Note of their Names who
" beftow'd their Benefactions on his *Difciple*, in order
" to their being repaid when he fhould be reftor'd.
" They were quickly apprehended, the Prieft hang'd,
" and the pretended King fent to the Gallies; this hap-
" pen'd in the Year 1585.

" THE very fame Year *Matthew Alvarez*, a Na-
" tive of the Ifland of *Tercera*, and the Son of a
" *Stone-Cutter*, was perfuaded to give himfelf out for
" King *Sebaftian*. This Man was a *Hermit*, and led
" in Solitude a harmlefs inoffenfive Life. Many of
" whom he begg'd believ'd they faw in his Counte-
" nance the Features of Don *Sebaftian*; they told him
" fo, but he very honeftly anfwer'd, that he was no
" *King*, but a *poor Hermit*. By Degrees however,
" Ambition got the better, both of his Reafon and of
" his Virtue; he no longer anfwer'd as he was won't,
" but on the contrary, gave all who interrogated him
" Caufe to apprehend that he was really the King.
" By Degrees he permitted them to pay him Royal
" Honours, fuffer'd his Hand to be kiffed, and dined in
" Publick; nay, he went fo far at laft, as to write to
" the *Cardinal Archduke Albert*, commanding him to
" quit his Palace, for that he intended to refume the
" Government. Upon this, a Body of Troops was
" fent againft him and his Adherents, by whom they
" were routed, and himfelf taken Prifoner. His Death
" quickly follow'd, accompanied with extraordinary
" Marks of Severity. He had his Right Hand cut off,
" after which he was ftrangl'd, and his Body quarter'd.
" By his Means the *Spanifh* Government reckoned a
" Stop

" Stop would be put to the Hopes of *Pretenders*, and
" to the credulous Folly of the *Portugueze*.

" In 1598, notwithstanding these Severities, there
" went a Report, that the true Don *Sebastian* had been
" seen in *Italy*. Upon this, one *Manuel Antonez*,
" who had served the Cardinal *Henry*, who succeeded
" Don *Sebastian*, declar'd publickly in *Portugal*, that
" *Sebastian* was not kill'd at the Battle of *Alcacar*, but
" that himself return'd with him into *Portugal*; and
" that the King put himself into a Religious *House* in
" *Algarve*, there to do Pennance for his Temerity,
" in Vindication of which Account, he produced an
" Act drawn up in Form, under the Hand and Seal of
" the Father, *Guardian* of that Religious House. This
" Affair making a great Noise, *Manuel Antonez* was
" directed to apply himself to the Court of *Spain*, which
" Order he obey'd, and having produced his Paper to
" King *Philip*, was seized, committed to Prison, and
" never heard of more.

" This new *Sebastian* appear'd first at *Padua*, where
" many pitied and reliev'd him. This making some
" Noise in the World, Directions were sent to *Padua*
" from *Venice*, to oblige the Person who called himself
" King of *Portugal*, to retire from thence in three Days,
" and in the Space of a Week, to quit the Dominions
" of *Venice*. He was sick when this Order was noti-
" fied to him, but as soon as he recover'd he went to
" *Venice*, in order to give an Account of himself to
" the *Seignory*. The Ambassador of *Spain* instantly
" applied himself to that *Senate*, demanding that this
" *Impostor* should be apprehended, and charging him
" with many enormous Crimes. He was accordingly

in

" in the Month of *November* thrown into a Dungeon,
" and Commiffioners appointed to hear what the *Spa-*
" *nifh* Ambaffador could prove againft him, which came
" at laft to nothing at all.

" HE was Eight and Twenty Times examined ; at firft
" he anfwer'd readily all the Queftions that were ask'd
" him concerning the Embaffies fent to him, while he
" was King of *Portugal*, the Meafures he had taken,
" the Letters he had written, and the Minifters he had
" made Ufe of. But at laft he refus'd to anfwer any
" more Queftions, addreffing himfelf to his Judges in
" thefe Words. *My Lords, I am* Sebaftian *King of*
" Portugal, *I defire you will fuffer me to be feen by*
" *my Subjeƈts, many of them have known, and muft*
" *remember me ; many others, Strangers to that Nation,*
" *have likewife feen and converfed with me ; if any Proof*
" *can be offered, that I am an Impoftor I am content to*
" *die ; but would you put me to Death meerly for having*
" *preferred you to the reft of the* European *Powers, in*
" *feeking Refuge in your Dominions ?*

" DOCTOR *Sampajo*, and other *Portugueze*, then Re-
" fident in *Venice*, folicited vehemently his being fet at
" Liberty ; the Commiffioners inform'd them, that
" without a Certificate of indubitable Authenticity, as
" to the *Marks* by which Don *Sebaftian* might be
" known, they could not fet this Perfon at Liberty ;
" becaufe they knew their Hatred to the *Caftilians* to
" be fuch, that if Need were, they would acknowledge
" a *Negroe* to be Don *Sebaftian*. Dr. *Sampajo* upon
" this went privately to *Lisbon*, from whence he return'd,
" and brought with him to *Venice* a *Canon*, and an In-
" ftrument fign'd by an *Apoftolick Notary*, containing an
" exaƈt

" exact Account of the Marks on Don *Sebaftian's*
" Body ; whereupon he renew'd his Requeft, which
" the *Seignory* evaded, alledging, they could not enter
" into fuch an Inquiry at the Requeft of private Perfons,
" but that they were ready to do it, if any of the Po-
" tentates of *Europe* interefted themfelves therein. The
" *Portugueze* upon this, applied themfelves to Foreign
" Courts with unwearied Diligence.

" At laft, on the 11th of *December* the fame Year,
" Don *Chriftopher* the younger, Son of Don *Antonio,*
" once King of *Portugal,* attended by *Sebaftian Figuera,*
" arriv'd at *Venice,* with Letters from the *States Gene-*
" *ral* and Prince *Maurice.* Upon this, a Day of Au-
" dience was appointed, on which the Perfon calling
" himfelf *Sebaftian,* was feated on the Right Hand of
" the Prince, and permitted to deliver his Pretenfions
" in Writing to the *Duke,* and two Hundred *Senators,*
" who when they fpoke to him gave him the Title of
" *Illuftriffimo.* This was on the *Tuefday,* on *Wednef-*
" *day, Thurfday,* and *Friday,* the *Council* was conti-
" nued. At *Ten* in the Evening of the laft mention'd
" Day, they made their Report to the *Senate,* who im-
" mediately fummon'd Don *Sebaftian* before them, to
" whom they gave the fame Injunction that he had
" before receiv'd at *Padua;* while this Order which
" was in Writing was read, the *Senators* continued
" ftanding, while he who call'd himfelf *Sebaftian* fate,
" and remain'd cover'd.

" When he came out he would not fuffer any to
" accompany him to the Houfe where he had firft
" lodged, where he found *Roderigo Marquez,* and *Sa-*
" *baftian Figuera,* who at the firft Sight of him were

ex-

" extremely furpriz'd : They faid he was much chang'd,
" but that they were pofitive he was the King, of which
" they advifed his Coufin *Don Chriftopher*, who there-
" upon ordered he fhould be conducted to the Lodgings
" of *Don John de Caftro*, which were in a more pri-
" vate Part of the City.

" THERE he fhew'd himfelf to all the *Portugueze*,
" obferving to them, that his Perfon was very remark-
" able, his whole *Right* Side being bigger than his
" *Left*; he meafured his Arms, his Legs, his Thighs,
" then kneeling down, he difcover'd that his right
" Shoulder was higher than his left by three Inches, he
" fhewed them the Scar of his right Eye-brow, and
" fuffer'd all who defired to feel with their Fingers,
" a remarkable Cleft in his Skull. He then fhewed
" them that he wanted a *Tooth* on the right Side of his
" lower Jaw, which he faid had been drawn by *Seba-*
" *ftian Nero* his Barber, all the reft of his Teeth being
" firm and ftrong. They would then have had him eat,
" but he refufed fo to do, becaufe it was *Friday*. As
" thofe who were about him came from different
" Countries, fome were Habited after the *Dutch*, fome
" after the *Italian*, others after the *French* Fafhion ;
" one whofe Name was *Francis Antonio*, was in the
" Garb of a *Pilgrim*, with a Staff in his Hand. *Se-*
" *baftian* ftanding by the Fire, after continuing a long
" Time filent, at laft faid with a Smile, *Tanto trage !*
" *What odd Fafhions !* Upon which, fome of the *Por-*
" *tugueze* Nobility, who had been to that Time filent,
" cry'd out, that from the Manner of his pronouncing
" thofe Words, they knew him to be the King. The
" *fecond* Night underftanding that all the Paffes into the

D   " Country

" Country of the *Grifons* were fecured, he went over
" into the *Terra Firma* in the Habit of a *Monk*, but
" when he quitted *Padua*, he refumed his Cloak and
" Sword, took the Road to *Florence*, and was there ar-
" refted by Order of the *Grand Duke*.

" THE King of *Spain* immediately demanded that
" he fhould be put into his Hands, which the *Grand
" Duke* refufed to do, juftifying himfelf by the Example
" of the *State* of *Venice*. However the Duke of *Savoy*
" preparing to invade his Dominions, he caufed *Seba-
" ftian* to be fent to *Orbitello*, and put into the Hands
" of the *Spaniards*. The Wits in *Italy* were mightily
" divided on this Accident, fome commending the
" *Grand Duke* for difcouraging an *Impoftor* ; others
" alledging, that it was a direct Breach of Faith. He
" who call'd himfelf King of *Portugal*, underftood it
" in this Light, he reproached the *Grand Duke's* Of-
" ficers in the fevereft Terms, adding, when he was
" deliver'd to the *Spaniards*, that he did not doubt but
" God would punifh the Houfe of *Medicis* for their Per-
" fidy towards him.

" AT *Naples* he was imprifon'd in the Caftle *del
" Ovo*, and as the *Portugueze* affirm, was lock'd up in a
" Chamber for *three* Days, without having any Sufte-
" nance given him, or fo much as feeing the Face of any
" Perfon ; only a *Rope* and a *Knife* of half a Foot
" long were left in a Corner of the Room. *Sebaftian*
" did not make Ufe of either of thefe Remedies, but
" bore with Patience and Refignation all the Injuries
" and Hardfhips which were put upon him. The
" *fourth* Day the *Auditor* General, accompanied by
" *two* Secretaries, made him a Vifit : This Magiftrate
" told

" told the Prifoner in few Words, that provided he laid
" afide the Chimerical Stile he had hitherto affumed,
" he might have Meat, Drink, a convenient Lodging,
" and other Accomodations. *I cannot do that,* faid he,
" *I am Don* Sebaftian *King of* Portugal, *whofe Sins*
" *have drawn upon him thefe fevere Chaftifements; I am*
" *content to die after what manner you pleafe, but to deny*
" *the Truth, that I can never do.* After this he was
" allow'd Bread and Water for fome Time, and then
" *five* Crowns a Month, and a Servant to attend him.

" THE *Conde de Lemos,* at that Time Viceroy of
" *Naples,* being defirous to fee him, he was conducted
" to the Palace, where ent'ring the Hall, and perceiving
" the Count bare-headed, which happened accidentally,
" on Account of the Heat of the Weather, he faid in
" a grave and majeftic Tone. *Conde de* Lemos *be co-*
" *ver'd.* The Spectators being aftonifh'd, the *Count*
" asked him with fome Difdain, by what Authority he
" bid him be cover'd ? *By an Authority,* replied the
" Prifoner, *to which my Birth entituled me. But why,*
" *Sir, do you pretend not to know me ? I remember you*
" *very well; my Uncle* Philip *fent you twice to me into*
" Portugal, *where you had fuch and fuch private Confe-*
" *rences with me.* The *Count,* touch'd with this Dif-
" courfe, continu'd fome Time filent; at laft, he faid to
" the Keeper who was with him, *Take him away, he*
" *is an Impoftor. No Sir,* return'd he, *I am the un-*
" *fortunate King of* Portugal, *and you know it well.*
" *A Man of your Quality ought on all Occafions, either*
" *to be filent, or to fpeak the Truth.* While the *Conde*
" *de Lemos* liv'd, except his Imprifonment, *Sebaftian*
" endur'd no great Hardfhip; he was allow'd to live

" as he pleafed, and was permitted to go to *Chapel*
" whenever he defir'd it. He fafted regularly *Friday's*
" and *Saturday's*, and during the whole *Lent* contented
" himfelf with *Herbs* and *Roots*, receiv'd the *Sacrament*,
" and went to Confeffion conftantly.

" THE *Conde de Lemos* was fucceeded in his Go-
" vernment by his Son, who treated *Sebaftian* with
" great Rigor. The Bifhop of *Reggio* was fent to ex-
" orcife him, (the *Spanifh* Miniftry on Account of his
" Anfwers, affecting to believe he was a Magician)
" This Prelate having perform'd his Office with great
" Solemnity, the Prifoner drew a little *Crucifix* out of
" his Bofom : *Behold*, faid he, *the Badge of my Pro-*
" *feffion, the Standard of that Captain whom to the laft*
" *Drop of my Blood I fhall ferve*. On the *firft* of *April*
" 1602, he was carried from the Caftle mounted upon
" an *Afs*, three Trumpets founding before him, and a
" Herald proclaiming thefe Words, *His moft Catholick*
" *Majefty hath commanded this Man to be led through*
" *the Streets of* Naples *with all Marks of Ignominy,*
" *and then to ferve on Board the Gallies for Life, for*
" *giving himfelf out to be Don* Sebaftian *King of* Por-
" tugal, *whereas he is a* Calabrian. The Trumpets
" founded before and after Proclamation. When the
" Heralds fpoke of his calling himfelf King, he cried
" out, *and fo I am*; when he came to the Word *Ca-*
" *labrian*, the Prifoner cried out again, *that is falfe*.

" AFTER this, he was put on Board the Gallies, and
" for a Day or two, chain'd to the Oar; but as foon
" as they were out of the Port, they reftored him his
" own Cloaths, and treated him like a Gentleman. In
" the Month of *Auguft* 1602, the Gallies came into
Port

" Port St. *Lucar*, where the Duke and Dutchess of
" *Medina Sidonia* defired to fee the Prifoner. When
" they had converfed together fome Time; *Sebaftian*
" asked the Duke if he had ftill the Sword which he
" gave him ? *I have,* reply'd the Duke cautioufly, *a*
" *Sword given me by* Don Sebaftian, *when he went to*
" Africk, *which I keep among other Swords prefented to*
" *me.* Let *them be brought,* faid the Prifoner, *I fhall*
" *know the Sword I gave you.* A Servant being fent
" upon this Occafion, return'd prefently with a dozen.
" *Sebaftian* having examin'd them, *one* by *one,* turn'd
" gravely to the Duke and faid, *Sir, my Sword is not*
" *here.* The Servant being remanded to bring the reft,
" as foon as he came with them, *Sebaftian* catched one
" out of his Hand, crying out, *This Sir, is the Sword*
" *I gave you.* When he came to be put on Board the
" Gallies, he faid to the Dutchefs : *Madam, I have no-*
" *thing to give you now, when I went to* Africk *I gave*
" *you a Ring, if you will fend for it I will tell you a*
" *Secret;* the Dutchefs faid, it was true the King of
" *Portugal* had given her a Ring, and ordered it to be
" fent for. When *Sebaftian* faw it, *prefs it with your*
" *Fingers Madam,* faid he, *the Jewel may then be ta-*
" *ken out, and beneath it you will find my Cypher,*
" which proved true. The Duke and Dutchefs fhed
" Tears at his Departure. When he took his Leave
" he faid to the Dutchefs, *Madam, the Negroe Slave*
" *who attends you, formerly wafhed my Linnen.* Seba-
" *ftian* was after this imprifoned, yet treated with Le-
" nity till he died, which happen'd at four Years End,
" always perfifting that he was in Truth what he
" gave himfelf out to be."

Mr.

Mr. *de St. Dennis* was the firſt who ſpoke to me of the Neceſſity of acting upon ſettled Principles, and propoſing ſome certain End to myſelf; a Thing eaſily apprehended by my Judgment, but hardly reconcileable to my Inclinations. I had left my Country young; had framed to myſelf no diſtinct Ideas, either of Civil or Eccleſiaſtical Polity; the Inſtructions I had receiv'd on one Hand, were hindered from making any great Impreſſion by thoſe given me on the other; the odd turn my Affairs had taken, had in a manner joſtled out both; ſo that when I came into this *French* Gentleman's Family, my Mind was a kind of Blank, in which, except the firſt Principles of Morality and the Chriſtian Religion, there was nothing written, or at leaſt nothing which might not eaſily have been effaced. To him I ſtood indebted for moſt of thoſe Maxims, which in ſucceeding Years preſerv'd me from thoſe Misfortunes which are too common to Wanderers, and which in Spight of that roving Temper, that I could never totally ſubdue, maintained me in a State of tolerable Tranquility in my own Breaſt, and hindered me from becoming offenſive to others. He directed my Studies, inform'd me what Books were worth reading, and what would only burthen my Memory without informing my Underſtanding. From him I learn'd to place Religion in my Heart, and in my Actions, without ſuffering it to dwell too much upon my Lips; to preſerve a reſpectful Behaviour towards the eſtabliſh'd *Form* of *Religion*, and towards the *Clergy* in all Countries; to habituate my ſelf to Acts of Charity, and to a Complacency for all ſorts of Perſons with whom I had Occaſion to converſe. Mr. *Fetherſtone* inſtructed me as to the Methods

of

of remitting Money, and of travelling with Eafe and Safety through *France* and *Italy*. After we had been at *Rouen* about fix Weeks, he fet out for *Paris*, and re-turn'd a few Days after with the News of his Uncle's Death, which happened fuddenly, the Day after he ar-riv'd, by which he became poffeffed of a little Fortune, which turned into ready Money, amounted to about 4000 *Livres.*

In the *Spring* of the Year 1663, I receiv'd from my Uncle, Bills of *Exchange* for about 1000 *l.* with a Secu-rity on his Eftate for the Remainder of my Fortune. I then determined to travel into *Italy*, not judging it proper to refide at *Paris*, on Account of the Influence of the *Englifh* Court, and the Pains which I knew had been taken to apprehend fuch as had been for the *Par-liament*, and had fled on that Account into *France*. We determined to fet out in *April*, and in the mean Time, Mr. *de St. Dennis* carried me to moft of the remarkable Places in *Normandy*, giving me proper Information as to the Antiquities, and other Particularities, whereby they were rendered remarkable.

The Caftle of *Ivetot*, with a pretty Lordfhip round it, lies at a fmall Diftance from *Rouen*, it was at the Time that I faw it in the Hands of Mr. *de Bellay*, a Perfon of great Family, and who feldom refided there. This Manor or Lordfhip, is the Glory of the *Pais de Caux*, having been formerly a diftinct Kingdom, and remaining to this Day a Principality, of which this is, as I was informed, an authentick Account. *Gautier de Ivetot* was Chamberlain to King *Clotaire*, and a Gen-tleman of great Courage, as well as wonderful Probity; Qualities which gained him the Love of his *Sovereign*,

and

and in Confequence thereof, the Hatred of his Courtiers, who devifed fo many Stories to his Prejudice, that the poor Man thought proper to retire from Court, and even to quit his native Country. Ten Years he travelled Abroad, and with equal Valour and Succefs, fought againft the *Sarracens*. At length being defirous to return into *France*, he went to *Rome*, where he was receiv'd by Pope *Agapetus* with great Honours, and obtain'd Letters recommendatory to King *Clotaire*, which he prefented him at *Amiens* on *Good-Friday*, as the King was at Chapel. At firft the King did not remember him, but perceiving by the *Pope*'s Letters who he was, he fuddenly catch'd a Sword from one of his Guards, and kill'd the unfortunate Gentleman, who was on his Knees before him. The *Pope* fo highly refented this Fact, that he immediately fent a *Legate* to inform the King, that he would put him and his whole Kingdom under an *Interdict*, if he did not give the Church Satisfaction for the Murder of *Gautier de Ivetot*. The King thereupon declared, that as he had violated the Bonds by which Princes and Subjects are united to each other, he was content to releafe the Defcendants of *Gautier de Ivetot*, from all Homage, Fealty, or other Obligation, in refpect of the Lands by him poffeffed at that Day, which he accordingly did by a folemn Act dated A. D. 553. Thus the Lordfhip of *Ivetot* was erected into a Kingdom ; but on the Extinction of the Family, the Title was reduc'd to that of a *Principality*.

THE *Pais de Caux* is one of the richeft Diftricts of *Normandy*, tho' not very large, the Worth of this Territory may be guefled from the following fhort and pleafant Defcription.

Au

Au noble pays *de Caux,*
Y a quatre *Abbayes Royaux,*
Six *Prieurez conventaux,*
Et six *Barons de grand arroy,*
Quatres *Comtes,* trois *Ducs,* un *Roy.*

The *English* of which is:

In the fruitful Pays de Caux,
 Royal Abbies *there are* four,
Six *fair* Priories *also,*
 Of *Baronies* as many more:
Four *Earls,* three *Dukes,* from thence their *Titles* bring,
And what is *greater* still——Here dwells a KING.

THE King hinted at in these Verses, is the King of
Ivetot before-mention'd ; I shall not pretend to set down
the Names of the other Places mention'd in the Verses.
It is sufficient to say, that *Diepe, Havre de Grace, Har-*
fleur, and other remarkable Places are seated in this Dis-
trict. The Estates of the Inhabitants descend to the
eldest Son entire, contrary to the Custom of *Normandy,*
by which Lands descend in *Gavel-kind.*

OUR next Journey was towards the other Side of
Normandy, viz. to *Caen.* It is certainly a very antient,
and remains to this Day, a very beautiful and pleasant
Place ; but to believe that it was built by an *Israelite,*
called *Cademoth,* or that the famous *Cadmus* laid its first
Stone, requires more Faith than an intelligent Man is usually Master of. Without troubling one's self farther, as
to a Point not easily to be settled, let it suffice that it is
strong,

ftrong, populous, rich, and pleafant, watered by *two* fair Rivers, and feated but at a very fmall Diftance from the Sea. Adorned with a Univerfity, and protected by a Caftle, which, if its Fortifications anfwered its Situation, could not be eafily taken. In this Caftle there is a *Donjon*, or high fquare Tower; in antient Times the Mark of a *Barony*, or Lordfhip. In this City, amongft other ftately religious Houfes, ftands an Abbey, dedicated to the *Holy Trinity*, which acknowledges for its Founder, *William* the *Conqueror*. In 1542, a Vault being opened in a Church of the faid Abbey, there the Bodies of that *Prince*, and of his Wife *Matilda*, were found. This City is the Capital of lower *Normandy*, and the Head of a *Bailiwick*, which derives it Name from thence, and is of a very confiderable Extent. Yet with all thefe Advantages, it is not a Bifhoprick, but makes a Part of the Diocefe of the Bifhop of *Bayeux*.

THERE are many Monuments of the *Englifh* Dominion in this, as indeed there are in moft of the remarkable Places in *Normandy*, and many of the *Gentry* are of *Sirnames* well known in *England*. This gives the Inhabitants a peculiar Affection for the Natives of our Ifland; but I cannot agree with fome fanguine Travellers, that they are defirous of returning under our Dominion, the *French* in general being as loyal to their Princes, as moft Nations in *Europe*.

At my Return to *Roan*, I expected to have found a Letter from my Uncle, in Anfwer to a long Epiftle I had written him, as to my Intention of vifiting *Italy*; but, to my great Surprize, no Letter was come, neither did I receive one in *three* Weeks; I was afraid of

writing

writing again, no Friend in *England* had my Addrefs, it was dangerous to make any Enquiries at *Paris*; at length, growing very impatient, Mr. *Fetherftone*, tho' his Affairs were rather in a worfe Situation than mine, I mean with Refpect to the Government, offered to go to *England* to obtain fome Satisfaction. I cannot tell, whether in Juftice I ought to have expofed him to fo great a Rifque as he ran; but being a young Man, and as yet little acquainted with Difappointments, I readily accepted his Kindnefs, and we immediately concerted the Means for his Paffage from *Calais* without Sufpicion.

M. *de St. Dennis* had fome Manufcripts relating to Chemiftry, which he caufed to be very fairly tranfcribed, bound in a Velvet Cover, and emboffed with Gold, the whole fo tinctured with a Solution of *Saffron*, that they appeared to have been written a long Time. Thefe Manufcripts Mr. *Fetherftone* carry'd to *Paris*, and by the Means of an *Englifh* Roman Catholick, whofe Name was *Talbot*, got himfelf recommended to an Agent of the Duke of *Buckingham*'s, who firft endeavour'd to buy the Manufcripts; and finding that impracticable, procured Paffes for my Friend under the Name of *Vincent le Blanc*, to go over into *England* with a certain fealed Packet directed to the Duke of *Buckingham*.

T H I S Scheme fucceeded perfectly well. Mr. *Fetherftone* came fafe to *London*, took Lodgings in St. *Martin's-Lane*, and after three Weeks Negociation with the Duke, fold him the Manufcripts for *fixty* Pounds. In this Time he learned that a *Plot* either real or pretended had been difcovered, and my Uncle, on Account of fome Remittances made to General *Ludlow*, had been apprehended and brought up to *London*, where tho' there was no Foundation for this Suspicion, after nine Weeks close Imprisonment, he was at length not totally set at Liberty, but admitted to *Bail*. When he was by this means at Liberty as to his Person, Mr. *Fetherstone* saw him, and receiv'd from him Instructions for me not to write any more by the Method hitherto used ; he likewise signified his Approbation of my going into *Italy*, and gave Mr. *Fetherstone* some Letters for *English* Gentlemen there. This Business being done, Mr. *Fetherstone* prepared for his Return, and upon Application to the Duke, easily procured such Licences as were necessary for his passing out of the Kingdom. The Day before he was to set out taking a walk in the Park, he was met and known by Lieutenant Colonel *Brown*, who had been an Officer in *Cromwell's* Guards ; the Colonel pressed him to dine with him, which after some Difficulty Mr. *Fetherstone* consented to, and fixed on a House in *Old-Palace-Yard*, promising to be there exactly at *One* o'Clock. But when he had thus disengag'd himself for the present, he sent his Cloak-bag to an Inn in *Southwark*, and taking Post-Horses, made the utmost Dispatch to *Dover*, where embarking, in *three* hours time he pass'd to *Calais*, and from thence came the next Day to *Roan*.

WHEN after the first Compliments, he told me this Story, and I asked him how he came to fatigue himself so excessively, when there was no appearance of the Colonel's betraying him ; he answered, That it was one of *Thurloe's* Maxims. *A Man should in nowise hazard his Safety for a Dinner, and a little idle Chat, which can never produce much Good, and may possibly issue in Ruin.* I was perfectly satisfied with his Conduct in this Journey, and on his Return began to prepare in earnest for my

Passage

Paſſage into *Italy*, where I flattered my ſelf I ſhould be extremely delighted, though I knew not why or wherefore ; which I take to be a Circumſtance no way peculiar to me, but common to moſt young Travellers, who ſeek Pleaſure in every Thing but *Quiet*, which on this Side of the Grave is moſt capable of affording true Satisfaction.

A little before I ſet out M. *de St. Dennis*, receiv'd Advice from *Paris*, that a Perſon of Diſtinction to whom he was well known, was to go ſhortly to *Italy* on the King's Affairs. The good old Man laid hold of this favourable Opportunity to procure for me a very commodious Method of Travelling. For the better effecting of this he invited M. *de St. Paul*, a very ancient Gentleman, and Uncle to him in whoſe Train I was to go, to come to his Houſe to Supper. This Gentleman, tho' he was little leſs than *fourſcore*, had abundance of Life and Spirit, and told us many entertaining Stories, eſpecially of the Court of *Henry* IV. in which he had liv'd four or five Years. I laid hold of this Opportunity to enquire into the Particulars of that Prince's Death. M. *de St. Paul* told me, that many things were remarked concerning it, which were truly extraordinary, of which he gave us a Multitude of Inſtances, the moſt remarkable were theſe.

ON *Thurſday* the 13th of *May* 1610, being the Day of the Queen's Coronation, and the Day before the Murder of the King ; his Majeſty in the Evening was ſpeaking with great Marks of Tenderneſs of the Queen, and of her Conduct, during the Ceremony ; *La Broſſe*, an old Phyſician, diſcourſing with the Duke *de Vendome*, ſaid, *If his* Majeſty *out-lives a Miſchief which threatens*

him

him at prefent, he will live thefe thirty Years. The Duke
de Vendome immediately defired the King to hear what
La Broffe had to fay. What is it? faid the King tartly.
The Duke held his Peace, but the King commanding
him to fpeak; he told him what La Broffe had juft before faid: He is an old Fool for telling you fuch Things,
and you are a young Fool (faid the King) if you believe him.
Sire, returned the Duke, One ought not to believe fuch
Things, but one may fear them. All France is bound to
take Care of your Majefty; and as for me, I am more
bound thereto than any other. Let me befeech you to hear
La Broffe. Hold your Tongue, cried the King, I will not
hear him. Well Sire, faid the Duke of Vendome then, I
will carry him to the Duke. If you do, faid the King haftily,
I will never love you more. He repeated thefe Words
in fo angry a Tone, that the Duke of Vendome defifted,
and La Broffe was not heard.

T H E fame Day as the King was going with the
Queen into his Cabinet, he ftopp'd to fpeak to fomebody,
upon which the Queen ftopp'd alfo, Paffez, paffez,
Madam la Regente, i. e. Go on, go on, Madam the
Regent, faid the King. A few Days before his
Death the Queen had two odd Dreams. She fancied
that the Diamonds, Rubies, and other Jewels in her
Crown, were changed into Pearls, and that fhe was
told Pearls fignified Tears. The Night after fhe ftarted
and cried out in her Sleep; the King waking, catched
her in his Arms, and asked her what was the Matter.
I have had a frightful Dream, faid fhe, but Dreams are
Delufions. I have always thought fo too, faid the King;
however tell me what it was. With much Intreaty fhe
proceeded. I dreamt, faid fhe, that you were ftabb'd
                                                    with

with a Knife under the short Ribs. Blessed be God, said the King, *it was but a Dream*, and so went to Sleep.

On the Day the King was kill'd, he was observed to be very uneasy; nay, he observ'd it himself, and said several Times, that something sat heavy on his Heart. When he was going out he asked if the Coach was below. The Villain who kill'd him was at the Foot of the Stairs, and was heard to mutter. *I shall have you, you are lost.* He thrice took leave of the Queen before he went into the Coach. He then seemed to resume himself, he forbid the Guards to follow him out of the *Louvre*; sent the Captain to the *Palais*; the Lieutenant was sick; the Ensign was gone with a Message to the *President du Harlay*; so that the Coach was open on all Sides; his Attendance went through another Street; the *Rue de la Ferronneire* being very narrow, was encumber'd with *two* Waggons, one laden with Wine, the other with Corn, which obliged the King's Coach to stop. At that Instant the King threw back his Cloak, and put himself into such a Position, as left his Side wholly exposed to the *Assassin*, who said himself afterwards, that he thrust his Knife into the King's Body, as into a *Sack* of *Corn*.

It was remark'd, that in the Space of a Week the *French* saw two Kings interred, who both died by the *Knives* of *Assassins*; for but a few Days before his own Death, *Henry* IV. had caused his Predecessor to be solemnly interred. It is certain that in *Flanders* the King's Death was spoke of as soon as it happen'd, and the Queen's Jeweller receiv'd a Letter the next Day from one of his Correspondents, desiring that he would inform him whether the King was kill'd or no. M. *de St. Paul* laid

laid great Stress on these *Omens*; and indeed I have heard others speak of them with Surprize; for my own part, I know not what to say; this I know, that many rash and ignorant People disregard and laugh at these Things, and that Men of great Wisdom and Learning speak of them with Diffidence, and strive rather to encourage others to slight them, than shew any real Contempt of them themselves.

By the Help of this Mr. *de St. Paul*, I was so effectually recommended to the Count *de Gaffion*, that he readily consented to my going with him into *Italy*, and even did me the Honour of his Intimacy and Friendship. Mr. *Fetherstone* had engag'd in some Concerns of Trade, and therefore chose to remain at *Roan*. When all things were ready, my private Concerns settled, and my Debt, tho' not my Obligation to my kind Host M. *de St. Dennis* discharg'd, I set out with my Man *Johnson* for *Paris*.

The City of *Roan* is as pleasant, populous, and well built as any in *France*. Ships of considerable Burden come up the River *Seine*, and lye close to the Key. The Bridge which rises and falls with the River, is venerable for its Antiquity, admirable for its Beauty, and valuable for its Conveniency. At *Roan* the Parliament of *Normandy* is fixed, it assembles in an elegant Building by far more beautiful and stately, as well as more neat and convenient than that at *Paris*, destin'd to the same Use. It is composed of *two* Presidents, *twenty* Counsellors, and as many Advocates as the Court thinks fit to admit. The *first* President takes Place of the Governor of the Province, unless in a Convention of the Estates, for there the Governor presides. The Archbishop of *Roan* is

is Primate of *Normandy*, and the firſt of his Predeceſſors
was conſecrated Archbiſhop during the general Council
at *Arles* under *Conſtantine* the Great.   The Revenue of
the See may amount to *three thouſand* Pounds *per Ann.*
of our Money.   Beſides the Cathedral and Religious
Houſes there are in *Roan thirty-two* Pariſh-Churches.
The Metropolitan Church is dedicated to *our Lady*, and
is remarkable for its having three fine Towers.   One of
theſe, becauſe it was built with the Money ariſing from
the Sale of Diſpenſations to eat *Butter* in *Lent*, is called
La Tour de Beurre, or the *Butter Tower.*   In the Tower
over the Porch hangs the great Bell ſo much talk'd of,
call'd from him who placed it there, *George Amboiſe*.
It is about *thirteen* Foot high, *eleven* in Diameter, and
weighs, as the old *French* Verſes upon it tell us, *Forty
Thouſand* Pounds.

   THE principal Abbey is dedicated to St. *Owen*, of
whom I am almoſt aſhamed to tell a Story that is however
univerſally received here.   They ſay there was a great
Dragon in the Neighbourhood which did prodigious
Miſchief, and which became at laſt ſo formidable, that
the People began to quit their Houſes, and to leave the
Country deſolate.   *Romanus* was then Archbiſhop of
Roan, who commiſerating the Diſtreſs of his Flock, reſolved to go in Queſt of this Dragon.   Before he ſet out
he choſe for his Companions, a *Thief* and a *Murderer*,
who were at that time in Priſon.   When he drew near
the *Dragon*'s Den, and that dreadful Creature came hiſ-
ſing towards him, the *Thief* took to his Heels, but the
Murderer ſtuck faſt by the Archbiſhop, who when he
had offered up his Prayers to *God*, took off his *Stole*, and
advancing directly to the *Dragon*, put it about his Neck,

E   and

and delivered him, thus made Prisoner, to the *Murderer*, who carried the Creature in Triumph to the *City*, where it was first strangled, and then burnt to Ashes. This Exploit is said to have been performed on *Holy Thursday*, in what Year I cannot pretend to say. Thus much is certain, that St. *Owen*, who succeeded St. *Romanus*, certified this Fact to King *Dagobert*, about the Year of Christ 635, and obtained from him a perpetual Edict, whereby the *Canons* of the *Cathedral Church* are vested with a Power of delivering on every *Ascension-Day*, any Criminal appointed to suffer Death. But the *Criminal* must give Security to assist either himself, or by *Proxy*, at the annual Procession in Memory of this *Miracle* for *seven* Years.

NORMANDY, divided into the *higher* and *lower*, is one of the most considerable Provinces in *France*, as well in Regard to its Fertility, as Extent, and always made a very distinguished Figure in the World. It was formerly reckon'd a Part of *Neustria*, or the Kingdom of *Soissons*, but in the ninth Century it chang'd its Name and its Masters, being yielded by *Charles* the Simple to the *Normans*, whereupon *Rollo* their Prince call'd it *Normandy*, and stiled himself *Duke* thereof. The Descendant and Successor of this Prince, *William* the *Conqueror*, annexed it to *England*. When *John*, the Grandson of that Prince mounted the Throne, he seized this Dutchy as well as he had done the Kingdom, in Prejudice to his Nephew *Arthur*, who in a short time after was murdered, with Circumstances strongly insinuating the Connivance at least, if not the Direction of his *Uncle*. Upon this King *John*, as a *Peer* of *France*, was summoned to answer before the *Parliament* of *Paris*, where

where by neglecting to appear, either by himself or Proxy, he was by *Arret* of *Parliament* declared Convict, and his Lands forfeited. Whereupon *Philip Augustus*, King of *France*, did in the Year 1202, seize the said *Dutchy* into his Hands.

It was afterwards however recovered by the *English*, and finally taken from them by *Charles* VII. and inseparably annexed to the Crown by *Lewis* XI. *Lewis* XII. fixed the *Parliament* at *Roan*, and succeeding Kings have honour'd it with other Favours. The *Normans* however do not forget that they were once a free and independent People, but have so vigorously insisted on their Privileges at all Times, that they have hitherto conserved most of them, particularly that of being governed by their own Laws, and being exempted from a great many Taxes. In other Respects the *Normans* are very good Subjects, and as they are an industrious trading People furnish to the Royal Revenue very large Sums. Wine is wanting to this Province, but the Deficiency is tolerably well supplied by a great Quantity of good *Cyder*, which is the common Drink of the Natives, and much more than compensated by the abundance of fine Wheat, which is the Glory of this Country, and which is produced with half the Cultivation necessary in our own. The People are strong, hardy, and industrious, fairer, and more fresh-colour'd than in other Parts of *France*, and less subject to the Gout and Stone, than the Inhabitants of those Provinces which abound in Vineyards, and are consequently well stored with Wine. Their great Vice is Litigiousness; and in Truth they need not have a worse, since it is the Parent of Fraud, Malice, and ill Neighbourhood.

DURING

DURING the Stay I made at *Paris*, I lodg'd at the House of Mr. *D'Aulnoy*; he was himself a Man of good Sense, great Worth, and much Learning; his Lady the most agreeable Woman in the World, and held to write the best Stile in *France* of any of her Sex, after Madam *de Scudery*. I remain'd at this Gentleman's House but three Weeks, and in that small Space I was sensible that I improv'd my self very much in the *French* Language. At my setting out for *Italy* I carry'd with me a hundred Pistoles and Bills for three hundred more on Mr. *Hobson* at *Venice*. The same Sum I deposited in the Hands of a Banker at *Paris*, having also some Money in the Hands of M. *de St. Dennis* at *Roan*. My Design was first to visit the principal Places in *Italy*, and then to return into *France*, that from thence, if the Times in respect to my Affairs were mended, I might pass over into *England*.

WE left *Paris* in the Month of *March*, in order to go to *Nevers*. The Count, and two other Gentlemen, were in one Coach, his Secretary M. *de St. Florentin*, my self and two others of his Attendants in a second Coach, and he had *nine* Domesticks besides. We were *eleven* Days complete in reaching *Nevers*, which is accounted *fifty eight Leagues* from *Paris*. We rested there *three* Days by reason of the Count's using some Waters in its Neighbourhood, which gave me an Opportunity of viewing the Place.

IT is an ancient and no very large City, though a Bishoprick, and the Capital of a Dutchy, and of the Territory call'd *Nivernois*. The *Ducal* Palace is a very fine Structure, and was richly furnished, but the most remarkable Rarity in it is a curious Marble Table, not

very

very large, but finely vein'd, and which is indeed furprifing, perfectly tranfparent, either by Night or Day,
for a Lamp being placed behind, may be diftinctly feen
through it. *Nevers* is likewife adorned with an ancient
Cathedral dedicated to St. *Cyr*. There is alfo a Bridge
over the *Loire*, which is very remarkable, confifting of
no lefs than twenty Arches. *Nevers* was a County or
Earldom under the firft *French* Kings, was firft erected
into a Dutchy by *Charles* VII. It paffed afterwards into
various noble Families, 'till at length it defcended to the
Houfe of *Gonzaga*, from whom a little while ago the
Cardinal Minifter acquir'd it not with much Reputation,
and hath procur'd it to be erected into a Dutchy and
Peerdom in favour of his Nephew *Philip Mancini Ma-*
zarine, a young Man who continues as yet unmarried.

F R O M *Nevers* we proceeded in five Days to *Lyons*,
which lies at the Diftance of *forty-five* Leagues. This
is beyond Comparifon the pleafanteft City in *France*,
perhaps I fhould not err if I faid in *Europe*. It differs
from all the Places I ever beheld, inafmuch as it is agreeable to every Tafte, having within its Walls all Things
that can delight the Eye, or pleafe the Imagination. Part
of the City ftands high, Part low. You may live on
the Side of a River, or out of Sight of Water. Some
of its Streets have all the Hurry of Bufinefs, others have
magnificent Houfes, and at very reafonable Prices, fo
fituated as to have the Air of a magnificent Metropolis.
And in the Skirts of this agreeable Place you may enjoy
a rural Habitation, furrounded with Fields, Gardens,
Vineyards, and yet at no great Diftance from the Heart
of the City ; furrounded as it is with Hills, it is continually warm, and as thofe Hills are extremely well

E 3 cultivated

cultivated, they afford the fineſt Proſpect that can be imagined.

THE *Saone* paſſes through the City; the *Rhoſne* waſhes its Walls; the Stone Bridge over the former conſiſts of nine Arches, and is remarkable for the Cruelty exerciſed thereon by *Caligula*, who cauſed all ſuch as diſputed before him and did not prevail, to be thrown from thence into the River and drowned, as *Juvenal* informs us. The Bridge over the *Rhoſne* is by far more remarkable; indeed there are few which can be compared with it, conſidering the Breadth and Rapidity of the River. It conſiſts of twenty-ſix Arches, nineteen large, and ſeven ſmall ones. The Beauty and Pleaſantneſs of *Lyons*, though they are certainly very great, are not however its principal Advantages. Its Commodiouſneſs for Trade deſerves particular Attention. The *Rhoſne* affords an eaſy Paſſage to the Sea, and conſequently opens a Gate to the *Mediterranean* Commerce, to that of *Africk* and the *Levant*. Twelve Leagues of Land-Carriage ſends all Sorts of Merchandize to the *Loire*, whereby a Communication is acquired, not only with the moſt diſtant Provinces of *France*, *Holland*, and *Flanders*, but alſo with *Britain* and the North. From *Montangis* Boats go through a little River into the *Seine*, and ſo to *Paris*. By this means *Lyons* is the Centre of a prodigious Trade, continually filled with Foreigners, and inhabited by abundance of Artificers, and Mechanicks of all Sorts. They have here *four* free *Fairs* every Year, one, which may be called the firſt, at *Twelfth-tide*, the ſecond at *Eaſter*, the third in *Auguſt*, and the laſt on the Day dedicated to the Memory of *All-Saints*. One principal Commodity at theſe Fairs is *Books*, the

Number

Number of which, without feeing them, it is impoffible to have any Conception of.

THE Privileges beftow'd on this City for the maintaining and encreafing thefe Advantages are great; and which is yet of more Confequence, well adapted. The Bufinefs of Exchange is wholly in the Hands of the *Florentines*, who are perfectly well fkill'd in that myfterious Branch of Traffick. The *Germans* have great Immunities, particularly this, that no Caufes in which they are Parties can be drawn out of their own Courts, whether their Nature be civil or criminal. The Government of *Lyons* is by a *Prevoft des Marchands*, and four *Efchevins*, the latter chofen annually, the firft once in two Years: When the *Efchevins* go out of Office, they are eannobled of courfe. All Caufes are decided here very fpeedily, and at a fmall Expence, which is done in favour of Trade, and hath a mighty good Effect. The Town-houfe is a very elegant Fabrick, having before it a large fquare Piazza with a noble Fountain; here all the City Courts are kept, and the publick Bufinefs tranfacted.

THE Cathedral, dedicated to St. *John*, is a large venerable Pile, remarkable chiefly for its Clock, placed in a ftately Tower, on the Top of which ftands a Cock, which every Hour claps his Wings and crows twice; then an Angel comes out at a Door, which opens of it felf, and falutes the Virgin *Mary*; at the fame Time the Holy Ghoft appears in the Form of a Dove; then a Figure, reprefenting the Eternal Father, bleffes her three Times. The Days of the Week are reprefented by feven Figures, each of which takes place in a Niche in the Morning of the Day it reprefents, and continues

there

there 'till the next Morning. But the greateſt Singularity was newly put up, *viz.* an oval Plate marked with the Minutes of an' Hour, which were exactly pointed to by a Hand reaching the Circumference, and which in its Revolution inſenſibly dilates and contracts it ſelf; the Difference of the Tranſverſe, and conjugate Diameters being *ten* Inches, half of which conſequently is the greateſt Extenſion of this Hand.

It appears by an Inſcription on the Clock it ſelf, that it was repaired and improved by *William Nouriſon, Anno Dom.* 1661. but it was contrived long before his Time by *Nicholas Lipp,* a Native of *Baſil.* The Report goes, that the Magiſtrates of *Lyons,* after he had finiſhed this curious Machine, cauſed his Eyes to be put out, that he might never be able to perform the like; but this is an abſolute Falſhood, invented by the Mob to magnify their Clock. As to *Lipp,* the Magiſtrates engaged him to fix at *Lyons,* by allowing him a very conſiderable *Salary* to look after his own Machine, which he is ſaid to have perfected at the Age of *Thirty,* or of *Thirty-two,* and in the Year 1598.

M. *SERVIER,* who invented the Minute-Motion, I have deſcribed lived at this Time in great Reputation at *Lyons.* He was in his younger Years an *Officer* in the Army, but all of a ſudden quitted the Life of a Soldier and came to *Lyons,* where he gave himſelf up wholly to the Study of the Mechanicks. The common People believed him a ſecond *Solomon,* and Perſons of the beſt Senſe admitted he had wonderful Abilities. As I was ſtill a very young Man, I had not the Confidence to apply to him for a Sight of his Curioſities, becauſe I heard he was an odd-temper'd Man, and not over-complaiſant to Foreigners, unleſs they were Perſons of very great Diſtinction.

I

I took Care however to find out a Person who had formerly liv'd with him, and who gave me an exact Detail of all his Rarities, the most remarkable of which were these, 1. A flat Ruler lying on a Plane like one of our Cribbidge Boards, mark'd with Hours, half Hours, and Quarters. The Hour of the Day or Night distinguished thereon by the Paw of a Mouse creeping forward, and returning backwards of its self. 2. A perpendicular Ruler mark'd in the same manner, the Time pointed out by a Lizard, ascending and descending. 3. A brazen Vessel with the Hours on the Sides, this being fill'd with Water, an artificial Tortoise is put into it by any Spectator, which after turning several Times, points the exact Time of the Day. 4. Two Dials at a Distance from each other, yet the Hand of one being moved to any Hour, the Hand of the other was instantly moved to the same Hour of itself. 5. A perpetual Hour Glass, which not only turns itself, but also changes in turning a brass Figure on its Top, shewing the Hour of the Day or Night. Most of these extraordinary Machines are thought to depend chiefly upon *Magnets* or *Load-stones*, properly disposed. I should not have mentioned them if I had not been persuaded, as well of the Possibility of such Performances, as of the Veracity of him who inform'd me.

After eight Days Stay at *Lyons*, we set out for *Geneva*, where we arriv'd in three Days, having passed through a very indifferent Country, and seen in that Space the Territories of three independant States exclusive of *France*, viz. of the Duke of *Savoy*, the *Canton* of *Berne*, and Republick of *Geneva*.

On

On my Arrival at *Geneva*, I met with Letters from Mr. *Fetherftone*, Mr. St. *Dennis*, and my Uncle, all advifing me to ftay for fome Time in that City, which of my felf I was inclined to do, in Order to learn the *Italian* Language, to revive my Acquaintance with ancient Authors, and to acquire fome Knowledge of the Mathematics. It was no difficult Matter to fettle here to my Contentment, the Inhabitants of *Geneva*, having a great Regard for the *Englifh*, on Account of their conftant Correfpondence with them fince the Retreat of the Exiles thither, in the Reign of *Philip* and *Mary*. Befides Lieutenant General *Ludlow*, and fome other Perfons of Diftinction, having refided there lately, and my Letters being addreffed to one of their Friends, I was prefently fettled in a Lodging, boarded in the fame Houfe, and recommended to the Profeffors of the feveral Sciences I intended to ftudy, during my Stay there.

At this Time the War broke out between *England* and *Holland*, ufually call'd the firft *Dutch* War. It appeared plainly enough, that the *Genevefe* were more addicted to the *Dutch*, than to *us*, which I conceive to be owning to two Caufes, their being under a Republican Government, and the *Dutch* having always fhewn a warm Affection for the People of *Geneva*, efpecially teftified by a new Baftion towards the *Rhofne*, the whole Expence of which was defray'd by the *States*.

The City of *Geneva* is as pleafantly fituated as its Inhabitants can wifh, furrounded by Mountains, which defend it from the *Eaft* and *Weft* Winds, and by which as they have many openings on the *North* and *South*, the Inhabitants are prevented from being incommoded with a thick and moift Air. It is divided into two Parts

by

by the *Rhofne*, that Portion which is on the other Side the River, is call'd the *Burgh* of St. *Gervafe*. There is a fine Bridge over the River; and on the Sides thereof, the most wholefome, as well as most agreeable Walks. The common Opinion is, that there is in this City between thirty and forty Thoufand Inhabitants, and confequently about fix Thoufand capable of bearing Arms; but thofe who have examined Things more clofely, think there are not quite fo many. In Point of Extent, it is not held to be above a third Part as large as the City of *Lyons*.

THERE is no Place in the World better ferved with Provifions than this; they have good Wine, and cheap, excellent wild Fowl, and incomparable Fifh; particularly *Trout*, which many believe to be better, and larger, than are to be had in any other Part of *Europe*; whereas fome affirm, there are larger in *Germany*: Certain it is, that the *Trouts* of *Geneva* weigh fometimes fifty Pounds, which are taken out of a kind of Weirs, placed in the River. The chief Church is that of St. *Peter*'s, remarkable for two very large Bells, the largeft requiring ten Men to Toll it; in the Steeple of this Church there is a Watch fet every Night, who in Cafe of any Danger, alarm the Citizens, either by ringing a Bell, or difcharging a Piece of Cannon, two fmall ones being placed on the Steeple for that Purpofe. At each Gate of the City there is a Guard, and when it is fet at Night, one of the Soldiers fays Prayers. Befides thefe Guards, which are compofed of the Garrifon Troops, there are feveral Guards in the City of *Burghers*, neither are fuch Precautions taken without good Reafon, fince they are in the midft of Enemies; and

fo

fo lately as 1602, in the Night of the 12th of *December*, the Duke of *Savoy* attempted to take the Place by Scalade, which he had infallibly done, if the *Savoyard*, who was to have fired the *Petard*, had not been kill'd in attempting to perform it. In the *Arfenal* they have Arms in conftant readinefs, for about five Thoufand Men, with eight Pieces of Cannon, and all neceffary Ammunition., The fcaling Ladders taken from the Duke of *Savoy's* Soldiers, with other Trophies of their Succefs on that Occafion, particularly the Arms of thirteen Men of Quality, who were taken and hanged, together with the *Petard* before-mention'd, yet undif-charged, are fhewn in the fame Place.

THE eftablifhed Religion of the State is *Calvinifm*. The publick Worfhip in their Churches is very decent and regular ; the Minifters pray either according to their own manner, or according to a certain Form which has been approv'd, tho' not impofed. In their Prayers they always mention the *French* King, the King of *England*, the Cantons of *Zurich* and *Berne*, the Pro-teftant Princes in *Germany*, his Highnefs the Prince of *Orange*, and the *States*. Every Day in the Week there is a Sermon at Seven in the Morning, except *Thurfdays* and *Sundays*, when there are two, one at five, and the other at eight. The Minifters are very zealous, and fometimes inveigh bitterly againft the Corruptions of the Age in which they live. Amongft thefe they reckon Mufick, Dancing, Shooting, and other Recrea-tions, to which the young People conftantly repair every *Sunday* in the Afternoon ; but it does not appear, that they have as great an Influence in this as in other Things ; for tho' the Minifters have long preached, yet the

the People continue to Dance in Spight of all that can be faid to them.

FOREIGNERS have Monuments erected for them in the Churches of *Geneva* ; amongſt others, in the Church of St. *Peter*, there is one for *Henry* II. Duke of *Rohan*, which is very magnificent. In an old Cloiſter hard by, there is the Tomb of M. *de Aubigny*, of Sir *Roger Townſhend*, who died in 1647, and Sir *William Maſſham*, Bart. who died A. D. 1662. But as for the *Genevefe* themſelves, they have no Monuments. The Grave of the great *Calvin*, having nothing to diſtinguiſh it from that of another Man. If any *Italian* Family embraces the Proteſtant Religion, they are readily received, and willingly accepted as Citizens of *Geneva*; nay, there are ſome of their Paſtors who have been *Popiſh* Prieſts and Jeſuits, of whom it is obſerved, that they are remarkably zealous in their Sermons, and ſpeak with greater Vehemence againſt the Corruptions of the Romiſh Church, than any of their Brethren.

THE Clergy here are far from having as large Salaries as in other Places, and yet they labour almoſt beyond Meaſure ; befides daily Sermons, and Catechizings, other publick Exerciſes are expected from them, and if a Man hath not a real Call, and conſequently an unfeigned Affection to the Miniſtry, he muſt under this Character live but unhappily in *Geneva*, where not only the leaſt Irregularity, but even a Suſpicion of Lukewarmneſs, or Uneaſineſs, would infallibly deſtroy him.

MY Stay at *Geneva*, tho' it wanted but little of Ten whole Years, was perfectly eaſy and pleaſant to me. At firſt the extraordinary Gravity of the People gave me ſome Diſquiet ; but by Degrees I began to conſider

it

it in quite another Light, and to perceive that what seemed an unneceſſary and burthenſom Auſterity, was in Truth no more than the Effect of a ſerious Diſpoſition, and a juſt Senſe of the Duty incumbent on us in this Life, to act prudently and juſtly. This compoſedneſs of Mind is only to be underſtood of the learned and better Sort of People, of whom, comparatively ſpeaking, there are more here than in moſt other Cities ; for as to the Commonalty, they differ little from thoſe in *Savoy* or *France*. The generality of the *Genevéſe* uſe in common Converſation the *Savoyard* Dialect, but all Perſons of Diſtinction ſpeak good *French*. Among the *Italian* Families that Language is ſpoken ; and there are many of theſe ſettled in *Geneva*, very conſiderable, on Account of their Antiquity and Fortunes: Such as the *Butini*, the *Cornelli*, *Diodati*, *Minutoli*, *Peliſſari*, &c.

IMPROVED by the wiſe Diſcourſes I daily heard, and encouraged by the Examples continually before my Eyes, I proſecuted my Studies with much Application, and began to form to myſelf a Reſolution of leading a more regular and ſettled Life, than hitherto I had done. The Folly of rambling about the World, to gratify a Deſire of ſeeing new Things, and hearing new Stories, appeared to me at this Time in ſo glaring a Light, that I can ſcarce Account for my relapſing ſo ſuddenly into that Paſſion for Novelty, which I had ſo juſtly diſcarded and diſpiſed. It may be that with Reſpect to his Manners, Man himſelf is a *Cameleon*, and having nothing permanent in his own Nature, eaſily receives from others, that Colour with which Cuſtom hath ſtained them, and as eaſily loſes it when he changes Climate to receive another Tincture from the ſame Cauſe.

IN

In the Month of *August* 1664, we had an Account at *Geneva* of the Murder of Mr. *Lifle* at *Laufanne*, it happened thus: That Gentleman had been one of the King's Judges, and even an Affiftant to Serjeant *Bradſhaw*, who was Prefident of the Affembly then called the *High Court of Juſtice.* He had withdrawn himfelf from his Countrymen, who lived in the Territory of the *Canton* of *Berne*, to the Place where he was murdered, on a Suppofition, that thofe Affaffins which had for fome Time hovered on the Confines of *Switzerland*, were employed to difpatch General *Ludlow*, not having any Apprehenfion that his own Death was fought; tho' no Man had been either deeper in the Meafures againft the King, or had expreffed himfelf with greater Warmth againft the *Royal Family.*

The *Wednefday* preceding the *Sunday* on which he was kill'd, two Men pretending to be the Grooms of a *German* Officer of Diftinction, came to the Town where General *Ludlow*, Mr. *Broughton*, and the reft of the *Englifh* refided; but the Regency of *Berne* being entirely in their Intereft, the Affaffins thought fit to decamp, and to make the beft of their Way to *Laufanne.* There they waited for an Opportunity of deſtroying Mr. *Lifle*, which they effected thus: They were informed that it was this Gentleman's Cuftom to go to the Church which ftood near the Town Gate; one of the Affaffins thereupon, fixed himfelf early at the Church Gate, and having waited 'till all the People were gone in, he mutter'd to himfelf, *Le Bougre ne viendras pas, the Rafcal don't come.* He then went to a Barber's, pretending to have the Tooth-ach, but turning his Head towards the Window, he faw Mr. *Lifle* had paffed him,

him, and was in the Church-yard alone; upon which he ran after him, pull'd out his Carbine, which was flung under his great Coat, and being close to the unhappy Victim, shot him through the Back; the Piece recoiling he fell down himself, but getting up hastily, pull'd off his Hat, and swinging it round his Head cry'd, *God save the King.*

He left his Gun behind him, and made the best of his Way to his Companion, who waited hard by on Horseback, with another Horse ready bridled and saddled in his Hand. On this the Assassin mounted, and they both rode off without Molestation. It was reported that the Government of *Lausanne* were not very industrious in their Endeavours to seize these Murderers; but whoever is acquainted with *Switzerland*, must know that before the *Regency* could be well appriz'd of the Fact, Men so well mounted might be out of Reach, and it is certain, that not contented with having kill'd Mr. *Lisle*, they actually insulted and abused the *Regency* of *Lausanne*, as they rode through the Country.

It was commonly reported, that these Men were commissioned from the *English* Court, to go and take off its Enemies in all Parts of the World, that in consequence of this Commission, one of them had actually murder'd, or at least desperately wounded one Mr. *Ker* in *Holland*, who had betray'd some of the King's Secrets, and had attempted to shoot Col. *Algernoon Sydney*, on the Road to *Paris*. But People of moderate Sentiments, conceived that they were encouraged only by Queen *Henrietta Maria*, and her Daughter the Dutchess of *Orleans*. This was the rather believ'd, because it was certainly known, that the very Man who kill'd Mr. *Lisle* on his Return to *England* was forbid the
Court,

Court, and died shortly after through Want and Despair.

THE other was advanced to a military Command,
but it was in the *French* Service, and had Money given
him, but not by the *English* Court.   For this Cause the
English Gentlemen who were Refugees in *Switzerland*,
spoke with some Degree of Triumph, when in a short
Space after the *Queen* died oddly at *Paris*, that is, by a
Prescription of one of her Physicians.   It was said she had
a Cold, and that a gentle opiat was ordered her, but
either the Drug or the Dose was mistaken, for she never
awaken'd after taking it.   The Wits at *Paris* did not
fail to give their Sentiments on so extraordinary an Accident.   Amongst the several Pieces written upon this Occasion the following Verses were held to be by far the
most poignant; and as they are exactly to my Subject,
I have transcribed them.

> *Le croirez-vous race future ;*
> *Que la Fille du grand Henry*
> *Eut en mourant meme avanture*
> *Que feu son Pere et son Mary ?*
> *Tous trois sont morts par assassin,*
> *Ravaillac, Cromvel, Medecin :*
> *Henry d'un coup de Bayonette,*
> *Charles finit sur un Billot,*
> *Et maintenant meurt Henriette*
> *Par l'Ignorance de Valot.*

> The coming Age will it believe,
> Great *Henry*'s Daughter could receive
> Her End, in the same fatal Way,
> Her Sire, and Spouse, did Death obey ?

F   Will

Will not its utmost Faith be try'd,
When it is told they all *three* dy'd,
By base *Assassins?* —— *Ravaillac,*
The cruel *Cromwell,* and a Quack.
Fatal to mighty *Henry's* Life,
The bloody Villain's treach'rous *Knife.*
Charles on a Block resign'd his Breath,
* *Valot* to *Henriet* gave Death.

But to pass from these melancholy Subjects, and to return to my own Affairs, and the natural Order of time, which tho' distant some few Years, I have, for the Sake of Perspicuity, brought all together.

While I remain'd in this City I frequently spent my Evenings with Mr. *Say* and Mr. *Melville,* the former a vehement Commonwealth's-Man, the latter strictly attached to the Royal Cause, but Men who loved each other; and though they generally differ'd in their Opinions, yet never grew angry, or transgressed in their Expressions the Bounds of Decency. I shall mention one of their Conversations for the Sake of a Fact not generally known. Mr. *Say* would frequently maintain that the War made by King *Charles* against the *Dutch* was ungrateful, because of the Assistance he had received, and the Kindness that had been shewn him from the *States.* He urged also, that it had been carried on unfairly on account of some secret Correspondence which his Majesty had kept up with Admiral *Trump,* and several other eminent Persons in the Interest of the Prince of *Orange,* which had been discover'd by a Spy putting into the Hand of the *Pensioner de Wit,* a Letter from

* *The Name of the Queen's Physician.*

one of the King's *Minifters* inftead of a Petition from himfelf, for which Miftake he paid with his Life, and Admiral *Trump*, and other Perfons of Diftinction, were removed from their Places.

MR. *Melville* obferved that this War was entirely owing to the *Dutch* themfelves ; that in the War they carried on againft the *Commonwealth* of *England*, they fought their own Caufe, not the King's ; that the Letter which occafion'd the Death of *Buat*, concerned folely the Intereft of the *Prince* of *Orange*, whofe Advantage, the King was bound in Honour, Duty, and Intereft, to promote. On the other hand, he alledged that the *Dutch* had encourag'd all that in them lay the Malecontents in *England*, to take up Arms, had actually concerted Meafures for fupporting a Rebellion in *England*, by an Invafion, and to that End had ftrongly folicited Lieutenant General *Ludlow*, Colonel *Algernoon Sidney*, and others, to come into *Holland*, in order to pafs into *England* with a great Body of Foot.

MR. *Say* reply'd, that the Rules of War permitted all this, and that his Moft *Chriftian Majefty* had as ftrongly folicited General *Ludlow*, as the *States*, and even fent him a Paffport that he might come fafe to *Paris*. For my Part, thefe Facts made it clear to me, that *Princes* and *States* prefer their prefent Interefts to all Things. In my Paffage through *France* I had feen *Oliver St. John*, who had been Lord Chief *Juftice* of the *Common Pleas* in the Time of the *Commonwealth*, and of *Cromwell*, treated with great Refpect, though under the Name of Mr. *Mountague*, while meaner People durft not fhew their Heads, leaft the *Englifh* Minifter fhould demand them ; in which Cafe they

would

would certainly have been delivered up. I have already taken Notice of the Terror that Cardinal *de Mazarin* was under with Respect to *Cromwell*. It seems from the following Instance, that either that, or a high Veneration for him, remained not only with the Cardinal, but his Successors in the Ministry after *Cromwell's* Death.

DURING his Protectorship, there happen'd a great Tumult at *Nismes*; the Papists had attempted to take from the Protestants the Right of chosing *Magistrates*, which the latter, rather than submit to, opposed Force to Force, and actually drove the Papists out of the City, not without the Effusion of Blood. Upon this the *Cardinal Minister* caused great Bodies of Troops to march on all Sides towards the City. The Inhabitants perceiving that it would be impossible to defend the Place, began to consult about their own Safety. At length they resolved to send Dr. *Mullins*, a Scotchman, to the *Protector*, to intreat his Interposition.

OLIVER immediately gave Directions to his Secretary to write in the most pressing Terms on their Behalf to the *Cardinal*, and sent this Letter, with a Postscript, in his own Hand, which he added, to shew that he was really concern'd as to the Issue of the Business, by Dr. *Mullins*. The Doctor, like a faithful Agent, scarce took Rest or Refreshment 'till he came to *Lockart*, who was *Cromwell's* Minister at the Court of *France*. *Lockart* instantly carried him and the Letters he brought to the Cardinal, who on opening the Epistle address'd to himself, found the Postscript in these Words: *As you treat these Protestants, you have me a Friend, or an Enemy.* Upon which the Cardinal dispatched Orders for the Troops which were marching towards *Nismes* to halt,

halt, and consented that the Affair should be amicably made up.

It happened that this Dr. *Mullins* was in *France* while I was at *Geneva*, and the Ministry being apprehensive that if he returned into *England*, he might give a very disadvantagious Account of the State of Affairs in *Languedoc*, where the Protestants were generally disaffected, they clapp'd him up in the *Baſtile*. A short Time after they offer'd him his Liberty upon Security given that he would not leave *France*, which he alledg'd was utterly out of his Power. At length they diſcharg'd him without any Security, only they order'd him to quit the Kingdom in a Fortnight. Mr. *Melville* was well acquainted with this Gentleman and his Tranſactions: He was, it seems, a Man of great Intrepidity, and conſequently a fit Engine for *Cromwell*.

From theſe Gentlemen Mr. *Say* and Mr. *Melville*, I had it confirmed to me, what Mr. *Fetherſtone* had often told me, that the *Protector* had the Confidence of the *Engliſh* Roman Catholicks, no leſs than that of the *French Hugonots*. He perſuaded theſe People, I mean the *Engliſh Roman Catholicks*, that only under his Government they could be ſafe ; that if the *Commonwealth* was reſtored, they would be expoſed to perpetual Harraſsments, if not to a general Baniſhment, and Confiſcation of their Eſtates. As for his Part, he declared he hated no Man on the Score of his Religious Principles, but on the contrary, would defend all who lived quietly and peaceably under him.

He afterwards made Choice of one Sir *Robert Talbot* for his Agent, a moderate *Papiſt*, a Man who loved Peace and Quiet, and who thought it became People to

F 3

ſubmit

fubmit to the Powers in Being. This Man accepted a Commiffion to go to the Court of *Rome*, whither accordingly he went, and by the Help of *Donna Olimpia*, infinuated himfelf into the good Graces of his Holinefs, whom he informed that *Cromwell* was quite another Man than he had been reprefented; that he was far from defiring to opprefs, or hurt the *Catholicks*; that he had no violent Averfion to the *Popifh Religion*; and that he was fo far from having any Intention, as had been reported, to attack the *Pope*, by fending a Fleet on his Coafts; that he was defirous of living upon good Terms with his *Holinefs*, and of doing him good Offices in all the Courts of *Chriftendom*.

At Home he engaged Sir *Richard Willis*, to give him exact Intelligence of all that paffed in the Council fettled by the King, confifting of the Earl of *Oxford*, Lord *Mordaunt*, Sir *Orlando Bridgman*, and *nine* or *ten* more, on a Promife that their Lives and Fortunes fhould remain untouched, which was however not over-well complied with. Sir *Henry Slingsby*, and Dr. *Hewet*, who were of that Number, being executed in confequence of certain Diftinctions which the *Protector* knew very well how to make, efpecially, confidering that Sir *Richard* could not fo much as expoftulate with him. Such were the Arts of this Man, who from a private Condition, advanced himfelf to the Sovereignty in his own Country, and made himfelf as much confidered throughout all the reft of *Europe*, as any other Sovereign in it.

When a little Relaxation from Study was neceffary, and the fine Weather invited, I ufed to make Excurfions either into *Savoy*, or into the Territories of the neighbouring

bouring Cantons, efpecially thofe of *Berne* and *Zurich.* In the former a very exemplary Piece of Juftice was done on one *Dupr.*, a *Savoyard*, who had attempted more than once to murder General *Ludlow*, and Mr. *Broughton* at *Vevais*, as fome of his Companions had done Mr. *Lifle* at *Laufanne.* This Man was defcended of a good Family, and had received a liberal Education; he had ferved as a Soldier with fome Reputation, but was moft abandoned in his Morals, diffolute in his Difpofition, void of all Principles, without Pretence to Religion, a Gamefter, Drunkard, and Bully.

One of his firft Exploits was carrying off a young Woman who was Heirefs of fome Lands in the Territory of *Berne*, whom he married by Force. He next engaged himfelf with thofe People who came from *France* to deftroy the *Regicides* in *Switzerland*, from whom he received confiderable Sums of Money on Account of his exact Knowledge of the Country, and his great Adroitnefs in extricating himfelf and his Companions, when it appeared that their Expeditions had mifcarried.

His Sifter had married a Gentleman of Worth and Fortune, who more than once had faved him from Banifhment or Imprifonment, which by a Variety of Crimes he had deferved. However, becaufe this Gentleman had once refufed to lend him a Sum of Money, on Account of his having fome Idea of the Ufe he intended it for, *Dupré* refolved to be revenged on him, which he effected thus.

He perfwaded a Gentlewoman, with whom he was very familiar, to invite his Brother-in-law to her Houfe, where he met him, begg'd his Pardon for what had pafs'd, and having engaged him to drink a Bottle with

him,

him, he of a sudden pick'd a Quarrel, and having given his Brother such abusive Language as was not to be born, that Gentleman rose up hastily in order to go away. *Dupri*, who watched for this Opportunity, struck him under the Right Pap with a Dagger, and as he turn'd to defend himself, shot him into the Left Breast with a Pistol. Having perpetrated this horrid Murder, he caused some of his Dependents to take the Body in the Dead of the Night, and carry it a considerable Space; he then directed it to be laid down, and himself and his People quarrelling over it in a high Tone, he at length discharged a Pistol, and left it and the Dagger by the dead Corpse; hoping that from these Circumstances it would be thought he was kill'd in a Fray at the Place where he was found.

His Artifice succeeded so well, that at first he was not at all suspected, nor is it probable that the Truth had ever come out, if he had not brought it about by refining upon his former Scheme; for after settling the Deceased's Affairs, and speaking upon all Occasions with the utmost Horror of his Assassination, he at length proceeded to offer a great Reward for discovering the Murderers.

This put many People upon enquiring into the Circumstances of the Fact, and at last he was cited to appear at *Chamberry*, to answer an Accusation preferr'd against him upon this Head. His Courage fail'd him here, for instead of going to *Chamberry*, he withdrew out of the Dominions of *Savoy*, and retir'd to *Fribourg*. The Process hereupon was quickly finish'd, his Estate confiscated, and himself condemned to be broke upon the Wheel.

At

At *Fribourg*, being exceedingly diftreffed for Money, he enter'd into new Schemes with fome defperate Perfons refiding in *Burgundy* ; in going to a Meeting which they had appointed, he was apprehended by a Party of Horfe, fent for that Purpofe from *Berne*, whither he was fhortly after conducted, and where a Procefs being commenced againft him for the Rape of his Wife, he was condemned to lofe his Head. He little regarded this Sentence at firft, believing, that as his Family was in good Circumftances, it would be bought off, but when he found that this was not to be done, but that die he muft, he loft all Patience, Prudence, and even common Senfe.

He uttered bitter Execrations againft the Lords of *Berne* ; he refufed to liften to the Minifters who came to pray with him ; he would not go to the Place of Execution, but was dragged thither like a Dog. When he was on the Scaffold, he ftamp'd and beat his Breaft like a Madman, 'till at length his Hands being tied between his Legs, and himfelf held down upon his Breech, the Executioner ftruck off his Head. It was hoped that this Execution would have tamed People of this Stamp for the future, but it did not, many of *Dupré's* Affociates continuing to ufe the fame Trade, which is but too commonly practifed in *Italy*.

As to the City of *Berne*, it is not very large, but wonderfully fortified by Nature, being almoft furrounded by the River *Aar*, which at once renders it fafe and pleafant. Over this River there is a fine Stone Bridge, and the Country about it is carefully cultivated. *Laufanne*, which alfo belongs to this *Canton*, is a very confiderable Place, though very oddly fituated, occupying

the

the Slope of *two* Hills and the Valley between them :
The reft of the Territory of *Berne* is full of large Burghs
and populous Villages, in the Neighbourhood of which
there is great Abundance of Corn, as well as of good
Wine ; Liberty and Induftry being the grand Character-
ifticks of the Inhabitants of this, and of the reft of the
Proteftant *Cantons.*

ZURICH is the moft confiderable Place in *Switzer-*
land, and therefore deferves to be the more exactly defcribed. It ftands at the Bottom of the great Lake
which divides it in two, Part lying on one Side, and
Part on the other. Both joined together by three
Bridges, one of them fo large as to admit of an Herb-
Market upon it ; there are abundance of Goldfmiths,
Paper-Makers, Dealers in Cloth, Makers of Wicker-
Ware, &c. in this Place, where Young and Old work
hard for their Livings, and where Idlenefs is not only
punifhed with Infamy, but with Imprifonment : Peace
and Plenty always abound. The City is well fortified,
and every Citizen is at Liberty to wear a Sword.

Here are two Councils, a Council of *fifty,* and a greater Council of *two hundred.* It is impoffible for People to
live with greater Unity amongft themfelves, or with more
Decorum than the Inhabitants of *Zurich* do, either in
temporal, or fpiritual Concerns. In their Churches a
Pfalm is firft fung, then the Minifter prays, being habited in a Gown with a Cap upon his Head, which however he puts off while he prays ; then he gives out the
Text, preaches a full Hour, then makes a concluding
Prayer, after which another Pfalm is fung, and fo the
Service ends. One Thing is very remarkable, that tho'
they are zealous *Calvinifts,* yet they bow very reve-
rently

rently at the Name of *Jesus*. It is generally believed that *Zurich* is three Times as big as *Geneva*; the Houses are many of them of Stone, with Portico's before them, and the publick Buildings are remarkably neat, and perfectly well kept in Repair. The neighbouring Country abounds with Corn, Wine, Fruits, &c. and the Lake, together with the River *Limagis*, furnishes it with excellent Fish.

As to the *Swiss* in general, though they are somewhat rude in their Manners, yet they are naturally honest, open, and sincere. It is said that their Virtues are liable to Injury from Travelling; for it is observed that in Foreign Service, the *Swiss* are crafty, avaricious, and a little inclin'd to Mutiny; whereas at home they are very patient and submissive. It is morally certain, that their Country in the Hands of other Inhabitants would be but a very indifferent Place, whereas by their Industry and Frugality, it is made to furnish not only the Necessaries, but the Conveniencies of Life. By Frugality I mean, that Sparingness which is observable amongst them in Regard to Clothes and Houshold Furniture, wherein Usefulness and Cleanliness are only expected; for as to Beauty and Magnificence, they are not affected with them, even where it is in their Power. As to their Table it is otherwise; they love to eat and drink well and plentifully, especially the latter, which sometimes they push to Excess, the Love of Liquor being their greatest Vice. They are hardy, couragious, extremely capable of military Discipline, War being a Trade to which they are all bred.

In the Cities there are generally speaking more Men, than Women, on Account of the Manufactures that are

carried

carried on; in the Country again there are more Women than Men; the former are no less industrious than the latter: They do not spare for Pains or Labour in such Businesses as they are able to execute; and as to the Care of their Families, the Women in no Part of the World excell them; for they are very affectionate to their Husbands, and very tender towards their Children, whom they do not suffer however to grow up in a Course of Idleness, but take Care to teach them to do somewhat for their Bread, as soon as their Strength and Capacities will permit them. What I have said relates to the Protestant Cantons only, for as to the Popish, I had not Occasion to visit them; but I believe the Inhabitants do not differ much in their Manners. As to the Government of this Country, I shall speak of it when I come to mention my leaving *Geneva*, having taken some Pains to make my self Master of the several Particulars relating thereto.

DURING the whole Time of my Residence at *Geneva*, my Letters came regularly both from *England* and *France*, 'till toward the latter end of the Year 1665, that I heard no more from M. *St. Dennis*. About three Months after, Mr. *Fetherstone*, whose Affairs had call'd him into *Lorain*, returned into *Normandy*, and gave me an Account that our Friend, after first suffering by a partial Palsey, which took from him the Use of one Side, died extremely lamented by all who knew him. He had the Precaution the Day after he was first taken ill, to place the little Sum of Money I had left in his Hands, in the Hands of Mr. *Hay*, a Scotch Factor at *Bourdeaux*, who happened to be at *Roan*, and who advised me of the Death of M. *de St. Dennis*, and of his

having

having *five hundred* Crowns of mine in his Hands, three or four Days after Mr. *Fetherstone*'s Letter came to Hand.

I t is impossible to express the Concern which the News of this old Gentleman's Death gave me: He was a Man of singular good Sense, and of the highest Probity; one who had lived long enough in Courts to detest them, and who knew perfectly well how to enjoy that Repose, with which Providence blessed him in his declining Years.

A s he had received great Favours from the *Marshal de Ancre*, while he was the Favourite of the Queen and of Fortune, he spoke of him always with much Tenderness. He commended his Affability and Sweetness of Temper, towards his Friends and Domesticks; his pleasant and familiar Manner of conversing with them, and his Readiness to serve them. He observed that the *Marshal* was not mistaken in Those whom he honoured with his Confidence; for that the Marshal Duke *de Estrees*, the *Marshal Hocquincourt*, and the *Marshal de Bassompiere*, were his firm Friends to the last; he had however Vices more than sufficient to bring upon him the Misfortunes which crush'd him in the End: He was a Man of excessive Vanity, addicted to the amassing of Money by any Means, as also to the making an immoderate Display of it. His Ambition had no Bounds, yet he had the Address to conceal it, declining ever to be admitted of the King's Council, and affecting not to enquire into Matters of State, though nothing relating to them was transacted without his Knowledge. The King always hated him, and the *Marshal* was not ignorant of it, but fondly hoped to overcome his Aversion

by

by his Complacencies, and by his affecting to render him all the perſonal Services in his Power; which however had no Effect.

It hath been much doubted, whether by his Birth he was a Gentleman; and the ſame Thing hath been ſaid of his Wife. The *Italians*, who ought to know beſt, affirm, that they were of mean Parentage; and yet nothing is more certain, than that their Names, *Concini*, and *Galigai*, ſpeak them of noble Families, as appears from all the Hiſtories of *Florence*. To ſolve this Difficulty, it is alledged that the *Marſhal* aſſumed the Name of *Concini*; that the Name of his Wife was really, *Doſi*; and that her Father being a very rich *Miller* when he left off his Trade, procured the Family of *Galigai* to acknowledge him for their Relation, and to permit him to bear their arms.

However, the Stations in which they both appeared in the beginning of their days ſeem to ſpeak theſe ſuggeſtions calumnies. It was by the aſcendency which his Wife had over the Queen her Miſtreſs, that the *Marſhal de Ancre* arrived at ſuch exceſſive Wealth, and at ſo exorbitant a Pitch of Grandeur; and as ſhe was the Foundreſs of his Fortune, ſo if he had taken her Advice, ſhe would have preſerved him, herſelf, and their Family from the Miſchiefs that befel them. They lived in the Midſt of Wealth, Power, and Splendour; not only in perpetual anxiety and uneaſineſs, from the open Teſtimonies of Hatred, which the People beſtowed very liberally upon them; but were alſo, on account of Family Differences, continually quarreling at home.

The grand Dutcheſs of *Tuſcany* had once the Goodneſs to ſend the *Marſhal* a Meſſage to this Purpoſe.
That

That since the Winds grew high, and the Waves began to roll, he would do well to think of steering into some Port. To which the Marshal answered, *That while his Vessel went before the Wind, he was resolved to keep out at Sea, and to push his good Fortune to its utmost Extent.* In this he really spoke as he thought, for at other Times, out of an Affectation of Moderation, he would speak of retiring, as a Thing which of all others he sought most, and that he was impeded therein by the Obstinacy of his Wife; whereas in Truth, she daily solicited him thereto.

At last many Circumstances concurring, his Ruin was determined. The King intended by his Destruction to make the first Essay of his Power, and to assert what to him appeared the choicest Jewel in his Crown, *an absolute Authority.* His Favourite *Luynes* eagerly desir'd to succeed in the *Marshal's* Place, and to enrich his Family by the Confiscation of the Favourite's Effects. *Vitry*, the Captain of the Guards, was the Man made choice of to perform this extraordinary Act, of staining the Royal Palace with Blood, which he readily accepted, in hopes of acquiring thereby a Marshal's Staff. Without Question, if this Affair had taken Air, the whole Plot would have been defeated; the whole Power being as yet in the Hands of the *Queen*, and her Favourite.

The King, though a young Man, behaved with profound Dissimulation; the Terror of a Miscarriage kept *Luynes* perfectly silent, but *Vitry* had the Imprudence to acquaint his Mistress with it the Evening before; happy for him that she had less of female Loquacity, than he of manly Prudence, otherwise this Scheme had never

ver

ver taken Place, as it did on the 24th of *April* 1617, when *Vitry* ftabb'd the *Marfhal* in the *Louvre*. This extraordinary Step was immediately followed by others, the Queen was removed and confined ; the *Marfhal's* Wife fent Prifoner to the *Baftile*, and fo totally deferted that fhe had not fo much as Change of Linnen there, 'till fhe procured from fome of the Keepers, a couple of ready-made Shifts, which coft a Crown. She behaved however with great Courage and Intrepidity ; and when fhe was brought, before her Judges to anfwer a long Charge, confifting of Variety of Crimes, at the Head of which were *Sorcery* and *Magick*, on a Suppofition that fhe had bewitched the Queen ; fhe could not help cry-ing out, *Alas! what* Witchcraft *! I governed her by the Superiority of my Genius. What Miracle was it that a Woman of Wit, fhould influence one who had* none ?

However, fhe was condemned to lofe her Head at the *Place de Grave*, and her Body to be afterwards burnt, which was executed ; and all the Eftates which fhe and her Husband had poffeffed were confifcated, amounting, as fome fay, to *half a Million* Sterling. The only Son of the *Marfhal d'Ancre* continued for fome Years a Prifoner, but being at length difcharged, retired to *Flo-rence*, where he poffeffed Eftates of the Value of *twenty thoufand* Crowns a Year, 'till the Plague carried him off in the Prime of his Age. It is pretended that the *Marfhal d'Ancre* fought to make himfelf a fovereign Prince. *Firft*, by Purchafe from the *Pope* of the Dutchy of *Ferrara*, and afterwards by feeking to get the Coun-ty of *Montbeliard* erected into an independent Princi-pality; however, both his Defigns mifcarried.

It

It is said that when the *Marſhal* was one Day preſſing the Queen earneſtly upon theſe Points, and her Majeſty ſeemed inclin'd to comply with his Requeſts, the *Marſhal's* Wife could not refrain from ſaying : *Madam, you approve too eaſily whatever Projects this Fool forms, and in the End his Vanity and Self-Conceit will ruin us all.* This Sentence doth not want Spirit, Senſe, and Loyalty, but at the ſame Time it is a full Proof of that Contempt of her Husband which muſt have made her a very bad Wife. A complaiſant Diſpoſition attones for many Faults ; but I confeſs I know not what Virtues can compenſate for the Want of ſuch a Diſpoſition.

My long Reſidence at *Geneva* had, as I have obſerved, a great Influence on my Temper and Manner of living ; I was no longer poſſeſſed with a Spirit of Rambling, but on the contrary followed my Studies cloſe, conformed my ſelf to the Manners of the People among whom I lived, and took a great deal of Pleaſure in making my ſelf acquainted with the Manufactures carried on there. It ſo happened that one Mr. *Roland*, a Jeweller, or rather a Lapidary, lodged at the next Door ; he was a Man very well skill'd in his Buſineſs, and had ſpent the Prime of his Years in the *Levant*. With this Man I frequently converſed, and as he was very frank and communicative, I learned from him abundance of Things relating to his Trade. It ſo fell out, that by reaſon of ſome Diſappointments he was greatly ſtraitned, and his Credit in the utmoſt Danger. Out of this Difficulty I extricated him, and thence forward he ſcarce kept any of his Secrets from me.

G

His

Hɪs principal Art lay in tinging Cryftals after they were cut, and in forming *factitious* Stones which in their Appearance fell very little fhort of thofe efteemed precious, efpecially of the *Opaque* kind. Though I had not the leaft Idea of profiting by thefe Lights, yet I often amufed my felf with Experiments in this Way, and as I fpared neither Labour nor Coft, by degrees I fucceeded as well as my Mafter. Mr. *Roland*, far from being difpleafed, affifted me all he could, explained to the utmoft of his Ability the Nature of *Gems*, and particularly of coloured Stones, which he beft underftood. To what I learned from Mr. *Roland*, I joined what I could difcover on the fame Subjects from thofe who were fkill'd in natural Philofophy, and from fuch Perfons of Tafte as had Cabinets, and were curious as to the Hiftory of the remarkable *Jewels* which they had in their Cuftody. I likewife went through a Courfe of Chemiftry, procured all the Books I could hear of relating to precious Stones, and began my felf to make a little Collection of Rarities by way of Amufement.

My Man *Johnfon* was at firft a little out of humour at the Trouble my new Employment gave him, but by degrees he began to have a Relifh for it, and was at laft never better pleafed than when employ'd in the Experiments I was, daily making. All this Time I proceeded with my refpective Mafters, and acquired fo ftrong a Relifh for the Sciences, that I had no further Thoughts of an active Life. But as Time and Chance have Dominion over all Men, fo it was not long before they exerted their Sovereignty over me, and fo effectually changed the Face of my Affairs, and at the fame time altered fo entirely my own Temper, that never were two

Men

Men more unlike each other, than I in my succeeding Years to my self while at *Geneva*.

In the beginning of the Year 1669, Mr. *Fetherstone* acquainted me with the Death of my Uncle, which happened suddenly, so that he left his Affairs in the greatest Confusion. He had two Sons, of whose Education he had taken all imaginable Care, and yet with very little Success. The eldest of them knowing, that at all Events he should inherit his Mother's Jointure, became a downright rural Squire, conversed more with his Dogs than his Neighbours, and lived the Year round in a State between drunk and sober. His Father dying without a Will, at least that could be found, he took Possession of his real Estate, and made over all Claim to what there might be of personal to his younger Brother.

This young Spark was quite of another Cast; he had been bred at *Venice*, where he had acquired abundance of *Italian Art*, and where, if ever he had any, he left all his Stock of *English Probity*. When Mr. *Fetherstone* first wrote to him on my Concerns, he pretended an absolute Ignorance of them. He could not apprehend how any Mr. *Brown* should stand in so near a Relation to him ; alledged that his Father's Accompts were in bad Order, and that he did not know whether his *Effects* would answer the Demands which had already been made upon him. After *six* or *seven* Months writing to and fro, he at length wrote Mr. *Fetherstone*, that he had found a *Memorandum* in his Father's Pocket-Book, purporting his Intention to remit *five hundred* Crowns to Mr. *Brown* at *Geneva*, in full of all his Demands, of which he desired Mr. *Fetherstone* to inform me ; as also that he had remitted that Sum to Mr. *Hales* at *Venice*,

G 2

who

who would pay it to me or my Order, on my figning
fuch Difcharges as he had taken care to tranfmit to the
fame Perfon.

I eafily underftood whereto all this tended, and faw
clearly my own Folly in leaving *thirteen hundred* Pounds
in my Uncle's Hands. The Mortgage I had was in the
Name of *Brown*, for I had been out-lawed during the
firft *Dutch War*, when it was thought neceffary to proceed with the utmoft Severity againft all who had been
any way concerned in the Protector's Government.
Thus in an Inftant I loft a comfortable Eftate, and was
left to look about me with no other View of a Subfiftance,
than what could be drawn from the fmall Stock of between *three* and *four* thoufand Crowns, and the Effects
which I ftill had in *France* and *Italy*. One Advantage
I had in the midft of thefe crofs Accidents, *viz.* my
Credit which the Tranfactions I had had with my *Uncle*
Mr. *Fetherftone*, Mr. *St. Dennis*, and Mr. *Hales* at
Bourdeaux, and other Merchants, had rendered pretty
extenfive : So that if I had been at this Time acquainted
with the Method of carrying on any fort of Traffick, I
might either have done pretty well at *Geneva*, or might
have removed to *Leghorn*, and have fettled there with a
tolerable Profpect.

B u t as I had made Books fo long my Study, all
the Profit I reaped from them was to know that they
could now be of very little Service ; and as I was fenfible that the difclofing my Affairs might be attended with
infinitely more Prejudice than Advantage, I did not
think proper to make at this Time any fuch Inquiries as
would have tended to the opening a Paffage to a new
Scene of Life, which nothing but Neceffity could have
                                                    prompted

prompted me to think of, and which Neceffity was of all Reafons in the World the moft unfit to be affigned to thofe I muft have confulted. It remained therefore thoroughly to confider Things in my own Breaft, and after mature Confideration immediately to put in Practice fuch Refolutions as Reafon dictated.

THE firft Thing I did was to fend *Johnfon* to *Venice*, with Orders to bring me Copies of the Papers tranfmitted to Mr. *Hales*, to whom I wrote in the moft refpectful Manner. While the Servant was gone upon this Errand, I fpent almoft all my Time at Mr. *Roland's*, where our Converfation turned chiefly on the Trade he had carried on in the *Levant*. He acquainted me with the Genius and Temper of the People; the Jewels which they moft affected; the Method of dealing with them; the Manner of travelling in Caravans; the neceffary Precautions againft fuch Accidents as Strangers were moft liable to; the Means of dealing with *Jews*, *Armenians*, *Greeks*, and other Chriftians, together with the Arts of concealing Things of Value, and avoiding thofe Snares which Governors, military Officers, and petty Princes make ufe of in order to plunder Travellers and Merchants. From thefe Inquiries I derived much Information, and as I was not over fleepy in the Night, I diverted myfelf with writing in my Journal my Queftions to Mr. *Roland*, and his Anfwers, and when I had fo done, I drew out in my Pocket-Book a new Lift of Queftions for the next Day.

I did not at this Time apprehend that thefe Remarks would at any Time be of Service farther than to divert me; but when I afterwards experienced many Advantages from them, I took a liking to the Method, and

purfued

purfued it all my Life. One Thing Mr. *Roland* over and over infifted on, *viz.* That whoever intended to travel amongft the *Turks, Perfians,* or other oriental Nations, ought by all Means to make himfelf Mafter of the Art of *Phyfick,* a *Science* little underftood, and confequently wonderfully admired by thefe Nations. As the prefent Diforder of my Mind hindered me from applying to my ufual Studies, I made Choice of fome Books of Travels, which I read with great Avidity, and perceiving from them how neceffary good Mapps were, I made the beft Collection I could in that Way, and had them bound fo as to roll in a leather Cafe, which lying in a fmall Compafs, might be conveniently carried without any Danger of fpoiling them.

THUS, without intending to travel, I furnifhed my felf with the Requifites for a diftant Voyage. On this I have fometimes reflected with Wonder, but I think I can now difcern that there was nothing in it ftrange at all. A Man difordered in his Mind never acts rationally, and therefore when he comes afterwards coolly to confider his own Conduct, he takes the Effects of his own Paffions for Things fupernatural, and would fain introduce Fate to take the Blame of his Folly. Thus Self-Love bubbles us when we are not upon our Guard, and when we are, attempts to perfwade us that we were bubbled by fomething elfe.

THE firft News I received from *Johnfon,* was that he had received a very fhort Anfwer from the Merchant, and that he was fallen fick at *Venice* of an Ague, which rendered it impoffible for him to travel. The Day after I received another Letter from a Merchant at *Roan,* with Advice that Mr. *Fetherftone* had failed, and was

gone

gone off. Both thefe Accidents gave me inexpreffible Concern. I was forced to remit Money to *Venice* for the ufe of *Johnfon* ; I was much at a Lofs for him to divert my Melancholy ; for as he was a Man of Senfe, and ten Years older than I, he was become a Sort of Companion, and indeed the only Companion I had. With Refpect to Mr. *Fetherftone*, my Grief was equal for his Misfortune and my own, above a third Part of the little Fortune I had being in his Hands.

However, my Apprehenfions with Refpect to him were quickly leffened, by a Letter inclofed in one from Mr. *Hales*, fignifying that his Loffes would not at all affect me, all my Effects being in the Hands of them on whom he could depend, and who would fhortly remit them to Mr. *Hales*. *Johnfon* continued five Weeks ill at *Venice*, and was at laft cured by the Surgeon of an *Englifh* Ship by Vomits only. As foon as the Surgeon told him it was fafe for him to travel, he fet out for *Geneva* ; and though he informed me of the Day of his Departure, he furprized me very much by his Arrival, which was four Days fooner than I expected. He told me that Mr. *Hales* had fhewn him the Writings which he apprehended to be Releafes in the moft ample Forms, but that he had refufed to let him have any Copies of them, and faid, that if Mr. *Brown* did not think fit to fign them he might let it alone. After we had talk'd over fome other Affairs that I had entrufted him with, and had received all the Intelligence he could give, we began to let Matters reft, and from talking of *Venice*, turned our Thoughts to our Affairs in *England*, *France*, and *Geneva*.

One

ONE Evening when we were deeply engaged in difcuffing Mr. *Fetherftone*'s Affair, *Johnfon* ftarted up of a fudden, and with an Air of Surprize cried out, *Lord! Sir! I forgot to tell you that Mrs.* Lucia —— *is at* Venice. At firft I was fo much confounded, that I did not make him an Anfwer; at laft, contrary to my Cuftom, I flew into a violent Paffion, upbraided him with Stupidity, and want of Thought in not telling me before; to which the Man very innocently anfwered, That it was twenty to one, confidering his Sicknefs, and the many Things he had upon his Head, that he remember'd it at all. However, I could not get him to any Temper that Night, and therefore went early to Bed, where I fpent the Night without Sleep, endeavouring to find what it was that had put me fo much out of my ordinary Road.

I was once or twice going to call *Johnfon* up, but reflecting that the Man would believe I was abfolutely mad, I defifted, and at laft, when it grew light, fell afleep, and did not wake 'till *Johnfon* came into the Room, to tell me it was eight o'Clock, and confequently above two Hours later than I was wont to rife.

WHEN I had dreffed myfelf, I did not as my manner was go out; but having called *Johnfon* into the Room, talked to him of indifferent Things, in Order to lead him to fpeak again of his Stay at *Venice*. But it fell out with me, as I believe it does with moft Men, when under the Influence of their Paffions; all I gain'd by my Arts, was to amufe and deceive myfelf, for before we had talked a quarter of an Hour, *Johnfon* return'd very bluntly to the Point I aimed at, thus. I can now, Sir, very readily account for the Paffion you were in laft

Night,

Night, as foon as I reflected on the manner Mrs. *Lucia* was fpirited away from her Fathers, and how briskly you thereupon rode to your Uncle's, the Secret was out, and I perfectly convinced, that I fhould have done better if I had fpoke of Mrs. *Lucia*, before I had given you an Account of your Bufinefs ; and perhaps it would have been beft of all, if I had been wife enough to have forgot I had feen her.

WHEN I found, that Circumfpection and Circumlocution fignified nothing, I came as roundly to the Thing as he. Acknowledged that I had an extraordinary Concern, as to every Thing which related to this Lady, and defired to know, how fhe came to *Venice*, and in what manner fhe liv'd there. Sir, anfwer'd *Johnfon*, I fhould be glad if my Intelligence furnifhed me with a Power of making you fatisfactory Anfwers ; all I can tell you I will, and affure you with great Sincerity, that if while I remained at *Venice*, it had come into my Mind, that the Affairs of Mrs. *Lucia* had fo near a Relation to yours, I fhould not have fpared any Pains to have been better informed about them ; but as I had then no fuch Thoughts, you muft be content with receiving from me, what by meer Accident I came to know. One Day when I went to receive the Money you were pleafed to remit me, I happened as I was going out of the Merchant's Houfe to meet Mrs. *Lucia*, fhe knew me fooner than I did her, called me by my Name, and asked me, if you were in *Venice* ; I told her you were not, fhe faid, fhe had been there three Years, and never had been able to hear a Word of you, the Caufe of which I readily apprehended to be your going by your Mother's Name. I promifed

her

her to call the next Day; but having only that Time
to provide for my Journey, my Head was so occupied
with other Things, that I really thought no more of
Mrs. *Lucia* till last Night; so that if I have committed
any Fault thro' indiscretion, I hope my telling you
plainly the Truth, will make some Atonement for an
involuntary Error.

It would have been very happy for me, if I had
thought as wisely as my Servant; but who ever does so
that is under the Dominion of Passion. From the very
Moment we had this Discourse, I began to frame a
Project of going to *Venice*, with no other View certainly than to see *Lucia*, and yet I had not Courage enough
to avow this, but began to reason with *Johnson* on Mr.
Hales's Conduct, and to drop some Hints, that very
possibly I might be able to bring him by Discourse,
to think better upon this Head.

After several Conversations upon this Subject, perceiving what I said made *Johnson* very thoughtful and
uneasy, I pressed him to speak his Sentiments freely and
candidly, and at last he did so. I have been about you
Sir, said he, ever since you were a Child, and when I
was very little more myself, you have had a great many
Difficulties to go through, and you have, blessed be
God, gone through them very happily. Your Conduct
hath hitherto been so right, that I never presumed to
question it; but you are of late so much altered, have
such nice and odd Notions, that I find myself absolutely obliged to impart to you out of your own Stock, and
to offer to you the best Advice I can, from the Principles you have heretofore taught me.

As

As to Mr. *Hales*, he is a Man of an inflexible Temper, swallowed up in Business, and will no more enter into the History of your private Concerns, than he would pay you the five Hundred Ducats upon an uncertainty. To make the Persuasion of this Man the Motive of your Journey, therefore would be a perfect Chimera; indeed if you settle your Affairs here, I should think you might as well reside at *Venice*, as any where else, or rather better; but to be making Journies to and fro, will answer no Purpose, but that of running into a large Expence, which is worse than none.

As soon as I had extorted from *Johnson* this plain and honest Judgment of my Affairs, the next Thing I did was, to seclude him from my Counsels, and to resolve with great Secrecy and much Diligence, to prosecute as far as in me lay, the Ruin of my Fortune, which was already in a bad Train. I found out, by the Means of Mr. *Roland*, a Gentleman who had very considerable Concerns with Mr. *Hales*, and from him I procured Letters of Recommendation, signifying that I had resided several Years at *Geneva*, had lived like a Man of Probity, on whose Word he might depend. From this Gentleman also, I took Bills on Mr. *Hales*, for upwards of a hundred Pounds Sterling; I likewise provided some Jewels, and having taken all the necessary Care for travelling with the utmost Expedition, the Morning before I was to set out, I acquainted *Johnson* with my Resolution, and at the same Time told him, that I should leave all my Concerns in his Hands, and did not at all doubt his taking a proper Care of them.

The Man seemed, as well he might, amazed at so odd and sudden a Step; but when he had recover'd
himself

himfelf a little, he faid it was the firft Time that he obeyed me with Reluctance; and that he fhould be glad that I took as much Care of my own Affairs at *Venice*, as he would be fure to take of all entrufted with him at *Geneva*. This faid, he immediately difpatched whatever was requifite for me to have with me in this Journey, fuch as Cloaths, Linnen, &c. with a Care and Alacrity, which rather gave me Pain than Satisfaction.

THE next Day I fet out, but my Mind was fo much diftracted, and my Head fo confufed, that I made no manner of Obfervation of Places, Perfons, or Things; and had much ado to regulate even the neceffary Concerns in my Paffage; fo much was I taken up with a Defire of reaching a Place where, properly fpeaking, I had no very great Bufinefs.

AT laft I arrived at *Padua*, where in Refpect to my Health, I ought to have continued for fome Time, having felt the firft Attacks of an Ague, which vifited me more rudely at *Venice*. However I remained in this famous City and Univerfity but three Days, the firft of which was far fpent when I arrived, and on the laft I was not able to travel. The fourth in the Morning, I fet out for *Venice*, where the Difficulties I met with in going afhore, partly through my own Inadvertency, and partly through the unneceffary nicenefs of the Officers of Health vexed me not a little, and contributed to make the next Fit of my Ague more violent.

As foon as I was at Liberty to go to the Factory, I did make fhift to go firft to Mr. *Hales*'s about Bufinefs, and then to the Merchant's Houfe where *Lucia* dwelt. At the firft I met with better Treatment than

I

I expected; when I came to explain myfelf upon the Reafons of not figning the Papers, Mr. *Hales* would have excufed himfelf from hearing any Thing, but when I promifed to be concife, and had entered a little into my Story, he faid I had been hardly ufed, defired to fee me fome other Time, and promifed he would think of fome Method to ferve me. *Lucia* was exceedingly furprized at the Sight of me, and tho' the great Errand I had at *Venice* was to fee her, I was much more fo at the Sight of her.

IT happened luckily that there were no Spectators at this Interview, which when fhe came to herfelf, the Lady defired might be fhort, advifed me in a Day or two to go and lodge at a certain Place where fhe promifed I fhould fee her, and hear from her a very fingular Account of what had happened to her fince our parting. In Compliance with her Requeft, I prefently took my Leave, and returned to the Place where I lodged for the prefent, which I found to be very little diftant from the Dwelling of an *Englifh* Statuary, at whofe Houfe *Lucia* had defired me to take Lodgings. I was at firft thinking to have fent for this Perfon, in order to have told him, that as I was much indifpofed, and had fome Matters of Confequence to tranfact at *Venice*, I fhould be glad to live in an *Englifh* Houfe for many Reafons. But reflecting that *Lucia* could not direct me to this Man's Houfe without having fome Knowledge of the Perfon who kept it, I judged it would be better to let it alone to the next Day, that in the intermediate Space, fhe might if fhe thought proper, give the Man fome Intimation of it.

IN

IN this for once I judged right, for having the next Day about Noon, sent for Seignior *Bushell*, and acquainted him what my Business was, he presently told me, that the Lady had spoke to his Wife upon this Head; and that in two or three Days, an Apartment should be fitted up for me, and he would do his best to make all Things as commodious as possible. In the Interim I received a Letter from Mr. *Fetherstone*, inclosed in one from *Johnson*, in which he informed me of a very extraordinary Accident which had happened to our Friend M. *D'Aulnoy*.

THE Marquiss *de Courboyere*, M. *la Mouisiere*, and M. *Lamiere*, three *Normans*, the two first Men of Family, and who had lived in Friendship with M. *de Aulnoy*; the last a Man in bad Circumstances, but who had a good Reputation, conspired the Destruction of this unfortunate Gentleman; the former out of Pique, the latter for a Reward of a thousand Crowns, half of which he had received: The Method agreed on was, to charge M. *d'Aulnoy* with Treason, which accordingly was done, and the Matter so cunningly managed, that tho' the Facts were absolutely false, yet the innocent Gentleman was on the very Point of being condemned: Then it was that *Lamiere*, a Stranger to him in Comparison to the other, began to relent; however Fear got the better of his Honesty, and he held his Tongue till M. *d'Aulnoy* was Condemned to lose his Head, till the Priest had confessed him, and till he saw his Grave dug.

HE then followed the supposed Criminal into the Presence of his Judges, who were met to examine him before his Execution. There *Lamiere* fell down on his

Knees

Knees, confeſſed his Perjury, and charg'd his two Aſſo-
ciates, who were likewiſe preſent, with the Conſpiracy,
of which he gave ſuch authentic Proofs, that M. *d'Aulnoy* was immediately diſcharg'd. The Marquiſs *de
Courboyere* was a few Days afterwards executed on the
Scaffold erected for the Execution of M. *d'Aulnoy*, on
which the Day following *la Muiſiere* ſuffered. *Lamiere*
was preſent at both theſe Executions; after the laſt, he
knelt down near the dead Body, and the Executioner
having paſſed his Sword over his Head, he was ſet at
Liberty. A moſt ſignal Deliverance this from a double
Execution of the Body and of the Reputation. What the
Motive of this Conſpiracy was, or whether any more
than M. *d'Aulnoy* were compriſed therein, I could never
learn. As to his own Affairs, Mr. *Fetherſtone* acknowledged, they were in very bad Order, but aſſured me,
my Money was ſafe, and that I might command it
when I pleaſed.

THE Day before I was to go to Mr. *Buſhell's* the
Statuary, went again to wait on Mr. *Hales*, who told
me he had reflected on what I ſaid, and by comparing
it with certain Circumſtances, within the compaſs of
his own Knowledge, was fully convinced it was true.
He added, that he was ſorry a Gentleman who had
been bred at *Venice* ſhould act after ſuch a manner; and
that if I remained a few Months there, he would endeavour to procure me Satisfaction. He would have
paid the Bills I brought with me from *Geneva*, tho'
they were not due; but I declined it, having no immediate Occaſion for Money.

HE adviſed me to be careful of my Health, and not
to ſuffer myſelf to be corrupted by the Pleaſures of *Venice*.

AFTER

AFTER Dinner I went to see a Play, which did not entertain me near so much as I expected. To have a relish for *Italian* Comedy, a Man must not only understand *Italian*, but be also thoroughly tinctured with their Manners, otherwise the pert Jokes, the obscene Jests, and that sort of manual Wit with a wooden Sword, which is there so much in Fashion, amounts to nothing. The *English* Comedy, especially as manag'd by *Johnson* and *Fletcher*, is infinitely superior to any Thing hitherto known in *Europe*.

ONE may be allowed to say this without Suspicion of Flattery, since to judge of Comedy, we must read the Rules laid down by the *Critics*, observe their Effects in the Works of the ancient Poets, who are by all allowed to excel, and then with those compare the *Moderns*; but if we except the *French*, there are none but our *English* Comedies that can be compared with the Ancients. The *Italian* Plays, nay, and the *Spanish* too, are written without Regard to rule, and depend much more upon the Action of the Player, than upon the Genius of the Author.

TIRED therefore with this Representation, I bought two or three Collections of Novels, that I might improve myself in *Italian*, and at the same Time divert that splenetick Disposition, which made me uneasy to myself, and no doubt disagreeable to others. Thus the same Passion which divested me of a Power of using Time, taught me how to murder it, just as the Folly which hinders a young Man from encreasing an Estate, puts him into the Road of spending it.

THE second Day after my Removal, *Lucia* came to see me, her Visit was short, and a meer Matter of
Form,

Form, fome of the Family being always prefent; but
fhe took Occafion to drop a Note in the Window, intimating, that the next Day at three o'Clock, fhe would
come and ftay two or three Hours. Thefe Delays
were infinitely grievous to me, yet as I apprehended
they were reafonable, it gave me a moft exalted Idea
of *Lucia's* Prudence.

At her Hour the Lady came, with a Servant, and
after having, paffed fome little Time with a Friend of
her's, who lodged in the Houfe, fhe paffed through that
Lady's Apartment to mine; and after fome previous
Introduction, and brief Inquiry into what had befallen
me fince I left *England*; fhe entred on the Story of
her own Life, and the Caufe of our ftrange and fudden
Separation. It may be my Recital of her Difcourfe,
may in fome Way tarnifh its Beauty, Women having
a peculiar Elegance in Narration, and the Detail of
Facts, likes Rays of Light receiving Colour from Reflection, yet if Truth be preferved, the Variations will
not be material, and as they are inevitable may be eafily
pardoned.

It would be to no Purpofe faid fhe, for me to give
you any Account of my Family, who are as well acquainted with it as myfelf, I will therefore briefly open
to you what hath been the Source of great Difquiet to
me, and I am perfwaded, no lefs Uneafinefs to yourfelf.
Colonel ——— when he went on the Expeditions to *Hif-
paniola*, left under my Father's Care his Son, a Youth
of about Nineteen Years of Age. What Education he
had before he came to live with us I know not, but
during that Space, we faw little Signs of any; Country
Sports he affected much, loved Drinking more than
youngfters ufually do, and was addicted to other Vices,

H   which

which made my Father very uneafy, left he fhould corrupt my Brother *Philip.*

It fo happened, that either by over heating himfelf, or fome other Irregularity, this young Gentleman fell into a Fever, which brought him to the very Verge of Death, and when it left him, had fo exceedingly enfeebled him, that the Phyficians were of Opinion, it would be followed by a Confumption. To prevent this, they recommended to him a very regular Courfe of Life, great Compofure of Mind, and all forts of innocent Diverfions. In Confequence of thefe Rules, he came much more into our Company than he was wont, and being much taken with the Romances and Books of Poetry which furnifh my Clofet, he fancied the Amufement he received from them, contributed to his Health, which being eftablifhed by Degrees, he fhewed a more than ordinary Regard for me, which was much fooner underftood by my Brother and Father than myfelf.

You muft know, that my Brother *Philip* hath fome Qualities in him which are not fuddenly fufpected. He is particularly addicted to Intereft, and was fo from his moft tender Years. He never defpifed Money, as young Lads are apt to do, but very carefully laid up whatever was given him, and was continually forming Projects to encreafe his Stock.

As foon therefore as he perceived his Friends liking to me, he informed my Father of it, took Notice of the confiderable Eftate the young Gentleman was to inherit, as alfo of his Expectations from a Relation at *Smyrna,* immenfely rich, and who had no other Relation. While he was inftilling thefe Notions into my Father's Head, Colonel ——— died abroad, and left his

Son

Son a clear Eftate of 1500 *l. per Ann.* and a very confiderable Sum in ready Money, which determined my Father to improve, what to him appeared the luckieft Accident in the World. As to me, they either thought my Confent not neceffary, or reckoned upon it as a Thing of Courfe ; and therefore they mentioned nothing of their Scheme till all was ripe for its Execution.

WHEN the young Man had difcovered that as a Secret to my Brother, which himfelf had found out, and reckoned upon long before, then it was thought proper to break the Matter to me, which was accordingly done by my Brother ; but in fuch Terms, as fhewed that I was not to be confulted, but directed. Whether this gave any Biafs to my Inclinations or not, I am unable to determine. The young Man had never been agreeable to me, tho' out of Refpect to his Family, I had always treated him with much Civility : An Accident had contributed to improve this Diflike into an Averfion, he had a Lad that waited on him, pretty near his own Age, and who was his Nurfe's Son ; this Boy upon every little Offence, he would lafh with his Horfe-Whip as if he had been a Slave ; which to me feemed a bad Prefident for his Wife, and therefore I told my Brother on the firft mention of this Bufinefs, that I could never have any Affection for him ; and therefore would never confent to marry him.

THIS unexpected Anfwer put them all into Confufion. The firft Refolution they came to was, to forbid me to explain myfelf to the young Man; which Command I received from my Father himfelf, not without fome very fharp Reflections on my Conduct, or as he was pleased to call it, my disobedience. As in the Course of my Life I had never deserved or received the smallest Reproof before, the old Gentleman's Discourse made an inexpressible Impression on my Mind, insomuch that I threw myself at his Feet, and bedewed them with my Tears.

WHEN I had recovered my Spirits a little, I told him I was so sensible of my Duty to him as a Parent, and of the Obligations laid on me by his Tenderness, that I had much rather submit to Death than do any Thing which might either offend or afflict him. I would be glad to know, Daughter, replied he, which you would have me believe, your Words, or your Actions; for as they are contrary, you cannot imagine I can believe both. Pardon me, Sir, returned I, if to me they seem very consistent; I wish *Lucia*, added he, that you could convince me of that; why, Sir, continued I, my refusing to marry this Man is not the Effect of Humour, Pre-possession, or Obstinacy, I am convinced in my Mind, that if I were his Wife, he would make me very unhappy; this Sir, would not fail to afflict you, and therefore I hope you will not attribute my Conduct to Disobedience. No, *Lucia !* said the good old Man, sighing, I shall not: You may depend upon it that I will never force your Consent; perhaps you may in Time change your Sentiments; in the mean time, all that I expect from you, is to conceal them.

WHAT Excuses they made to my Suitor, I know not; but about two Months after, came a Letter from his Relation at *Smyrna*, desiring him to come thither with all possible Expedition, with an Assurance that he would be well recompensed for the Fatigue of his Voyage.

Voyage. My Father and Brother advifed him to comply with his Relation's Defire, and the rather, becaufe they thought his Abfence added to his Youth, might be ferviceable in protracting certain Suits that they were apprehenfive would be commenced, in relation to fome part of his Eftate; they promifed to furnifh him with a proper Expedient for returning in a Year, or a little more, and my Brother very roundly undertook to him, that the Marriage he defired fhould then take Effect.

As to the Management of his Eftate, his Father had fettled it by Will on certain Truftees, with whom my Father would have nothing to do, having naturally no great pronenefs to Bufinefs. He and my Brother accompanied the young Gentleman to *London*, and the Spring following my Father would have *Phillip* go and ftudy in *Scotland*; for he perceived that notwithftanding a more than ordinary Sagacity in his Nature, he had not a fufficient Stock of Learning, nor a competent Knowledge of the World, both of which he thought he might acquire by refiding a little at one of the Univerfities in that Country.

I NEED not tell you what paffed while you were at my Father's Houfe; but as you are ignorant of the manner in which I was carried away, I will acquaint you therewith, and of what happened to me fince I have been here. When you inadvertently communicated to my Brother your Thoughts concerning me, he inftantly flew to my Father, and having given him very difadvantagious Impreffions of our innocent Correfpondence, brought him to order me to remain in my Chamber, where he was pleafed to watch over me himfelf. About five in the Morning my Brother carried me in

H 3   the

the Coach to *Spalding*, from whence, when you were gone into the *North*, I was carried to *London*, and as narrowly watched, as if either some mighty Fortune had depended upon my Marriage, or I had been engaged in some scandalous Intrigue.

IN three Years Space I heard little or nothing from Home, whether at last I returned almost without knowing why I had been banish'd, or wherefore I was recalled. The good old Man received me on my Return with great Tenderness; he said he was sorry he had been so long deprived of me, and hoped I would still be a Comfort to him, since he had lost my Sister. This surpriz'd me, for in the Letters my Brother thought fit now and then to write to me, he had never mentioned a Word of any Thing befallen my Sister; I therefore asked my Father with some Amazement, how long she had been dead? She is not dead my Child answered he, tho' she is dead to me, she has married one Captain —————— whom you must have seen, a great Royalist, a boon Companion, and one of a small Fortune, who will quickly waste what her Grandmother left her, and leave her to be a Burthen and Disgrace to my Family.

I HAD not been long at Home before, after much Inquiry, I was inform'd that you were gone abroad under a borrowed Name, but whither, or under what Name, I could not then, or ever after learn. After a few Months, my Brother was obliged to go into the *West* on some Affairs of Consequence, and a Day or two after his Departure, my Sister came privately to make me a Visit. As we had always loved each other tenderly, I received her with all the Marks of Affection possible, and met the like in her, she told me, that being

ing

ing quite tired with my Brother's fevere governing Temper, she determined with herself to take the first Opportunity that offered of gaining her Liberty. While she was in this Temper, the Gentleman she married met her by Chance at a Neighbour's House, and being surprized to fee a Woman whose Family had been always of the Puritan Side, so chearful and debonnaire, he took a Pleafure in converfing with her, and by Degrees became much in Love with her, she told him candidly and plainly the State she was in, her Defire of being fettled, and the fmall Fortune she had.

THE Captain as fairly told her, he had a Relation lately dead, who had left him wherewith to clear his Eftate, that he was very fenfible of the idle manner in which he had formerly fpent his Time; and that he was juft in her Condition, waiting for an Opportunity to fettle himfelf. This Similitude of Circumftances joined to the peevifhnefs of my Brother, and the abfolute Command he had over my Father, brought Things to a fpeedy Conclufion; they married privately, and my Sifter having left a moft dutiful Letter behind her, retired to the Captain's Houfe, about a quarter of an Year before I was fent for Home.

WHEN fhe had vifited me twice or thrice, I took a Opportunity when I knew my Father was coming down Stairs to leave the Door open. The old Gentleman, as foon as he faw her, came into the Room, and tho' he at firft would have been very angry, yet in half an Hour his Paffion was fo far loft, that he asked her to ftay all Night, and offered to fend a Servant to acquaint her Husband, fhe very readily complied, and the next Morning came the Captain.

We

WE were from this Time all very good Friends, and my Father's Temper began to alter very much. His Son-in-law and he converſed very freely on Tranſactions of an ancient Date, and the more they converſed, the better they were ſatisfied with each other. My Father found that the Captain was neither debauched in his Morals, nor addicted to arbitrary Power, and he on the other Hand ſaw nothing of that Stiffneſs or Contempt of the Government which he expected in the old Man. Thus Things went for a Time happily enough in our Family, excepting that my uneaſineſs on your Account, encreaſed the natural Gravity of my Temper, and by cauſing a great Depreſſion of Spirits, brought on an Indiſpoſition of Body which threatened a Conſumption.

My Brother, whoſe fertile Brain would never ſuffer him to be ſtill, and whoſe Notions with Reſpect to Church and State had not received much Improvement from his Studies in *Scotland*, embarqued himſelf in an Affair which had well nigh effected his Deſtruction. It happened that ſome of his Acquaintance had mentioned him to the *Duke* of *Bucks*, who was then in Diſgrace, as a Man of lively Parts, and one zealouſly devoted to the Common-wealth Party; upon this he ſent for him, careſſed him, gave him a Share in his Buſineſs and his Pleaſures, 'till the King iſſued a Proclamation for apprehending his Grace; and Warrants from the Council were ſent to ſeize his Dependants, among whom *Philip* had the Honour to be one.

IN this Diſtreſs he retired into his native Country, and coming to a Farm-houſe about a Mile's Diſtance from our's, ſent for his Father; the old Gentleman though

though he went to see him, did not afford him that Countenance he was wont, but spoke to him very roundly, told him he was reconciled to Capt. ———— and that he would speak to him of his Business. My Brother took all in good Part, and being well acquainted with the Captain's Character, desired to lodge at his House, as knowing it would not be searched.

But in a few Months the Scene was changed; the Duke of *Bucks* was declared Prime Minister; governed all Things at his Will; and my Brother going up to *London,* was well received by the Duke, and is, I believe, still in his Confidence. What the Designs of his Grace are, it is well if himself can tell; but as to *Philip,* I dare say his Aim is to aggrandize himself by the Favour of his Patron, who hath already made such Promotions as have given Birth to a Proverb: *That to have a Place at Court a Man must be known not to love the King.* My Distemper encreasing, my Father was desirous I should come to *London* for Advice; I did so, and lodged with an Aunt of my Brother-in-Law the Captain's. She had the Honour to be allied to the *Newcastle Family,* and by that means I was introduced to a great deal of good Company, to whom otherwise I should never have been known.

My Brother, during my Stay in Town, visited me very assiduously, and gave me extraordinary Marks of Tenderness and Affection. His former Conduct towards me made me at first entertain some Doubt of his Intentions, but by Degrees the great Change I saw in his Manners engaged me to hope he was really become a new Man; for though he still affected to live upon good Terms with his old Friends, yet he was become a great

Courtier,

Courtier, spoke very advantagiously of the *Duke* of *York*, and sometimes hinted that his *Royal Highness* had an extraordinary Kindness for the *Presbyterians*.

Though these Things served for some Time to amuse me, and though on my first coming to *London* I was visibly better, yet in a few Months I relapsed, and the Physicians unanimously agreed that nothing could restore me to a sound State of Health, but residing some Time either in the South of *France*, or in *Italy*. Tho' this was not very agreeable to me at first, yet my Brother perfuaded me to comply with it, promising to make it his Care that I should be perfectly eafy as long as I ftaid abroad, and that he would procure me such Recommendations, as should secure to me a good Reception where-ever I came.

I did not care, however, to be wholly at his Difpofal, and therefore I very gladly accepted my Brother-in-Law's Propofal of going to *Venice*, and refiding in the Houfe where I now am, the Gentleman's Wife being the Captain's firft Coufin. I have been here near fix Months, have heard regularly from my Brother, whofe Letters are continually accompanied with Prefents; and the Air hath had fo proper an Effect on my Conftitution, that I really think that I am perfectly recovered.

Thus, without telling me any thing very extraordinary, *Luvia* charm'd my Attention, and I liften'd with more Satisfaction to the plain Narrative of what had befallen her fince my leaving *England*, than I fhould have done to the beft wrought Story of any *Italian* Wit, though it had abounded with furprizing Incidents, and had been embellifhed with that captivating Elegance deriv'd to this Nation, not more from Art than Nature.

I N

In return to this Detail of *Lucia's* Adventures, I made a brief Recital of my own, from the Time of my leaving her Father's Houfe, to that of my fettling at *Geneva*. When I had finifh'd, You have not told me, faid fhe, any of your Amours. Come! come! You muft not perfuade me, that in fo many Years you have feen no-body who could efface the flight Impreffions you are pleafed to fay I made upon your Mind. If Nature had formed you without Regard to our Sex, you would have had no Paffion for me; and having this Bent from Nature, Love could never have been all this Time idle.

Your own Relation, *Lucia*, faid I, affords me a proper Excufe; you have told me nothing of the Addreffes which your Beauty muft have every where attracted, and therefore the Credit I afford your Silence ought to derive the like to mine. To fpeak freely, I believe our Coolnefs hath had but one Caufe. The Impreffion your Charms made on my Heart, join'd to the ill-omen'd Events which follow'd it, gave me I know not what Prejudice to the Ladies, and hindered me from reaping thofe Advantages from their Converfation in my Travels which I might otherwife have done. Believe me, Madam, I look upon this to be an Injury for which you are accountable to me, and which you can only repair by making me happy in your felf. All Prejudices of this Sort deprive a Man of the higheft Pleafure Converfe with the World affords: There is a certain dry Gravity attendant on the Difcourfes of Men of Senfe, which difgufts, though the parting with it would introduce a Levity far more difguftful; but with the Ladies it is otherwife; they animate Converfation with an innocent

nocent Liveliness, more effectually prevalent against Spleen than all the Wisdom in the World. To Men a Man submits from Custom and a Principle of good Manners, which like the Homage paid to a Usurper, is accompanied with a secret and unextinguishable Regret ; but Regard for Women is the Dictate of Nature, and like the Duty paid to a natural Prince, issues from the Fullness of our Hearts, and is scarce received with so much Pleasure as it is given.

I AM obliged to you, replied *Lucia*, for these Compliments; but since you have mentioned *Italian* Love-Stories, permit me to give you a short Account of one, the Particulars of which fell under my own Cognizance ; and the Son of the unhappy Lady whom it concerns was your Predecessor in these Lodgings. I told her that I should be very glad to hear any thing that might be depended upon, because the *Italian* Wits having a fruitful Invention, and being also naturally fond of surprising incredible Adventures, I had not hitherto given much Faith to many of the Stories I had heard.

I believe you are not much in the Wrong, continued *Lucia* ; but upon what I assert in Respect to my Story you may depend ; as to the less important Circumstances, you may judge as you please ; and the whole will leave you such a Field for Conjecture, that your Faith will not be at all over-burthen'd by the Load my Credit will bind upon it.

LUCRETIA Donde was a Lady whose Beauty, though it distinguished her from all the Women in *Padua*, was very far inferior to her Virtue, and to the amiable Qualities of her Mind. Her Cheerfulness, which was the Effects of her Innocency, made her always a-
greeable

greeable to others; and the Tranquility of her own Life was such, that as she always seemed, so she was always perfectly easy and well pleased.

THE Marquis of *Orciano* fell in Love with her, and marry'd her when she was very young. Her Parents laid no Restraint on her Choice, though they had recommended one Signior *Lorenzo*, who was also deeply in Love with her. The Lady, in Consequence of the Liberty left her, made Choice of the Marquis, though before and after her Marriage, she always spoke of Signior *Lorenzo*, in Terms of very high Esteem. Eighteen Years this Couple lived together with all the outward Appearance of Content; several Children they had, the eldest a hopeful Youth, who had prosecuted his Studies with great Applause, and who to the Love of Books joined also a suitable Affection for all such Things as it became a Gentleman to know.

As for *Lucretia*, the gentleness of her Manners, her spotless Character, her artless inoffensive Conduct, made her the Darling and Delight of all *Padua*. The Men spoke of her in Raptures, the Ladies held her the Honour of their Sex, and *Signior Lorenzo* persevering in his romantick Gallantry, affected to admire her now no less than when she was single. It happened that the Marquiss of *Orciano* had Occasion to make a Journey to this City, and in his Absence the poor Lady fell a Victim, whether to Lust or Jealousy, none can tell.

THE Night after her Husband's Departure, her Son hearing her give a violent Shriek, jumped out of Bed, and ran to her Chamber-Door, which opening upon him, somebody came out, pushed him over the Stairs, besmearing befmearing his Face with his Mother's Blood, and fo went out. The Servants alarmed, and bringing Lights, the Lady was found half out of Bed, with three Stabs on her Left Breaft, two of which were held to be mortal. She was not quite dead, but fpeechlefs, and unable to give any Account who was the Author of her Death.

SIGNIOR *Lorenzo* being proved to have walked frequently under her Windows, was apprehended, and put to the Torture; which he fuftained with incredible Firmnefs of Mind, acknowledged it the juft Reward of his Folly, but declaring that he knew not any Thing of *Lucretia's* Murder, though he might be the innocent and involuntary Author of it. This Expreffion occafioned new Sufpicions; Signior *Lorenze* was difcharged, and the Marquis of *Orciano* imprifoned in his Stead. He proved himfelf here at *Venice* on the Night of the Commiffion of the Fact, and was thereupon difcharged.

A while after fome of the Servants put it into the Son's Head, that Signior *Lorenzo* was both the Murderer of his Mother, and the Affaffin of his Father's Reputation. The Youth unfortunately mention'd it to fome of his Fellow Students, who far from moderating the ill Impreffions he had received, exhorted him as a Man of Honour to take Vengeance of the Enemy of his Family.

THE poor young Gentleman, thus miffed, hired certain *Bravo's* to affift him in his Enterprize, which fucceeded but too well; for furprifing Signior *Lorenzo* as he came from Mafs, they fhot him in the Street; fome Gentlemen, who were with him, purfued and kill'd two of the Murderers, but the young *Orciano* efcaped, and for fome Time lived privately here.

Hā

HE feemed to be a very well-inclined young Man, but a little difturbed in his Head; however, being known, and proclaimed a *Banditto* at *Padua*, he was forced to fly, and is now at *Rome*. His Father leads a very difconfolate Life, having never been able to clear himfelf from the Sufpicions brought upon him by this unfortunate Affair: To perpetuate, however, the Memory of fo excellent a Perfon, the Government of *Padua* have in their Hall of Juftice erected a Statue of the amiable *Lucretia*, with a fuitable Infcription.

AFTER fome Reflections on this melancholly Story, I obferved to *Lucia*, that I was certainly a little unlucky in my Lodgings, fince the Houfe I lived in at *Geneva* belonged to the Grandfon of a Man whofe Adventure had not only made himfelf remarkable, but was at every Turn brought up on the Mention of any of his Family. *Lucia* defired to be acquainted with it; and though the Story was common, I gave her an Account of it, having formerly fet it down in my Diary as a Proof of this Obfervation. That Vice is ever productive of Mifery; and that fuch have Reafon to be well pleafed with their Situation, who diftinguifh the Hand of God in their Punifhments in this World. The Inftance was this.

THE Hero of this Hiftory was a Native of *Rimini*, a City in the *Papal* Territory, and a very accomplifhed Gentleman, his Name was Signior *Pandolfo*. He had ferved fome Years in the *French* King's Armies, and with Reputation. He refided fome time afterwards at *Rome*, but finding, that though his Mind had improved, his Eftate had been impaired by fo many Years Abfence, he retired to *Rimini*, refolving to pafs the Remainder of his Years in his native Soil. He was then about *thirty*

fix,

fix, and as active and fprightly as when a Lad. It fo fell out that his Houfe joined to that of an old Gentleman who had married a young Wife, the Daughter of a Man of great Quality, though but mean Fortune.

Signior *Pandolfo* had not been long at home e'er this Lady caft her Eyes upon him. She was a Woman addicted to Pleafure, and without any Regard either to the Laws of Honour or Religion. She made therefore no manner of Scruple of acquainting Signior *Pandolfo* with her Kindnefs for him; and he, much too fine a Gentleman to feel any Reftraint from Confcience, contrived a Method for their better Acquaintance, by breaking a Paffage into her Maid's Chamber, whence he was eafily conducted to her's.

But to prevent all Poffibility of Surprize, the Lady caufed feveral Holes to be bored in a very large Cheft, where fhe kept her choiceft Clothes and her Jewels, which was all the Fortune fhe brought her Husband, that upon any Emergency *Pandolfo* might be lock'd up therein, and yet not fuffer for Want of Air.

Things went on in this Courfe for about two Years, when the Lady fell dangeroufly ill. Finding her End approach, fhe would needs take Leave of *Pandolfo*; but in the Midft of this Interview, hearing her Hufband coming, he was forced to betake himfelf to his Cheft, in which he had not lain long before he heard the Lady addrefs herfelf in thefe Words. *My tenderly loving and much beloved Lord, I find Life retiring; gratify me in one Requeft dying, to whom living you denied nothing.* Speak, faid the good old Man, and be affured, that whatever you afk fhall be granted. *Let then*, faid fhe, *that Cheft be fet upon my Coffin without any Body's being fuffered to look in it.* It fhall be fo, replied the Husband. Prefently

Prefently, fome of her Relations came to vifit her, and in a couple of Hours fhe expired.

As her Diftemper was a kind of malignant Fever, it was refolved to bury her about Midnight of the next Day, which was accordingly done, and the Cheft, un-opened, placed upon her Coffin in the Vault where fhe was interr'd. Before her Amour with Signior *Pandolfo*, fhe had fhewn fome Marks of Favour to her Hufband's Page, who had thereby an Opportunity of feeing the Jewels that were in her Cheft. This Man conceiving that fuch Things were of little Ufe to the Dead, went to the Sexton, and having promifed him and his Son a Share in the Booty, prevailed on them to take a Share in the Enterprize of fearching the Cheft.

Signior *Pandolfo*, in the mean time, gave himfelf up for dead, and befought the Almighty to pardon him his manifold Sins, and to fuffer them to be expiated by this cruel Punifhment. Such were his Meditations when he heard the Door of the Vault open, and foon after found them tampering about the Lock of the Cheft. Conceiving thereupon a fudden Hope of Deliverance, he pufhed back the Spring of the Lock, and throwing up the Lid of the Cheft, ftarted up all at once.

The Thieves, fuppofing it was the Devil come to punifh them for their facrilegious Attempt, fled without looking behind them. *Pandolfo* having put as many of the Jewels as he thought fit into his Pockets, went and hid himfelf in a private Part of the Church 'till Morning, and then retired to his own Houfe fecretly. His Son, for he afterwards married, being a Prieft in the fortieth Year of his Age, retired to *Geneva*, where he became a

I   Prote-

Proteſtant, married a young Woman, and left a numerous Family.

THE Evening began now to wear apace, and *Lucia*
at length took her Leave, with a Promiſe of giving me
another Viſit in two or three Days. In the Intervals between her Viſits I diverted myſelf with ſeeing whatever
was curious in *Venice*; the *Duke's* Palace, the *Arſenal*,
the Church of St. *Mark*, and many other Places; which
as Books inſpired me with a Curioſity of examining, ſo
they left me little of Novelty to treaſure up amongſt my
own obſervations. Some Remarks, however, I did
make, and in the Number, theſe.

THE *Venetian* Commerce, which is now little ſpoken
of, deſerves the Attention of *Foreigners*; and the Liberty
of *Venice*, which is exceſſively cry'd up, hath indeed
very little in it, or to ſpeak with greater Propriety, is it
ſelf nothing at all. This may ſeem very ſtrange, but it
is notwithſtanding very true. For, in the firſt place,
the Duke himſelf is a *Slave*; he hath, it is true, a fine
Palace, and when he goes abroad doth it in much State,
but then this State reflects Honour only on the *Republick*;
and as to the Palace, he is in fact a Priſoner in it, having
Counſellors continually about him who pry into all his
Actions, and from whom he neither can, nor dare keep
any Thing.

ON the other hand, the Nobility dare not converſe
with Foreigners, eſpecially of Diſtinction, for fear of
rendering themſelves obnoxious to the State. Many of
theſe Noblemen, notwithſtanding they boaſt ſo much of
their Honours, go about to Stranger's Lodgings, and beg
of them privately with very great Humility; nay, ſome of
them

them will do this who live in good Credit, keep hand-some Houses, Servants, and *Gondolas*.

As to the People, they are the fartheft from enjoying *Liberty*, taking that Word in a juft and proper Senfe, of any in the World. As for their Coin, it rifes and falls two or three Times in a Month ; many of the poorer Noblemen go into Shops and buy what they think fit, fend it home, and pay for it at the *Greek Kalends*, that is, *never* ; he from whom they take it neither daring to refufe them *Credit*, nor demand his Debt when he has given it them.

As for Strangers, they may do what they pleafe, fo they meddle not with the State, the fmalleft Offence againft which meets with the quickeft and fevereft Pu-nifhment. It is indeed a very glorious City in all Re-fpects, and very far richer than in the northern Parts of *Europe*, we are apt to think. It is about eight Miles in Extent, contains not lefs than feventy Churches, fixty Religious Houfes, the one half for Men, the other for Women, between four and five hundred Bridges, and at leaft ten thoufand *Gondolas* or *Boats*, which are very convenient, and which they manage with great Dexte-rity.

In the few Weeks Stay I made at *Venice*, I had ma-ny Interviews with *Lucia*, all at my own Lodgings, whither fhe came under Colour of vifiting a Lady who lived there likewife. She faid fhe had Reafons for my not vifiting her at home ; and indeed what fhe alledged on this Head was very reafonable, *viz.* That we could not talk freely there, and that it would have rendered it impoffible for her to have vifited fo frequently, and fo long as fhe did at the Houfe where I lodged. The Iffue

of

of thefe Interviews was, that we fhould return together to *England*, and that after being privately married, fhe would, by her Brother-in-Law's Intereft, procure me a Pardon, which would have put me in a Condition to have dealt with my perfidious Coufin.

Her Fortune in Poffeffion and Reverfion might amount to between fourteen and fifteen hundred Pounds; and if this Project, which either was, or Love made me believe was practicable, had been carried into Execution, we might have lived comfortably enough, our Tempers fuiting at leaft as well as moft of thofe who make Bargains for Life. But firft of all it was neceffary that I fhould return to *Geneva*, and fettle all my Affairs there; which, however, was not to be gone about, 'till I had received Mr. *Hales*'s Anfwer.

This arrived at the End of the Space I mentioned, and contained in Subftance, that my Coufin was very much furprized at his Correfpondent's Letter; and tho' he found nothing among his Father's Papers to warrant moft of the Facts ftated therein, yet, for the Sake of Peace, and to fhew his honeft Inclinations, he was content to pay me a thoufand Chequins, provided I would fign an Agreement to make no farther Demands in three Years, in which Space all his Father's Affairs, he hoped, would be thoroughly fettled.

Mr. *Hales* advifed me to accept of this Propofal; and indeed I thought it very reafonable my felf; fo I figned the neceffary Papers, and received the Money.

When there was nothing to hinder my fetting out for *Geneva*, I made the neceffary Preparations for it, and the Evening preceeding my Departure, had a long tender Interview with *Lucia*, to whom at her going

away

away I prefented a Ring fet after the *Turkifh* manner, that is enigmatically. It confifted of a large Saphire perforated, a Diamond filling up the Middle, the whole furrounded with Rubies, which according to the Language of oriental Gallantry, is thus explained.

THE Rubies which firft falute the Eye, fignify a ftrong and ardent Paffion ; the Saphire reprefents Fidelity ; both of which are infinuated to be everlafting in their Nature by the Diamond : Alluding to a *Turkifh* Verfe, which litterally render'd, runs thus,

My faithful Love fhall ever laft.

Lucia gave me a fquare Gold Box, in the Lid of which was her own Picture. Our parting ftruck me with a deep Melancholy, but fhe either was not, or did not feem to me fo much affected.

I LEFT with her Directions how to write to me, and fettled likewife a Correfpondence with my Landlady. I propofed to return to *Venice* in five or fix Weeks, and I paid for the Lodgings before-hand for that Time. Such is the Confidence of Man, who knows not where he fhall live or lodge on the Morrow. It would be Labour loft for me to go about to defcribe the heavinefs of Mind, the Dejection of Spirit, the Irrefolution of Heart, which attended this Separation. I am almoft afhamed when I recollect, that the great Source of all this was neither more nor lefs than a Dream.

IT happened the Night before my taking Leave of *Lucia,* and in few Words was this : I thought myfelf in a large Meadow, with a Bow and Arrow in my

I 3
Hand ;

Hand; at a confiderable Diftance I faw a Pillar, to which a white Efcutcheon was affixed, and on the Top of the Pillar ftood a large Goblet of Gold; I fhot with a fingle Arrow, and fixed it in the Efchuteon; but when I went to take down the Goblet which I fup-pofed I had won, I found a deep, tho' narrow River in my Way, too rapid to think of fwimming over, and for croffing which, I could not fee either Bridge or Ford except at a very great Diftance down the Stream, fo that going thither and coming round on the other Side, feemed an endlefs Undertaking.

I TOLD this to *Lucia*, who fmiled at it. The Impref-fions faid fhe of our waking Thoughts, amufe us in our Sleep. I too have dreamt, and my Dream corre-fponds with yours. But what Wonder is it our Thoughts correfpond? Thofe who fuffer themfelves to be deluded by the Shadows of Things, are frequently deprived of the Subftance, and then impute to the Malice of For-tune, what in Truth proceeded from their own Folly. This appeared to me fo fententious, fo different from *Lucia*'s manner of fpeaking, and fo appofite to the Subject, that in that Inftant I defpifed my own Weak-nefs, and fo far banifhed all Thoughts of my Dream, that I never afked *Lucia* how it refembled hers. But afterwards it recurr'd with its firft Force to my Remem-brance, and like the Vifion of *Brutus*, rid my Imagi-nation fo ftrongly, that I could never throw it of, by Reafon, Philofophy, or Religion. But enough of thefe vain Things.

THERE was nothing of any Moment happened in my Return to *Geneva*, where *Johnfon* had managed every Thing with great Prudence and Circumfpection.

I

I gave him an Account of all that had paſſed at *Venice*, and of my Intention to return to *England*,. with which he was mighty well pleaſed ; and on my enquiring how long he thought it might be before our Affairs would be ſo well ſettled, as to admit of my Return to *Venice*, he demonſtrated to me, that it could not take up leſs than ſix Weeks or two Months; for as all the ſeveral Threads which my former Occaſions had obliged me to ſpin, were now to be wound upon one Bottom, the Operation would not admit of a Lover's Haſte, without breaking moſt, if not all of them.

PATIENCE therefore was abſolutely neceſſary, and I began to frame to myſelf many Schemes of Amuſement, till my Buſineſs could be brought into ſuch Order, as ſuited the Project upon which I was Intent. At Mr. *Roland*'s particularly, I ſpent a great Part of my Time, and laid out a conſiderable Sum of Money in compleating a Cabinet of Curioſities by his Directions. I flattered myſelf that theſe would not turn to my Loſs on my coming back to *England*, and in the Proſecution of my Deſign, I happened to purchaſe a fine *Onyx* from Signior *Pucci* an *Italian*. Tho' theſe People are not very communicative, yet in ſeveral Viſits he made me, I did him ſo many Courteſies, eſpecially in preſenting him with a Book of Drawings, which had fallen into my Hands by Chance, that by Degrees I became much in his Favour, and he ſeemed diſpoſed to deny me nothing in his Power.

MR. *Roland* had told me, that this Man, who was very rich, was reputed to have a Secret for clearing all ſorts of precious Stones of Clouds and Milkineſſes. Amongſt other Jewels I had a very large white Saphyr,

which

which I bought at *Venice* for twenty Ducats, tho' had it been perfectly clear, it would have been worth ten Times that Money. This Stone I one Day shew'd to Signior *Pucci*, and told him frankly that I had heard he could make it perfectly bright.

At first he was a little confused, but when he had recollected himself, he told me he was pleased with my frank manner of speaking, and that since I had obliged him, it was but reasonable he should oblige me. Accordingly he took the Stone, and in a Fortnight returned it perfect. When he gave it me, he addressed himself to me in these Words: You must certainly be very much surprized at what you see, it will doubtless convince you of an Error you may have been in ; I mean believing such an Operation as this impossible ; but have a Care of falling into another Mistake, *viz.* an Opinion that this may be done by all sorts of Stones, which so far as my Notion reaches, is impracticable. My Secret came to me by Chance, the Skill of using it by deep Observation and long Experience. I know, generally speaking, what I can perform, and where it would countervail the Expence ; this hath turned to my Advantage; my Secret in the Hands of a rash and avaricious Man, instead of enriching, would destroy his Substance ; and he would then charge that upon the Operation, which he ought to have charged on his own want of Judgment. If you have any Stones by you in which I can do you the same Kindness, I shall very freely serve you.

About a Fortnight after my Return to *Geneva*, I was much surprized on my coming from Church, to find Mr. *Fetherstone* in my Lodgings, from whom I had

not

not heard for some Time. We embraced each other, and when he had refreshed himself with Chocolate, he gave me the Detail of his Misfortunes.

He said his Affairs went on perfectly well, and that he was worth a confiderable Sum of Money when his Ruin broke upon him like a Cloud big with Lightning, which blafted all his Hopes. He told me that in the Year 1657, he had fome Acquaintance with a Perfon who had lived in *Holland*, and had a Penfion from *John de Wit*, who was known by the Name of M. St. *Marcelle*. This Perfon did him fome very confiderable Services, and would accept of no fort of Gratification.

Mr. *Fetherftone* in the Courfe of ten Years had almoft forgot him, when a Perfon came to him one Day on the *Exchange* at *Rouen*, and prefented him a Letter figned St. *Marcelle*. The Purport of the Letter was, that the Bearer would deliver him a Pacquet, addreffed to a Perfon of Diftinction at *Paris*, which he defired might be fent by a fpecial Meffenger, and that he would be pleafed to give the Perfon who brought thefe Letters, what he thought a reafonable Compenfation for bringing them from *Diepe*.

Mr. *Fetherftone* having received the Pacquet, gave the Perfon five Piftoles, and fent the Letters by his Servant to *Paris*. About fix Months after, it was difcovered that this St. *Marcelle* either was engaged, or pretended to be engaged in a Defign againft the *French* King's Life. Upon this, the Perfon to whom his Letter was addreffed, was conducted to the *Baftile*, and a Perfon fent to apprehend Mr. *Fetherftone* at *Rouen*, who miffed him but accidentally, and who conceiving that

he

he was fled, made a precipitate Diſcovery of his Errand, of which when Mr. *Fetherſtone* had Advice, he thought it very expedient to fly in earneſt.

Notwithstanding the Confuſion this Step brought on his Affairs, he found Means to prevent any Body's being a Loſer by this Miſchance but himſelf, whoſe whole Fortune by this Means was reduced to the narrow Compaſs of a Hundred Piſtoles, or thereabouts. A melancholy Revolution this, and one that would certainly have overturned the Underſtanding of a Man of leſs Firmneſs; but for Mr. *Fetherſtone*, he ſupported himſelf under it with a *Roman* Conſtancy, and comforted himſelf, by repeating often this Saying, *That the Character of an honeſt Man was an Eſtate which Fortune could not take away.*

This Gentleman had not been long at *Geneva* before he diſcovered an old Acquaintance of his, whoſe Name was *Alonzo Perez*. He had been a Merchant at *Seville*, and Mr. *Fetherſtone* had frequently Bills drawn upon him. By Degrees they entered into a cloſer Acquaintance, and *Perez* entruſted Mr. *Fetherſtone* with the Care of ſome Jewels of very great Value, which he ſent over into *England*. His Appearance at *Geneva* was very indifferent, which mightily ſurprized my Friend, who had known him a very conſiderable Man in the richeſt City of *Spain*.

PEREZ quickly explained to him the Cauſe of his leaving his Country, and the Means by which his Fortune had been reduced, both the Miſchiefs flowing from the ſame Source, which was this. The Uncle of *Perez*, who had given 18000 Crowns for the Title of *Marquiſs* to the King of *Spain*, and who had been for

many

many Years Farmer of part of his Catholic Majesty's Revenues, was suddenly apprehended by the *Holy Office*, on a Suspicion, as it was supposed, of *Judaism*, which so terrified his Nephew, that tho' he had acquired a great Estate, and was on the Point of being married to a rich Heiress; yet he chose to leave all behind him, and by the Favour of an *English* Vessel escaped to *Genoa*.

THERE he received a Bill of a thousand Pistoles; but the Day after, having Notice that the *Spanish* Government would leave no Means unessay'd, in order to bring him back; finding also great and visibly affected Delays in such as ought to have delivered him the rest of his Effects in that City, he thought himself no longer safe there; and therefore withdrew as expeditiously as he could to *Geneva*, where he lived in very great Privacy, and was not a little pleased to find there so faithful a Friend as Mr. *Fetherstone*.

To him he communicated all his Affairs, and particularly informed him, that his Diamonds having been sold in *England* to a Person in great Authority during the Interregnum, his Correspondent had informed him, that he was very apprehensive the Money would be lost. Mr. *Fetherstone* advised him not to despair, and promised him that he would make Use of the few Friends he had to serve him in this ticklish Business.

IT was not long before Mr. *Fetherstone* introduced his old Friend to me; and as *Perez* was a Man of mighty good Sense, much Learning, and great Experience, tho' not above forty Years old, I was extremely taken with him; the rather because he had a strong Tincture of amorous Madness, and talked as much of his Mistress at *Seville*, as I thought of mine at *Venice*.

ONE

ONE Thing in his Conduct seem'd to me inexplicable, he had always liv'd in *Spain* like a good *Catholic*, he had fled from thence on an Apprehension that he was suspected of *Judaism*, here at *Geneva*, he was a regular *Calvinist*, and behaved so well, that no Body doubted of his Religion. My Curiosity on this Head got the better of my good Manners, and I could not help intimating to him one Day, that I wondered he was not tired with the length and Vehemence of a certain Dominican's Sermons, who having quitted his Order, and abjured the Errors of the Church of *Rome*, declaimed against them with a never ceasing Vivacity.

PEREZ could not avoid smiling at my Question, for he immediately penetrated the Drift of it. My Friend, said he, you have a Mind to know my Religion, come we are not in *Spain!* I will therefore tell you my Sentiments freely, I have a Religion of my own, the first Article of which is, that I confide in God's Mercy.

I AM a *Christian*, but as I am descended of the House of *Israel*, I think myself obliged to observe the *Mosaic Rites*, which I believe to have a perpetual Obligation, because I think them perpetually rational. As to Popery or Protestanism, tho' I have comply'd with both, I acknowledge neither, for I am truly a *Catholic*, holding those Principles fundamental in Religion wherein all Christians are agreed; and supposing that I may follow the *Mosaic Rites* without Danger of Salvation, because they were observed by the *Messiah* and his *Apostles*, from the same Motive as I apprehend which inclines me to them, *viz.* My Descent from *Jacob*, and my Conviction of Mind, that they are perfectly reasonable.

fonable. Thefe Sir, are the Articles of my Faith, from which I believe I fhall never depart, and for which the Inquifition without doubt would have put me to Death without Mercy.

I LOOK'D upon myfelf to be very much oblig'd to the Gentleman for this Act of Confidence; for tho' as he obferved, there was no Inquifition at *Geneva*, yet it is very certain, the Magiftrates would have look'd upon a Man who held fuch Opinions as thefe in a very bad Light, as is apparent from their punifhing *Servetus* with Death, for hammering out a Syftem not very wide of this of *Perez*.

I DID not fail to give my Friend the ftrongeft Affurances, that nothing he faid to me fhould ever prejudice him here or any where elfe; upon which he opened himfelf very freely on many Subjects; efpecially the number of *Jews* in *Spain*, which he affirmed to be very great; adding, that the Superftition of the People, and the Immorality of the Priefts, were the grand Obftacles to their Converfion; the Practice of the former placing the Exteriors of Chriftianity in a very bad Light, and the latter inducing a Sufpicion that thofe who were moft zealous for its Propagation, were leaft inclined to the Belief of its Doctrines, fince their Lives and their Leffons were fo diametrically oppofite.

WHILE I was amufing myfelf with my Friends at *Geneva*, till fuch Time as I could bring together all my Effects, which by engaging in feveral little Branches of Traffick, were pretty much fcatter'd, I wrote, and receiv'd conftantly Letters from *Venice*, till fuch Time as I informed *Lucia* that my Affairs would be wholly adjufted in a Fortnight; and therefore intreated her by the

next

next Conveyance, to send me whatever Commands she would have executed before my Return to that City. But as it often happens, having suffered *Hope* to cast up this Account, there was a very considerable *Error* in the *Calculation*; for after three Weeks Disappointment of Money from *Lyons* on the one Hand, and of Letters from *Venice* on the other, I found myself still at a Loss, as to fixing the Day of my Departure.

IN this Situation I was, when a Letter from my Landlord at *Venice* Thunder struck me at once. It ran in a Stile of high Resentment for my having carried on, as he expressed it, a very suspicious Correspondence at his House with a married Woman; that a Week before Mrs. ————'s Brother and Husband had arrived, with whom she was sailed for *England*. The Evening before her Departure, she sent, as he acquainted me, a Letter for me, enclosed in one for his Wife, which she entreated might be carefully transmitted me ; because she was afraid it would be a long Time before an Opportunity would offer of writing to me again ; but as he thought it a great Indignity put on his Wife, he had commanded her to burn it in his Presence, which she had accordingly done ; he concluded with desiring me to trouble him with no more Letters, and if I came again to *Venice*, not to find the Way to his House.

THE oddness of the Matter, and the Rudeness of its Form, made this Letter appear to me in the Light of a Sentence of Destruction; it took from me all Hopes at present, and not only so, but in some sort deprived me of all Expectancy of Hope, a Circumstance which sunk me below even a Slave at *Algiers*. I determined how-

however to conceal this Misfortune as carefully as if it had been a Crime, and notwithstanding the Treatment I had received, to write in Terms the most preſſing, and the moſt moving, it was in my Power to invent, to Mr. *Buſhell*, with a View to the procuring a thorough Inſight into this dark Affair. Accordingly that very Evening I wrote near a Sheet of Paper in the firſt flow of my Diſtraction, and in a Tenderneſs of Stile and Thought, which I never remember but with Regret.

'TILL I could receive an Anſwer, I determined to exert the utmoſt Force of my Philoſophy, in preſerving ſuch an Evenneſs of Temper, as might not only keep my Secret from being known, but from being ſuſpected, even by *Johnſon*, who knew my Diſpoſition, and the Situation of my Affairs ſo very well.

THE better to ſucceed in this Scheme, I ſent to invite my Friend *Perez* to come and paſs a Day with me, which he very readily did, having already formed in his Mind that Project to which he afterwards procured my Conſent. He came in the Morning, and till Dinner we diverted ourſelves with looking over ſome Medals and other Curioſities, which I was packing up in Caſes; and after Dinner was over, we fell upon the Affairs of *Spain*, when Mr. *Fetherſtone* who dined with us, took this Occaſion to aſk Mr. *Perez* ſome Queſtions, as to the Conduct of the Inquiſition. This inſenſibly turned the Converſation altogether upon that Head; and what our Friend, who was born a *Spaniard* ſaid thereon, made on me ſo great an Impreſſion, that after my Company were gone, I amuſed myſelf till late in the Night, with ſetting down the Subſtance of what I learned; to which I was the rather inclined, be-

cauſe

cause there was fcarce any Subject of which in the Courfe of my Life I had heard more, or underftood lefs : The Proteftants generally fpeaking, declaiming in the moft violent Terms againft the Injuftice and Barbarity of the Inquifition ; while on the other Hand, moft Catholicks decline fpeaking on that Head, or elfe endeavour to apologize for the *Holy Office*, by denying moft of the Facts alledged againft it, and by dreffing in the beft Colours poffible, the grand Argument in its Favour. *The preferving the Purity of the Faith, and preventing the Peace of Society from being difturbed by religious Jars.*

THE Inquifition was eftablifhed in moft of the Provinces of *Spain*, towards the Clofe of the fifteenth Century, by the Power of *Ferdinand* and *Ifabella*, who were directed in the Affair by Cardinal *Torquemada*, a Man of enthufiaftic Refolution, and who had fuch an Afcendancy over the Spirit of the Queen, that he engaged her to carry his Projects into Execution, maugre all Oppofition.

PHILIP II. who had a ftrong Prejudice to his Father's Memory, fuffered the Inquifition to proceed not only againft the Archbifhop of *Toledo*, and two of the deceafed Emperor's Chaplains, but alfo to form a Procefs againft the late *Charles* V. as a Favourer of Hereticks, and who had been fufpected of Herefy himfelf. His Son *Don Carlos*, his natural Brother *Don John*, the Prince of *Parma*, and fome other Perfons of great Quality, took Fire at this, and expreffed their Refentments a little too openly. The Confequence was, that the King by fair Means and much Interceffion, pro-

procured the Procefs on the Emperor's Will to be ftaid, though he fuffered one of his Chaplains to be burnt alive, together with the Bones of the other, the Archbifhop of *Toledo* faving himfelf by an Appeal to *Rome*.

As for the Princes, they were for the prefent obliged to retire from Court, and the Inquifition purfued them with unrelenting Hatred to the laft Hour of their Lives. Sanctifying the Death of *Don Carlos* by their Decree, and acting on all other Occafions with fuch Fiercenefs, that King *Philip*, with all his Policy and Refolution, had much ado to reftrain them within any Bounds.

FROM the Time of his Death, having had lefs able Princes to deal with, they have pufh'd their Authority ftill farther, and have prefumed not only to cenfure, but to punifh Kings of *Spain*, while on the Throne. As for Inftance, *Philip* III. who having been fo far moved by the Cries of the Condemned, at an *Auto de Fe*, as to fay, *How hard for Men to die for their Belief, a Thing which they cannot help !* The Inquifitor General being informed of it, fent to acquaint him, that the Holy Office expected Satisfaction ; nor would he defift till the King confented to have fome Ounces of his Blood drawn from his Arm, which the Executioner of the *Holy Office* threw into the Fire before the Inquifitor-General, and his Officers.

IN *Portugal* they formed a Procefs againft the Infant *Don Juan* ; but their Behaviour towards the Duke of *Braganza*, after he affumed the Regal Dignity, was ftill more extraordinary. He was call'd *John* the IVth ; and as he owed his Crown to the People, fo there never lived a Prince who was more truly the Father of his People. On this Account he was no great Friend to the Inqui-

K   fition.

fition. The Practice of the Holy Office in feizing at once the Perfon, and the Effects of thofe whom they fufpected, feem'd to him not only unjuft and unreafonable, but even highly prejudicial to the State. He therefore publifhed an Edict, whereby he pofitively forbid all fuch Confifcations for the future.

THE *Holy Office* therefore apply'd themfelves to the *Pope*, who thought fit to redrefs what they call'd a Grievance, though he refufed, notwithftanding the moft prefling Inftances of his moft Chriftian, as well as his *Portuguefe* Majefty, to furnifh *Portugal*, or any of its Dominions with Bifhops, though for Want of them the People were in Danger of becoming *Heathens*. The Relief he gave the *Inquifitors* was this: He by a *Brief* directed the former Method of Confifcation to take Place, declaring, that whoever oppos'd it, fhould ftand excommunicated *ipfo facto*.

THE Inquifitors, as foon as they had this *Brief*, went directly with it to the King, whom they met on his Return from Chapel. When he had read the *Brief*, he demanded of them to whofe Ufe they pretended to convert the Goods of their Prifoners; they anfwered, to his Majefty's Ufe. Very well, faid the King; then let the *Brief* be punctually obeyed; direct your Officers, when they feize, to make always exact Inventories of thofe which you fay are to be my Goods, and let them deliver them together with the Goods themfelves, to my *Affignees*, whom I declare to be the next of Kin, to the Prifoners; and my Pleafure is, that they enjoy them as a Gift from the Crown. While the King lived, they durft not difpute his Orders; but as foon as he expired, the Inquifitors told the Queen, and the Infants *Alphonfo*,

and

and *Peter*, that his Majesty had incurr'd the Guilt of Excommunication, and could not be buried till they thought fit to abfolve the *Dead Body*, which they did in the Prefence of the Queen and Royal Family, with much Solemnity.

THE Means by which the *Holy Office* maintain fo abfolute a Dominion in *Spain* and *Portugal*, are thefe. Firft, their being fupported on all Occafions by the Papal Authority, which on the other Hand is exceedingly fortify'd by the Authority of the Inquifition. Secondly, by the Holy Office retaining fuch a Number of *Informers* under the Title of *Familiars*, who are Men of all Profeffions, and many of them of the higheft Rank. Thirdly, the Afcendency they maintain over the Minds of the common People, who from their Cradles are imbued with fuch a Reverence, and fuch an enthufiaftick Paffion for the Service of this awful Tribunal, that it gets the better of all Sentiments of Religion and Honour, nay, even of that Tendernefs which feems natural to the human Species.

As all the *Tribunals* of the *Inquifition* correfpond with, and are fubject to the *Congregation* of the *Holy Office* at *Rome*, it follows that the *Roman See* naturally protects thefe zealous and devoted Promoters of her Intereft. To fay the Truth, this is one of the fundamental Maxims of the *Roman* Policy ; and without it, it is impoffible to form any Idea how not only the Catholick Religion, but fuch a blind Devotion for the Papal Decrees as reigns at prefent in *Spain* and *Portugal*, could have been kept up, efpecially if we obferve the Temper and Difpofition of thefe People, who are as knowing, as thinking, and at

K 2

the

the fame time at leaft as proud as any of their Neighbours.

THAT this is not Conjecture, but a Judgment eftablifhed on Facts, will appear from comparing the Credit of the *Pope* with the Power of the Inquifition; for wherever we find the latter great, we fhall find the former indifputed, whereas in Countries where there is no Inquifition, or where its Power is very much circumfcribed, the papal Authority is alfo kept within pretty ftrait Bounds, even though the Prince and People are zealous Roman Catholicks.

IT cannot but feem ftrange, that Men in good Circumftances, and of good Families, nay, even Men of Quality, fhould enlift themfelves as Informers; but they have their Reafons, and fuch as in thofe Countries appear far from contemptible. For firft, they ftand themfelves exempt from all Fear of Informations; they enjoy an extraordinary Liberty, and have alfo a large Meafure of Authority through their Intereft with the Inquifitors. Again, they are privileged Perfons, and cannot be proceeded againft in any other Court than that of the Inquifition, let them do what they will, Murder not excepted. And though for very atrocious Crimes the Inquifitors will vouchfafe to commit them to Prifon, and even to fentence them to perpetual Imprifonment, yet that does not hinder their being found at five hundred Miles Diftance from their Prifon-Gates; the *Holy Office* claiming a Power of being as extravagantly indulgent to its own Creatures, as it is fuperabundantly fevere towards fuch as fall under its Difpleafure. Laftly, the Familiars of the Inquifition are extremely well rewarded for their Services out of the Effects of Heretics; for though it is

pretend-

pretended that thefe are confifcated for other Purpofes, yet it is certain that the Office divides the greateft Part of them amongft its Attendants.

As to the Afcendency which the Inquifition maintains over the Minds of the People, it is undoubtedly one of the moft ftrange and unintelligible Things in the World; it is as if a Flock of Sheep fhould be fuborned to affift three or four Wolves in deftroying their Fellows; it is as if Men could be wrought on by fome Kind of Sorcery, to affift at the Immolation of fome of their Fellow Creatures to an infernal Spirit; but ftill, as it is an indubitable Fact, we muft admit it, how little foever we can account for it.

My Friend *Perez* affured me, that in *Portugal*, where *Auto de Fe's* are more common than in *Spain*, the People not only willingly affift at the moft cruel Executions, but do it with a frantick Kind of Joy, not to be defcribed, and fcarce to be imagined; perhaps after all, this very Joy may be excufable, fince if we attentively confider it, we can fcarce fuppofe the People are in their Senfes. On the Whole it is certain, that there never was any Judicature fo odious, or fo terrible as the *Holy Office*.

PEREZ had for his Rival a Perfon whofe Brother was a *Familiar*; this Man afked one of *Perez's* Servants whether he had not feen his Mafter read *Abarbinel's* Commentary; this Queftion being reported to *Perez*, and he having compared it with other Circumftances, it induced him to leave *Spain*, and an Eftate of near two hundred thoufand Dollars. His Fears, however, were far from being ill grounded, for within *fix* Hours after he quitted his Houfe, it was invefted by the Officers of

K 3

the

the Inquifition, who immediately poffeffed themfelves of his Effects, and proceeded againft him as a Perfon whofe Flight had declared him guilty.

THE next Day I fpent in adjufting all my Effects, being determined to quit the prefent Place of my Refidence, though I had no particular Reafon for fo doing, neither knew I whither to go where I fhould be either better received, or live more at my Eafe. In the Evening Mr. *Fetherftone* came and fat with me two or three Hours, in which Space we ran over a great Variety of Subjects, and I remember that he was particularly concerned at the Approach of old Age, before he had made any Provifion for its Reception. He faid, that when Want threatened, a Man ought by all Means to double his Induftry, and inftead either of reproaching Providence, or of pretending indolently to wait for Relief from thence, to fhew a Difpofition of meriting the divine Favour in the Way of natural Caufes, without vainly expecting Miracles never wrought in Favour of the Lazy.

WHEN he took his Leave, he told me that Mr. *Perez*, who lived on the other Side of the River, defired that I would pafs the next Day with him, having fomething of Importance to communicate to me. I readily accepted the Propofal, and promifed to wait on him as foon as I came from Church. When Mr. *Fetherftone* was gone, and I had Time to ruminate on what he had faid, I plainly difcerned that his Mind was under fome unufual Oppreffion, and that, not without ftruggling, it had delivered itfelf of thefe Reflections, which had either Reference to the Situation of his own Affairs or mine. With all my Induftry, however, I could not penetrate

the

the true Source of them ; and therefore, as I found my self little difposed to Reft, I refolved to apply his Reafon-ing to my Condition, in Order to form from thence fome Judgment as to the Principles on which I ought to act in the future Conduct of my Life.

WITH fuch Speculations I amufed, or rather wearied my Underftanding, 'till at laft I was ready to drop afleep, without being able, from all my Reflections, to form any more than this fingle Rule : That a Man, whofe Fortune is in Diforder, fhould never fuffer his Thoughts to be diverted from the Means of fetling it, to the Con-fideration of the Methods of employing it when fettled.

THE next Day I went according to my Appoint-ment to the Apartment of my Friend *Perez*, where I found him and Mr. *Fetherftone* difcourfing together on Chemiftry, at which I was furprized, for 'till then I had never fufpected that either of them knew any thing ex-traordinary of this Matter. Mr. *Fetherftone* feemed to make very light of the pretended Miracles of that Art.

HE faid, that as to Medicines, he had obferved the greateft Cures done by Simples, and the worft Acci-dents following from Drugs *chemically* prepared ; that as to the Curiofities of the Chemifts, they ferved rather to divert and amufe Men, than to inform their Underftand-ings ; and as to the Tranfmutation of Metals, he afferted, that Reafon and Experience had convinced him of the Impoffibility of the Thing, as well as of the Folly of thofe who converted real Wealth into Smoke in the endlefs Search of imaginary Treafure. He clofed thefe Obfervations with a very fhrewd Remark, *viz.* That the Profeffors of all other Sciences began with laying down Self-evident Truths, or at leaft fuch Maxims as

K 4

were

were eafily fhewn to be true, whereas the Chemifts began
they ended, with Dreams and Chimeras; and inftead of
inftructing their Pupils in the right Ufe of their Reafon,
endeavoured to deprive them of it, in order to fill their
Heads with enthufiaftic Notions without Foundation,
Connection, or the fmalleft Appearance of Veracity.

OUR Friend *Perez*, who had really lefs Vehemence
than is ufually found in a *Spaniard*, could however fcarce
bear this with Patience. Chemiftry, it feems, was his darling Study, and he was almoft as paffionately fond of it
as of his Miftrefs. If I were not acquainted with you,
Sir, faid he, to Mr. *Fetherftone*, and did not greatly admire your good Senfe in other Things, what you have
faid upon this Subject, would have given me a very
wrong Idea of your Merit. Confider, my Friend, that
every Science hath its Defamers. With the *Libertines*,
the *Jewifh*, *Chriftian*, and *Mohammedan* Divinity, feem
all alike Fables. To the Wits, Mathematics is a dry,
ufelefs, and barren Sort of Knowledge. Poetry, and
the *Belles Lettres*, are to Men of rigid Sentiments in all
Communities, Trifles unworthy of Notice; and, in
fhort, we have known Men, who, like *Cornelius Agrippa*, have firft fought to acquire Reputation by addicting
themfelves to univerfal Science, and have afterwards
attempted to raife their Fame ftill higher by perfuading the
World that they had feen through all Sciences, and found
them no better than myfterious Vanities. General Prejudices, Sir, prove nothing, becaufe they prove too
much; and as to particular Obfervations, I am perfuaded that Chemifts have as much to fay for themfelves, as
any other Tribe of learned Men. To them, Sir, Mankind owes moft of thofe ufeful Inventions which are the

Boaft

Boaſt of latter Ages, and which, as they were unknown, ſo they were unhoped for by the Antients. What you ſay of Amuſements certainly does Honour to this Art, ſince Men of Senſe are then only amuſed when they ſee Things atchieved, for which their Underſtandings can no way account. The Tranſmutation of Metals ſurpaſſes your Faith, but the moſt intelligent *Spaniards* readily admit it, not from Credulity, but Conviction. You muſt know, Sir, that ſuch as are acquainted with the Method of refining the Silver at *Potoſi* in *Peru*, unanimouſly confeſs that Art brings Nature to mature in a much ſhorter Time, that precious Metal, than ſhe would otherwiſe, that is, without Aſſiſtance do; and I my ſelf can ſhew you an Experiment of a Silver Tree ſhooting out Branches of the ſame Metal from the bare Addition of Lead; though, as you ſay, this is of the Tribe of Amuſements, ſince it is ſo far from being attended with Profit, that the *Silver* might be bought at a cheaper Rate. However, this is not the Caſe at *Potoſi*, and where it is the Caſe, it ſtill proves the Poſſibility of Tranſmutation, which is neverthleſs wonderful, neverthleſs certain, for its being expenſive.

Mr. *Fetherſtone*, either not knowing how to anſwer theſe Arguments, or which I rather believe, deſirous of quitting a Topic that appeared diſagreeable to his Friend, turned the Converſation, by addreſſing himſelf to me. Mr. *Perez*, ſaid he, did not intend by this Invitation to diſturb you with our Diſputes, and therefore I take the Liberty of adjourning the Debate to ſome other Opportunity, when I ſhall have had more Leiſure to conſider and examine what he has at preſent advanced upon this Head. As I was extremely pleaſed with what

each

each of them had said, I would have had Mr. *Fetherstone* returned to the Charge, but Mr. *Perez* also declined it; he considered the last Expression of his Antagonist as a Mark of his being at present unprovided with Matter, and therefore from a *Spanish Punctilio* refused to press him farther at this Time. Chocolate, therefore, was called for, and not a Word mention'd of Chemistry for that Day.

The rest of the Morning was spent in talking of our several Adventures, which had this in common, that without any great Misdeed, each of us was become an *Exile*. *Perez* regretted nothing but the Loss of his Mistress, for the Dread of the Inquisition had extinguished in his Bosom all Love for his Country; so that without the Abolition of that Tribunal he could never frame a Wish of returning to *Spain*.

Mr. *Fetherstone* observed that he was alike banished from *England* and from *France*, and from both by cross Accidents, or rather by Mistakes; yet, as he remark'd, it was easier to satisfy Strangers than one's own Country-men; for, on his sending an Account to the *French* Court of the Manner by which Monsieur *St. Marcelle* became known to him, he was immediately informed that he might return in Safety, for that this unhappy Man had given the same Account both on his Examination and at the Time he suffered Death.

As to my self, I took Notice that I suffered for the Faults of my Father, which I took to be the harder, because at the Restoration all old Offences were washed away, and Those received into the highest Favour who had been deepest in those Measures which had driven the Royal Family abroad.

Our

Our Dinner was flight, for our grand Repaft was in the Evening ; and this being over, *Perez* defired Mr. *Fetherftone* to acquaint me with the Bufinefs on account of which he had defired my Company. For my Part, I had quite forgot what he had told me the Evening before, and was therefore a little furprized when *Perez* mentioned Bufinefs ; however, I joined with him in defiring Mr. *Fetherftone* to explain it to me, adding, that I fhould have been better pleafed if it had been difcuffed in the Morning. *Perez* fmiled, and faid, it was a Thing would require both Evening and Morning Confiderations ; and then Mr. *Fetherftone* taking the Difcourfe, proceeded thus :

My Friend Mr. *Perez*, and I, had been for fome Time confidering of a certain Project offered us by a Gentleman in *France*, who is our common Patron ; and as we are now at the Point of entering on its Execution, we were unwilling either to keep it longer a Secret from you, or to refufe you a Share in it, if it fhall appear in the fame Light to you that it does to us. In few words then, our Friends propofed that we fhould make the Tour of a Part of the *Ottoman Empire*, beginning with *Egypt*, in order to collect Medals, Stones, Manufcripts, and other Curiofities, for which there never was fo great a Demand as at prefent throughout all *Europe*, particularly in *Italy*, *France*, and *England*, where for genuine Relicks of Antiquity no Price whatfoever is held to be extravagant.

Mr. *Fetherftone* making here a little Paufe, I was going to fpeak. Stay Sir, faid he, let me finifh what I have farther to offer you upon this Subject, and you fhall have Time enough to fay what you pleafe. You muft

not

not imagine Sir, that at this Seafon of Life I fhould be
fond of feeking Adventures in unknown Parts of the
World, if I had not a very probable Profpect of making
myfelf eafy, in Confequence of my going through fuch
a Fatigue. I have a Friend at *Lyons*, who will lend
me 200 Piftoles, I have another at *Marfeilles*, who will
furnifh me with as much, what I have of my own will
make up the Sum between five and fix hundred ; my
Friend *Perez* will venture the like Capital, and we are
well informed of the Goods in which our Money ought
to be vefted ; we have likewife a Memorial, containing the fulleft Inftructions as to the Curiofities we are
to purchafe, we are neither of us unacquainted with
thefe Things, and we have the ftrongeft Recommendations to the *French* and *Venetian* Confuls ; fo that tho'
at firft Sight this Project may feem a little chimerical,
yet it is in Truth as well founded, and will be as well
fupported as any Thing of its Nature can be. Our
own Induftry muft indeed be the Sheet Anchor of our
Hopes, and if we cannot depend upon ourfelves, it is in
vain for us to expect Succefs in this, or in any other
Undertaking. As it is, my Fortune is Shipwreck'd, it
can be no worfe if I fhould be miftaken in my Conjectures as to the Project before us ; whereas if Things
go right, I fhall be fure of paffing the reft of my Days
in quiet in *France* or in *Italy*, or it may be in *England* ;
for I am not of Opinion, that the Government there
will always purfue the fame Meafures which they have
hitherto done.

A s for me, added *Perez*, I have fuch a Source of
perpetual Difquiet in my own Bofom, that Reft is painful, and a State of Agitation only affords me Quiet,
by

by refcuing me as it were from myfelf. It is this, full
as much as any View of Profit, which hath determined
me to take this Voyage. If I fhould not fucceed I fhall
ftill have fomething left to preferve myfelf and my
Friend here, from being quite quelled by the Frowns
of Fortune, and as Time is the Parent of many ftrange
Events, I cannot tell what, againft our Return, it may
bring forth ; perhaps fome Accident as favourable to me
as that was unfortunate, which drove me from my Family and my Hopes. You have heard our Project,
and our Reafons for embracing it ; now Sir, if Similitude
of Circumftances fhould incline you to take a Share
with us in this Defign, we fhall have a better Opinion
of it, and fcarce entertain any Doubt of fucceeding under your Aufpice. It is impoffible that you fhould refolve in a Moment; it will be a Fortnight or three
Weeks before we fhall think of quitting this Place ;
and therefore, if in eight or ten Days you will come to
a Refolution, we fhall hear it with Pleafure.

I THANK'D my Friends for this new Mark of their
Confidence and Affection, promifed to take the Matter
into my Confideration, and to acquaint them with my
final Refolution, within the Space of twelve or fourteen
Days. I defired Leave however, to ask the Advice of
certain Perfons, whom I took to be proper Judges of
an Affair of this Nature, declaring at the fame Time,
that how much foever I thought it might import my
Intereft, yet I would never think of doing fuch a Thing
without their Confent ; they readily gave it me, with
this Caution, that I fhould not defcend into Particulars,
or mention any of the Perfons concerned. Thefe Pre-
liminaries fettled, we parted, and I fpent a great part of
the

the Night in ruminating on the Probability of carrying
this Project into Execution, and the Turn of my own
Capacity for bearing a part in it. The great Point that
perplexed me was, the forsaking *Lucia*, whom notwithstanding the strong Probability of the Thing, or rather
Proof of it, I could not believe married.

THE next Day, as soon as I had brought myself into
some Temper, for in the Morning the Reflection of
what had passed the Day before, confused me not a
little, I went to visit Mr. *Roland*, who had been a Pre-
ceptor in the Theory, and my sole Master in the little
practical Knowledge I had of Stones and Medals. It
so happened, that I came to him very opportunely,
he was embarrassed for want of a small Sum of Money,
which because of a former Debt, he would not mention
to me ; it came by Chance to my Ears, and with some
Difficulty he was perswaded to make Use of my Assistance. We spent the Afternoon together, and as nothing was more common than for us to talk of the
Affairs of the *Levant*, and the Method of carrying on
a Trade there, I easily turned the Conversation on
that Subject, on which my Friend talk'd as freely and
fully, as if I had particularly asked his Advice on the
Business then in my Head.

HE discoursed of the Cautions necessary for preser-
ving Health in the Oriental Countries, and for famili-
arizing one's self to their Customs ; he described at large
the Virtues, Vices, and Manners of the *Turks*, *Jews*,
and *Greeks*, and never did any Painter hit Likeness
more exactly. He explained the Method of dealing
with all these People, their respective Artifices, and the
Means of guarding against them ; above all, he recommended

mended the Study of *Physic*, as the shortest and safest
Method of being introduced into the Houses of Persons
of Distinction, with whom he alledged it was always
best to converse, and through whom it was easiest to
acquire whatever one sought for in those Countries.

FROM this Conversation I was thoroughly convinced, that such an Expedition as my Friends had proposed to me, might turn to great Advantage under prudent Management, and a steady Regard to the main
Design. When I returned Home in the Evening, I
looked over all the Notes I had formerly made upon
Subjects of this Nature, planned out a Method for dif-
posing them into Order, and drew out such *Queries*
as might lead to a thorough Knowledge of all Points in
which I had been hitherto deficient, for want of being
acquainted with the proper Head of Inquiry. I likewise prescribed to myself a Task still more laborious,
that of digesting all my other Memorandums into Method, so that they might lie in a narrow Compass,
knowing that if I ever carried this Design into Execution, it would be impossible for me to have the Use of
many Books.

A DAY or two afterwards I went to visit Mr. *Pucci*,
whom I found in a very declining Condition, he had
some Months before a Fit of an Apoplexy, from which
with Difficulty he was recovered. Soon after he fell
into a Dysentery, which tho' the Physicians had found
Means to alleviate, yet were they unable to cure. It
was this Disorder which had brought my Friend so low
as to be scarce able to walk cross the Room. In this
Condition he had his Senses as clear as ever, and spoke
to me with his usual Affection and Tenderness. The

Concern

Concern I was under to see him so weak, hindered me from mentioning any Business, and occasioned my enquiring particularly into the Causes of his Distemper. The good old Man said, that he believed his Constitution was quite worn out, and that he was thankful to Providence for affording him this soft and gentle Death.

BEFORE I was aware I answered, that it was not impossible he might recover, for that I had known extraordinary Things done by taking daily a very small Dose of prepared *Opium*. Senior *Pucci* catch'd at this, and would immediately have the Medicine, which when I saw he was not to be moved I comply'd with, and having weigh'd out exactly three Doses, he took one of them immediately, and the other two on the next succeeding Days. After the last Dose, he was apparently much better, and by keeping to this Medicine in the same Proportion it was at first given him, he recovered wonderfully.

BY this lucky Accident I became exceedingly in his Favour, he would have presented me with a Ring of very great Value, but I absolutely refused it, telling him at the same Time, that I would put it in his Power to gratify me farther than the Value of that Ring. I then began to explain to the old Gentleman the Business I had at Heart, and he very kindly furnished me with all the proper Instructions I could desire, and answered all the Questions I thought fit to ask. At the close of the Conversation he gave me a little Note, which in three Lines contained the Secret of cleansing colour'd Stones, the Value of which, if I had attentively considered, I might have spared myself the Pains of leaving *Italy* to acquire a Fortune.

BEFORE

BEFORE the Fortnight was expired, in which I had promised to give my Answer to my Friends, I receiv'd a Letter from *Venice* unsigned, which informed me, that my Landlord threw my Epistle into the Fire without reading it, that all I could write would meet with the same Fate, that *Lucia* was undoubtedly married; and that to make myself easy and happy, I ought never to think of her more. At this Time I steadfastly believed this Letter came from my Landlady, who had always professed a very great Esteem for me, but it seems she really knew nothing of the Matter; on the contrary, as soon as he had burnt my Letter, my Landlord went to the House of the Gentleman where *Lucia* lived, and in a Passion, gave an Account of the whole Transaction, which coming to the Ears of the Lady with whom *Lucia* lived in the strictest Friendship, she had the Goodness to write the Letter I have just mentioned, in order to put me out of Pain.

THE next Morning I sent my Man to invite Mr. *Perez* and Mr. *Fetherstone* to Dinner, and before we sat down to it, declared to them my fixed Resolution to embark with them in the Design they had proposed. They appeared extremely satisfied with this Resolution, and we drank that Evening to the Success of our Affairs, not indeed to a Degree of downright Drunkenness, but pretty much beyond our usual Extent; so that it was thought proper for them to remain all Night in my Apartment, and the next Morning it was agreed that we should immediately enter on the necessary Preparations for our Voyage.

HITHERTO I had suffered myself as often as I was alone, to be haunted with Dreams of returning to *Eng-*

L

land,

land, and living fomewhere in the Country with *Lucia*. But now as this appeared abfolutely impracticable, I refolved to rid myfelf of thefe idle Notions, and to apply folely to the Point in Hand, as to that on which my Fortune entirely depended, having at prefent, little or no Hopes of receiving farther Advantage from the Effects of my Uncle, notwithftanding the Juftice of my Demand.

Mr. *Fetherftone* who had undertaken to negotiate with Mr. *Mountague* (for fo the *Lord Chief Juftice St. John* was called) after he had retired into *France*, the Payment of the Money due from a certain great Perfon to Mr. *Perez* for his Diamonds, happily concluded that Affair ; I fay happily, tho' he could not procure the whole Debt; but 1500 Piftoles, for which it was compromifed, proved a great and unexpected Addition to *Perez*'s Fortune, who till his Flight from *Spain*, had looked upon this in the Light of a defperate Demand. All my Effects were by this Time either come to Hand, or remitted to Mr. *Hayes*, on whom I could depend ; and therefore it was agreed that Mr. *Fetherftone* fhould immediately fet out for *Venice*, to provide all Things there for our Departure from *Europe*, and that Mr. *Perez* and I fhould follow him as foon as conveniently we could.

This Refolution was executed almoft as foon as it was taken, and we had no Reafon to repent of having placed our whole Confidence in Mr. *Fetherftone*, whofe Integrity and Capacity appeared very remarkably in the Management of a Bufinefs fo new to him, as well as to ourfelves. It is true, he had the Help of the *French* Memoir, which was very exact, as well as comprehenfive,

five, but with the best Instructions, it is necessary that he who is to execute them should have Honour and Prudence, for otherwise they will be of little Use.

It fell out in our Affairs as it does in most new Undertakings, half the Difficulties relating to it were not foreseen. Mr. *Perez* and I therefore were exceedingly surprized, when after a Stay of Seven Weeks, Mr. *Featherstone* informed us that it would much better answer our Purposes, if we made Choice of *Leghorn* for our Port, from whence in the succeeding Month there would sail a *French* Ship for *Alexandria*, on Board of which we might enjoy all imaginable Conveniency; whereas according to our former Scheme, we must wait till the Beginning of the next Year before we could embark from *Venice* as commodiously. The Reasons he assigned were so just, and our Confidence in him so great, that we instantly returned him an Answer conformable to his Desires, and he thereupon quitted *Venice*, and repaired to *Leghorn*, for which Place, as soon as we received Advice of his Arrival, we determined immediately to set out, having had all Things for some Time in readiness.

Among the parting Visits I made to my Friends, one was to Signior *Pucci*, which because it was attended with some Consequences worthy relating, I will mention here. As during my Stay at *Geneva*, I had a great deal of spare Time on my Hands, I employed part of it in visiting such of the States and Principalities in *Italy* as lay not at too great a Distance. By Degrees, either on Business or Pleasure, I saw them all, excepting only the Territory of his *Holiness*, and the Kingdom of *Naples*. As my Intention was to inform myself

as

as thoroughly as I could of their prefent Condition, I conftantly made a Lift of *Queries* drawn from the Deficiences, Variations, and Contradictions of the Accounts I had read, and by fatisfying myfelf on thefe Points, I looked upon it as a Thing certain, that nothing very material could efcape me. Thefe at my Leifure I reviewed, and from them compofed *two* diftinct *Treatifes*, one in *Italian*, the other in *Englifb*, of the State of *Italy* in the Year 1672.

The former of thefe I had formerly fhewn to Seignior *Pucci*, who either out of Regard to its Author, or becaufe he really had a better Opinion of the Piece than it deferved, defired to have it tranfcribed, that he might have a Copy of it for his own Ufe, which at this Vifit I gave him. The old Gentleman received it very kindly, and at the fame Time he placed it in his Cabinet, took from thence a Paper, which he put into my Hands.

This faid he, my Friend, next to the Manufcript you have given me, I look upon to be the choiceft Piece in all my Collection; it is a Difcourfe of a *French* Virtuofo on the *Philofopher's Stone*, and is efteemed by the *Literati* of *Italy* a Mafter Piece. I think I cannot make you a more acceptable Prefent, otherwife I would endeavour to do it.

A Dissertation *on the natural Production of Metals, and of the Poffibility and Probability of there being fuch a Univerfal Tincture as is commonly called the Philofopher's Stone.*

" **A**S Credulity is the *Mother* of *Error*, fo *Scep-*
" *tifm* is the Parent of *irrefolute Ignorance*, as
" homely a *Baby* as the *other*. *Truth* is only difcover'd
" by

" by thofe who are content to join the *Lights* of *Expe-*
" *rience* and of *Reafon*, and who are as much difpofed
" to *receive* for certain, what of their own Knowledge
" they are *told* by *others*, as they are inclined to expect
" from *others* an immediate Belief of what they *affirm*
" themfelves. I have premifed this for two Reafons,
" *Firft*, becaufe the little Knowledge I have hath ac-
" crued to me from practifing thefe *Maxims*; and *Se-*
" *condly*, becaufe I intend to deliver the Fruits of my
" *Studies* to *others* in the fame Way, and not by the
" fatiguing round-about Road of the *Schools*, wherein
" *Form* is fo much prefer'd to *Matter*, that we are of-
" ten difgufted with *Truth* itfelf, through the *Weari-*
" *nefs* we are under from the *tedious Journey* taken in
" *Search* of her.

" In all the Parts of the *Univerfe* we diftinguifh
" *Matter* and *Spirit*; by *Matter* I underftand thofe
" *grofs* Particles which are only fit to be *acted* upon;
" and by *Spirit*, thofe *fine* and *lively Effluvias* which
" are properly fuited for *Action*. A warm and humid
" *Vapour* fteeming continually from the *Centre* of the
" *Earth* gives *Spirit* to all Things; which are the fame
" in this Refpect, tho' they differ from each other, ac-
" cording to the variety of Matter wrought on by this
" *Ætherial Spirit*, or *Mercury* of *Nature*.

" This *Breath* or *Vapour* paffing over a dry fubtil
" and fulphureous *Earth*, it carries Part thereof along
" with it, becaufe all *dry* Bodies adhere to *Moifture*,
" being forced by the *Central Heat* ftill upwards, and
" meeting in the *Caverns* of the *Earth*, continual Re-
" fiftance, whereby it is often beaten back on that dry
" and fulphureous Earth, which it at firft gently touch'd;

L 3 " at

" at laft, after many *Sublimations* and *Precipitations,*
" this *Mercury* is abforbed and fwallowed up in the
" *Earth,* and by the internal *Heat,* becomes the *Seed*
" of *Metals,* of which the *Matter* as well as the *effen-*
" *tial Form* is the fame in all, their Differences arifing
" only from the *Accidents* of *Denfity* and *Colour.*

" A s to the *firft* Point, the *Difference* in the *Weight.*
" Such as are called *imperfect* Metals are *fpecifically* ligh-
" ter, than thofe which are ftiled perfect Metals; and
" the Reafon is, becaufe they are compofed of *grofs*
" and *heterogeneous* Parts, that is, the Bulk and Contra-
" riety of the Particles caufe in fuch Metals more *Va-*
" *cuities* than there are in thofe compofed of *fmaller*
" and *homogeneous* Particles. To make this perfectly
" plain, confider that a Basket filled with *Apples* hath
" evidently more void Spaces, than the fame Basket
" fill'd with *Corn.* Again, a thoufand *ivory Dice*
" might be pack'd up in much lefs Room, than if the
" fame quantity of *Ivory* was wrought up into *five*
" *hundred* Dice, *three hundred* Billiard Balls, and *two*
" *hundred* little Eggs. This Comparifon, as it ex-
" plains the lightnefs of *imperfect* Metals, fo it fhews
" alfo how they come to be more brittle and frangible;
" for in a Body full of *Vacuities,* any Stroke from
" without eafily occafions a *Seperation,* whereas it
" would more clofely *unite* a Body compofed of *fmall*
" and *homogeneous* Particles, as Experience alfo veri-
" fies.

" T h e *Second* Difference is *Colour.* For if all *Me-*
" *tals* could be made as *heavy* as *Gold,* and as *yellow,*
" they would undoubtedly be turned to *Gold.* At pre-
" fent we fhall not enter into the Caufes whence are
" de-

" derived the different *Colours* of *Metals*, it is sufficient
" to obſerve, that the *yellowneſs* of *Gold* ariſes from its
" being compoſed of *homogeneous* Parts, and from its
" *humid Spirit* being effectually ſwallow'd up in its
" *Earth*. To explain this, let us conſider *Bread*,
" which is compoſed of *Flower* and *Water* properly
" tempered; when by the Operation of *Heat*, the *Moiſt*
" is thoroughly abſorbed in the *Dry*, the Reflection of
" the *Rays* of *Light* exhibit to us a *yellowiſh Colour*;
" whereas when *raw* it was *White*, and if it had been
" *over-baked*, it would have been *Black*.

" THIS then being a fair Account of the manner in
" which *Nature* acts in the *Formation* of *Metals*, if
" we propoſe to ourſelves to do the ſame Thing, we
" muſt imitate her; we muſt take a dry ſubtil and ſul-
" phureous *Earth*, and this warm and humid *Vapour*
" or *Mercury*, and having cauſed the *one* to *imbibe* the
" *other*, we muſt ſublimate and circulate theſe till they
" fix in a *metalick* Subſtance, which by Degrees may
" be dryed till it becomes *Gold*, and this the more cer-
" tainly and the more expeditiouſly, if the *Earth* were
" properly purified before, and the *Operation* performed
" by a *Heat* ſtronger and more conſtant than that
" proceeding from the *Central* flame.

" BUT our *Philoſophy* pretends not to carry Things
" ſo far; it aims only at making a *Powder* fuſible, ſub-
" til, penetrating, fixed, and with a Power of *Ting-*
" *ing*. By its Fuſibility, it melts with a ſmall Degree
" of *Heat*; by its Subtilty, it is render'd fit to enter
" into the ſtreighteſt *Pores* of any *Metal*; by its pene-
" trating Quality, it forces through them, and mingles
" itſelf with all their *Particles* to the very *Centre*,

L 4

rendering

" rendering them fix'd and solid, by the Expulsion of
" *heterogenous* Particles; and finally, by the Diffusive-
" ness of its *Tincture* drying the *imperfect Metal*, and
" tinging it throughout with the *colour* of Gold.

" IT is apparent from what hath been already said;
" that for the Formation of the *Philosophic Powder*, so
" far transcending *Gold*, it is necessary to have a proper
" *Spirit*, and a proper *Matter*. The *Spirit* or *Mer-*
" *cury* of the Philosophers is, as we have shewn, en-
" closed in every Thing which *lives*; but then this
" *Spirit* acquires a specific Quality from the *Matter*
" which it animates; and if we could seperate a *vege-*
" *table Spirit* from the Matter in which it is envelo-
" ped, and mix it with a smaller quantity of the *Mer-*
" *cury* of the *Air*, it would operate on the *latter*, so as
" to assimulate it, and make it become a *vegetable Spi-*
" *rit*. But to cut Things short, if it could be so con-
" trived as to seperate the *Mercury* of *Gold* from its
" subtil and sulphureous Earth, we might by small
" Additions of the *Mercury* from other Things, greatly
" encrease this *Mercury* of *Gold*, and then by a long
" and ingenious *Process*, managed with a proper Re-
" gard to *Nature* in her *Formation* of *Metals*, force
" this accumulated *Spirit* or *Mercury*, to unite itself
" again with the aforesaid subtil homogeneous and sul-
" phurous *Earth*, after which it would be no longer
" *Gold*, but the spirituous, penetrating, fixed, and tin-
" ging *Powder* which we want.

" SUBSEQUENT to this short and distinct Account,
" there is no need of running through the *Experiment*
" of *Transmutation*, in order to shew how this *Pow-*
" *der* would operate on an *imperfect Metal*; this we
" have

" have already done in the Description we gave o
" the Philosophic Powder ; and we would equally avoid
" Obscurity and Repetition. The Intent of this little
" Essay is not to divulge the *Secret* of making this
" Powder, but to shew that the supposing the Possibility
" of preparing it, is no *Absurdity*, as some who affect to
" be thought *Philosophers* would persuade the World it
" is ; and having done this, there is nothing more to
" be said. Let him who would be farther instructed,
" consider seriously this Account, and prosecute his
" Studies with an *humble Mind*, and a due Resignation
" to the *Will* of *God*."

A Day or two before we were to set out for *Leghorn*,
as I was talking to *Johnson* of our Expedition, I apprehended by the Coldness of his Answer, that he had no
great Opinion of our Success, upon which I intreated
him to deal freely with me, and give me his Advice in
this as he had in other Things. He began with observing that I ask'd it a little too late ; that if, as I suspected, he had conceived an indifferent Opinion of this Project, his confessing it would only serve to discourage me,
since my Fortune was already embarked ; but Sir, said
he, it is not so, my Uneasiness is on my own Account ;
I find my Constitution much weaken'd and impair'd ; I
am apprehensive that travelling will encrease this Indis-
position, and that instead of being for the future what I
hope I have hitherto been, a useful, and diligent Servant,
I shall be a Clog and Burthen to you. You will stand
in need of a Person more active and more knowing than
my self, though you are sensible, Sir, that I am not
wholly

wholly unacquainted with the Nature and Value of those Rarities you are going to collect. However, Sir, that you may see I mean nothing less than to desert your Service, I will propose to you what I hope may advantage it as much, or rather more, than my travelling with you, which in few Words is this. I will, if you think proper, remain at *Leghorn*, whither we are now going, in order to take care of your Effects, which are at present unemploy'd, and to receive and execute such Commands as you may find it necessary to give me ; but of this, Sir, you will think at Leisure, for I pretend only to offer you my Sentiments, desiring that you should be guided only by your own. There will be Time enough for you to weigh this Matter maturely, which I recommend to your Consideration so warmly, because I think your Interest much more concerned in it than my own.

In the beginning of the Month of *November*, Mr. *Perez*, and I, accompanied only by *Johnson*, arrived at *Leghorn*, where we lodged in the House of Messieurs *Varillon*, *French* Merchants, where we were treated with all imaginable Kindness, and had all the Conveniencies we could possibly desire. Mr. *Fetherstone*, since his coming hither from *Venice*, had been extremely troubled with a kind of bastard Pleurify ; but as he was a Man of great Firmness and Resolution, he was so apprehensive of delaying our Affairs as well as his own, if he should have Recourse here to the Advice of Physicians, that he contented himself to the Use of such simple Medicines as either Reason or Experience acquainted him with, in hopes that these, with the Help of a very regular Diet,

might

might reftore him to Health. But in this he was deceived, for by the frequent Returns of his Diftemper, he was fo exceedingly weaken'd, that in the Space of a Fortnight he was obliged to keep his Room.

In this Condition, I, without acquainting him, fent for an eminent Phyfician, whofe Name was *Ricardi*, who declared the Patient in a very dangerous Way, order'd fome Blood to be taken away, and the next Day prefcribed him a kind of Poffet-drink, which by its Smell and Tafte appeared to be ftrongly loaded with urinous Salts; by the Ufe of this, and fome oily Draughts, my Friend recovered flowly, and at the fame time the Phyfician declared that it would by no Means be fafe for him to think of going to Sea, efpecially at this Seafon of the Year; which induced a new Change in our Affairs, and engaged us to refolve that Mr. *Fetherftone* fhould remain at *Leghorn*, and that *Johnfon* fhould attend him. There was a Neceffity of coming to this Refolution, becaufe the *French* Ship, in which we were to make our Paffage, propofed to fail by the tenth of *December*.

In the Time that upon this Occafion I ftaid at *Leghorn*, I was entirely acquainted with one Mr. *Wood*, the Grandfon of Capt. *Wood*, fo famous for his many long Voyages, which turned, however, but little to his Profit. This Gentleman lived on a fmall Fortune, acquired by his Father in the Service of the Duke of *Northumberland*, whofe Son I faw more than once in *Italy*, and whofe Grandfon was at this Time Page of Honour to the Elector of *Bavaria*. As I was always jealous of the Honour of my Country, I could not help hearing with the greateft Satisfaction the Praifes given to the late Duke; nor was I lefs amazed at my own Ignorance in
this

this Point, who knew not 'till I came into this Country, that there was any such Person as this Duke in the World.

As for Mr. *Fetherstone*, he was tolerably acquainted with his History, and for my Friend *Perez*, he almost adored his Memory on account of his being one of the *Adepti*, and who was generally held to have possessed, if ever Man did, the Philosopher's Stone. Having collected from my Friends the best Materials I could, and compared them with such Books as I could get a Sight of at *Leghorn*, I drew up the following Memorial concerning this extraordinary Person, and his most wonderful Adventures.

ROBERT Dudley, Earl of *Leicester*, so well known to the World by the Favour he lived in with his Mistress Queen *Elizabeth*, cohabited for many Years with the Lady *Douglass Sheffield*, as his Wife, and had by her a Son and Daughter. The Son was called after his Father, *Robert*, and bred up with as much Care as if he had been intended for the Heir of his Father's Fortunes and Titles; and so indeed he ought to have been, since his Mother, who was the Daughter of the Lord *Howard* of *Effingham*, and the Widow of the Lord *Sheffield*, was no unworthy Match for his Father, and as certainly married to him as ever any Woman was to her Husband. But it was the Earl's Misfortune frequently to change his Views in Love, as well as Politics, and to stick at nothing to carry the Points which at any Time struck his Imagination. The Wife of the Earl of *Essex* eclipsed not only the Lady *Douglass*, but his many Mistresses; so that being desirous to transfer his Honours and Estates to his Issue by this Lady who was with Child by him

during

during her Husband's Life, he is said to have procured the Death of that Earl; and thus, notwithstanding his former Marriage, he took the Widow twice to Wife; Once privately for his own Satisfaction, and again to please her Father Sir *Francis Knolles*, in his, the Earl of *Warwick's*, and the Lord *North's* Presence.

As for the Lady *Douglas*, he first offered her seven hundred, then a thousand Pound *per Annum* to deny her Marriage, and bastardize her Children; but she refusing these and all other Conditions, another Method was try'd, familiar enough to his Lordship, whereby she lost her *Hair* and *Nails*, and was so effectually frighted, that to save him the Trouble of any future Attempts, she married Sir *Edward Strafford*, a Man of noble Birth, and of distinguished Abilities, the Queen's Ambassador to *France*.

All this Time the young *Robert Dudley* remained under the Care of his Father, who though he took Care on all Occasions to call him his *base Son*, yet in other Respects he abated nothing of his Tenderness towards him. When he grew up, he was sent to *Christ-Church* College in *Oxford*, of which University his Father was Chancellor. There the young Man very early distinguished himself by his surprizing Abilities, rivalling while a Youth, the most knowing in the University, especially in the Mathematics. What was still more wonderful, he excell'd no less in Studies of another, or rather opposite Nature, *viz*. Politics, at the same time that he surpassed in his Exercises the most sprightly of the Nobility.

When he was but a very young Man, he addicted himself to Chemistry, affected much all new Discoveries

in

in Navigation, and, after his Father's Death, who tho'
he again declared him his *base Son* by his Will, left him
all that was in his Power, exerted himself in a very lau-
dable Manner in the Encouragement of Trade, Manufactures, settling of Colonies, and whatever else contributed to national Glory. His Knowledge made him
esteemed by the wisest Men, his Beneficence caused him
to be surrounded with such ingenious Men as were in
Distress, whom he liberally relieved, and with whom he
familiarly conversed ; at length, in the Year 1594,
taking to heart the many Miscarriages of the *English* in
the South Seas, he fitted out three small Ships at his own
Expence, determining also to hazard his Person for re-
trieving the Reputation of the *English* Seamen in that
Part of the World, and for making such Discoveries as
might redound to the Service of the State.

BUT when all Things were ready, Queen *Elizabeth*
absolutely refused him a Licence, saying, It became her,
as the Mother of her People, to prevent their lavishing
away their Lives in such vain Expeditions ; however,
she gave him Leave to sail into the *West Indies*, which
he accepted, though he knew that Voyage could not
possibly turn to his Account. At his first sailing from
England, he lost the Company of his second Ship, and
never recovered her ; however, he proceeded in his
Course, and with his two small Vessels took and sunk
nine *Spanish* Ships, and in his Return engaged in his little Frigate a very large Ship of War, 'till such Time as
all his Powder was spent, and then out-sailed her, tho'
it was afterwards known that she founder'd at Sea, and
was lost with all her Crew. In 1595, he returned safe
to *London*, and was some time after knighted.

DURING

DURING the reft of Queen *Elizabeth's* Reign, he diftinguifhed himfelf by encouraging to the utmoft of his Power all the new Branches of Trade which were opened by our Merchants, either to the Eaft or Weft. He married the Lady *Alice,* by whom he had two Daughters, and for ought I know other Children. On King *James's* coming to the Crown, he attempted in the Court of *Star-chamber* to prove the Legitimacy of his Birth. To this Purpofe, his Mother, the Lady *Douglafs,* was examin'd, who depofed, that fhe was lawfully and folemnly married at *Afher* in the County of *Surry,* to the Earl of *Leceifter,* in the Prefence of Sir *Edward Horfey,* who gave her in Marriage, *Robert Sheffield,* Efq; and eight other Perfons. It appeared likewife in Evidence, that the Ring with which fhe was married, was fet with five pointed Diamonds, and a Table Diamond; which Ring had been given to the Earl of *Leicefter* by the old Earl of *Pembroke,* with this Injunction, never to part with it but to the Lady he made his Wife. The Lady *Parker* depofed at the fame time, that fhe had feen and read at the very Time it was delivered to the Lady *Douglafs,* a Letter felicitating her on the Birth of her Son *Robert;* fubfcribed, Your loving Hufband, *Leicefter.*

BUT on a fudden, the King fent an Order to ftay all Proceedings in this Caufe, and forbid the Publication of any of the Depofitions. Soon after an Information was exhibited againft fuch as had been examined for entering into a Confpiracy againft the Honour of *Lettice* Countefs of *Leicefter;* whereupon Sir *Robert Dudley* refolved to leave his native Country.

WITH

WITH this View he procured a Licence to travel for three Years, though he certainly intended not to return so early at least, if at all. He took with him the Daughter of Sir *Robert Southwell*, and left his Wife, by whom he had two Daughters, behind him, with her Children. Travelling into *Italy*, after visiting other Courts, he settled at that of the great Duke of *Tuscany*, where he lived with such Lustre, that it was currently reported, and generally believed, he either had the Philosopher's Stone, or some other Secret of the same, though it might be of an inferior Nature. Here it was that he made a grand Display of his vast Abilities in the practical Mathematics, by projecting the Re-establishment of *Leghorn*, for Those who pretend it was built by him, are in a prodigious Error.

IT anciently belonged to the *Pisans*, and was by them rendered a commodious Port, and a tolerable City ; falling into the Hands of the *Florentines*, it sunk into a very low Condition ; from whence it was recovered by the Interposition of Sir *Robert Dudley*, who contrived a Method of cleansing the Marshes, and thereby amending the Air, the Unwholesomeness of which had been the chief Occasion of its Desertion. He likewise advised the declaring it a *Free Port*, and pointed out the vast Advantages which would accrue to the Grand Duke thereby. One grand Objection that he overcame was this, that even according to his own Project the Port of *Leghorn*, however fair in Shew, would never be capable of receiving large Ships ; and if these again were suffered to ride in the Road, they would not be under the Command of the Guns from the Fort ; so that after a vast Expence the Grand Duke would have no Security of

seeing

feeing any Part of his Money return'd, but lye in a Manner at the Mercy of Strangers.

Sir *Robert* obferved that it was on this very Situation he built all his Hopes, that what was called Want of Security, was the beft Security in the World, for it would induce Traders to anchor there rather than in any other Port. Two other Things he advifed, which have been pretty well kept up to, *viz.* the laying but one Piafter on a Bale of Goods, let its Bulk or Value be what it will; the other, that *Meffieurs* the *Inquifitors* would be pleafed to wink at Strangers, and not pretend to inquire into the Religion of Thofe who came to do their Bufinefs, and not to make or be made Profelytes. This Nobleman afterwards built a very fine Houfe at *Florence*, where he was very confpicuoufly the Patron of the Learned, the Induftrious, and the Ingenious. For his rare Merit the Emperor *Ferdinand* the IId, created him a Duke of the *Holy Roman Empire*. The *Englifh* generally ftile him Duke of *Northumberland*, but the Inhabitants of the Country called him Duke *de Berlich*. But it is now Time to return to his Affairs in *England*.

He had not been long out of the Kingdom before the Enemies of his Family procured a privy Seal to recall him; which he not obeying, his Eftates were feized. Afterwards, however, Prince *Henry* having a Mind to purchafe the Caftle of *Kenilworth*, and Lands belonging thereto, Sir *Robert* was treated with in order to part with his Right, which for *fourteen thoufand five hundred* Pounds he confented to do, though the Purchafe was worth *forty* thoufand. His Highnefs had thereupon Poffeffion given him, yet Sir *Robert Dudley* never received one Shilling. *Three thoufand* Pounds, Part of the Purchafe

Money,

Money, was paid to an *English* Merchant who failed; and Prince *Henry* dying, the Estate descended to Prince *Charles*, and all Hopes of the Money were lost.

In the Year 1621, however, a new Agreement was made with the Lady *Alice*, Wife to Sir *Robert Dudley*; in Consequence of which, an Act of Parliament passed to enable her to convey all his Estates as if she was a single Woman, and legally possessed of them, in Consideration of certain perpetual Annuities granted to her and her Daughters; which, however, neither she nor they ever received. But a long Time afterwards, I think, after the breaking out of the *Civil War*, this Lady, who was still living, was by Letters Patents under the Great Seal, created a Dutchess, with Precedency to her self and Daughters, according to the Patent granted by the Emperor *Ferdinand* to her Husband. These two Daughters, *viz.* the Lady *Catherine*, and the Lady *Anne* were married, the former to Sir *Richard Leveson*, the latter to Sir *Robert Holbourn*.

This Duke, who spent the rest of his Life for the most part at *Florence*, had Issue two Sons, and several Daughters, by the Lady he carried from *England*. The eldest of these Sons succeeded him in his Title, the second was an Ecclesiastick in *France*; his Daughters married Persons of great Quality, and the eldest of them was at this Time living, being married for the second Time to the Marquis *Paleoti*, by whom she has Issue. The present Duke of *Northumberland*, as he is called, was formerly High Steward to the Queen of *Sweden*, from whom he had a Pension of six hundred Crowns *per Annum*.

He

HE also hath two Sons, but is not esteemed rich, and therefore I think the *English* do not pay him much Court. I have known many who took him for a Knight-Errant, and a Man of no Birth. This strange Inaccuracy amongst our Countrymen makes Strangers conceive oddly of them ; and indeed not without Reason. For undoubtedly, never any Man was worse treated than Sir *Robert Dudley*, who was punished for the Crimes of his Father, contrary to the Law of Nature, of Nations, and of his Country. To deny therefore to him or his Descendants, those new Honours which he merited from Foreign Princes, is a Mark not only of Injustice, but of Unpoliteness, or rather Brutality. But enough of this.

L E G H O R N is a very pretty Town, extremely well built, and appearing so much the more beautiful, because the Streets are broad, uniform, and strait, all leading to the large Piazza where the Merchants meet. The Place is very well fortified, and the Citadel is of considerable Strength. The Mole is a wonderful Work, and of great Security to the Ships which lie within it ; the Road is tolerably safe ; but in truth it is the Privilege of its being a free Port which causes such a mighty Resort to *Leghorn*. Should any of the Grand Dukes venture to encrease their Revenues by breaking in upon this Privilege, we should see it deserted, as many of the Ports of *Italy* are already. On the Key there is a very fine Statue of *Ferdinand* I. Grand Duke of *Tuscany*, supported by four Slaves.

THERE were at this Time several very eminent *English* Merchants in *Leghorn*, viz. Mr. *Foot*, Mr. *Brown*, Mr. *Serle*, Mr. *Sidney*, Mr. *Hatton*, Mr. *Dethick*, &c. But our Business lay with *Jacob Francia* a Jew, a very

rich

rich Man, and of a fair Reputation. Of his Nation there are great Numbers at *Leghorn,* who have a Quarter to themselves, and are not troubled on Account of their Religion. There are many *Turkish* Slaves who go up and down with a little Lock upon their Legs, and are permitted to ply as Porters for their Bread, paying an Acknowledgment to their Patron. This is an excellent School for such as intend to understand the *Levant* Trade, because they have here greater Opportunities of conversing with Foreigners, such as *Greeks, Armenians,* and *Jews,* who have travelled through the *Turkish* Empire, than any where else, and therefore, though we remained longer than we at first expected, it was with very great Regret that I left it so soon, before I had Time to make many Acquaintances, or could furnish my self with such further Instructions as I thought necessary for pursuing with Success the Business I went about.

In this City there resided one *Jacobi,* who had been Captain of a trading Vessel, but had now raised an Estate on which he lived very handsomely. He was a great Lover of Chemistry, and understood it pretty well. This Gentleman affirmed, that five and twenty Years before, I think in the Year 1646, a Person lodged in the House of a *Jew* of his Acquaintance, the Man was a Stranger, without Recommendation to any Body, but of very courteous Behaviour, and who appeared to have more than ordinary Learning. This Stranger having heard of Captain *Jacobi's* Inclination for Chemistry, and that he was very desirous of knowing whether there was such a Thing practicable as *Transmutation of Metals,* desired to speak with him; and having first obtained his

Promise,

Promife, that he would fay nothing of what paffed between them 'till a certain Time after his Departure. He defired the Captain to bring him a brafs Candleftick, which having melted before his Face, he turned immediately into *fine* Gold.

I HAVE heard many fuch Stories without giving much Credit, or indeed without taking much Notice of them; neither can I abfolutely believe this; but I have fet it down, becaufe Capt. *Jacobi* was efteemed a Man of Honour.

THERE was alfo in *Leghorn* one *Veneroni*, a *Venetian*, whom himfelf ftiled a Phyfician, and whom the Phyficians called a Quack: He had a *Noftrum* for curing the *Neapolitan* Difeafe, which he performed with very gentle Phyfic; of which it was known the chief Ingredient was *Senna*, and a Diet Drink very pleafant to the Tafte. He likewife cured Leprofies, and all extraordinary Foulneffes of the Skin, chiefly by a Diet of Chickens and Capons, nourifhed with the Flefh of *Vipers*. The Phyficians would have bought his *Noftrum*, but he refufed to part with it, upon which they decry'd him; however, he has got a great deal of Credit as well as Money. It was obferved, that of late Years this Man affected to appear very religious, which fome attribute to his Fear of the *Inquifition*, to whom, on the leaft Scandal, the Phyficians would get him denounced, and thereby rid themfelves of fo troublefome a Rival.

THREE or four Days before we left the Place, my Friend *Perez* grew very uneafy. He had at a Coffee-Houfe refufed a *Jew* his Price for a Watch; and the Fellow being very importunate, he at laft bid him be gone in a pretty quick Tone. Upon this the Fellow

turned

turned about and told him, he was as much a *Jew* as himself; that he had fled from the *Inquisition* in *Spain*, and that he should. not remain long at Liberty if he staid in *Leghorn*. It seems this Fellow had been at *Genoa* when Endeavours were used to seize Mr. *Perez* there. We were much alarmed at this Accident ; but it had no ill Effects, by reason the *Jews* of their own Accord obliged the Fellow to go immediately to *France*, fearing that he should expose themselves to the Resentment of Strangers ; and that if this Affair made a Noise, it might prejudice some of their own Relations in *Spain*. However, to rid Mr. *Perez* of all Apprehension, I got an Apartment for him in the House of a *British* Merchant, where he remained till the Vessel was ready to fail. This is an Instance of the natural Insolence of the *Jews*, which renders them so hateful where-ever they reside.

T H E Day preceding that on which we should have gone on Board, a *Corsair* failed out of the Road, and carried with him abundance of Seamen belonging to the Ships then in the Port. I, who heard the Complaints of most of the Captains, and particularly of him with whom I was to fail, took all the Pains I could to be acquainted with the Nature of the Business, there appearing to be in it the strongest Contradictions in the World. For, on the one hand, it was asserted, that Seamen were no where better treated than on board the Vessels in the Merchants Service trading to the *Levant* ; and that on the contrary, in these *Corsairs*, or *Crusals*, the Men were used like Slaves, detained sometimes five or six Years, and at length set at Liberty without a Farthing in their Pockets.

THAT

THAT Sailors of all Nations should quit the Merchants Service to go on Board these Privateers, was therefore to me the oddest Mystery in the World, especially considering the Infamy attending that Profession, which hinders Sailors who have ever been on Board them from being employed elsewhere, for fear some of their old Maxims should stick with them, and put them upon inviting their Companions to mutiny, which Experience, as well as Reason, hath shewn to be but too practicable in these Parts.   In order to inform my self on these Heads, and of the Nature of these cruising Voyages, of which I had heard so many extravagant Stories, I resolved, as I was to go in the Afternoon to take my Leave of Captain *Jacobi*, to desire him to set me right a little, and to give me some Idea of the Charms in this kind of Life, which were so strong as to engage Men to leave an honest and comfortable State of Life for immediate Want, and the future Prospect of perpetual Slavery, impaling alive, or at least Indigence and Infamy, as long as they lived.

CAPTAIN *Jacobi* enter'd readily into the Matter, and gave me a very full and very distinct Account of the Management of the Crusals.   He began with observing that they were fitted out from several *Ports* of the *Mediterranean*, particularly from this of *Leghorn*, under Colour of cruising on the *Turks* and other *Infidels* ; but in truth, to make Prize of all Vessels weaker than their own. The first Thing, said he, considered on such an Undertaking is the Choice of a Captain, who, together with the Lieutenant, and other Officers, are to be Men of Experience, such as have made at least one Voyage before.   For these Voyages lasting often nine Years, one is sufficient for a Man to gain Experience.   The Captain

M 4

and

and Officers being fixed, a Ship is bought, an old one generally, which is well fitted up, handsomely painted and sixteen or twenty Brass Guns put on board, besides Patareroes. As to the Number of Men, it is uncertain, however, they rarely go to Sea with less than *one*, or more than *three* hundred. I perceive what you want to know is, how they come by these.

In the first place, the Captain and his Officers pick out a *dozen* or *twenty* daring desperate Fellows who know not how to live, and these are stiled *Volunteers*. Next he stands out to Sea with his Vessel, and perhaps hovers on the Coast of *Corsica*, or of *Sicily*, where he takes on board such as are in great Fear of the Gallows, such as have been condemned for Murder, Robbery, or Sacrilege, and, by the Interest of their Friends, are permitted to escape out of Prison. By this Time the Captain has Soldiers enough; the next Thing is to get Seamen.

With this View he comes again into this Road, and sends on shoar a Dozen or Fourteen of his Volunteers, who insinuate themselves into the Company of Sailors; tell them Miracles of their Captains Valour, Generosity, and good Fortune; swear that they are bound by their Agreement with their Proprietors to return to *Leghorn* in *three* Years, and that at the End of this Space they propose to divide at least *three thousand* Ducats a Man.

As soon as a Seaman listens to his Discourse, and begins to talk of Wages, he tells him they live on Board like Gentlemen, and at the End of the Cruise receive their Proportion of the Prizes; but that as they may at present stay some Time in Port, the Captain will readily advance a Seaman he likes forty or fifty Crowns, or to a

very

very clever Fellow (such a one to be sure as the Volunteer talks to) *fourscore* or a *hundred*, if he stands in need of them.   Upon this, the Sailor desires to be introduced to the Captain, who at his Audience hath three or four of his People by, ready to catch the Words before they are half out of his Mouth, and to swear to the Truth of all he says. This Interview issues in an Agreement with the Stranger, and an Advance of fifteen or twenty Crowns, which the Man is suffered to spend in running up and down *Leghorn*, but never without a Spy in his Company, whom he generally treats as his Friend.

WHEN the Money is out, this Fellow puts him upon asking for more, pursuant to the extravagant Agreement made with him at first.   Upon his Application to the Captain, he is very probably kept to Dinner with him, and invited to drink pretty freely after it; when he is mellow, the Captain goes to reach him the Money, but finding he has not much on Shore, he gives him an Order upon the Lieutenant for the Sum he desires, and at the same Time another very express Order, that after receiving the Money he shall be permitted to come on Shore, which however the Lieutenant construes into a very strict Command to keep him close on Board, which he does not fail to do, without giving him a Dollar.

By these Practices the Ship is mann'd with *French*, *English*, *Dutch*, and *Flemish* Sailors, for *Italian* Seamen are not so easily trapanned, and then they stand away for the *Arches*, where tho' every Thing they lay hold of is good Prize; yet so much Care is taken to look up all the Sailors Shares, that they seldom or never see a Dollar,

Dollar, or get a Shoe or Stocking of their own. The *Volunteers* are their *Guards*, and treat them like Slaves. After *eight* or *nine* Years the Ship returns into Port in better Condition than she sail'd, for they frequently break up new Vessels to repair her, and make Use of all the Carpenters they can lay hold of *Gratis*. The *Seamen* are then turned adrift, and the *Proprietors*, besides a considerable Sum of ready Money, have *three* or *four Hundred*, sometimes many more Slaves, divided amongst them,

To make this the more easily comprehended, the *Captain* was pleased to give me an Account of a very strange Accident which befell Monsieur *Thevenot*, a very learned French Traveller, who returning from a Pilgrimage which he had made to the *Holy Land*, was taken on Board a *French* Saique, almost in Sight of the Coast of *Syria*, by a *Maltese* Caper, that is a *Corsair*, fitted out from *Malta*, not one of the *Vessels* of the Order. These Pirates not only seized the Vessel and Cargo, but stript also the Passengers, and amongst others M. *Thevenot* stark naked, and the next Day sent them ashore with only a few Rags to cover their Nakedness. The *Port* they landed them at was *Acra*, or *Ptolemais*, where there happened to be two or three French Merchant Ships in the Harbour. The *Turkish Aga* thereupon apply'd himself instantly to the *French* Consul, and told him, since this Insult had been offer'd to his Master's Subjects almost within Sight of the Place, he must insist on his giving Orders to the *French* Captains to give Chace to the *Corsair*, offering to accompany them in Person with three or four small arm'd Barks. The *Consul* could not avoid complying with
this

this Requeft, the *French* Captains fpent the Night in putting their Veffels in order, and in the grey of the Morning ftood to Sea with the *Turkifh* Barks. As foon as the *Corfair* faw them, her Crew cut the Cables, and crowded all the Sail they could ; they chaced them however fome Hours, and the *Turkifh* Barks fired at them, tho' to no Purpofe ; at length they gave over, and returned into Port. As foon as the *Aga* had debarqued his Troops, he went to pay his Compliments to the *French Conful* which he did to this Purpofe. *I am obliged to you for the Affiftance you fo readily accorded me, I have done my Duty, and am not forry we did not fucceed, fince how much Villains foever thefe People may be, you could not help feeing with Regret fo many Men, fome perhaps of your Country, all of your Religion, impaled alive, a Fate from which I could not poffibly have excufed them.* The *Conful* on his Part congratulated the *Aga* on his Integrity, and fo this Bufinefs ended.

NOT long fince a *Frenchman* of Birth, addicted himfelf to this Way of living, and became Captain of a Veffel which carried *Livorneze* Colours. As he was a very enterprizing Man, he quickly rendered himfelf very famous throughout the *Archipelago*, having fometimes adventured to land, and take Prifoners within a Day's Journey of *Conftantinople*. At length it fo happened, that he went afhore on a *Greek* Ifland, where fometime before the People had rifen, and put the *Grand Seignior's* Officers to Death. Confcious of their own Demerits, and dreading the Revenge the *Turks* were about to take, the faithlefs *Greeks* feized this unhappy *Captain*, and made their Peace, by delivering him up to the *Sultan*.

HE

HE had made himself so terrible to the *Turks*, that the *Grand Seignior* had a Desire to see him ; he was then absent from *Constantinople*, and the Prisoner was carried where the Court resided. When the *Grand Seignior* had look'd upon him, a Man of the Law was ordered to tell him that he must become a *Turk*, to which he answered, *I am in your Power, you may put me to what Death you please, but God forbid I should redeem my Body at the Expence of my Soul.* Three Hours afterwards he was beheaded, and his Corpse by the *Grand Vizir's* Order exposed for three Days, after which the Christians were suffered to inter it. Such was the Account my Curiosity procured me of the *Corsairs* of the *Levant* and their Affairs. Now to my own.

ALL our Effects and Baggage being on Board by the 8th of *December*, the Captain called upon us in the Evening, to desire we would not fail to be ready before Noon the next Day. We spent the greatest Part of the Night in conversing with Mr. *Fetherstone*, to whom we promised to send from *Alexandria*, whatever we met of Value, with Instructions how to dispose of it, that it might be without the Reach of Fortune. He and my Servant *Johnson* on the other Hand, gave us all possible Assurance of their Industry and Care of our Interests, of which we were perfectly well assured, and I think no People ever did trust each other so much, and found less Occasion to repent of it. The Week before we parted I had taken into my Service one *Antonio* a *Portugueze*, who had been Servant for many Years to the last *Venetian* Consul at *Cairo*. This Man was recommended to me as a Person sober, diligent,

gent, one who underſtood the Language, and was well acquainted with the Country, which Character I confeſs he anſwered ; but he had ſo many odd peeviſh Humours, that Mr. *Perez* and I were rather his Servants than he ours.

It had been my Study to put our Effects in the leaſt Compaſs poſſible, and with that View I had contrived four Cheſts, which being placed two on the Top of the other Two, made an exact Cube, and by the Help of Steel Rods and Rings were faſtened ſo, as to make a convenient Bale if put on Board any Veſſel, or where they were to paſs by Land Carriage, they were ſo fitted as to make two Bales ; or if that was inconvenient, might be divided into four.

Besides this Mr. *Perez* had two large Cloak Bags to himſelf, and I one, with a portable Cabinet bought at *Verona* of a *German* Chemiſt for *fifty* Ducats. It contained a compleat *Apothecary*'s Shop, furniſhed with *Galenical* and *Chemical* Medicines ; and beſides its Conveniency, was of admirable Uſe in ſtriking the *Turks* and *Arabs* with Wonder, the Doors, Lids, Bottoms, and Pedeſtals being all filled with Drawers, Cells, and other Conveniencies, which turning out ſuddenly, and as it were of themſelves, by touching Buttons fixed upon Strings, ſeemed very pleaſant and ſtrange, eſpecially to a Beholder unaccuſtom'd to ſuch Things. All theſe Matters, together with ſuch Proviſions as were neceſſary in the Paſſage, we got on Board by the Time preſcribed.

On the 9th of *December*, about Seven in the Morning, the Wind blowing fair, the Captain came to hurry us on Board, we chearfully obeyed his Summons ; but the

the Wind chopping about, he was in some Doubt as to putting out to Sea, but between three and four it blew fair again, and we failed with all the Tokens of a prosperous Voyage ; the tenth, eleventh and twelfth, the Wind continued fair, but sometimes it blew pretty hard, the thirteenth we passed the *Scheirches*. The same Day we saw *Masata*, a Maritime Town in *Sicily*. The fourteenth in the Morning we had the Island *Gozo* in View, and in the Afternoon we entered the Haven of *Malta*, where Mr. *Perez* and I immediately went ashore, and took up our Lodgings at the House of one Mr. *Nicolas* a *Frenchman*, with whom also our Captain lodged while we staid. It seems he had more Business in this Island than we were aware of; for the same Evening at Supper he told us, that he believed he should not fail in a Fortnight, or perhaps twenty Days, which determined us to visit the Island, and gave me an Opportunity of practising first the Rules I had laid down to myself, as to the Method of my Inquiries during my Travels.

THERE are about the Haven of *Malta* three Cities, of which in the Order we saw them. *First*, the City of *Valetta*, so called from the Grand Master who so gallantly defended the Island against the *Turks*, it was built *Anno Domini* 1566, and stands between the great and little Ports, extremely well fortified, and farther secured by the Vicinity of the Castle of St. *Elmo*, which many Engineers have pronounced impregnable, yet I believe its greatest Strength lies in the Valour of the *Knights* who guard it. It is built upon the very Point of Land, with a grand *Piazza* before it, under which is a vast Magazine of all sorts of Commodities. In it
the

the *Knights* are imprifoned for Offences, and in the midft of it is a Tower, from the Top of which there is a fair Profpect of the whole Ifland.

As to the City itfelf, it is as regular as the Nature of its Situation, on a Rock will allow it. The Streets are not paved, nor is it very neceffary, they are a little uneven, except the two chief Streets, where live the Merchants and moft eminent Citizens. There may be in this Place about 2000 Houfes, and 10000 Inhabitants, allowing five to a Houfe; thefe for the moft part are low built, and tho' tollerably convenient, yet not beautiful to the Eye, by Reafon of their flat Roofs covered with a neat white Plaifter, which render them very convenient in the Summer Time, the People fleeping there for the Sake of Coolnefs, happy in the clear and conftant Temperature of their Air, which prevents their fuffering by a Cuftom which in other hot Countries would be extremely fatal. Towards the South Weft there is a very ftrong Wall with Baftions, half Moons, and other Out-works, and beyond it about half a quarter of an *Englifh* Mile, another Wall running from Port to Port. Within the Space included within thefe Walls, the Inhabitants of the Ifland in Cafe of a Seige, have Room to encamp when forced out of the open Country. All the Baftions are hollow, that in Cafe of Neceffity they may be blown up, moft of them have triple Batteries, and fome have four, well mounted, and in good Order.

THEY are in Time of Peace kept in excellent Order, and on fome of them there are Convents and Gardens, which are very airy and pleafant. The Cathedral Church of St. *John* is fmall, but very fine, neither can

one

one Figure to one's self a grander Sight than the beholding the *Grand Mafter* and the *Great Croffes*, with
the Knights of the Order at their Devotions. There
are in this Cathedral feveral neat Chappels, in adorning
of which no Expence hath been fpared. The Palace
of the *Grand Mafter* doth not make a great Figure,
but it is well contrived, and well furnifh'd ; there is in
it a large Hall finely painted, and an Armoury which
deferves to be viewed, there being Arms kept in exact
Order, which would accommodate 25000 Men at leaft,
befides the little Armoury, which belongs to the *Grand
Mafter's* Houfhold, and is alfo very curious.

THE Infirmary ftands on an Ifland, and the great
Hofpital is a noble Building ; to fpeak the Truth, the
very Glory of *Malta*. Here the fick are provided for
much better than they could be in their own Houfes;
there are but two in a Room, which is large and commodious, every Patient having two Beds for change,
and a Clofet with a Lock and Key to himfelf. The
fick are ferved by the Knights in Perfon, their Diet is
prefcribed by the Phyficians, and brought up in Silver
Difhes ; fuch exact Order being obferved, and every
Thing being performed with fuch Magnificence, as
furprizes Strangers, and gives them a high Idea of the
Charity of this illuftrious Order.

THE Prifon for the Slaves is a very confiderable
Place, it is a fine fquare Building adorned with a Piazza,
and at leaft 2000 Slaves belonging to the Order lodge
therein, fometimes there are three or four Thoufand ;
when thefe are out at Sea, as they muft be when the
Gallies of the Order go on any Expedition, then the
Slaves of the Inhabitants are permitted to lie here,
otherwife

otherwife they lodge at Home. Thefe People, as at *Leghorn*, have only a fmall Lock on their Ankles, and are permitted to go at large in the Ifland, it being almoft impracticable for them to make their Efcape.

CROSSING the Harbour, you go over another City, called formerly *Il Borgo*, but fince the repulfing of the *Turks* in 1565, *Citta Vittoriofa*; it is not very large, built upon a Tongue of Land thruft out into the Sea, at the End of which is the Caftle of St. *Angelo*; it may contain about 800 Houfes, and between 3 or 4000 Inhabitants; here are four or five Churches, and the moft confiderable Place in the City is the *Palace* of the *Inquifitor.* Oppofite to the Neck of Land whereon this City ftands, there is another Neck juts out, upon which ftands a third City or great Town, called *L'Ifola,* i. e. The Ifland, covered by the Caftle of St. *Michael,* called fince the raifing of the Siege by the *Turks, La Citta Invitta,* i. e. The unconquered City. It may contain about 1000 Houfes, and between 4 or 5000 Inhabitants.

IN the Haven between the Cities laft mentioned lye the Ships and Gallies of the Order, and a great many other Veffels fhut up with a Chain, fo that none can go out without Leave; higher up in the Ifland ftands *Citta Veccia,* i. e. The old City, the ancient Capital of the Ifland; here is a Cathedral dedicated to St. *Peter,* the Bifhop hath a Palace here, and the Place is furrounded with very ftrong Walls, and good Fortifications; tho' the Houfes are but very indifferent, and there are but few People of Diftinction that live here, tho' the Place is large, and feems to have been formerly much better peopled than at prefent.

N

HAVING thus spoken briefly of the Cities or great Towns in this Island, I return to my own Affairs, and shall then give a summary Account of the Soil, Climate, Inhabitants, Government, Wealth, Trade, &c. of *Malta*, having taken extraordinary Pains to be well informed as to all those Particulars.

A *Sicilian* Physician whose Name was *Sprotti*, and who was very intimate with my Landlord, undertook to shew me the *Curiosities* of the Island, which he accordingly performed. We rode on Asses, which carried us perfectly well, especially for the first Hour or two ; for at length the poor Creatures are apt to tire. We saw the several *Houses of Pleasure* which the *Grand Master* hath in *Malta*, the Grotto of St. *Paul*, the petrified Serpent's Heads and Teeth, the Salt-Pits, and other Curiosities, of which I shall speak hereafter. This Physician, tho' a *Sicilian* by Birth, and educated at *Rome*, had spent the far greater part of his Life in *Malta*, for he was upwards of fifty, and had resided thirty five Years in *la Valetta*. He had taken abundance of Pains in collecting whatever had been publish'd, relating either to the Place, or to the Order of St. *John* ; so that if I had remained there three or four Months, I might have known all that could well be known in relation to either. His two great *Heroes* were the Grand Masters *Valette* and *Vignacourt*, of whom he spoke continually in Raptures.

THE first of these, *John de la Valette Parisot*, was a *French* Gentleman of a good Family, he was *Knight* of the *Language* of *Prouence*. He was a Man who, if I may be allowed the Expression, had the *Signature* of a *Hero* ; he had a Majesty in his Presence which raised him

him above Envy, a Felicity in his Conduct which afforded Malice itfelf no Opportunity of fpeaking, a Candor in his Behaviour, which made him beloved by his very Enemies, Courage invincible, and yet fo modeft, that it never affected his Words, or hindered him from liftening to his Prudence where a Shew of Courage would have been fatal. With thefe great Qualities, and the happinefs of exerting them to Advantage, in the Space of two Years Time he paffed through all the Dignities of the *Order*, and on the 21ft of *Auguft* 1557, was chofen *Grand-Mafter* with univerfal Applaufe.

In the *eight* firft Years of his Government, the *Gallies* of the *Order* made fuch terrible Depredations on the *Turks*, that *Solyman* II. refolved at laft to rid himfelf of fuch terrible Enemies at all Events. With this View he fent *Piali* Bafhaw in the Month of *May* 1565, with a Fleet of eleven *Sultanas* to convoy a Land Army embarked on a hundred and fifty large Tranfports, which was to be commanded by *Muftapha* Bafhaw, who had Orders not to ftir from the Siege till he had reduced the Place. The Army debarqued on the 20th of *May*, not without confiderable Lofs, the *Maltefe* Horfe behaved extremely well, and a Troop of *Sicilian* Banditti, confifting of 300 Men who had tranfported themfelves thither, performed Wonders, and diftinguifhed themfelves by their Fidelity and Regularity during the whole Siege. The *Grand-Mafter* fhew'd his great Wifdom, by his abandoning all the Pofts of fmall Importance, and withdrawing his Troops into thofe where they might be ufeful. The Caftle of St. *Elmo* was taken the 23d of *June*, after having fuftained five Affaults,

faults,

faults, in which the *Turks* loſt as many thouſand Men. The *Grand-Maſter* then ſlighted the Caſtle of St. *Angelo*, and withdrew his Forces into the *Burgh* and the *Iſle*.

THE *Turks* next attack'd the Caſtle of St. *Michael* with incredible Fury, but being repulſed, they bent all their Force againſt the *Burgh*, where the *Grand-Maſter* was in Perſon; and having made ſeveral Breaches, gave a general Aſſault on the 21ſt of *Auguſt*; where, after a gallant Defence, they entered the Place, and fixed ſeven *Horſe Tails* on the inner Gate. Then it was that the *Grand-Maſter* put himſelf at the Head of the *Corps de Reſerve* of *Knights*, to whom with a very loud Voice, tho' at other Times he ſpoke very low, he ſaid, *I ſhall not put you in Mind that you are Gentlemen, and the Flower of* European *Knights, I tell you only that you are Chriſtians, and that Death is a Thing you ought rather to hope than to fear; come then my Brethren, let us die together in the Cauſe of* CHRIST, *like Men who have no Truſt but in him.* This ſaid, he fell upon the *Turks* with his handful of Men, and while this unequal Engagement laſted, all the People in *Malta* Men, Women, and Children, ran at once to the Breach with Weapons in their Hands, and drove the *Turks* from their Lodgments with prodigious Slaughter.

YET this would not have ſaved the Place, the *Grand-Maſter* having now a Town in Ruins, and not above 6000 effective Men, whereas the *Turkiſh* Army conſiſted ſtill of between 70 or 80,000 Men, had not on the 7th of *September* Don *Garcias de Toledo* appeared before *Malta* with his Fleet, and having waited till the

Suc-

Succours he debarqued, were fafely arrived in the old City, he hoifted Sail for *Meffina*, leaving a Meffage behind him, that as furely as he had vifited the *Chriftians* now, in fourteen Days he would vifit the *Turks*. But they faved him the Trouble, for *Muftapha* Bafhaw, having on the 13th of the fame Month made a general Difcharge of his *Artillery* in the Morning, embarqued all his Troops at Midnight, and fet Fire to his Camp, after having loft between 20 and 30,000 of his beft Troops. After the Siege was raifed, the *Grand-Mafter* immediately refolved to build a new City on the Point of Land which ran out into the middle of the Sea; accordingly on the 28th of *March* 1566, he laid the firft Stone in Perfon, over a number of Gold, Silver, and Copper Medals, whereon was his own Buft with an Infcription to this Effect; *He hath founded it on a Rock*, the People fhouting all the while, *Long live the great* VALETTE.

ALL the *Chriftian* Princes in Communion with the Church of *Rome*, promifed to contribute largely towards defraying the Expence of this Undertaking; but the Money coming in flowly, and the Wages of the Workmen amounting to 2000 Crowns a Day, the *Grand-Mafter* coined fmall Copper Pieces with this Infcription, *Non Æs fed Fides*, i. e. *Not Coin but Faith*; and upon giving his Honour that they fhould be exchanged for Crowns, carried the Affair through with the fame Expedition with which it was begun.

THE *Pope* to fhew his high Efteem for fo deferving a Perfon, offered the *Grand-Mafter* a Cardinal's Hat, who modeftly refufed it, faying, *Ecclefiaftical Honours fuited not a Man whofe Hands were ftained with Blood.*

Two

Two Years after, *viz.* in 1568, on the 21ſt of *Auguſt*, the Day on which he was choſen *Grand-Maſter*, *La Valette* yielded up the Ghoſt, behaving in his laſt Sickneſs with ſuch exemplary Devotion, that if he had not before acquired the Character of the greateſt Soldier, he would certainly have been eſteem'd from thence, the greateſt Pattern of Piety of the Age in which he lived. He was ſucceeded by *Pietro de Monte* an *Italian*, who on the 18th of *March* 1571, entered the City of *Valetta* at the Head of his *Knights*, and eſtabliſhed there the *Reſidence* of the *Order*.

ALOPHIUS de Vignacour, Chief of the Language of *France*, was elected *Grand-Maſter* of the Order of *Malta* in *February* 1601, during his Reign, the *Turks* had frequently a Deſire of invading this Iſland; but the *Grand-Maſter* being a Man of much Complaiſance, would not give them the Trouble of coming ſo far to prove the Courage of his Knights, for equipping larger Squadrons than uſual, he took now one Place in the *Morea*, then another in the *Archipelago*; the next Year he invaded *Barbary*, and by and by threatened *Egypt*, making an infinite Number of *Turks* Slaves, and drawing immenſe Treaſures into the Coffers of the Order. He did not however ſuffer them to remain there long, but expended them in fortifying all the Coaſts, and adorning all the inland Part of the *Iſland*.

He it was who releaſed the Inhabitants of *la Valetta* from the Slavery of preſerving Rain Water, which was all they had for Uſe, by building an Aqueduct which ſupplies the City with Water, and by an Engine of his Invention is forced near its Fountains into *leathern Troughs*, which being carried over the Rocks,

fill

fill without farther Trouble the Water Veffels of Ships which lie in the Harbour. He repaired all the publick Edifices in *Malta*, reftored decaying Infcriptions, and having governed with the higheft Reputation and Felicity 21 Years, died univerfally regretted in the Year 1622.

AFTER our Vifit to the feveral remarkable Places in the open Country of *Malta*, Seignior *Sprotti* and I returned to the City, and found there my Friend *Perez*, and the Family not a little embarraffed. Our Man *Antonio* grew enamour'd of a *Fleming*'s Daughter, who lived at next Door, which being difcovered by her Father, he caufed a Billet to be thrown over the Wall into our Landlord's Yard, inviting *Antonio* in the Name of his Daughter to his Houfe at Midnight, affuring him that the Door fhould be left open, and a Perfon wait there to conduct him to his Miftrefs. *Antonio* was too much a *Cavalier* not to be punctual; when he came he found the Door and the Servant as he had been promifed, faw his Miftrefs, and was conducted by her into a Bed-chamber, where by fome Accident the Light went out; however he found his Way to Bed in the Dark, but in the Morning opening a Lettice that he might have Light enough to drefs himfelf by, he faw in the Bed an old *Negro*, the moft ugly that ever was beheld of the whole Race.

HE flew home with all imaginable Speed, but found the News of his Adventure had out-run him; whereupon he raifed a terrible Out-cry, vowing Revenge, and threatening Death to the Man and all his Family. When I came home, however, he became a little quieter, and told me at Night, as I was going to Bed, that his Paffion

N 4

was

was all a Feint, that his Miftrefs had ftaid with him all Night, and that the whole was a Contrivance to deceive her Father. With this Story *Antonio* fatisfied himfelf, and talk'd no more of Blood and Slaughter. Happy for him that our next Door Neighbour was not a *Maltefe*, if he had, *Antonio* would have been difmifs'd to the other World without the Ceremony of fuch an Appointment. The reft of the Time I remain'd in the Ifland, I employed in drawing up the Notes, which ferv'd for frameing, when I had more Leifure, the following Account of *Malta*, as to its ancient and prefent State.

It is, I think, univerfally agreed, that the modern Name of this Ifland is taken from its ancient Appellation, *viz. Melita*. But whence this Name is derived, is a Difpute not fo eafily decided ; the moft probable Account, however, is, that it comes from *Mel, Honey* ; of which there is great Plenty, and that excellent in its kind. The Learned alfo difpute, whether it is a *European* or an *African* Ifland ; Cuftom hath carried it in Favour of the former, but Reafon feems to be on the Side of the latter, fince the People look like *Africans*, and fpeak a broken kind of *Arabick*.

As to its Situation, it hath 35 d. and 50 m. North Latitude, and 14 d. of Longitude Eaft from *London*. In the Summer it is extremely hot, as appears from the Complexion of its Inhabitants, though it is affirmed that all the Summer long there are Breezes which render the Mornings and Evenings not only temperate, but pleafant ; but in the Spring and Winter, inftead of Breezes, they have very furious Winds, which take their Paffage like a hoftile Army through the Ifland, and carry all before them.

THE

THE Soil cannot be stiled unfruitful, though it is commonly reported so by Authors, whereas there are some who cry it up as the most fruitful in the World; the Truth is, the greater Part of *Malta* is a down-right Rock, and consequently barren; but the Ground where there is any, though it be but a Foot deep, is fertile to Admiration. It bears all sorts of Corn, but especially *Barley*, *Cummin* wild and sweet, *Cotton*, esteemed the finest in the Universe; also Vines, from whence they have *Raisins*, as large as *Prunes*, both red and white, which bear a great Price; *Olives*, *Almonds*, *Figs*, the finest that can be imagined; *Peaches* as large as our ordinary *Melons*, *Apricots*, *Dates*, and most *European* Fruits. Flowers and Herbs every where abound, especially *Roses*, which in Beauty and Odour surpass those of *Europe* very much.

To be more particular, the *Maltese* spare no Pains to remove the natural Imperfections of their Country; they suffer no Dung to remain a Moment in the Streets or Highways, but gather it like Treasure in their Baskets, and immediately carry it to their Gardens or Fields. They import also Earth from *Sicily* as Ballast, and carry it to such bare Places of the Island as are best seated for receiving Water as well as Sun-shine. By these Helps, and the Industry of their *Turkish* and *Moorish* Slaves, they raise yearly *eighty thousand* Measures of Corn, of which half is Barley; *fifteen thousand* hundred Weight of *Cummin*, and about *fourteen* hundred thousand Weight of Cotton, amounting in all to the Value of 760000 *Scudi* or 152000 *l.* Sterling.

As to Animals, they have the same, and the same Plenty as in other Parts of *Europe*. Their *Horses*, employed

ployed in carrying Burthens, and in drawing Carriages, are unfhod; their Affes ftrong, and very fit for riding; to make them the more fo, they flit the Side of each Noftril, by which Means the Creature breaths more freely. The *Dogs* and *Cats* of *Malta* are particularly handfome, and for that Reafon are much coveted in *Sicily*, and *Italy*. The *Grand Mafter* has a good Stable of Horfes for the Saddle and Coach, as have alfo the *Great Croffes*. The Inhabitants of the Ifland maintain a thoufand Horfe fit for Service, or any Emergency, and which are review'd twice a Year.

IN ancient Times the Inhabitants of *Malta* were famous throughout all *Europe* for their Skill in maritime Affairs, their extenfive Commerce, and for their refined Luxury, as appears from one of the Orations of *Cicero* againft *Verres*, in which he upbraids him with being as voluptuous as a *Maltefe*. *Appian* informs us, that *Cæfar* had much ado to reduce thefe People when they had revolted; by degrees however, they grew low and poor. At length they became fubject to the *Spaniards*, by whom the Ifland was transfer'd to the Knights of St. *John*, tho' an annual Prefent of a *Falcon* is referved to the King of *Spain*, as a Recognizance of his Sovereignty. The prefent People of *Malta* fpeak a Sort of barbarous *Arabick*, are altogether *Africans* in their Manners, and are without queftion as luxurious and debauched as any Nation can be. The Women are handfome, well-fhaped, and for the moft part very amorous, though they affect to be exceffively religious, which hinders not their Hufbands from being outragioufly jealous; and this being join'd to their natural Cruelty and Love of Revenge, produces frequently very direful Effects.

Aa

As to the Government of the Island, it is entirely in the Hands of the *Grand Mafter*, who ftiles himfelf Prince of *Malta* and *Goza*. He is not, however, abfolute, but is in moft Cafes affifted by his Council, in fome by a *General Chapter* of the *Knights.* The *Grand Mafter* at this Time was *Nicholas Cottoner*, a *Majorcan*, who fucceeded his Brother *Raphael Cottoner*, who governed but three Months, and died 1663. He was a Perfon of low Stature, but a handfome Man, very affable and courteous to Strangers, who vifit him always as foon as conveniently They can after their Arrival. The Knights are diftinguifhed into *three* Claffes. The firft, ftiled *Knights of Juftice*, are obliged to prove their Nobility for four Defcents; they bear a Crofs of Gold, with which They are not invefted, till they have been abroad *three* Years. The fecond are Priefts of the Order, who bear alfo Croffes of *Malta*, but not of Gold, without the Permiffion of the *Grand-Mafter.* The third Clafs are ftiled *Servitors*, and Thefe again are divided into *Servitors* of *Arms* and of *Office*; and the former take the fame Oaths with Knights, and are capable of being admitted to the leffer Dignities of the Order, which the *Servitors* of Office are not. The Knights are alfo divided into eight Languages or Provinces, each of which hath its *Albergo* or *Inn*, where the Knights eat together in Publick under the Government of one who is ftiled chief of the Language. Of thefe the firft is *Provence*, and the laft *Germany.* The fixth was *England*; and there is ftill a void Space left for the *Albergo* of our Nation, of which there is alfo a Prior, who piques himfelf much on paying great Civilities to fuch of the *Englifh* as at any Time come hither.

THE

THE Number of the Knights is uncertain, but there are generally some Thousands, of whom eight or nine Hundred are usually resident in *Malta*, the rest are at their Commanderies with their Relations, or serve aboard the Gallies. Of these seven belong to the Order, each of which is a fine stout Veſſel, carries twenty or thirty Knights, and about five hundred Men. Besides these there are thirty or forty Ships fitted out by Licence from the Grand Maſter, to cruize upon the *Turks*, which they do with such Effect, that the Order is extremely rich in Money, as well as in Revenues, which are held to be not much leſs than one hundred and fifty thouſand Pounds *per Annum*, of which thirty thouſand belong to the Grand Maſter. It is ſuppoſed that twenty thouſand fighting Men may be levy'd in the Iſland, and that there are in it not leſs than ſixty thouſand Souls. For the Maintenance of theſe three Fourths of the Proviſion comes from *Sicily*, which yet come plentifully to Market, and at moderate Prices. I will now ſpeak of the Curioſities of the Iſland, natural and artificial, and ſo leave it.

OF the firſt we may reckon the *Scorpions*, and as ſome ſay, the *Speckled Snakes*, which are now and then found in this Iſland, perfectly harmleſs, and free from Venom. Nay, it is ſaid that the native *Malteſe* are invulnerable from theſe Sort of Creatures where-ever they go.

ABOUT ten Miles from *Valetta* is the *Cala di ſanta Paolo*, or the Grotto of St. *Paul*, near the Place where he is ſuppoſed to have landed ; though ſome will have it that he was never here, but that the Iſland on which he was ſhip-wreck'd is that call'd *Melita*, in the Gulph of

Raguſa ;

Ragufa; but this Notion is rather fingular than probable. In the Neighbourhood of this Place they pretend to fhew Serpents turned into Stone, as alfo petrify'd Eyes, Teeth, and Eggs, of Serpents, which are believed to have a great Efficacy in curing the Bites of thefe Sort of Creatures, and are therefore exported in great Quantities. There is alfo a Spring of very fweet Water, which is faid to have rifen miraculoufly at the Command of St. *Paul*, for whom the *Maltefe* in general have an extraordinary Devotion. From thefe natural Curiofities let us proceed to thofe of Art; and amongft thefe I know none that deferve Confideration more than the Pleafure-Houfes of the Grand Mafter, of which he has feveral.

BOSCHETTO, or *Monteverdala*, is the moft admired. It ftands two Miles from the old City, and is without queftion one of the fineft Places that can be imagined, that is, all Things confidered; for though this Pleafure-Houfe and its Gardens would make a very fine Shew in *Italy*, or in *France*, yet what is admirable, what amazes and ravifhes the Spectator is, to find it and them in *Malta*. On this Account I call them Curiofities of Art, becaufe they not only borrow little or nothing from Nature, but are on the other hand made in Spight of her; fo that whereas elfewhere fhe appears like a Queen and a Miftrefs, here fhe acts like an obedient Servant, or rather like a Slave, forced hither againft her Will.

THE Cafe, not to deal longer in general Defcriptions, is this, the Place Cardinal *Verdala*, who was once Grand Mafter of the Order, chofe for his Pleafure-houfe, was a Rock abfolutely barren, and alike expofed to the Sun and to the Winds; fo that except its lofty Situation, it had nothing to recommend it; and, in the Eyes of

any

any but Cardinal *Verdala*, this would have passed for an extraordinary Inconvenience, considering the Heats of *Malta*. But he was a Man of exalted Underftanding, and had fuch Ideas of Magnificence, that, by endeavouring to do it Honour, he had like to have ruin'd the Order. In the firft place, he hewed his Palace out of the Rock, a fquare Building with four Towers, having in the Middle a grand *Salon*, finely painted with the Stories of this Cardinal's Life. From the Houfe, towards the Sea, he caufed the Rock to be cut down, fo as to have a Defcent from his Houfe through a Range of fine Pillars to that Part which overlooks the Sea, and affords a Profpect of the neighbouring Ifland and *Sicily*. All this being performed, he had the hollow Part of the Rock filled up with fine Mould, brought thither in Ships and Barks; the Skirts of the Garden he planted with Olives, adorned all its Walks with Orange, Lemon and Citron Trees; of Flowers and fweet-fmelling Herbs there never was fo great a Quantity any where amaffed, but what gives an inexpreffible Air of Paradifaical Beauty to this Place, is the Difpofition of the Vines, which being planted at the Feet of the Pillars, turn round them; and being platted at the Top, form a covered Arbour of a Mile, opening, as I have obferved, upon the Sea. In this Garden there is not only very fine frefh Water, but it is alfo put to all the Ufes of Fountains and Cafcades that could be devifed by the teeming Imagination of a luxurious Cardinal. All the Apartments of the Caftle are difpofed Terras-wife for the Enjoyment of the Garden; and that this Pleafure-Houfe may be diftinguifh'd from all other Pleafure-Houfes, its Battlements are furmounted by fixteen Pieces of Brafs Cannon, over which, on any Solemnity, flies

the

the Banner of *Malta*. There are in the Island many other beautiful Pleasure-Houses, but none comparable to this, with the Description of which I will take Leave of the Place.

The Island of *Goza*, which belongs also to the *Grand-Master*, is divided from *Malta* by a narrow Channel of the Sea ; it is of an oval Form, about three Miles long, somewhat more than half as broad, and about twenty-one in Circuit. Its Coasts are so steep, that one may look upon it as fortified by Nature. In respect to its Air, its Soil, and its Products, it very much exceeds *Malta*, it being every where wholesome, pleasant, and fertile. The Number of the Inhabitants may be about five or six thousand, but they live dispersed thro' the Island, and not in *Casals* or Villages, as they do in *Malta*. The *Grand-Master* bears the Title of Prince of *Goza*, and its Commodities, notwithstanding its small Extent, yield annually about a third Part as much as those of *Malta*. There are also on the Coasts of this Island, as well as *Malta*, some Rocks and little Places under the Jurisdiction of the *Grand-Master* ; but as they produce little, they are not worth mentioning.

The last Day of the old Year we sailed from *Malta* with a fair Wind, the next Day, and the Day following, we had the Wind still fair, but a little fresher ; on the third it blew very hard, especially towards the Evening. On the fourth we had a Sight of *Candia*, and 'till Noon we had fine Weather, from thence, till Midnight, the Wind gathered Strength every Moment. In the Morning we had a terrible Storm, attended with what the *English* Seamen, who use the *Levant* Trade, call *Bastard-Spouts*. These are occasioned by the Air's drawing
ing

ing up into a Cloud a great Quantity of Water as it were with a Pump, which being carried a confiderable Way in the Shape of long Tails hanging down from the Heavens, at length difcharge all their Water either into the Sea, or into a Veffel, if it is fo unfortunate as to come in the Way. Thefe are called *Baftard Spouts*, to diftinguifh them from the true ones, called fimply *Spouts*, which are infinitely more terrible. Thefe appear like Pillars defcending from Heaven, and in proportion as they drop towards the Water, the Water boils up to meet them. At length thefe Spouts dip as it were into the boiling Water, and having filled themfelves therewith, pafs along fometimes with a very brifk, at other Times with an interrupted or languid Motion. It is faid that Ships of great Burthen have been extremely damaged by thefe Spouts, and it is conjectured that many fmaller Ships have perifhed by them. The leffer Sort, which we faw, happen ufually after Storms, but thefe larger Spouts are moft frequent in ftark Calms. On the fifth, the Weather grew fine again, but on the fixth we had very bad weather, with much Rain and Hail. The next Day, by Noon, all was fair again; and it being the Birth-Day of our Captain, he gave a handfome Entertainment to all on board. The Paffengers dined as ufual at his own Table, and their Servants with the Seamen and under Officers. Our Feaft began about Evening, and lafted 'till Morning. We had very good Provifions, and excellent Wine of feveral Sorts. But what diverted me moft, was the Converfation at Table which was fo much the more agreeable, on account of its being inftructive, every Body taking Pains to furnifh fomething worth hearing; and being as they were Men of different

Profeffions,

Profeffions, and who had fpent their Days in an active kind of Life, their Difcoveries were above the ordinary Level, and deferved not only Attention, but Prefervation. The Captain particularly entertained us, but not till he was thoroughly opened by Wine, with a very fingular Story, which he had from the very Mouth of the Man whom it concerned: It pleafed me fo well, that I committed it to Writing, as a wonderful Inftance of the Divine Providence in ordering the Affairs of Men, and as a noble Encouragement to preferve our Spirits, and the Ufe of our Reafon in the Midft of the greateft Dangers, out of which, if we truft in God, and ufe the Means he has given us, we may frequently efcape notwithftanding the ftrongeft Appearances of inevitable Ruin.

It is, faid the Captain, about 30 Years ago, that being in Company at *Rotterdam* with feveral Merchants, Captains of Ships, and Pilots, at an annual Feaft, my Companions were very urgent on an old Man whofe Name as I remember was *William Boutiko*, to relate to them his Sufferings in the *Indies*, which they had all heard much of from others, and concerning which they were very defirous to have a diftinct Recital from his own Mouth. The old Man was eafily intreated, and when he perceived the Company filently attending the Detail of his Adventures, he delivered himfelf very gravely to this Purpofe. In the Month of *November* 1619, I failed in Quality of Mafter on board a Veffel of 1200 Tuns, bound for the Streights of *Sunda*. On the 19th of that Month, when we were in the Height of five Degrees and a half, and thought ourfelves near thofe Streights, by fome Accident or other our Powder took

O   Fire,

Fire, and blew up myself and 119 Persons, those who escaped this Disaster betaking themselves to the Yawl and the Skiff. I was very sensible as I rose in the Air of my Misfortune, and cry'd out aloud, *This Lord is my Road, have Mercy on my Soul, and receive me into Heaven.* When I fell it was in the midst of the broken Pieces of our Ship, which in a few Minutes was torn to Shatters. The Water revived me, and finding myself between the great and the mizen Masts, I with much ado got upon the former. When I had settled myself thereon, I looked about me, and I perceived at a small Distance a young Man of my Acquaintance sitting upon a Plank; I immediately called to him and desired him to come as near to me as he could, for that I was so wounded that I was incapable of making any Effort to come to him. The young Man did so, and with very much ado I got upon the same Plank.

By this Time those in the Yawl and Skiff perceived us, and immediately rowed towards us, not daring however to approach too near, left they should suffer by the floating Wreck. My Companion flipping off the Plank easily swam on Board, but as for me I was forced to cry out, that my Wounds had disabled me from swimming, and that if they had a Mind to save me, they must come nearer. Upon which a *Musician*, my old Acquaintance, laid hold of a Rope, and jumping at once into the Sea, swam to the Plank on which I sate, and having fastened the Rope about my middle, dragg'd me after him to the Yawl, where with some Difficulty they took me in, my Spirits being so far spent, that I was absolutely incapable of helping myself. As soon as I was on Board, they laid me under a little Auning, and

and did what they could to give me Eafe; I had two dangerous Wounds in my Head, and it was the Opinion of my Companions, as well as of myfelf, that they were mortal; however, I did not fail to exert, as I conceived, my laft Breath for their Prefervation, by recommending it to our Factor, and the reft on Board, to keep all Night as near as poffible to the Wreck, that when it fhould be light the next Day, they might be able to get a Compafs and fome other Inftruments on Board, as alfo Provifions, of all which they ftood in great need.

But while I repofed myfelf as well as I could, the Factor hoping the next Day to gain the Shore, and either not heeding, or not believing what I had faid, commanded the Men to row with all their Might, which accordingly they did, and the Confequence was, that when it grew Light, we could not fee either Wreck or Land. In this Diftrefs the People caft their Eyes upon me as the only Perfon capable of advifing them. All I could do was to encourage them in general Terms, to exhort them to Conftancy, and to befeech them to act unanimoufly for their common Safety. I then directed that the Number of Perfons fhould be counted, which was accordingly done, and it appeared from thence, that there were 46 in the Yawl, and 26 in the Skiff. Our Provifions, which confifted chiefly in Bread, were very fhort, and as for Water we had none. I faw it was impoffible without Food for us to fupport much Labour, and therefore I propofed laying afide our Oars, and trying to make Sails with our Shirts joined together. This Motion was immediately agreed to, and I was thereupon going to pull off my Shirt, but

Q 2

my

my Companions would not permit me on account of my Wounds and Weakneſs. They gave me moreover a Watch Coat, and a Fur Cap, which they found in one of the Lockers, and our *Barber* tore a Piece of his Shirt, and having ſpread thereon ſome Bread which he had chewed, applied it by Way of Poultice to my Wounds, whereby, or rather by the Providence of God, they were ſpeedily cured.

THE Yawl and Skiff being provided with theſe poor Sails, we kept as well as we could before the Wind, ſteering by the Stars, and ſuffering much from the Weather, which if it fry'd us in the Day, froze us in the Night ; ſo that in 24 Hours we felt the utmoſt Rigour of Summer and Winter. By Chance a Perſon in the Yawl had a pair of Compaſſes in his Pocket, as ſoon as I was informed of this, I began to think of making Inſtruments. Accordingly, having deſcribed a Circle on a Board, I divided a Quadrant pretty exactly into Degrees, by the Help of which I made a Croſs-Staff, with which we took Obſervations. I alſo laid down on the Top of an old Box a ſort of Chart, whereon I deſcribed the Iſle of *Sumatra*, that of *Java*, and the Streight of *Sunda* between thoſe two Iſlands, ſuppoſing the Shipwreck to have happen'd at about the Diſtance of ninety Miles from Shore. I likewiſe kept as good a Reckoning as I could, that in caſe we made Land we might have ſome Notice where we were. As for Proviſions and Water, that was without my Power ; what Bread we had was quickly gone, tho' we husbanded it to the utmoſt, Rain Water we ſaved when it fell, in two empty Barrels, but this Relief we often wanted.

ONCE

ONCE a great Number of *Sea Mews* came on Board both our Veſſels, where we knock'd them on the Head, pluck'd them, and eat them raw. Another Time when we had taſted nothing a whole Day, a great ſhoal of flying Fiſh came croſs our Veſſels, of which we catch'd a good Number, and eat them too raw. Thoſe in the Skiff having none amongſt them who underſtood Navigation, and being ſometimes in Danger of ſeperating from us, deſired as the Yawl was large to be taken on Board, which Requeſt, after ſome Intreaty we granted. After this, abſolute Famine ſtaring us in the Face, I had much ado to hinder the Crew from eating the Boys ; and at laſt Deſpair carry'd it ſo far, that the Men abſolutely declared, if we ſaw not Land in three Days Time, they would preſerve themſelves, by killing and eating thoſe unhappy Youths. In the Afternoon of the laſt Day it began to rain, and we ſlackened our Sails in order to fill our Caſks.

TOWARDS Evening, as I was at the Helm, I perceived evident Signs of our being near the Shore ; but finding myſelf ſo cold, as to be no longer able to perform my Office, I put the Rudder into the Hands of an experienced Sailor, and lay down to Reſt ; but I had not quitted the Helm an Hour, before I heard him cry aloud, *Courage my Lads, we are near the Land* ; indeed we were ſo near, that before it was quite dark, we reached the Shore, and found a convenient Creek, from whence without Difficulty we got on ſhore. We preſently found ſome Cocoa Trees, and refreſhed ourſelves with their Nuts and Liquor. For this Relief I bleſſed God, whom I ſaw to be the beſt Pilot, and who by his Mercy delivered the Boys amongſt us, from that Death

they

they would inevitably have undergone the next Day. When it was light the next Morning, we perceived that we had ran on Ground in an uninhabited Island, which produced nothing fit for Food, excepting only the Cocoa Nuts before-mentioned ; of these we took a sufficient Number into the Boat, and then made all the Sail we could for the *Continent*, which lay over-against this Island.

WE sailed along the Coast the greateft Part of the Day, without being able to find any Place where we might attempt to land. At laft fome of the Crew fwam on Shore, and having difcovered the Mouth of the River, made a Waft to inform us thereof, and we bearing away according to their Signal, found the Mouth of the River, but choak'd with fuch a Bar of Sand, as gave but little Hopes of our being able to pafs over it, without expofing ourfelves to total Deftruction. Upon which I thought it convenient to fpeak to all our Crew after this manner : *My Friends, I will not undertake to run our Veffel over this Bank into the Mouth of the River, without the Confent of you all, and your Promife not to upbraid me let what will happen, fince I give you this previous Notice of your Danger.* They all cried aloud, that they were determined to rifque this Paffage ; and that they would no Way make me accountable for complying with their Commands. Then I went to the Helm, having ordered an Oar to be put out on each Side, at the other End of the Veffel, two of our ftrongeft Men being placed at each Oar, to keep the Veffel fteady, this done, we fteered for the Bar.

IN

In passing, the first Wave fill'd the Vessel half full of Water, which our Men emptied as fast as they could with their Hats, and the little Barrels in which we kept our Water. The second Breach of the Water fill'd us as full as we could hold, and overset us on one Side into the Bargain ; upon which I cryed out, *At it my Lads, clear the Vessel of the Water or we are all lost.* They laboured with all their might, and having with much ado got her upright, quickly cleared her of the Water. The third breaking of the Sea happily missed our Vessel, and the Water rising suddenly under our Keel, we were speedily over the *Bar*, and presently got all safe a shore, through the Protection of divine Providence. We found in the Neighbourhood of the Creek a good quantity of *Beans*, a Fire lighted, and some *Tobacco*, which we judged to be left there by some of the Inhabitants. We sat down without Ceremony, and made Use of all we found. Two old Hatchets that were in our Vessel proved of great Use to us now ; with them we cut down Wood enough to supply the Fire, as also to arm ourselves with each a tough Staff, for we were apprehensive that the *Savages* might attack us.

WHETHER our Hurry lessened or encreased our Disorder I know not, but at the coming in of Night, we were all terribly sick with the *Beans*, and incapable of taking Rest. In the midst of this Distress, the *Savages* came down to cut our Throats, two Hatchets, a rusty Sword, and the Staves we had cut, were all the Arms we had, the latter we thought fit to stick in the Fire, and when they were thoroughly on Flame at the Top, we drew them out, and marched towards the Enemy, who either terrified with our Appearance, for

the

the Night was prodigious dark, or whether they apprehended that we were better armed, fo it was, that they retired into a Wood, and we back to our Fire. The next Day three of the *Savages* advanced out of the Wood, to whom we fent three of our Seamen to treat with them. The firft Enquiry they made was as to our Country; our Seamen who were very well acquainted with the Tongues commonly fpoken in the *Indies*, told them that we were *Hollanders*, and that our Ship blowing up at Sea, we were obliged to put in there for Refrefhment. Upon this they faid fomewhat of *Java*, and repeated two or three Times the Name of *Hans Coen* our General there, then they enquired what Arms we had, we anfwered, a good Number of Mufquets, and Powder and Ball in abundance.

On board I put every Thing to Rights as well as it was poffible, that we might hide our Weaknefs from them as far as we were able. Some Rice and Fowls we bought and paid for, having about 80 Crowns amongft us. The next Day I went with four of our Sailors to the Village with all our Money, to buy Provifion for our Voyage. After Dinner we agreed for a Buffalo, but it proved fo wild, that we were not able to manage it, for in going back to the Veffel it broke loofe; we purfued it till it was Night to no Purpofe, the Seamen then begged me to return to our People, refolving to ftay themfelves, in order to catch the Buffalo in the Morning. With much ado I complied with their Requeft, and on my Return to the Veffel related our Adventure, our People were mighty uneafy at the Accident, and grew more fo when all the next Morning paffed without any News either of the Buffalo, or our Companion.

In

In the Afternoon however came two *Savages* with another Buffalo, I told them I was pofitive that was not the Beaft I bought the Day before, upon which they readily confeffed that it was not, but faid, as we bought that, they did not know but we might buy this, we then enquired what was become of our Sailors; they anfwered, that they had not yet got the Buffalo, but they would come by and by. With this we were forced to be content, being able to get no better, and having agreed with them for the other Buffalo, and paid them for it, we found the Creature fo unruly, that we were forced to get our *Butcher* to knock it down with one of the Axes. As foon as the Beaft fell, the two *Savages* fet up a horrible Cry, upon which inftantly 2 or 300 of their Companions iffued out of the Wood, where they lay in Ambufcade, and came rufhing furioufly upon us, difcharging as foon as within Reach a whole Shower of Darts, and then attempting to board our Veffel, which with much ado moft of us had gained before they reached us.

I cannot fay we fought couragioufly, for in Truth we were in fuch Defpair, that we thought of nothing but felling our Lives as dear as we could; the Men who had the Hatchets did terrible Execution, and our *Baker*, who was a very ftrong Fellow, dealt his Blows with our rufty Sword fo freely, that he twice or thrice clear'd the Veffel of the *Savages*, and thereby faved us from Deftruction. All our Efforts however would have been ufelefs, if there had not fprung up a brisk Gale from Shore, which quickly carried us out of the Reach of our Enemies, and gave us Leifure to confider our new Situation. We loft in the Engagement 16 Men, including the 4 who

who were left the Night preceding, and who without Doubt had their Throats cut by thefe barbarous People. We failed along the Coaft, our Stock of Provifions confifting only of eight Fowls and a little Rice, a poor Supply for 56 Perfons who were yet left; however we divided it equally, and husbanded it as well as we could for feveral Days.

HUNGER at laft forced us once more to think of going afhore, which we accordingly did, on a little Ifland inhabited indeed but thinly, where we found plenty of frefh Water, fome wild Fowl, and Fruit; but what rejoiced us moft, was the great plenty of large Canes, called *Bamboos,* of thefe we cut Numbers, and having burnt through their Joints, filled them with Water, for which they were the moft excellent Casks that we had feen for a long Time. While our Men were thus employed, I went alone to the Top of a very high Hill, where looking about me, I faw at a Diftance blew Mountains, I then remembered that I had heard *William Schouten,* the famous Pilot fay, that in two or three Voyages he had made to the *Indies,* he had obferved two Mountains of that Colour, over-againft the Point of the Ifland of *Java.* This made me ftill more attentive, I remarked that thefe Mountains were on my right Hand, that we had failed along the left Coaft of *Sumatra,* and that in the middle there appeared a fair opening in the Sea; upon this I went down, and acquainted our Factor with what I had obferved, and with my Reafons for believing that we were at the Mouth of the Streight of *Sunda.* He readily came into my Opinion, whereupon we drew together our People, and having got our Water on Board put to Sea.

ABOUT

About Midnight we faw Fire at a Diſtance, which we conceived to have been in ſome Veſſel, but it proved to be an Iſland in the Streight of *Sunda*. We paſſed by it, and came in a ſhort Space to another Iſland. In the Morning I ordered one of the Men to the Maſt Head, who had not been there long before he cryed out, *Courage my Lads, I ſee Ships riding in a Road, and I have counted twenty-three.* Theſe Words revived us all, and becauſe the Weather was quite calm, we betook us to our Oars, that we might ſooner reach the Fleet. It lay before *Bantam*, with which we were then at War, and was commanded by *Frederick Houtman* of *Alckmar*. The General happened to be at this Time in his Gallery, and having viewed our Sail with his Perſpective, he was ſo ſtruck with the Oddity of its Form, that he ſent his Shaloup to know what we were. We were quickly known to the Crew of that Veſſel, having ſailed with them out of the *Texel*, and kept them Company as far as the Coaſt of *Spain*.

The Factor and I therefore went with them on Board the Admiral, who received us very kindly, and ſet us down to Table with him ; but when I ſaw the Bread, the Meat, the Wine, and the Beer, my Heart was ſo full, that I burſt into Tears, and could not eat at all; in a few Days however I recovered pretty well, and went with the Factor in a Veſſel diſpatched to *Batavia*, where we gave an Account of all that happened to us to the General of the *Dutch Eaſt-India* Company, who provided for us all Things in great Plenty, till our Return to *Holland*. The Company, ſaid the Captain, to whom this Story was told, would have preſented the old Man with ſome Money, but he abſolutely

lutely

lutely refufed it, faying his Circumftances did not require it. All the Company heard this Relation with great Attention, and I the rather committed it to Writing, becaufe our Captain affured me, that to the beft of his Knowledge it had not yet been Printed.

Doctor *Salviati* a *Genoefe*, who had been both in the *Eaft* and *Weft-Indies*, and was a Man of great Wit and Learning, entertained us with many Stories of his Adventures, as likewife did Seignior *Altoviti*, a *Neapolitan*, a moft ingenious Man, with whom my Acquaintance took Birth in this Paffage, and proved much more pleafant than ufeful. The 7th the Weather was fair, and our Captain declared to us in the Evening, that he thought himfelf about fourfcore Leagues from *Alexandria*. But tho' there was little Wind, the Sea ftill ran high; fo that we durft ufe but little Sail, tho' we were defirous enough of getting into Port. The 8th the Wind was fair, and we made a great deal of Way. On the 9th we were in Sight of Land, and about Noon came into the Port of *Alexandria*.

For the prefent Mr. *Perez*, myfelf, and our Servant *Antonio*, went to lodge with one *Veneroni*, an Acquaintance of our Captain's; thither alfo came Seignior *Altoviti*, who was our Companion in feeing all the Curiofities in and about this famous City, among which he could find none which deferved Admiration more than himfelf. He paffed with us for a Traveller, whom Curiofity only led to vifit *Egypt*; but he difcourfed on all Subjects with fuch Fluency, and with fuch Appearance of Knowledge, that it was not eafy to conceive he fhould make this Voyage with no other View. His peculiar Excellency was in finding out, and fuiting

himfelf

himſelf to every Man's Genius, Temper, and Pleaſures ; ſo that he was not only the Companion, but the
boſom Friend of Dr. *Salviati*, Mr. *Perez*, our Captain, myſelf, and even of *Antonio*, whom he knew how
to play off for the Diverſion of every Body without
offending him, which was no light Secret.

HE loved Expence, came into all Propoſitions where
Pleaſure was in View, and paid for every Thing frankly, and like a Man of Quality. He liked Play as a
Diverſion, and tho' he did not ſhew any great Skill in
it, he was generally ſucceſsful. Tho' he never pro-
poſed high Stakes, yet he would readily make them to
gratify a Loſer, nor was it till after a very long Acquaintance, and upon a very particular Occaſion, that I
learned this was his Philoſopher's Stone, and the Mine
from whence he drew wherewith to ſubſiſt. He could
not be at this Time above 50 Years of Age, and yet
he was ſo well known in all Parts of *Europe*, that he
was forced to take this Method for opening a new Vein
as the Miners phraſe it.

DR. *Salviati* came hither on the Buſineſs of his Profeſſion ; he had been invited by two Brothers, who reſided as Factors at *Alexandria*, to come and live with
them, in order to take Care of their Health. The Doctor was about forty-fix, had all the *Italian* Politeneſs,
with a great deal of good Senſe, and as much Sincerity as
any Man could wiſh in a Friend. He went immediately to his Patrons, who received him with as much Affection as if he had been their neareſt Relation, cauſed all
his Things to be immediately brought to their Houſe,
and my great Bale with them at his Requeſt, aſſigned
him a large Apartment, and, in fine, did every thing
for

for him which would have contented the moſt troubleſome Man in the World, whereas of all Men he was the
leaſt ſo. The Doctor had but one Fault, which was,
that he liked Play. This brought him to us every Day,
though he generally loſt his Money, and would have
loſt it always, if the *Neapolitan* had not had Skill enough
to looſe now and then to him, at leaſt double as much
as he won of him at any ſingle Time.

OUR Affairs went on very happily from the very Moment of our Arrival. Signior *Altoviti*, to make his
Court to us, exerted all his Diligence in procuring graved
Stones, Medals, and ſuch like Curioſities which he had
Addreſs enough to buy much cheaper than we could, and
with which he furniſhed us at the Price he bought them,
ſuppoſing us to be Men of Fortune, who collected them
for our own Cabinets. The Doctor, who was not
very curious this Way, having his Head turned entirely
to Phyſick and Chemiſtry, frequently did us Favours in
the ſame Way. As for *Antonio*, we gave him ſeven or
eight Piaſters, and in two or three Days he brought in a
large Cargo, amongſt which we generally found ſomething of Value. From our firſt coming hither, I remark'd Mr. *Perez* did not much care for converſing with
any of the *Jews*; and indeed where-ever he came he
ſeemed to ſtand no leſs in Fear of them than of the Inquiſition. He never condeſcended to give Reaſons on
this Head ; but by putting together Things I have heard
him ſay, it appeared to me that the *Jews* allowed of no
Latitudinarians amongſt them, but thought themſelves
at Liberty to puniſh any Man who in the conſtant Te-
nour of his Life diſobey'd the Laws of *Moſes*. On this
Account, whenever I had any Tranſactions with *Jews*,
I took

I took care to keep them at a Diſtance, which I had all the Opportunity in the World of doing, Mr. *Perez* being a Man above Suſpicion, as believing firmly that a Perſon who called himſelf his Friend, would never forfeit his Honour ſo far as to deceive him ; and as I was conſcious to my ſelf that I deſerved the Truſt he repoſed in me, I took my Meaſures ſo as to ſerve our common Intereſt, without giving him any particular Cauſe of Diſpleaſure.

THOSE People, I mean the *Jews*, carry on the greateſt Part of the Trade of *Egypt*, and therefore all who have any Concerns therein have conſequently ſomething to do with them. We were recommended to one whoſe Name was *Abraham*, through the Means of Mr. *Fetherſtone* ; and, on our firſt Arrival, I thought myſelf extremely happy in having Buſineſs to tranſact with him. He ſpoke *Italian*, *French*, and *Spaniſh* perfectly. He was known to, and had great Intereſt with not only the *Venetian* Conſul, and the *French* Vice-Conſul, but alſo the *Turkiſh* Officers, Civil and Military ; able in his Profeſſion, polite in his Manners, and much better acquainted with Books than any *Jew* I ever met with who was not a *Rabbi*. With all theſe Qualifications, he was one of the moſt cunning, artful Knaves, that ever exiſted ; Many ſuſpected him, but few or none durſt publiſh their Suſpicions, for he was ſo ſubtile in his Contrivances, and had ſuch a mighty Intereſt, that whoever offended him, ſeldom eſcaped ſome great Miſhap or other.

FOR my part, the firſt Affair I had with him, was the Sale of a Parcel of Coral which had been ſorted by Mr. *Fetherſtone*, and was not only excellent in its kind, but alſo very neatly wrought. He was ſo pleaſed with the

Samples

Samples I shew'd him, that he readily undertook to dispose of all that we had, which was somewhat more than two Quintals; this accordingly he performed much to my Satisfaction, for he sold it for a thousand Piasters, whereas the *Venetian* Merchants, with whom Dr. *Salviati* lived, assured me that the Coral would not fetch above eight hundred and fifty. Before we came to make up the Accompt, my *Jew* shewed me abundance of Curiosities, some truly antique, but the greater Part of them evidently Counterfeits; those which were of any Value, he set much too high a Price on; and when I refused to take them, seemed to be not a little displeased; however, he shewed me afterwards some colour'd Stones, such as *Chrysolites* and *Amethists*, and at last some *Emeralds*, of which there are in *Egypt* some of great Value. Amongst these there were two, which if absolutely perfect, would have been valuable; as they were, he asked three hundred Piasters for the one, and two hundred for the other; I offer'd him two hundred and fifty for the largest; to which, with some Difficulty, he agreed.

WHEN I brought the Stone home, I shew'd it to Mr. *Perez*, and asked him what he thought of it, he said, it might possibly be sold for one hundred and fifty Piasters, but that he would not give so much for it; upon which I told him that I bought it for my self, in order to send it into *England* for a Present. I am sorry for it, said Mr. *Perez*, we must sell Stones as we find them, foul or clean; but when we make Presents they should be absolutely perfect; at which I smiled, telling him it was a *Spanish* Nicety; but that there were many People who loved large Stones, rather than small ones of greater Value. My real Design in buying this Emerald was to try the

the Secret I had of freeing it from its Imperfection, but, at the same Time, I found the *Jew* had imposed upon me near half in half; notwithstanding which, and my allowing him a Half *per Centum* more than usual in the Sale of the Coral, he was so displeased at our not putting all Things into his Hands, that he could not forbear doing us privately ill Turns which we had no Way deserved, and which *Antonio* would have revenged in his own Way if I had not prevented him.

DURING our Stay in this City, which was longer than we at first conceived necessary, and which was much shorter than it ought to have been, since no Place was fitter for our Purpose. I say, during our Stay here, and within three Months after our Arrival, there happened a singular Adventure, which served to give us a great Idea of our own good Fortune, and proved, I think, the principal Motive to our taking abundance of needless Trouble in hopes of meeting with still better Luck, of which there would have been much more Probability if we had never left *Alexandria* at all.

THE Adventure was this: When I had Occasion to go abroad, I hired always the Ass of an old *Arab*, or, as they are call'd there, *Bedouin*, who spoke a sort of *Lingua franca*, and with whom I could, though not without some Difficulty, converse. This Man, on account of my giving him now and then somewhat more than the Hire of his Beast came to, which was in Truth very little, began to have a great Liking to me, the rather, I believe, because of my being more reserv'd and grave than the *Franks*, as they call the *Europeans*, usually are. It so happened one Day, that this poor Fellow having got Cold, complained

P   much

much of a Pain in his Stomach ; with some Difficulty I got him to take a little of a Cordial in which Rhubarb had been also infused, which presently relieved him. When we came home, he told me that he would the next Day bring me some of the *Franks* Treasure, by which he meant Medals, and other Curiosities, which Travellers usually enquire for in *Egypt.* Accordingly the next Day he came and brought tied up in a coarse Cloth, as many Things as would have filled a Man's Hat : I did not examine them very carefully, because at first Sight I perceived that they were genuine and curious, but asked him what he would have for them ; he asked twenty Piasters, which in his Judgment was a vast Sum. I gave him twelve, and he went away not only satisfied, but over-joy'd.

THESE poor People live in the Vaults and Caverns among the Ruins of the ancient City of *Alexandria.* In these Places they have great Opportunities of finding Medals, Stones, Idols of green Earth, and other Curiosities. It seems a little before our Arrival there had been a very great Storm, accompanied with Rain, which washed down the Things the *Arab* sold me, with many more, into his Vault or Cellar, where he treasured them up till he had an Opportunity of selling them.

MR. *Perez,* when he saw these Things, and considered them, looked upon this as a singular good Omen, and indeed there were two Medals of *Lysimachus* in Silver, and one in Brass of *Cleopatra,* which were valuable ; neither was there any thing false, or which could be said to be of little Value. There were likewise three Tablets of Cornelian, harder, and of a much deeper Colour than is usual, which seem'd to have been prepared

for

for engraving; but, by some Accident, were left plain, and were the finest I ever saw. We sent these, and a great many other Things, to Mr. *Fetherstone*, from whom we receiv'd Advice, that by proper Asortments, and sending them to different Places, our Collections would in all Likelihood produce very considerable Advantages.

B y this time our *Neapolitan* began to discern somewhat of our Business, and therefore pressed Mr. *Perez* to go to *Cairo*. It was indeed high time for him to be gone, since he had already staid longer than seemed consistent with the Account he gave of himself, and of his Business; but as for us, there seemed to be no great Cause for our removing, nor had I any Idea of it 'till Mr. *Perez* mentioned it, and assured me that we should find our Account therein. But after all, the *Neapolitan* was forced to depart without us, having won a large Sum of Money of a *Jew*, who did not bear his Loss with that Patience which our Friend expected. The Cause of our longer Stay was my falling ill of an Ague, which proved very troublesome, for I relapsed twice. To facilitate my Recovery, Dr. *Salviati*, with the Consent of his Patrons gave me a Share in his Apartment at their House. Here having the Opportunity of a small Furnace, I made an Experiment of the Emerald my *Jew* had sold me, but it did not succeed so happily as I expected, though it improved the Stone very much. *Two* or *three* large *Topaz*'s, which were very foul, and as it were muddy, I tried in the same Manner, and succeeded therein beyond my Expectation, for they became perfectly clear and well-colour'd. Some Experiments also I made on *Amethists* and *Chrysolites*, but to no Purpose at all. When I was perfectly recovered, I consent-

ed,

ed, at the Requeſt of my Friend *Perez*, though againſt my own Opinion, to go to *Roſetta*, and thence to *Cairo*.

THE Time we ſtaid at *Alexandria*, including the beſt Seaſon of the Year, I had before me all the Opportunities I could deſire of informing myſelf concerning the ancient and preſent State of that moſt famous City ; neither did I let them ſlip, but as far as in my Power lay improved what I heard, what I ſaw, what I read, and what from the Compariſon of theſe I was able to conjecture to the beſt Advantage. Hence I often amuſed myſelf with framing Ideas of the different Situation Things have been in, in this Part of the World, and of the Power, Grandeur, and Riches, of the ſeveral Potentates who have either ruled in *Egypt*, or made it a Part of their Dominion. On mature Deliberation, I am perſuaded myſelf, and I think I could prove it to any reaſonable Perſon, that the ancient Kings of *Egypt*, before the Times of *Alexander*, were by far the moſt conſiderable Princes that ever ſwayed here. At firſt Sight it will ſeem odd to deduce this from the Conſideration of *Alexandria*, a City built after the Extinction of their Government, yet have I certainly Reaſon on my Side, ſince if the ancient *Egyptian* Princes had not taken Care to confer on this Country thoſe Benefits which Nature had denied it, it would have been ſo far from affording a Situation proper for the Metropolis of a great Kingdom, that there could not have been ſo much as a Village, no not a Houſe here, or any where hereabouts.

THE Maps we commonly have of *Egypt* are ſo erroneous, that it is really a difficult Thing to have a juſt Comprehenſion of what Travellers ſay of that Country ; and

and I have been sometimes not a little surpriz'd to see Charts inserted in Book's directly contrary, as to the Situation of Places, to what was said in them. The City I am speaking of lies without the *Delta*, towards the *Lybian* Desarts. The Soil about it was naturally as sandy and barren, as unfit for Cultivation, and as absolutely void of Water as can be imagined. To remedy these Evils, and to turn this Wilderness into a habitable Country, the ancient Kings of *Egypt* devised Methods of supplying it with Water ; and as a very great Quantity was necessary, they caused a large and deep Lake to be sunk within a few Miles of the Sea, to be a proper Receptacle for the furnishing the Canals they had designed with Water, at such Times as they could not be drawn directly from the *Nile*. This Lake still remains a Monument of their Wisdom and Power, and is called *Mareotis*. It was fill'd by the Waters derived to it from two grand Canals, the one drawn from the Lake *Moeris* in the upper, and the other discharging the Waters collected in the lower *Egypt*. From the Lake *Mareotis* again there was a Canal to the Sea, and several other Cuts for the Conveniency of Agriculture and Navigation. Thus the Country became inhabitable, by Degrees was filled with Villages, and lying conveniently for Trade, especially with the *Greeks*, served to circulate the Commodities of the higher *Egypt*, and perhaps of *Ethiopia*, and to return in their stead the Manufactures and Wealth of *Europe*.

It was in this State that *Alexander the Great* found it, and very wisely contrived to build a new City here to be the Seat of the *Grecian* Governors, and a kind of Check upon the rest of *Egypt*. Whoever is well

acquainted

acquainted with his History, will perceive that he pur-
chased no part of his great Dominions at so easy a Rate as
he did *Egypt.* The true Reason of which was, that the
Egyptians naturally inclined to rid themselves of the *Persian* Yoke, and to submit themselves rather to him than
to any body else. Their old Masters had always treated them with great Severity, and were besides open Enemies to their Superstition. The *Greeks*, on the other
hand, were their old Friends, and little less superstitious
than themselves. However, as *Alexander* thought of
keeping as well as getting, he saw clearly that the *Egyptians* were not to be depended upon, and that it would be
an indiscreet risquing of his *veteran* Troops to leave a
small Number of them encamped in the open Country
scatter'd up and down in Garrisons, or in any great inland City, where, in case of Rebellion, they might be
presently block'd up, and easily famish'd before they could
receive any Succours. There was nothing therefore
either of Pride or of Vanity in *Alexander's* building this
City, but it was purely a Work of Policy, which he executed with as much Spirit, as he projected it with
Sagacity. I know very well that there are some Dis-
cordances in the Accounts given us of this Transaction
by the Ancients ; but he who will exercise his Understanding and attend rather to the Reason of Things than
to the Niceties of Expression, and those Ornaments which
Historians usually endeavour'd after, such as Prodigies
and miraculous Accidents, will find this Account probable enough.

This City, as laid out by *Dinocrates,* at the Command of *Alexander,* stretched from the Lake *Mareotis*

to the Sea, thereby affording all imaginable Conveniency for correfponding with the *Upper* and *Lower Egypt*, at the fame time that effectual Provifion was made for eftablifhing a ftrong Garrifon, and a numerous and flourifhing Colony, open in refpect to *Greece*, from whence at Times it could receive Succours fufficient not only to preferve itfelf, but to fecure the Dominion of the *Greeks* over *Egypt*. As it owed its Foundation to one of the greateft Princes in the World, fo from the very Beginning it was adorned with the nobleft publick Buildings which the *Greek* Tafte for Architecture then at its greateft Height, and fupported by all the Riches of the Eaft, could fupply. This great Conqueror, fo long as he lived, continued his Care to this Child of his Policy, according to it fuch Privileges and taking fuch Pains to furnifh it with Inhabitants, that as it was built, fo it was peopled in fo fhort a Space, that the Account we have of it would be incredible, if we knew not that the whole was carried on by him, who with *thirty fix thoufand* Men attempted and atchieved the Conqueft of the beft Part of the Univerfe.

His Succeffor in this Part of his Dominions, *Ptolemy Lagus*, if he was not rather the Son of *Philip*, and the Brother of *Alexander*, made *Alexandria* his Capital, and the Care of fortifying, adorning, and augmenting it, the grand Bufinefs of a long and profperous Reign. It was he who made its Port the Wonder of the World, and erected over a moft magnificent Palace built on an artificial Ifland, that celebrated *Pharos* of which Authors fpeak with fuch Rapture and Amazement.

His Succeffors purfued the fame Plan, that is to fay, they improved and adorned *Alexandria* to the utmoft of

their

•their Power, transferring hither by degrees all the *Greek* Arts, and erecting that celebrated Library which was at length encreased to five, some say to seven hundred thousand Volumes, and which is affirmed to have perished by Fire when *Julius Cæsar* was in this City, tho' neither that Prince, nor the Consul *Hirtius*, who continued his Commentaries, say any thing of it. *Cleopatra*, the last *Greek* Sovereign of *Egypt*, exerted her utmost Force in order to excell all her Predecessors in magnificent Buildings, the Ruins of which (if they be truly the Ruins of her Palace which are commonly called so) remain to this Day.

AFTER *Egypt* became a Province of *Rome*, *Alexandria* of course declined from its former Grandeur, but remained still, as the *Roman* Authors frequently confess, the next City to *Rome*, containing not less than three hundred thousand free Citizens, and of all Sorts of Inhabitants, a Million at the least. Its Commerce, its pleasant and convenient Situation, its being the Metropolis of *Africa* after the Ruin of *Carthage*, drew to it such a Flux of Riches, and all other Utensils of Luxury, that, as *Quintilian* informs us, *Deliciæ Alexandriæ*, the *Delights* of *Alexandria*, became a Proverb. Thence forward it shared the Fate of the *Roman* Empire, or rather of the *Constantinopolitan*, of which it remained a Province 'till it was over-run by the *Saracens* in the *Caliphat* of *Omar*, when with all the rest of *Egypt* it fell into their Hands, and suffered from thence all the Calamities a barbarous Enemy could inflict, an Enemy equally cruel to Buildings and to People. This is to be understood of the Condition of this People at the Time of their Eruption into *Egypt*; for by degrees, when they were settled there, and

and tafted the Bleffings of civil Government, Peace and Riches, they became quite another People.

However, their Succeffors, who came thus to underftand the Value of the *Greek* Learning, could neither reftore the Buildings their Predeceffors had overturned, or thofe innumerable Works of Literature which they had deftroyed. For as all the Princes to whom *Alexandria* had been fubject endeavour'd to render it famous for being the Seat of the Mufes as well as of Government, fo the Libraries which they piqued themfelves on erecting had all of them alike ill Fate. Of the firft, Mention hath been made already, the fecond, begun by *Cleopatra*, and augmented by the *Roman* Princes and Governors, was I know not how deftroyed by the Zeal of Chriftian Priefts, from a Notion that heathen Learning muft nourifh heathen Superftition. What was faved from this general Wreck of Literature, fell into the Hands of the *Saracens*, who here, as well as at *Cairo*, heated their Ovens and their Bagnio's with Heaps of invaluable Manufcripts. In the Wars, which almoft continually vexed *Egypt*, after it fell under the Dominion of thefe new Mafters, *Alexandria* fuffered not a little; and at length one of the Succeffors of *Saladin*, as the *Europeans* call him, enclofed a Part of the City with Walls, which are yet ftanding, well fortified with Towers, after having demolifh'd every Thing without them, as well to prevent any Rebels from fortifying themfelves amongft them, as to furnifh himfelf with Materials for the Works carried on by his Command.

I know very well that many Travellers have reported, that the Walls now ftanding are thofe built by *Alexander*; but they are really what I fay, as appears not
only

only from the *Arabian* Historians, but from the Walls themselves, which are plainly composed in great Measure of the Fragments of an ancient Building, and have in many Places *Arabick* Inscriptions, all of a Date inferior to that assigned for their Erection. Under the *Mamalukes* it is said, that the ancient *Alexandria*, or rather the magnificent Ruins of it, suffered new Outrages. These People, greedy of Money, and having strong Suspicions that the *Obelisks* they saw covered with *Hieroglyphics* were erected for no other Purpose than by their *Talifmannick* Virtue, to preserve the Treasures buried under them, broke and threw them down wherever they could, and defaced all the Statues they met with, if they had the least Suspicion that they were hollow.

THE *Turks* since they became Masters, have acted upon the same wise Plan, and it is hard to say whether they have been more industrious in destroying the noble Monuments of Antiquity, or careless in erecting publick Works themselves. The true Source of which left-handed Policy is this, that they look upon *Egypt* not as an Estate, but as a Farm, of which they may one Day lose the Possession; and therefore while they have it, they are for making as much of it as they can. For we are much in the wrong to suppose that the *Turks* are a dull, senseless People, whereas in Truth, they are quite otherwise; the Things from which we make such Inferences, have Causes that we don't suspect; and therefore in this Light they are not Fools, but we. It is true, that if we establish for our Rule this Maxim, *that such Things only as are vertuously done, are wisely done*, we shall condemn the *Turks*, yet may they not also alfo pray Judgment againſt us on the ſame Statute. But if the purſuit of Riches be an allowable End in them, as from our Practice it ſhould ſeem we ought to admit, then I am afraid it will be found, they are at leaſt as wiſe as ourſelves. For not to ramble too far from my Subject here, in the Port of *Alexandria* the Grand Seignior acts with as much Policy as any *European* Prince, for he impoſes Duties upon all foreign Commodities ; ſo that if his Subjects will deal in Superfluities, they muſt pay him, but he gives all manner of Encouragement for the vending the rich Commodities of their own Country, whereby the Balance of Trade is brought on their Side, and conſequently the Well furniſhed with continual Supplies of Water, to be firſt ſuck'd up by inferior Spunges, and at laſt ſqueez'd at once into the *bottomleſs Ciſtern* of the *Imperial Treaſure*, acquired by draining and employed in oppreſſing the People. Madneſs which would be incredible if it was not ſo common.

BUT to return to the City, its ancient Magnificence appeared but in part from the noble Structures erected on the Surface, ſince it was wholly built on Vaults of ſtupendous Contrivance, and wonderful Beauty. As the Buſineſs of Navigation and Agriculture could not have been carried on without the many Canals above deſcribed, ſo their Domeſtic Occaſions required Supplies of Water nearer at Hand, and in Quantities proportioned to the Number of Inhabitants. Subterraneous Aqueducts furniſhed theſe, nay, and furniſh them ſtill, for there is not a Drop of Water in the Modern *Alexandria*, but what is drawn from the ancient Ciſterns fill'd once a Year, by the riſing of the *Nile*, towards which Time the Water remaining in theſe Repoſitories

corrupt-

corrupting, renders the Air unwholefome, and the City very fickly.

THE old *Alexandria* was a Square of about a League, but its Suburbs ftretch'd very much towards the Tower of the *Arabs* on the one Side, and towards *Rofetta* on the other, furrounded on all Sides by pleafant Gardens, full of the moft delicious Fruits. The Modern *Alexandria* is in a manner without Walls, ftretched along the Sea Side, and after gradually declining for a long Time, had well nigh funk into a Village 40 Years ago; but it is fince much recovered, and continues daily to increafe, Experience having taught the *Turks*, that nothing can be more advantagious than this, for the augmenting their Revenue.

THE moft remarkable Things in this new City are, the Remains of thofe ancient Structures which are yet in a Condition of being confidered. Among thefe, that which deferves firft to be taken Notice of is, what the Chriftian Inhabitants ftile the *Palace of the Father of St. Katherine*, which is fituated almoft in the middle of the Space comprehended in the prefent Walls; a moft pompous Colonade of Pillars, no lefs admirable for their Workmanfhip, than for their extraordinary Height and Bignefs, amufes the Eye of the Spectator; it extends at prefent 500 Feet, but Numbers of the Pillars are entirely demolifhed; fome there are which retain half their ancient Height, and one only is left entire. Overagainft thefe are found the Remains of another Range of Pillars, which heretofore fronted thofe before fpoken of, whence it is probably enough conjectured, that they included a Space of Ground 500 Foot in Front, and 200 in Depth, in the midft of which it is thought there

was

was a noble Fountain, as, from many concurring Circumstances, inquisitive Men think they have Grounds to affirm, that these were the *publick Baths* built by the *Romans*. Over-against this glorious Relique of ancient Architecture, stands one of the finest Churches in *Egypt*, formerly dedicated to St. *Athanasius*, now a *Turkish* Mosque; of the Inside of this we know nothing more than can be perceived through certain Openings over the Gates. Hence we are enabled to say, that the Roof of it is supported by four Rows of Porphyry Pillars, as fair and beautiful as can be imagined. As to the Churches, or rather Chapels, in the Hands of the *Christians*, they are very far from being considerable, and as to the Port, all that it hath either of Safety or Beauty, it derives from its ancient Masters. At present there is a modern *Turkish* Fortification on the Island, where stood the ancient *Pharos*, the *Franks* call it *Farillon*; it is neither very strong, nor very beautiful, but serves well enough for the Purpose to which it is used. Here are two Ports, each covered by a Mole. That which is called the old Port is capacious as well as very comodious and safe, into which only the *Turkish* Gallies and other Vessels are suffered to come; as for the new Port, it is far from having any of these Advantages, tho' they might be procured to it if the *Turks* would be at any Expence, which is scarce to be expected.

To what has been said, I shall add only an Account of two Remnants of Antiquity more, the one within, the other without the Walls of *Alexandria*. The first the Obelisk, or as the *Franks* call it the *Aiguilla*, and our Sailors the *Needle* of *Cleopatra*. There is one standing,

ſtanding, and another lying on the Ground. That which is upright is without a Pedeſtal, and in all probability there is a great Part of it in the Earth. It is four ſquare, pointed at Top, each Face is covered with *Hieroglyphicks*, and the Stone of which it is made wonderfully beautiful, what is above Ground may be 56 Feet high. The other, which is almoſt buried in the Sand, lies about 12 Yards farther, and is evidently of the ſame kind. I have ſeen in other Parts of *Egypt* ſeveral of theſe Needles, and I think there is a Correſpondence between the *Hieroglyphic* Figures on the Faces of them all; from whence I have been led to conjecture, that they were ſet up by the ancient Kings of *Egypt*, to make certain Things known to their Subjects for the common Good; for I cannot apprehend, that the *Egyptians* would expoſe any of the Myſteries of their Religion in the Highways; perhaps I may be miſtaken, and perhaps a learned Man who ſhould attempt to confute me, might be miſtaken too; let us leave then theſe obſcure Points to Time, and the Antiquarians, who pretend to be of his Council.

The other Antiquity is the famous Pillar of *Pompey*, which lies about half a Mile without the City, towards the Lake of *Mareotis*; this is at once the fineſt, and the faireſt Pillar, not in *Egypt* only, but in the Univerſe. I cannot take upon me ſo much as to conjecture whether there be or be not Foundation for the Title given it. Whenever it was erected, it certainly was the Work of a very great Architect, ſince it is alike pleaſing to the Eye of every Beholder, and no Critic that I know of hath preſumed to cenſure its Proportions, tho' it is not reducible to any of the Orders in Uſe amongſt us.

As

As to its Height two *French* Engineers meafured it, as each of them affirm'd, very exactly while I was here. The one afferted it to be 94 Feet high, and the other 106. Both thefe People could not be right, by my Admeafurement it fhould be 110 of our Feet. A Mountebank who afcended this Pillar with marvelous Facility, found it hollow at the Top; it may be there was fome Image fixed thereon when it was originally fet up. The *Turks*, according to their old Cuftom, have been battering its Foundation, in order to look for Treafure, but without Succefs. One may guefs from this Monument, how far the Skill and Addrefs of the Antients in thefe fort of Things tranfcends thofe of the Moderns; for I never heard any Body pretend, that a Work of this kind could be executed by any Artift in *Europe*. As this Pillar is perfectly plain, it is reafonable to believe, that it was fet up to perpetuate the Memory of fome extraordinary Event, which makes the Learned fo dubious as to the Propriety of the Name given it, fince in this Senfe it feems to correfpond with it well e-nough, in other Refpects the Pillar might be thought to fuit better with the *Grecian* Times.

As to the Inhabitants of *Alexandria*, I forbear fpeak-ing of them, till I come to fpeak of the People of *E-gypt* in general. I fhall only add, that our Sailors com-monly call this City *Scanderoon*, in Imitation of the *Arab* Name *Scanderani*, which is a Tranflation of the *Greek* Name, a Liberty the more allowable in them, fince the *Greeks* themfelves ufed it very freely, in alter-ing the Names of all the Places which fell under their Cognizance, either in their Wars, or in their Travels.

WE

WE left this famous Place, in order to travel by Land to *Rosetta*, having sent our Effects thither in a Bark by Sea; we had in our Company 21 Persons, and amongst them Dr. *Salviati*, who went to *Rosetta* on some Concerns of his Patrons. We past by a considerable Lake, out of which there is a Canal cut to the Sea. All the low Country lies much exposed to that Element, and we were informed, that it sometimes rushed in with incredible Fury. The *Doctor*, Mr. *Perez*, and some other intelligent Persons in our Company, gave it as their Opinion, that some Time or other this would be fatal, not only to the Country between these Cities, but to *Alexandria* itself. At that Time I said nothing, but having thoroughly considered the Thing, I came to entertain quite a different Notion, of which I still am, *viz.* That the Sea will lose Ground here instead of gaining it. To this I was first led by reflecting on what the Antients have delivered, as to the growing of the *Delta*, by the continual Accession of Mud brought thither by the *Nile*. I was confirmed in it, by comparing the Distances of Places, mentioned in antient Authors, from the Sea, which I found to be much encreased; and as to the Certainty of this, again I thought that there was no room left for me to doubt, since several old Captains of Ships assured me, that when they first knew the City of *Rosetta*, that Part of it which was now half a Mile from the Sea, was within a quarter of it at most. Besides, it is not above 60 Years since *Rosetta* became a Port, on account of the Difficulty there was found in navigating Barks of considerable Burthen up the River to *Fouhe*, where the *Grand Seignior*'s Officers of Revenue were formerly settled. But of this Subject enough.

FROM

From *Alexandria* to *Rosetta* are 10 Leagues, which with some Difficulty we travelled in one Day, and took up our Lodgings in a publick Inn, from whence we removed to the House of a *Scotch* Merchant, where we were very much at our Ease, and Dr. *Salviati* with us, for the Time he staid, which was about three Weeks. Directly behind this House lay certain Gardens, more regular, and kept in better Order then any we had hitherto seen. This induced us to enquire of our Landlord to whom they belonged, he told us to one *Hassan* a *Moor*, who had retired thither from *Tetuan*, and who lived with such Lustre, that the *Arabs* said he had the Art of making Gold grow, a Conceit which the meaner sort of People take in a litteral Sense, and which those of more Learning use to express the Art of Transmutation. It was not long before I obtained a better Account of this *Moor*, and of the manner by which he had acquired his Riches.

A *Spanish* Slave of his named *Matthew Vasquez* about 70 Years of Age, but of a robust Constitution, and who had been 38 Years in Slavery, came to the House of a *Jew*, with whom I had some Dealings, and was easily persuaded to visit me at our Lodgings. He told me that his Master was the Son of a *Spanish Renegade*, who fled voluntarily from one of the *Spanish* Garrisons, in order to abjure his Religion, which he did publickly at *Tetuan*, and in the Space of a few Years, came to be a very considerable Person. He took the Name of *Ibrahim*, and being a strong well made Man, and of an undaunted Courage, addicted himself to Piracy with astonishing Success. He married the Daughter of his Patron, who had given the

Q first

firſt Riſe to his Fortune; her Name was *Zaide*, and ſhe was at once as handſome and as virtuous as an Angel; by her he had this Son *Haſſan*, but loſt her about a Year afterwards by the Plague, which carried off alſo three of his Concubines. For ſome Months after *Ibrahim* was very diſconſolate, 'till hearing that a Neighbour of his, a Moor of great Quality, had a moſt beautiful Daughter, he would needs ſee her, which, by the Help of an induſtrious old Woman, he effected, being for that purpoſe placed on the other Side of a Hedge which ſurrounded her Father's Garden.

F A T I M A, that was the Lady's Name, appeared to the *Renegade* ſo charming a Perſon, that, by the Inſtigation of the old Woman, he inſtantly made his Addreſſes to her, offered her the richeſt Preſents, and ſwore to marry no other Wife if ſhe would conſent to become his. *Fatima* was deaf to all his Intreaties, refuſed his Preſents, and treated him for a long Time with the moſt haughty Diſdain. At length ſhe ſent him word by the old Woman that ſhe ſuſpected he was ſtill a Chriſtian in his Heart, and that he kept up a Correſpondence with his Family in *Spain*. *Ibrahim* anſwer'd, that he had indeed a Father, Mother, and two Siſters, living when he left *Europe*, but that he had never heard of them ſince; to which *Fatima* reply'd, that as a Proof of his Love ſhe expected he ſhould bring them over to *Tetuan*, and that they ſhould ſerve them as Slaves.

I B R A H I M was ſo drunk with his Paſſion, that he immediately order'd his Veſſel to be got ready, and under the Favour of the dark Nights run over to the *Spaniſh* Coaſt, and landed as near as poſſible to his Father's Houſe, which ſtood about fifteen Miles from *Gibraltar*.

He

He immediately debarqued twenty Men, and having posted them at the Foot of a Hill, about a Mile from his Father's House, he went thither alone. Upon his Admittance he told his Family, that he, with six other Christian Slaves, had made their Escape from *Tetuan*, that they had brought with them in their Bark a great Quantity of Gold and other Commodities of Value ; he therefore begg'd that they would go with him to bring off his Share, to which, after embracing him with the warmest Testimonies of Affection, they joyfully consented.

But as it required some Time for them to find Baskets and other Conveniencies for transporting these Goods, *Ibrahim* proposed that his Father should go before, and offered to go with him in order to have the Things set on Shore, if his Companions did not incline to land at the same Place. The poor old Man, not in the least suspecting his Son, readily yielded to his Request, and went with him towards the Sea-side. When they came to the Foot of the Hill, *Ibrahim* delivered his Father to his Crew, with Orders, if he made any Resistance, to cut his Throat ; his Men, however, had more Humanity than himself, for notwithstanding the old Man cry'd out, they did not kill him, but gagg'd him as soon as they could. Not so soon, however, but that he alarmed the Country ; so that before they could reach their Vessel, they saw three or four hundred Men, Horse and Foot between them and the Shore. Upon this they abandon'd their Prisoner, and observing where their Enemies were thinnest, made a brisk Push, and got to their Vessel.

The old Man finding himself at Liberty, quickly got the Gag out of his Mouth, and then told his Deli-

verers

verers after what Manner he had been betray'd by his perfidious Son. Upon this Intelligence they posted themselves at the bottom of the Hill, till *Ibrahim* came with his Mother and Sisters, who supposing them to be his own Men, order'd them to carry those Women to the old Man. *No thou Miscreant !* cry'd his Father, *They shall carry thee back to be burnt for a Traitor to thy Country, and thy Faith !* He was after a Time conducted to the Prison of the Inquisition at *Seville*, and there being at that Time a Project of making a Descent on *Africk*, he was offered his Life if he would abjure the Religion of *Mohamed*. To which he reply'd, *I scorn it, I will die a Moor for the Sake of the most lovely Lady in* Africk. To this Resolution he adhered, and was accordingly burnt a Year afterwards, without any Signs of Remorse, or of any Sense he had of his Condition.

My Master *Haffan* was not above two Years old when his Father was taken Prisoner in *Spain*. He was taken Care of by his Uncle on the Mother's Side, who was alike attentive to his Education, and to the Increase of his Fortune. When he attained the Age of twenty, he was settled in a House, married the Daughter of his Uncle, whose Name was *Dilferiba*, i. e. *the Ravisher of Hearts*, and they had eight thousand Sequins given them to begin the World with. *Haffan* fell to the same Trade which his Father had exercised ; and being full of Moorish Resentment, made frequent Descents on the *Spanish* Coasts, and brought away great Numbers of People, and much Booty. At length, his Uncle being suspected of an Intercourse with Prince *Gailand*, was put to Death, whereupon *Haffan* embarquing his Wife, four Female Slaves, my self and another, together with his own and his Uncle's Treasure, which had been confided

to

to him, on board his Veffel, failed hither under *Spanifh* Colours, where he lives rather like a Prince than a private Man, being the Protector of the *Arabs* and *Moors*, and keeping a ftrict Correfpondence with his Relations in *Barbary*, receives from them whatever is moft faleable in *Egypt*, and fends them in Return the richeft Commodities from hence. In order to this he travels four Times a Year to *Cairo*, and refides there a Fortnight each Time.

FROM this Man, in the feveral Converfations I had with him, I learned abundance of curious Particulars with Refpect as well to *Barbary* as *Egypt*, he having fpent a great Part of his Life in that Country ; but what I valued moft was his Account of the Caravans which pafs annually to and from *Cairo* to *Tripoli*, *Tunis*, *Algiers*, *Fez*, and *Morocco* ; a ftupendous March, not only thro' an uncultivated Country, but through burning Sands, abfolutely void of Shade or Water, and yet far from being free from noxious Animals, which add to the other Plagues, more than fufficient to exercife the Patience even of an *Arab*. My Difcourfes with *Vafquez* take up an hundred Pages in my Diary, but I fay no more of them here that I may purfue the Thread of my Narration.

AFTER the Departure of Dr. *Salviati* for *Alexandria*, I fpent moft of my Time with Mr. *Perez*, and this *Vafquez*, who came every Day to our Houfe, and brought us feveral Perfons who fold us Curiofities at a reafonable Rate ; fo that we quickly fent another Cargo to Mr. *Fetherftone*. One Day *Vafquez*, who was informed that I ftudied Phyfic, came earlier than ufual, and defiring to fpeak with me, told me I muft go with him

Q 3

that

that Moment to his Mafter. This I did not hefitate to do, though I had fcarce dined, and the Weather was exceffively hot. He conducted me to a back Door, which opened into his Mafter's Gardens, and ftriking crofs them, brought me to a Summer-houfe, where his Mafter waited for me.

HE was a Man extremely well made, about thirty Years of Age, and had all the Politenefs of an *European*. He fpoke *Italian* and *Spanifh* well, and *French* indiffe-rently. He received me with great Civility, and after we had drank Coffee, enter'd upon the Bufinefs for which he had fent for me. He told me that his Wife was in a very bad State of Health, and that though he had had the beft and moft skillful in the Art of Phyfick, both Men and Women, (for Men and Women practice alike in *Egypt*, and the latter are thought to underftand the Difeafes attending their own Sex beft) his Wife grew daily worfe, which induced him, on the Report of his Slave *Vafquez*, to defire my Affiftance.

UPON inquiring of him as to the Symptoms of his Wife's Difeafe, I found that it was a complicated Cafe, arifing from a Dropfy ill treated. He conducted me himfelf into an Apartment where the Lady was, whom I found about twenty-three Years old, a Native of *Sienna* in *Italy*, of an Olive Complexion, yet wonderfully beautiful, though not a little dejected. After encoura-ging her a little, and receiving an Affurance both from herfelf and her Hufband, that fhe fhould obferve an exact Method as to Eating and Drinking, I undertook, and happily effected a Cure in a very fhort Space. This procured me the Confidence and Favour of *Haffan*, the moft generous *Moor* I had ever Occafion to converfe with.

His

His Mother's Brother, by whom he was brought up, had much Correspondence with the Christians, and taught his Nephew early to despise that Rudeness and Contempt which the *Moors* naturally have for all People of another Religion. He likewise engaged him to learn *Italian* and *Spanish* from his Slaves, as also to play on the Lute ; withal he instructed him in the Policy of their Country, and exhorted him, in case any Accident befel himself, to quit it as early as he could, and to retire into *Egypt*, where he held a Correspondence with some of the *Arab* Princes.

HASSAN made the best Use of so happy an Education ; and having himself a great Genius as well as a deep Fund of Generosity and good Nature, he brought all the Instructions that he received from his Uncle to operate for his Advantage. Though he was but a young Man, he had establish'd an Intercourse unthought of before. For going to *Cairo* as often as the Caravans arrived from *Barbary*, *Nubia*, *Mecca*, or *Syria*, he drew the chief Merchants the Beys or Princes of *Egypt*, and the petty Lords of the *Arabs*, to have a Confidence in him, and to make use of him as a common Friend in all their Negotiations, whereby he secured to himself a powerful Interest as well as great Riches. He took Care also to live upon mighty good Terms with the *Turkish* Governors, made annual Presents to the Bashaw at *Cairo*, and to his Officers, and secured the Friendship of every *Aga* he had Occasion to transact with, by the never-failing Method of gratifying him with Money.

He did not, however, converse much with any of the Inhabitants of *Rosetta*, being afraid lest some of the Vice-Consuls of the Christian Powers should penetrate

the

the Methods by which he furnifhed the *Tunifeens*, and other Piratical States with Ammunition, in which he had often Addrefs enough to make themfelves bear a Part. Having one Day talked to me pretty freely on the Subject of my Voyage to *Egypt*, he obferved that it appeared to him, as well as to the *Turks*, a very whimfical Thing, that Men fhould with fuch Pain and Hazard to themfelves, make fuch long Journies purely to look at the Ruins of ancient Structures, and to carry home a few Medals, and fuch like Curiofities. I took a great deal of Pains to remove this Notion out of his Head, tho' it was vifibly againft my Intereft, but to no manner of Purpofe; he remain'd firm in his firft Sentiments, which he fupported by fuch Arguments as thefe. That Life was fhort and uncertain, and that therefore Men ought not to wafte it as Children fpend their Hours of Play in picking up Bits of Metal, and broken Pieces of painted Earth, meerly to look upon them. That the Neceffaries of Life were firft to be fought, then its Conveniencies; and thefe being obtained, it was more reafonable to fit down and enjoy them than to run up and down the World hunting for Baubles. That there were many ufeful Arts and Sciences highly profitable to the human Species ftill unperfected, which therefore he thought deferved our Attention much more than thefe Matters of Curiofity, which he faid muft have very little in them becaufe he could not underftand them; whereas he readily comprehended the Ufe and Service of other Things.

But when he was informed that I fent all my Collections to a Correfpondent in *Italy*, who difpofed of them in feveral Parts of *Europe*, he underftood this to be highly reafonable. For, faid he, whatever Men will

buy

buy is worth the buying for them. He gave me. a great many Curiofities, and procured me others at very fmall Prices, taking no more of me than the Trifles with which he prefented Thofe who brought them to him, and who were glad, by this or any other Method, to recommend themfelves to his Protection.

IT happened, that as I vifited him one Day, and he was fhewing me feveral Things that he received from the upper *Egypt*, I took Notice of three Emeralds, fmall indeed, but of a Hardnefs and Beauty inexpreffible, and far fuperior to any thing I had ever feen. I make no queftion but they were placed on purpofe for me to look upon them, for as foon as I took them in my Hand, and began to confider them, *Haffan* fixed his Eyes full upon me, and did not withdraw them 'till I laid down the Stones. You *Franks*, faid he, upbraid the *Turks* with Avarice, and yet you can fee nothing valuable yourfelves but prefently it takes up all your Thoughts. Tell me, what would you think of a Country where thefe were to be had in Plenty? I fhould think my felf, faid I, very happy in the Difcovery of it, provided too many of them were not brought from thence. Well, replied *Haffan*, I will think of it, and fome time or other, perhaps, I may talk to you further on this Subject. That fome time or other, faid I, muft not be far diftant, fince within a very few Days I intend to fet out for *Cairo*. Well, faid he, I fhall fee you there, and it will better ferve our Purpofes to difcourfe of that Matter there than here. I would gladly have renewed the Converfation, but was afraid it might make him uneafy, and therefore I readily turned our Difcourfe to another Subject.

HE

He had often asked me about the Aftrologers in *Europe*, and on my telling him that they were a Race of Cheats, and were only able to impofe upon the Vulgar, he feemed amazed, and immediately enquired how it came to pafs, that fuch as were fo well acquainted with the Motions of the heavenly Bodies, as the *European* Doctors were, fhould yet know fo little of this Art. I then told him plainly my Sentiments, that there was really nothing folid in this Art, and that notwithftanding the Prepoffeffion of the *Turks* and *Perfians* in its Favour, it was, and had been always rather a Species of Villainy than a Service. I never faw *Haffan* difturbed or angry upon any Occafion but this, I had no fooner done fpeaking, than looking upon me with an Air of Difdain and Contempt, *Chriftian* faid he, I thought thou hadft been wifer, but I find there are Men every where, who believe juft what they receive from their Priefts ; I know Aftrology is againft thy Law, and therefore thou contemneft it. In order to appeafe him, I affured him that was not the Cafe, for that in *Europe*, the far greater Part of the People were ftrongly prejudiced in Favour of Aftrology, Why then faid he, art thou an Infidel ? Doft thou prefume to fet thy own Wifdom above that part of the World and this ? With much ado I brought him to hear my Arguments againft the Solidity of this Art ; but they made no manner of Impreffion on him, he would needs have it, that the disbelief of Aftrology was a kind of Atheifm, and in Effect denying the Providence of God. This Difcourfe had like to have been fatal to me, for it feems, Aftrology was his favourite Study, and whenever he had any leifure Moments, this and Chemiftry were his only

Care ;

Care; but as yet he concealed his Affection to and Skill in these Arts from me, as from a Person full of Infidelity.

In Order to regain his good Opinion, I bethought myself of enquiring whether he had never heard of *Geomancy*, and upon explaining what I meant, he was mightily surprized, not conceiving that this sort of Divination had ever been practised in *Europe*. But when I assured him it had, and that several Books had been written upon it, which however were scarce, and very secretly preserved for fear of the *Inquisition*, he seemed mightily pleased, telling me he would give a 100 *Sequins* for a good Manuscript on this Subject in *Italian*; I promised him to write to my Correspondent, tho' I had previously settled the Matter in my own Head, having accidentally among my Books, the Treatise written by Dr. *Flood* on that delusive Art, printed at *Venice*, which I resolved to translate into *Italian* for his Use, tho' not without some Reluctance. I could not finish it before the Time came in which we were to set out for *Cairo*. When therefore I took my Leave of him, I told him that I had sent Instructions to *Alexandria* to dispatch the Book I had writ for after me, when it should arrive, to *Cairo*. He thanked me, seemed mightily pleased, gave me Instructions how to find his House, and a Letter for an *Aga* of the *Janissaries*.

In the beginning of the Month of *August*, we embarked at *Rosetta*, having hired a Boat to carry us and our Things, and a *Janisary* to attend us. As we treated this Man with more than ordinary Generosity, he was on his Side very kind to us, and readily went ashore
with

with us, when and where we pleafed. All the Banks
of the *Nile* up which we navigated, were covered with
Villages fo thick, that it looks almoft like a continued
Town, and as I have been informed, the Heart of the
Delta is as thoroughly inhabited, there being a multitude of Canals, which ferve not only to pafs from one
Place to another, but which alfo unite the two great
Branches of the *Nile*, particularly one which is greater
than the reft, called the Canal of *Rofetta*, whereby one
croffes the *Delta* into the other Branch of the *Nile*,
and then fall eafily down it to *Damietta*.

At *Fezzara*, where we made fome Inquiry after Curiofities, the People brought us fome broken Stones, and
counterfeit Idols, which we refufed to buy; our *Janiffary* thereupon told us, that he would carry us to a
Place where lately a great many of thefe Things had
been difcovered, and to which as yet no *European* had
come. We readily accepted his Offer, and by his Direction the Mafter of the Veffel turned out of the *Nile*
into a large Canal on the left, paffing between two great
Villages; when we had failed up this Canal about 20
Miles, the *Janiffary* went afhore with us, and after walking 3 or 4 Miles, he brought us to a Place called *Balken*,
which as he told us ftood in the Centre of the *Delta*, at
equal Diftance from *Rofetta*, *Damietta*, and *Cairo*.
Here we firft repofed ourfelves at the Houfe of another
Janiffary, and afterwards went with our Conductor,
and 3 or 4 other People, to a Place without the Town,
where afcending a little Eminence, we faw a fort of
Well, into which we were all let down; it was paved
with *Roman* Brick, and appeared to have been antiently
a very elegant Structure; but thefe new Difcoverers had
broke

broke to Pieces the Wall and Pavement, and besides it was so damp, that it was with great Difficulty we could keep the Lights which we carried down with us from going out. Mr. *Perez* therefore concluding we should make no great Discoveries, declined staying any longer. In our Return to *Balken*, we bought of those who went with us, near 100 Medals of different Sizes, and different Metals, that is of Silver and Brass, of most of the *Roman* Emperors, from *Augustius* to *Valerian*; and of several Empresses, as also some fine Pieces of *Cornelian*, and an *Amethist*, on which was engraven the Head of the Empress *Agrippina*. The whole did not cost us 20 *Piasters*. The next Day we returned into the *Nile*, and continued our Voyage to *Cairo*, without meeting with any Thing remarkable.

In ten Days after our Arrival in this City, where we received all imaginable Civilities from the *Aga*, to whom I was directed, my Patron *Hassan* himself arrived, and sent *Vasquez* immediately to find me out, and to conduct me to him. The first Thing he asked for was his Book; I told him I expected it every Day, he then fell to other Things, and at last asked me if I knew nothing of the great Art, by which I found he meant Transmutation. I told him ingenuously that I did not, but that I had a Memoir upon that Subject, which was held very curious by those who were well versed in Chemistry. He desired to see it, and I accordingly carried it to him the next Time I went to see him. It was the Paper I received from my good Friend Mr. *Pucci*, and as *Hassan* understood *Italian* very well, he read it with great Facility, and seemed to be charmed with it. When he had considered it a while, do you

believe

believe my Friend, faid he, it is poffible to make this Powder? I told him, I could not tell, but that I had heard fome very intelligent Perfons affirm that it was. You begin faid he, to be fomewhat lefs of an Infidel than you were, but I will tell you what will perhaps make you give ftill more Credit to this Opinion.

My Uncle was acquainted with a *Frank* who had fome of this Powder, tho' as he faid, he knew not how to make it. The Method in which he ufed it was this, he took an equal Quantity of Gold Duft, and of fine Silver, he melted firft the one, and having put into it a little of his Powder, he caufed the other to be melted, and pour'd in alfo; when it was taken out, the whole Mafs was Gold finer then any of your Coin. The Quantity he had of this Powder was but fmall, and when he died, which was at *Tunis*, he defired a Perfon in whom he confided, to carry it to my Uncle, which accordingly he did, and he actually performed the fame Experiment therewith, as the *Frank* had formerly done. I did not fhew any Signs of disbelief, tho' I was exceedingly furprized to find fuch Notions fpread into thefe Countries; tho' I have been fince well informed, that there are abundance of Alchymifts in *Perfia*, and *Grand Tartary*, and above all in *China*, where it is common for Men to fpend great real Eftates in the Purfuit of thefe imaginary Treafures.

By the Way I muft take Notice, that it is not impoffible that the Story told by *Haffan* might be true, and yet that Powder is far from being the Philofopher's *Arcanum*; becaufe it is certain, that a Powder capable of fuch a Tranfmutation, hath been, and may be made. As to the Method of projecting, by putting equal quan-

tities

tities of Gold and fine Silver, it was in all likelihood no more than an Artifice, to give the greater Weight and Solemnity to the Experiment; the Essence of which consisted in this. Some *Chemists* in *Germany* have found out a Method of concreting Gold, that is, of throwing off its grosser Parts, and retaining only the Essence of the Metal. We will suppose, that out of 2 Ounces of Gold, 10 Grains of this *Semen* could be extracted; this then being put into a Crucible, wherein 2 Ounces of fine Silver melted were before, would produce 2 Ounces of Gold, which with some sort of Propriety might be stiled a *Transmutation*. But then this is an introductory Experiment only; for it is plain, that the Transmutation is so far from being beneficial, that there is a considerable Loss thereupon, first in working upon the Gold, and secondly, of the whole Price of the Silver wrought upon. Yet am I persuaded, that it is a Powder of this Nature which hath given the greatest Reputation to *Alchymy*, a Study which so intoxicates the Head of those who profess it, that they take those for their Enemies who endeavour to undeceive them; this together with an Enthusiastick Opinion, that this kind of Knowledge is bestowed by GOD, and that *Faith quoad hoc*, is the most certain Means of obtaining it, keeps them everlastingly chain'd to the Furnace, till they have nothing left where with to make it smoak.

HASSAN's great Foible was his Love of the *occult Sciences*, of which I had the strongest Proof, when I presented him the *Treatise* on *Geomancy*, which I had translated into *Italian*, and illustrated with Notes, taken from the Works of *Cornelius Agrippa*, and Mr. *John Heydon*. He received it as a new *Revelation*, he studied

it

it intenfely, and in a fhort Time practifed it exactly, preferring it greatly to the Method he had before ufed, and afluring me, that he would tranflate it into *Arabick,* which was far from giving me any Satisfaction, fince I could not help thinking, that I had already committed a very great Fault, in thus condefcending for the Sake of temporal Views, to further and fupport a fuperftitious Practice, which I knew to be fuch, and in myfelf condemned and defpifed. However I was conftrained to conceal my Thoughts before *Haffan,* who like all Bigots, held it Impiety to queftion or fufpect the Certainty of his darling *Sciences ;* and I confefs I did it the rather, becaufe I faw myfelf now perfectly in his good Graces, and began to hope, that I fhould reap confiderable Effects there from.

A s the Weather permitted, and Occafion offered, I went with Mr. *Perez* to vifit all the Curiofities, not only in the Neighbourhood of *Cairo,* but at a confiderable Diftance, and we were fo lucky as to fall on a Method of buying Rarities, which ftood us in great ftead ; it was this, we conftantly refufed to buy any Thing of a Perfon who had attempted to impofe upon us, and we paid more generoufly than the *Franks* ufually do, for fuch Things as were brought us in a fair Way, and of thefe we had as many, or rather more Offers than we well knew how to comply with. For all thefe Things Mr. *Perez* and I traded out of the joint Stock ; but as to other Things, efpecially precious Stones, we made fuch Purchafes as we thought fit at our proper Expence, and at our proper Rifque. Mr. *Perez* was extremely well fitted for the Bufinefs he had undertaken; he had as great a Propenfity to the occult Sciences

ences as any *Arabian* or *Turk* of them all, and under-stood them much better. This was fufficient to re-commend him, fo that except going now and then to the *French* Confuls, and a *Venetian* Merchant's, he was continually taken up with thefe Virtuofi. Amongft thefe there was one *Solomon Effendi*, who paffed for the moft skilful Aftrologer in *Cairo* ; he even pretended to have a Power of compelling the Spirits of Perfons depart-ed to appear before him, and anfwer in any Language the Queftions he propofed to them ; he likewife boafted of mighty Secrets in Chemiftry, which for a while took up Mr. *Perez*'s Attention ; but at length he was convinced that he was a meer Pretender, and at the Bottom knew little or nothing except how to amufe the People, and by a cunning Train of Queftions to draw from them-felves thofe Anfwers they expected from him. He like-wife had fome Acquaintance with a *Polifh* Renegade, whofe Name was *Muftapha*, who was become an *Aga* of the *Janiffaries*, and very rich, and this by an Acci-dent fingular enough to deferve mention.

HIMSELF and his Sifter were carried away by the *Tartars*, when they were about feven Years of Age, and were fold at *Conftantinople* ; the Girl growing up prov'd an exquifite Beauty, and falling by Purchafe into the Hands of the Captain Bafhaw, he became fo much in Love with her, that he preferr'd her to all the Women he had. It fo happened, that on the Return of the Bafhaw from making a Tour in the *Archepelago*, a black Eunuch who was with him, acquainted the *Polifh* Lady that he had feen among the Slaves who rowed the Gal-ly, one perfectly like her, and much of the fame Age. This put her upon recollecting, and a Day or two

R

after-

afterwards fhe told the Eunuch that fhe remembered when fhe was taken out of her own Country, her Brother was taken with her, and that becaufe he lay down, and would not follow the *Tartar*, he nipped a Piece out of his Ear. The black Eunuch taking Occafion to find out the Slave he had mentioned, examin'd him, and found in his left Ear the Mark. The Captain Bafhaw thereupon immediately fet him at Liberty, and having perfwaded him to turn *Turk*, and recommended him to his Brother, who was then a *Sanjack* in *Egypt* ; he by Degrees, and frequent Demonftrations of an extraordinary Valour, was raifed to this Poft, in which however he was not beloved, by reafon of his exactnefs in Point of Difcipline ; he was a Man of good Senfe, tho' of no Learning, mightily addicted to Aftrology, and furioufly zealous for the Religion which he had embraced, whether thro' Ignorance or Policy, I am not able to determine.

SOME Times we went attended by a *Janiffary* to vifit the *Monks*, if I may be allowed to call them fo, who live in the Skirts of *Cairo*, and are indeed the moft learned of any *Mohammedans*. Thefe by the *Arabians* are called *Dervifes*, concerning whom our Travellers fall frequently into Miftakes, by confounding them with the *Santons*, from whom in reality they differ only as much as a wife Man does from a Fool. In the Road which leads to *Suez*, there is a Monaftery, wherein live between 30 and 40 of thefe *Monks*, who fpend all their Time in Prayer, in Study, or in manual Labour, when they go abroad they walk two and two, but then they generally feek out folitary Places, and they feldom enter the Cities or any of the Villages about them.
They

They are remarkably kind to, and fond of the Converfation of *Franks*, efpecially fuch as have Learning, and
are not Priefts. With thefe they converfe freely on all
Subjects, particularly Religion, of which they think as
freely as any People in the World. All their Difcourfes
are either of Divinity or Philofophy; fometimes they
difpute concerning the Immortality of the Soul, at others
of the apparent Juftice of Providence, moft of them have
much higher Ideas of JESUS CHRIST, than are common
amongft the *Turks*; and in general thefe Men greatly de-
teft that Impurity of Manners which prevails fo much
among thofe of their Religion. In their own Conduct
they are moft exemplary, meek, pious, charitable, and
continually ready to do any good Office that is defired of
them.

As to the *Santons* again, they are a fort of Hermits
living fingly in Caves or Woods, and coming frequently enough like Beafts out of their Dens to run through
Villages and Cities. They are moft of them really, or
in Shew at leaft, dementated, which amongft the *Turks*
is a ftrong Sign of Sanctity. They enter what Houfes
they pleafe, feat themfelves without Ceremony, fay
what they will, eat and drink whatever they can lay
Hands on; and all this is taken in good Part. They
carry their Brutality fo far as to lay hold of Women, and
deflour them in the open Streets, but above all, they
diftinguifh themfelves by a furious Hatred to Chriftians,
whom they will fometimes wound or kill in publick
Places, and this with Impunity; fo that it is always a
prudential Maxim to keep out of thefe Fellows Way.

ONE need not wonder fo much at this Superftition
among the *Turks*, if one recollects that the fame Hu-

mour

mour prevailed among the ancient *Greeks*, who fancied that there was fomething of Divinity in the Anfwers given by Idiots. To fay the Truth, almoft all the Notions of Divination amongft the Ancients or Moderns are as whimfical as this, and as much irreconcileable to good Senfe; however, in this Cafe, let us try to reconcile it. A Man quits that Guide God has given him, his Reafon, and what then? Why he liftens to thofe who have not the Ufe of Reafon. Methinks the Change is natural enough; perhaps it would appear more fo if we could compare enough of thefe Predictions with their Events. In *Europe* a Man who lofes his Senfes is fent to a Prifon, in *Afia* and *Africk*, he paffes for a Saint; thefe are certainly Extremes. In *Europe* we degrade human Nature by our treating Madmen like Beafts; in *Afia* and *Africk* Men degrade themfelves into Beafts by fuffering themfelves to be mal-treated by thofe who are no longer on a Par with them. None of thefe Evils could poffibly happen if we liftened to the Dictates of Nature, which never incline us either to injure others, or to fubmit tamely to Injuries which it is in our own Power to prevent.

ABOUT the Middle of the Month of *March* we received from *Alexandria*, by Means of a Veffel arrived there from *Legborn*, a Packet from Mr. *Fetherftone*, it contained a Letter from him to Mr. *Perez*, another directed to us both, and a third addreffed to me. The firft, I fuppofe, related to the private Affairs of my Companion, the fecond brought an Account of the Produce of what we had configned to him, with two Memoirs enclofed, one concerning the Value of Mummies, the other relating to the Choice of Medals. Mr. *Fetherftone*
observed,

obferved, that the Humour of forming Cabinets, and making great Collections of Curiofities of all Sorts encreafed daily not only in *Italy*, but in *France*, and in the *North* ; fo that provided they were judicioufly collected, all Sorts of Rarities might, by a prudent Management, be difpofed of to a greater Profit than any Merchandize whatfoever. In my Letter was enclofed fome Remarks on the Value of colour'd Stones, wherein, amongft other Things, my Friend noted, that the moft judicious Perfons were at a Lofs as to the Ground of that Diftinction, which had hitherto been made between oriental and occidental Emeralds, there being a great Doubt whether there were in truth any oriental Stones of that Sort. That, however, it was held reafonable to preferve the Diftinction, becaufe it was evidently founded in Nature, there being one Kind of Emerald harder, brighter, and clearer, than thofe commonly brought from the *Weft-Indies* ; which kind was yet in great Efteem, though the other, by being become common, were much funk in their Value. At the fame time we received certain *European* Goods, fome Toys, and other Curiofities.

AMONG thefe was a Gold Watch made at *London*, which ftruck the Hour and half Hour ; this I carried to my Patron *Haffan*, who was extremely pleafed with it, and who for it and the Manufcript of *Geomancy* gave me the three fmall Emeralds I fpoke of, which were worth 250 Sequins, or better. As foon as an Opportunity offered, I fent two of thefe to Mr. *Fetherftone*, affuring him, that they were of that kind which were ftiled oriental. The next Time I went to vifit *Haffan*, who was juft returned from *Rofetta*, he opened to me

the

the Defign he hàd formed when I had firft Admittance to him, and of which, though I did not apprehend them, he had given me frequent Hints fince. At this Vifit he took Notice to me of the infatiate Avarice of the *Turks*, and of their expecting annually greater and greater Prefents for the Favours he received from them, which in the End, he faid, would make it impoffible for him to continue longer in *Egypt*. He fpoke next of the Difficulty of retiring from thence without leaving the beft Part of his Effects behind him ; and at laft, as if he had been weary of this Difcourfe, and intended to have talked of fomewhat elfe, he asked me what I thought of the Emeralds I had had of him, and whether larger ones of like Beauty were not valuable in *Europe* ; I told him they were, but that they were not eafily to be had. I know it, reply'd he, and I know both what they are worth and how to difpofe of them, and if I knew a Man whom I could truft, perhaps I would fay that I know where to find them. I then began to apprehend what it was he aimed at. I told him that I did not doubt, that after having fo long and fo happily managed fo extraordinary a Commerce, he knew many valuable Secrets, and alfo a great many Perfons to whom they might be confided. You are miftaken, my Friend, faid he, I fcarce know any of the former, and for the latter I know none. Our *Arabs* and *Moors* know perfectly well their own Affairs, and how to manage them ; there are alfo among them Men of great Probity ; but, with refpect to the Bufinefs I would have performed, there are none of them fit to be employed. There is fhortly a Caravan to fet out for *Syria*. Under pretence of fending certain Commodities therewith, I can fend fome of my People
with

with fix or eight Camels laden with Money, if you will
go with them to *Suez*, where, on prefenting a Letter
which I will give you to an *Arab* Chief, who lives not
far from thence, he will fhew you fome of thefe Stones,
and you will, no doubt, make the beft Bargain for me
you can.   I confent alfo that you fhall employ as much
Money of your own as you pleafe in the fame Way.   I
immediately accepted this Propofal, without well weigh-
ing the Confequences of trufting my felf alone with the
Dependants of a *Moor*, People with whom no *Frank*
in *Cairo* would have ventured himfelf in the Defart.
But Avarice, like all other Paffions, fo choaks up the
Paffages of the Underftanding, that no Thoughts which
wear not its Livery can have Entrance.

WHEN I had once taken this Refolution, I endeavoured as ftudioufly to conceal the Motives thereto from
Mr. *Perez* and our Servant, as if they had been my
Enemies, and why? becaufe I knew them too well to
believe they would ever fuffer me to expofe my felf to fo
imminent a Danger.   I provided, therefore, privately,
two hundred Sequins in Gold ; and having informed Mr.
Perez that I had a Mind to travel to *Suez*, he at firft
oppofed it, but when he faw I continued firm in my Refolution, he yielded to it, and affifted me in providing
for my Journey.   The Reafons I offered to him were,
that I had heard many valuable Commodities were to be
bought there ; that I was in hopes of picking up Curiofities which might efcape us in this Part of *Egypt*, and
that I had an earneft Defire to look upon the Red Sea.
While I waited for the Departure of the Caravan, my
Thoughts were fo much difturbed with the Ideas of this

R 4   Journey,

Journey, that I found it very difficult to sleep, and was thereby much incommoded.

Of this I one Day complained to *Hassan*, who immediately rallied me thereupon, as a Physician of small Experience, or at least as one who did not care to practise much upon my self. He then asked me if I had not yet learned the *Turkish* Method of calming the Mind. I thought at first he meant Opium, or some other Drug of that Sort; but he presently call'd for a young Man, and, as soon as he appeared, ordered him to read where he left off the Night before. The Lad took up a Book, and did as he was directed; *Hassan* explaining to me every Period. When the Boy had done reading, *Hassan* raised several Questions on the Story we had heard; and perceiving that my Humour was quite changed, You see, said he, my Friend, that we are not such Barbarians as many of the *Franks* believe us. It is indeed the worst Property your People have that they are extremely vain and conceited, wedded to their own Customs, and yet provoked to see others tenacious of theirs. I know that many *Franks* laugh at our Histories, and at this Method of soothing our Cares; yet I conceive that it is as natural and as innocent as drinking great Quantities of Wine, or Gaming, which are your common Diversions. And though our Histories differ much, as I am informed, from yours, yet that is no Reason that they should be either fabulous or foolish. Our Manners have always differed, as also our Methods of conducting War and Peace, our Learning and our Pleasures. Why then should our Histories be like yours? Or why should they be despised for being unlike them? Is not this a Mark of

your

your Vanity and Pride, rather than of your Knowledge or Politeneſs ? I could not help admitting that he had Reaſon for what he ſaid ; and I do confeſs that there is to me nothing more ſtrange, than that our Writers of Travels ſhould cenſure the *Turks* for their Inclination to hear Tales and Stories read to them at their Leiſure Moments, when at the ſame time if this very Inclination did not prevail among Chriſtians, their Books could not be read at all. How eaſily do we ſee Motes in others Eyes without minding the Beams in our own.

THE Book which the Servant of *Haſſan* read had for its Title *Tarik-al-abbas*, i. e. The Hiſtory of the *Abaſſides.* The Story that he read was this. The famous *Caliph al-Mamon* had for his Uncle one *Ibrahim*, the Son by the Mother's Side, of a black Slave, a Man of a dusky Countenance, a little unweildy, but of great Parts, generous, good-humoured, a great Lover of Muſic, and one who had an excellent Voice. It ſo happened that the *Caliph*, by a ſingular Strain of Juſtice, which probably never enter'd the Head of any Prince but himſelf, declared for his Succeſſor the eldeſt of the Family of *Ali*, conceiving him to have a juſt Right to the Throne ; and this he did in Prejudice to his own Children, and all his Relations. The Family of *Abbas* were not in the Humour of doing Juſtice at the Expence of that great Power which they had got into their Hands. They therefore took Advantage of a Meeting they had at *Bagdat*, and having ſolemnly depoſed *Al-Mamon*, elevated *Ibrahim* his Uncle to the *Caliphat.* This Prince reigned upwards of two Years with great Mildneſs, and much Applauſe ; at the end of that Space *Al-Mamon* came at the Head of a great Army to beſiege *Bagdat.* *Ibrahim* finding

finding himfelf two weak to refift his Nephew, abdica-
ted the Government, and for fome Time hid himfelf
amongft his Friends ; but the *Caliph* having given ftrict
Orders to fearch for him, and having promifed a vaft
Reward to the Perfon who fhould difcover him, he was
at laft taken, and delivered to *Al-Mamon.* As foon as
the *Caliph* knew that his Uncle was taken, he fent for
Achmet, his Grand Vizir, and afked him what he fhould
do with him. *Father of the Faithful*, anfwered the Minifter, *if thou fhouldft put him to Death, thou wouldft
therein follow the Example of many great Princes ; but if
thou fhouldft pardon him, and take him into Favour, thou
wilt leave thy Example to all that are to follow thee.* The
Caliph fmiled, *I had already determined*, faid he, *to receive him not as the Ufurper of my Throne, but as the
Brother of my Father* ; having faid this, he ordered *Ibrahim* to be admitted, and having embraced him cordially,
they fupped together that Night.

WHEN the Repaft was finifhed, *Uncle*, faid the Caliph, *one good Turn deferves another ; I have freely pardoned you, tell me then frankly the moft extraordinary
Adventure that hath befallen you during the Time you hid
yourfelf.* With all my Heart, faid *Ibrahim.* You muft
know that I made it a Rule with me to lye but one
Night in one Place, and the Time at which I chofe to
retire from my Lodgings was about Noon, when there
are but few People in the Streets. One Day when I
had thus fallied out, and was looking for a frefh Place of
Refuge, I found myfelf over-againft a Houfe, the Shop
of which was fhut up, and the Mafter was ftanding at
the Door, a Man of a dusky Complexion, flat Nofe,
fat, and not unlike myfelf. I afked him if it was not

poffible

poffible for me to repofe my felf a little in his Houfe, he anfwered me very civilly in the affirmative, conducted me to an Apartment which lay quite behind, and having defired me to make my felf perfectly eafy, fhot through the Houfe out of the Door, and locked it behind him. I confefs his Conduct made a greater Impreffion upon me than his Advice. I took it for granted he was gone to call the Guards, and I fpent the Moments very reftlefsly 'till his Return. It was not long before he came back loaded with Victuals, and attended by a Man who brought a Bed, Coverlid, and other Things. I thought, faid the Man, that it was not proper to ferve you with what others had ufed, and therefore have bought every Thing new for you ; I get my Living as a *Barber*, but I endeavour to live like a good Man, therefore fet your Mind at Reft, and when you find you have a Stomach let us eat together and be merry. The Behaviour of the Man correfponded fo exactly with his Language, that I could not help giving Credit to him, and therefore as foon as I had compofed myfelf a little we fpread the Table, and made a very hearty Meal. While I was eating, the *Barber* asked me if I did not fome times drink Wine, I told him I did, and he immediately produced fome as good as could be wifhed. When we had finifhed our Repaft, my Hoft entreated me to grant him one Favour, I told him I would with all my Heart, then prefenting me a Lute, this faid he, is a good Inftrument, but to render its Harmony compleat, it fhould be accompanied by a Voice like yours. This furprized me exceedingly, and I could not help asking, how he came to imagine that I had fo good a Voice? My Lord faid he, you cannot be concealed, I know that

you

you are *Ibrahim,* the Uncle of our *Caliph,* and that he has promised 100,000 Pieces of Silver for discovering where you are. There needed no more than this, I instantly took the Lute, and accompanied it with my Voice. The *Barber* was mightily pleased, and when I had done singing, offered to sing himself if I would accompany his Voice with the Lute, to which I readily yielding he performed with incredible Sweetness, and I asked with Astonishment where he had learned those Airs, but he easily satisfied me, by informing me that he had lived for some Years with *Moussouli,* the most excellent Musician of our Age.

THE next Day, when at my usual Time I was about to depart, I offered my Landlord a Purse of Gold as a Reward for his Kindness and Fidelity, but he refused it with an Air of Anger and Disdain. *How odd, my Lord said he, is your Behaviour, you see I have done every Thing in my Power to discharge what the Laws of Hospitality require, and you would rob me of the Fruits of all my Pains, by treating me as if I kept an Inn.* This said *Ibrahim* was the most extraordinary Event which befel me while I suffered under your Displeasure. The *Caliph* was extreamly pleased with this Recital, and lived thence forward with his Uncle, in the strictest Friendship to the Day of his Death, and left him as a Counsellor to his Successor.

FROM this Time forward I took the Advice of my Patron, and whenever I found myself uneasy and incapable of Repose, I instantly had Recourse to one of the many Books of entertaining Narrations which are to be met with in this Country, most of the Oriental Histories being indeed no other. There are many in *Arabick,*

but

but the beſt of theſe ſort of Writings are in the *Perſian*
Language. This, if I may be allowed the Phraſe, is the
Court Language of the Eaſt, as the *Arabick* is the learned, ſo that we may compare the former to the *French*,
and the latter to the *Latin*, without a tolerable Underſtanding of both which, there is no paſſing for an able
Man. In *Egypt*, ſuch as apply themſelves to Study,
take Care firſt to acquire the *Arabick*, then the *Perſian*,
and laſtly the *Turkiſh* Language in Perfection ; then
they proceed to the Sciences, of which they have Sy-
ſtems as regular, their Method of teaching conſidered,
as ours. Learning is however very expenſive, becauſe
they have nothing but Manuſcripts, from which they
will hardly be beaten by any Reaſons that we can offer
them, ſince tranſcribing Books is a great Trade, employs many Hands, and is the firſt Reward of Learning,
by producing to a diligent Perſon, and a good Scribe, a
Livelihood on the Spot. Above all I think their Dictio-
naries are dear, the beſt and moſt comprehenſive cannot
be bought under 100 *Piaſters*, not but ſometimes Manuſcripts are to met with pretty cheap. Many of the
Learned boaſt of their Secrets in Phyſick and Chemiſtry, but if they have any, they are very tenacious of
them, and they frequently prove but Trifles when they
are known. I bought three Secrets for fixing Mercury,
two of them were abſolutely falſe, and the third fala-
cious ; for after three Weeks, the Mercury became fluid
again by the meer Operation of the Air. As ſoon as I
was acquainted with *Haſſan* ſo far as to converſe with
him about theſe Things, I received from him a fourth
Method of performing the ſame Thing, *viz.* by boyl-
ing Mercury in the Juice of the Herb *Lunaria*, called

by

by the *Greeks Sellenitis* ; but I never made the Experiment, becaufe I have Reafon to think, that this Notion is built on the Doctrine of Signatures, which I confefs I do not much efteem, becaufe I fcarce comprehend it at all; and I am perfwaded, that in moft of the Inftances which are produced to favour it, thofe who produce them are miftaken ; but enough of this.

In the beginning of the Month of *April*, the Caravan fet out, and on the 3d Day of the fame Month I departed from *Cairo*, attended by two *Arabs*, who were privately recommended to me by *Haffan*. Mr. *Perez*, two *Italian* and three *French* Merchants, with *Antonio*, came to fee me on my Way, and I obferved, that Mr. *Perez* when he took Leave of me, was under an extraordinary Concern. As for poor *Antonio*, he was all in Tears. All that Day we travelled through a fandy Plain, every Grain of which feemed to be perfect Cryftal ; fo that the Reflection of the Light from thence exceedingly hurt my Eyes. In the Evening we overtook fix Camels, with feveral *Arabs* who belonged to them, and a Man, who immediately faluted me, told me his Name was *Morat*, and that he was my Slave. At firft I did not underftand him, but he foon let me know that he belonged to my Patron *Haffan*, and that the Lading of thefe Camels were to be difpofed of by me, according to a Letter of Inftructions which he delivered to me.

We flept together under a Tent, but found the Night exceffively cool. Our Supper was very light, confifting only of Dates, and dried Fruits. As for the *Arabs* they mixed fome Water and Flour, and having kneaded it into a Pafte, left it on a Cloth to heave
while

while they lighted a Fire, then throwing it on the Embers, and turning it often, at laſt they took it off half baked, kneaded it again in Salt and Oyl, and breaking it into little Pieces, eat it as comfortably and as merrily as if it had been the fineſt Proviſion in the World. The *Moor* entertained me the firſt part of the Night with many ſingular Stories of the Riches of *Egypt* which he ſaid were buried in all thoſe Vaults, and under all the Needles, about which the *Franks* were ſo curious ; he alſo apprehended that our copying Inſcriptions was meerly with a View to diſcover the Contents of the Places from whence they were taken. He likewiſe ſeriouſly aſſured me that our Friend *Haſſan* had a Book containing an Inventory of all the hidden Treaſures in *Egypt*, with Copies of the *Taliſmans* by which they were ſecured, and an Account of the manner by which their Force might be diſſolved. I confeſs at this Time I thought all he ſaid the Effects of pure Imagination, but I have been ſince informed, that there is in reality a Book of this ſort, and that ſome Copies have been carried into *Europe*.

THE fourth of *April* we continued our Journey ſlowly, pleaſantly, and with great Unanimity amongſt ourſelves, for I went into all the Folly of the *Arabs*, and liſtened attentively to every Thing they told me, as if I had regarded all their Sayings as the moſt authentick Oracles. We ſlept that Night on a little Slip of Land, on which there was Graſs, and where a few Sheep were feeding. I taſted that Graſs out of Curioſity, and found it brackiſh ; I bought one of the Sheep and gave it to the *Arabs*, who dreſſed it after their manner, I eat of it, and found it very good. Upon cutting up a

Turf

Turf it appeared that the Earth was wonderfully charg'd with Nitre, I tafted that too, but excepting its coldnefs, it left no relifh on the Palate at all.

THE fifth, we jogg'd on foberly as before, my *Arabs* advifing me to walk fometimes by the Side of the Camels, which change of Pofture refrefhed me exceedingly. We dined in a Valley, and as I apprehended, fhould have fupp'd and lain in one; but either I miftook them, or our Guides themfelves were miftaken, for we were obliged to fleep in the Plain, and I found the Air very nipping, tho' the Day had been hot. We eat at Night fome Salad, which we pick'd by the Way, and found it very cool and refrefhing.

THE fixth, we began to travel early, and three Hours before Noon came to the Foot of the Mountains. They make a ftrange Figure, many of them being hollow, as if Channels of Water had run under them, and to fay the Truth, the Valleys we met with feemed to have been formerly the Beds of little Brooks. In the Afternoon we defcended again into a great Plain, which extends quite to the *Red Sea*.

THE feventh, we arofe early, and travelled very hard, in order to be at our Journey's End that Evening, which we with much Difficulty effected; but as it was late in the Evening before we came in fight of *Suez*, and as the *Arabs* never enter Towns, I chofe to remain with them under their Tents, with which they were mightily pleafed; for they efteem nothing fo much as a ready Conformity to their Cuftoms.

THE next Day I went with my *Moor* to *Suez*, who conducted me to the Houfe of a Perfon who correfponded with *Haſſan*, and who received us with all imaginable

ble

ble Kindnefs and Refpect, and difpatched, as foon as we
arrived, his Son to carry Advice to the *Bey* of our Arrival.   We remained with this Man two Days, in which
Space I eafily took a View of the Town or Port of
Suez, than which nothing can be conceived more contemptible in its appearance, or of higher Confequence in
its felf.   It ftands about a Mile from the Sea without
Fortifications, and with a very indifferent Garrifon.
There were at this Time three Ships there one *Turkifh*,
one *Arabian*, and one *Indian* Veffel, a heavy, clumfy,
ill built Thing, fit only for thofe Seas, where upon the
leaft Squal of Wind they run into Port, and are fometimes fix Months in making a Voyage of a Week.
Here are however vaft Magazines of rich Goods, and it
is wonderful that this Port being in the Hands of a Po-
tentate who loves Money fo well, is not made more
beneficial, tho' as Things ftand, he raifes a vaft Revenue from it. But what to me appears ftill more amazing
is the want of Attention among the Chriftian Traders ;
for nothing can be plainer than that the fettling a Factory here would be of prodigious Confequence, and
might in fome Meafure alter once again the Trade of
the *Indies*.   Land Carriage by Camels is very eafy and
cheap, and the Diftance between *Suez* and *Damietta* not
above 130 Miles ; fo that for ought I perceive, *Indian*
Commodities might be carried from thence to *Marfeilles*
in three Weeks, or a Month at fartheft.   I know very
well that there is much Difficulty in treating with the
Turks about altering old Cuftoms, but I know full as well
that there is no Cuftom they will not alter, for the
Sake of getting by it ; but this by the way, having in
another Place confidered this Matter more at large

S   with

with a View to the Enlargement of our *English* Commerce, which publick Ministers treat as Men of Quality do their Wives, with much outward Respect, and very little real Affection, often throwing away twice as much in their private Pleasures as would be necessary to fulfil all the Ends, which if it were not for Expence, they pretend they would make it their Glory to obtain, as if every *Mistress* had a Right to be profuse except the *Publick*.

THE *Turk* at whose House I was, had better Notions of Trade than are common to People of his Nation, which without question was the Reason that *Hassan* chose him for his Correspondent. He shewed me a great many curious Things, and amongst others a Drawer of small Pearl, which were very perfect, and were all bored ; and therefore he valued them at a high Rate, Pearls being grown scarce of late Years at *Suez*, tho' the grand Fishery for them is in the *Red-Sea*. He said the *Arabian* Ladies were passionately fond of them, and making Use of them in Embroideries, occasioned their bearing a much higher Price here than in *Europe*, where they were suddenly grown into disesteem. To say the Truth, I perceived plainly, that as to valuable Commodities which lay in little Room, they could not be bought to any great Advantage ; but then again, as to more bulky Wares, very large Profit might without doubt be made upon them. *Isouf Aga* had a very convenient House, tho' it made but a very mean Figure. In an outward Apartment there was a Fountain of Water, which in those Countries affords peculiar Pleasure to the Eye, at the same Time that it is of the greatest Use ; this Apartment was neatly paved and lined

with

with a kind of Mats chequer'd Green and Straw Colour. Behind it was the Apartment in which he received Company, it was fprinkled with fweet fcented Waters, and he was ferved with Coffee and Tobacco of a kind fuperior to any Thing I had ever tafted. His Coffee was roafted, ground and boyled in the Space of 7 or 8 Minutes; fo that it had an Oil upon it extreamly grateful to the Tafte, and comfortable to the Head. His Tobacco was made up into Rolls ftrongly twifted, fo mild and pleafant to the Tafte, that I thought fome peculiar Art had been made Ufe of in curing it; but he affured me, that it was the natural Flavour of the Leaf, which he faid grew in *Arabia*, but my *Moor* affirmed the contrary, and I believe he was in the right.

In Difcourfe the *Aga* acquainted me, that he had a young Son, whofe Head was much out of Order at the full and Change of the Moon. I defired to fee the Child, and after having examined him ftrictly, as to the Nature of his Complaints, I found Means by a Snuff to difcharge a great quantity of fætid Matter by the Nofe, whereby the Child was immediately relieved, and I gave the Father Directions how to proceed in Cafe the Diforder fhould return, together with fome Obfervations as to the Diet and Exercife of the Child, till fuch Time as his Conftitution was thoroughly fettled. In return the *Aga* made me a Prefent of feveral Curiofities, and of a quantity of Papers which had belonged to a *Frank* who died at his Houfe. He could not tell of what Nation he was, tho' by his Papers it fhould feem he was a *Frenchman*, by Profeffion he was a *Surgeon*, and had lived in *Ethiopia* upwards of 25 Years, from whence with fome Difficulty he had efcaped to

S 2 *Suez*

Suez, in hopes without queſtion, that from thence he might find a Way of returning into *Europe*. This Man on Account of his Profeſſion was admitted into the Houſe of the *Aga*, and remained there three Months, moſt of which Time he was on a declining Condition, and at length died with great compoſure of Mind. What Effects he had, which I could not find were very valuable, came into the Hands of his *Hoſt*, who not being able to make any Uſe of his Papers, laid hold of this Opportunity of obliging me, which he did very effectually, there being in them abundance of curious Obſervations, with which otherwiſe I could never have been acquainted.

THE Meſſenger he had diſpatched to the *Bey*, being returned with an Account of the Place where we might find him, and with an Order that we ſhould immediately attend him, it was agreed that the very next Day we ſhould ſet out. I would have been glad to have been exactly informed whither we were to go, or at leaſt how far, but the Meſſenger declined giving me any Anſwer to either of theſe Queſtions, only he told us in general, that he would conduct us as ſafe and as ſpeedily to the *Bey* as we could deſire.

ON the 10th of *April* in the Morning, we returned to our *Arabs*, and about nine o'Clock ſet out, our Guide being mounted on an *Arabian* Courſer, and all the reſt of our Train on Camels. We travelled all that Day towards the Mountains, and encamped in the Evening near the Foot of them. The next Day, about Noon, we reached them, and having marched very ſlowly through a narrow troubleſome Road, we paſſed the Evening near the Ruins of an ancient Edifice. I went accompanied

by

by our Guide, and by the Moor *Morat*, to take a View
of them. They were of confiderable Extent, and feemed to have confifted of a Square compofed of fmaller
Buildings in the fame Form with that in the Centre,
which was ftill pretty entire, and which was therefore
the chief Object of our Curiofity. It was built in the
Form of a Beehive, and might be about a hundred and
eighty Feet in Height. There was an Entry, but it
was quite choaked up with Sand, and we had not Time
to let the *Arabs* remove it, which otherwife might eafily
have been done. I was affured, that in the Infide of this
Building there was a large Hall, and in the Centre of it
a Stair-cafe defcending into another Hall underneath,
from whence there were Galleries of Communication,
which led to all Sides of the Squares. All thefe Structures were built of that which is called *Thebaic* Marble,
or the Stones hewed out of thofe very Rocks through
which we travelled. Early the next Morning we fet out
again, and foon enter'd a large plain Road cut with infi-
finite Labour in the Rock, in which we travelled all that
and the next Day.

On the 14th, about two in the Afternoon, we turned off on the Right, and having without much Difficulty defcended the Mountains, we came to the Habitation or Palace of the Bey *Mehemed*, to whom being
prefented by our Guide, we were very gracioufly receiv'd,
and had the Honour of eating with him. At Supper
he only enquired generally of the Health and Welfare of
Haffan, whom he ftiled his Brother, and of whom he
fpoke with the warmeft Tokens of Affection. At parting he told us that he would fpeak to me the next Day
on the Bufinefs of my Journey, accordingly the next

S 3   Morning,

Morning, after I had eaten some dried Fruits and Bread, which were brought me by an *Abyssine* Slave, together with a pleasant kind of Sherbet, I was conducted to a Summer-house, where the *Bey* sat on a Sofa smoaking. He was upwards of fifty Years old, well-shaped, and a venerable Person in his Aspect. He treated me with much Civility, and after some Discourse on different Subjects, he asked me whether *Hassan* had not charged me with another Letter than that which I had given him the Night before: I told him he had, but that my Instructions were not to part with it 'till he had solemnly promised not to discover its Contents. This he readily complied with, and I thereupon immediately put the Letter into his Hand. He read it with some Emotion, and when he had read it, continued for some time silent and thoughtful. At length he renewed the Conversation.

FRIEND, said he, *Hassan* need not have commanded thee not to part with his Epistle 'till I had promised to conceal its Contents. He knew well enough that I dare not mention them ; and I suppose he knows thee very well, otherwise he would not have put my Safety and his own into your Hands : Tell me, therefore, how you became acquainted with him ; how long and how far you have served him. Upon this I entered into a genuine Detail of my Correspondence with *Hassan*, and did not fail to mention the Book I had procured him from *Europe*, and our Discourses on Chemistry, in hopes that this might be the Foible of *Mehemed*, as well as of *Hassan* ; in which I happened to judge right.

THE *Bey* heard me with great Attention, and without once interrupting me while I was speaking, but he kept his Eyes very steadily fixed upon me ; and when I had

finished

finifhed my Narration, told me he was glad that *Haffan* had fent him fo intelligent a Perfon, and that he would take another Opportunity of converfing with me upon thefe Subjects. I was then conducted back to my Apartment by the Slave, who had attended me the Night before, and who in my Abfence had brought into my Room a Chair, a Table, and fome other Utenfils neceffary to a *European*. This Slave was about 30 Years of Age, extremely diligent, modeft and docile; fo that he furnifhed me with whatever I afked for, and informed me of fuch Things as I thought fit to afk about, with a great deal of Franknefs. I acted, however, with great Caution, on Account of what the *Bey* had faid, which to me implyed little lefs than that I was upon my good Behaviour, and that according as he conceived of my Conduct, he fhould either truft me, or provide for his own and his Friend's Security at my Expence.

At Noon we eat together with *Morat*, and two other Perfons, in the Evening he fent for me, and we had a long Converfation, wherein I difcovered that he was a univerfal Scholar, a Thing not fo rare as we imagine among the *Arabs*, efpecially thofe of Quality, fuch as him of whom I am fpeaking, whofe Anceftors had been immemorially Lords or Governors of this Part of *Egypt*, and were held to be defcended from its ancient Princes. *Mehemed* told me amongft other Things, that he had in his Youth ftudied *Elm-al-Nogioum*, i. e. The Science of the Stars, or what we call Aftrology. But he faid that it created a great deal of Uneafinefs, hindered him from acting according to the Rules of Prudence, and filled him with Sufpicions. To divert his Mind from a Science fo little productive of Pleafure or Profit, he apply'd him-

S 4

felf

felf to ftudy *Al-Ecfir*, i. e. *Alchymy*, whence our Word Elixir. This perfectly anfwered his End. For as it involved him in a long Train of Speculations and Experiments, fo it kept him, by a continual Succeffion of Purfuits, from returning to the Study of Aftrology, and, at the fame Time, furnifhed the Means of diverting his leifure Hours. He was far from being fo great an Enthufiaft as *Haffan*. Time, Experience, and a larger Fund of Knowledge, had eradicated that Fiercenefs and Obftinacy fo natural to the *Arabians*, and taught him a philofophical Calmnefs rarely to be met with in Chriftendom. One of his Maxims was never to difcourfe on a Subject he did not underftand, or to conceive that he underftood any Thing fo well as not to want farther Inftruction. With all this Wifdom he feem'd to be thoroughly perfuaded that Tranfmutation was very poffible ; that it had been formerly known and practifed in the *Indies*, and that there was Reafon to believe the *Bramins*, whom he called *Gioghis*, i. e. Religious Perfons, were ftill acquainted with it. He informed me, that one of thefe becoming a *Mohammedan*, had tranflated the whole Body of their Philofophy into *Arabick*, under the Title of *Merat-al-Maani*, or the *Speculum* of Science, which Book he purchafed at a very high Price, but found it written in a dark and figurative Stile ; fo that it was not of great Ufe to him. A Proof upon which he principally infifted, was the Treafures found in the *Indies* by the Sultan *Mahmut* the *Gafnavite*, which by authentic Authors were affirmed to exceed fixty Millions of Sequins in Gold, coined and uncoined. Thefe Treafures, in his Opinion, were not the pure Effects of Nature, but were rather owing to the Art of the *Indian* Sages. In fuch

Difcourfes

Discourses as these we passed away a Fortnight, which would have been spent pleasantly enough if I had not been apprehensive that not only *Hassan*, but my Friend *Perez*, would be extremely alarmed at my Stay ; of which, to say the Truth, I knew not what to think my self.

To divert the Time as well as I could, I began to look over the Papers of the *French* Surgeon, which had been given me by *Isouf Aga*. Amongst them I found an exact and concise Description of the Empire of *Abyssina*, concerning which I had assiduously enquired at *Cairo*, but was able to learn no more News concerning it there than if I had been at *Geneva* or *London*, except that the Riches of this extensive Empire were brought into *Egypt* by the *Nubian Caravans*. In reading this Discourse, I collected a small Paper of Queries, upon which I interrogated *Melec*, the *Abyssine* Slave, who attended me ; his Answers served as a kind of Annotations to the Account afore-mention'd, and set me perfectly at rest as to many Points which 'till then I thought utterly unintelligible, *European* Authors being extremely confused in all that they deliver concerning this Empire and its Inhabitants.

On the last Day of *April*, being sent for by the *Bey*, to confer with him in the Afternoon, I found him, as I thought, in a little Hurry, and after some previous Conversation, he told me that he intended the next Morning to carry me abroad with him, in order to shew me the Ruins of an ancient City at no great Distance ; therefore he desired I would be ready as early as I could. I confess I knew not what to make of this Invitation, nor could I sleep all the Night : So that when *Melec* came in the Morning to awaken me, he found me already up and

and dreſt. It was once in my Head to have aſked this Slave ſome Queſtions, but not knowing what Conſequences might attend it, and dreading, though I knew not why, the Severity of the *Bey*, I held my Tongue. However, while I was eating my Breakfaſt, *Melec* told me that he was to go with us ; that we ſhould return at Night, and that he believed I would ſet out for *Cairo* on the Morrow. This pleaſed me very well, for I began now to wiſh myſelf out of theſe unknown Parts, where I was entirely at the Mercy of Strangers, and in a Condition to which no Man in his right Wits would have reduced himſelf.

A T the Cloſe of his Diſcourſe, *Melec* informed me that he had himſelf ſome Curioſities to diſpoſe of, which he had caſually met with in going to a City called *Siouf* with a Meſſage from his Maſter : Theſe, he ſaid, he was content to let me take at my own Price when I ſhould return. A Propoſition which ſuited me very well. As ſoon as it was perfectly light, the *Bey* was ready to depart, attended by a Troop of *Arabian* Cavaliers, conſiſting of ſixty Men well armed. *Morat*, and myſelf, had Horſes provided for us, and coaſting along the Mountains we came by Noon to a Road which ſtruck as it were into the Heart of them. There the *Bey* gave Orders for his Guards to halt, and then proceeding with his Slave *Melec*, he conducted *Morat* and myſelf to a Cave at ſome Diſtance, one of the moſt ſtupendious Works which yet remains of the ancient *Egyptian* Magnificence. It is hewn out of the ſolid Rock, ſupported by Pillars of the ſame Stone, wrought with all imaginable Art and Beauty, and filled with hieroglyphic and other Characters. Here we ſat down in the Cool, and eat a ſhort

Repaſt

Repaſt, after which *Melec* and *Morat* went to give Orders to the Guards, and left the *Bey* alone with me in the Grotto.

As ſoon as they were gone, my Friend ſaid he, if Time would permit I could entertain you with a pleaſant Account of the wonderful Stories that are told us of this Grotto, wherein it is ſuppoſed there are greater Treaſures buried than in the Grand Seignior's Coffers. The moſt intelligent are of Opinion, that ſome where in this Neighbourhood lies that famous Mine of Emeralds ſo much ſpoken of in the *Eaſt*, and ſo fatal to its Owners. But I can aſſure you, that the laſt Story is full as ill grounded as the firſt ; for I am well ſatisfied, that the Mine of Emeralds is not here, nay as far as my Information reaches, it is not oſſ this Side the *Nile*, tho' one of my Predeceſſors loſt his Life on a Suppoſition that he was poſſeſſed of it. The Ground of this Story was, his having collected a great quantity of Emeralds, which tho' in other Reſpects he was a wiſe Man, ſhewed him to be extremely deficient in true Policy. The then Baſhaw of *Cairo*, whoſe Name was *Muſtapha*, was avaricious in the higheſt Degree, and on a Suſpicion that he ſhould poſſeſs himſelf of immenſe Wealth, he made War upon and deſtroyed the unhappy Prince, yet without gaining the End he ſought, for his Treaſures could never be found, and the Baſhaw himſelf was the Year following ſtrangled at the *Porte*. On this Account I am not a little tender of owning, that I have any of theſe fatal Stones, at the ſame Time I am not averſe to the ſale of them upon reaſonable Terms ; becauſe any other Commodity of Value ſuits me better.

HAVING

HAVING said this, he produced a little Casket from under his Robe, and having opened it, shewed me a great many of these Jewels, some of them wonderful perfect, and others larger, but cloudy and full of Specks. We were not long in bargaining, for he asked me at first a very moderate Price, and at last I agreed for 30 Stones on the part of *Hassan*, and 3 for myself. One of 40, one of 50, and the other for the Price of 70 *Sequins.* Those I bought for *Hassan* were absolutely perfect, those on my own Account were large but foul, and I bought them with a View to make Use of the Secret I had from M. *Pucci*, which I was sensible would render them of much more Value than they were sold to me. After our Business was over, the *Bey* shewed me another Parcel, consisting of 19 large Stones, but far less perfect than those I had seen before. He seemed very desirous of selling me these altogether, I told him frankly that I had gone to the Extent of my Commission, and that I had laid out all my own Money also. He then shewed me 5 Stones tied up in a Bag of a still larger Size, very thick but foul, and of different Colours. If these said he were perfect, they would be worth more Money than you have given me for all the rest, as they are I will sell them for 500 *Sequins.* This I confess tempted me exceedingly, and immediately brought into my Head what I never once thought on before, *viz.* That I had about me a Pearl Necklace which had been my Mothers, and which I had determined never to part from. I remembered that *Isouf* had told me Pearls bore a very high Price in these Parts, and thereupon I took a Resolution of beseeching the *Bey* to refer this Negotiation till our Return to his

Castle,

Castle, which at first he declined, but afterwards putting up the Stones with those I had bought, he delivered the whole Parcel to me in a Bag, bidding me take Care to let no Body suspect our Business there to have been any other than to gratify my Curiosity with a Sight of these Grottos, for there were several within our View, and we went afterwards to look upon them.

AFTER a Stay of 3 or 4 Hours, we mounted our Horses again, and returned to the *Bey*'s Palace just as it was dark. It happened that the *Cheik* of an adjacent Village, and a Friend of his came that Afternoon to visit the *Bey*, and staid for his Return ; so that our Conversation was put off till the Morning. I retired earlier than usual on Account of the Strangers, and that I might have Time to speak to *Melec* about the Things he had promised to sell me. When I was come to my Chamber, I put him in mind of his Promise, and he assured me, that as soon as the *Bey* was retired to Rest, he would come and shew me what he had mention'd. He came accordingly, and brought the better half of a broken Urn, with about 180 Medals of Gold, Silver, and large Brass, I was extremely surprized at so unexpected a Sight, and the first Question I asked was, whether the *Bey* knew any Thing of them? the poor Fellow trembling, affirmed he did not, and began I believe to apprehend that I would betray him ; I bid him be of good Courage, and asked him what he valued these Curiosities at, he said 10 *Sequins*, I immediately gave him 20, and observed to him, that we were alike in Danger if we broke our Faiths. I put the Medals amongst my Equipage, and gave him the broken Urn to bury in the Place from whence he had taken it, after which

which he departed, and I being exceedingly fatigued, went to my Reft.

In the Morning *Melec* waked me by coming into the Room, which he feldom did, and I was at firft extremely furprized, fuppofing that fome Accident had happened, I was confirmed in this, when he told me, that the *Bey* defired to fpeak with me in an Hour. The Slave's looking perfectly eafy and compofed, alarmed me ftill more, from an Apprehenfion that he had betrayed me, and that this was one of thofe Artifices of which I had been fo often forewarned, from my Propenfity to converfe with *Moors* and *Arabs*. I dreffed myfelf with much Hurry and Confufion, and addreffed myfelf to my Prayers with much Diftraction of Mind; when I had finifhed them with much ado, it fhot into my Mind that the *Bey* had fent for me about the large Emeralds, and thereupon I immediately grew eafy again, wondering at my former Difquiet and fully perfuaded that a Man's own Sufpicions excruciate him much more than any real Evils to which he ftands expofed, from the ordinary Events in Life. The firft Thing I did was, to unrip the Lappit of an old Waiftcoat which I wore over my Shirt, and in which the Necklace was fewed at full length; it confifted of 5 Rows of Pearl with Pears at each End, they were extremely fine, and at the Time they were bought, of a very high Price. I could not help fhedding Tears at the Sight of it, and began to charge myfelf with the want of filial Tendernefs, in parting thus with my Mother's Necklace to an Infidel. But when I had recollected myfelf a little, when I confidered that the Value of all thefe Things was imaginary, and that a Parent if living could not but

approve

approve an Advantage gained by an Exchange of Things uſeleſs in themſelves ; I recovered my Tranquility, and taking off the two Pears, reſolved to produce only five Rows of Pearls.

By that Time I had done this, *Melec* came to haſten me, ſo I went directly to the *Bey*'s Apartment, carrying the five Emeralds with me, which as ſoon as we were alone I produced. Well my Friend, ſaid *Mahemed*, what is it you have to offer me for theſe Children of the Sea? alluding to the Colour of the Stones. I have anſwered I, ſome of the true Children of the Sea, preſenting him at the ſame time the Necklace ; he looked upon it with an Air of Pleaſure and Aſtoniſhment, from whence I gathered, that I ſhould be ſucceſsful in my Negotiation. After looking at them for ſome Time, my Friend, ſaid *Mehemed*, here are about 300 Pearls, if I value them at a *Sequin* a piece they will purchaſe only 3 of thoſe Stones. True my Lord, ſaid I, but you will conſider that you ſet a Value on your own Emeralds and on my Pearls. Very well, replyed *Mehemed* gravely ; and are you not a great Gainer by the Value which I have ſet ? I then ſhewed him the two Pears, and our Buſineſs being quickly adjuſted, he deſired me to bring the reſt of the Emeralds with me when I came to Dinner, which I accordingly did, and after our Repaſt was over retiring to a Summer-houſe, he put up each of the Stones in Paper, affixed his Seal or Mark, for it is taken off only with Ink, on the Folds of each of them, and wrote within to whom it belonged, when he had ſo done, he put them all into the Bag, and that again into a little Caſe which he alſo ſealed with four Seals, and delivered it to me. He then

then demanded whether I would return to *Cairo* the next Day, or repofe a Day longer, I chofe the latter for the Sake of fome Queftions which I had to ask *Melec*.

THE *Bey* then told me, that all the *Arabs* I brought with me muft remain with him ; but that *Morat* fhould return with me, and that he would fend a Perfon in whom he could confide, to fee us fafely embarked on the *Nile* with our Baggage, for that he thought it would not be fafe for us to return by Land. This fomewhat furprized me, for I had no Idea of returning any other Way than that by which I came ; but when I had confidered the Neceffity of the Thing, and that the Return of thefe *Arabs* with their Camels might be fatal, not only to them, but to me. I very readily acquiefced, and thanked the *Bey* for his Care. When all thefe Things were adjufted, he told me, that in the Grotto's where we had been before, he had difcovered fome fubterraneous Paffages, in which he at firft fuppofed fome Treafure might be hid ; but that upon a ftricter Scrutiny, he difcovered they were meer *Catacombs*, and that he had taken out of them fome embalm'd Birds, certain Idols, and figured Stones, which he promifed to fhew me, as he did the next Morning, and afterwards made me a Prefent of them, in return for which I gave him a little filver Cafe of Inftruments which I carried in my Pocket.

IN the Evening fome Strangers arrived, which was the Reafon that I did not fee the *Bey* any more that Night, which gave me an Opportunity of finifhing at leifure all the Inquiries I had to make from *Melec*. He told me, that about five Years before, as he was going with his Sifter to meet a young Man to whom fhe was

to

to be married, they were all surprized by a Body of barbarous People which border on *Abyssinia*, and that after living in Servitude with them some Months, they sold him to a *Nubian* Merchant, who brought him into *Egypt*, and having received many Favours from the *Bey*, presented him and his Sister, whom he had also bought, to *Mehemed*, with whom they had lived ever since.

THIS Sister I understood remained in the Women's Apartment constantly, and tho' *Melec* did not tell me so, yet from various Circumstances I conjectured, that she was one of the *Bey*'s Concubines. In this I was confirmed by the small Desire the *Abyssine* expressed to return into his own Country, or of obtaining his Liberty. He was perfectly satisfied with his present Condition, and was only desirous of having a little Money by him, in Case any Accident should happen to his Master, a Thing frequent enough among these little Princes, who when united are powerful enough to give Law to the Grand Seignior's Governor; but when at Variance with each other, as they generally are become Victims to their own ill-timed Resentments, and either die in the Field against some of their Neighbours and Competitors, or are strangled at *Cairo*, on some pretended Conspiracy.

THE next Day being the third of *May*, I spent almost entirely in the Company of the *Bey*, who seemed to open himself with unusual Confidence. He said he looked upon it as a Thing certain, that he should not hear often from *Hassan*, that he thought his Design of retiring out of *Egypt* prudent; but that it required great Caution in the Execution of it, because the *Turks* were equally suspicious and barbarous, and having conceived

strange

ftrange Notions of his Wealth, would not fail on the flighteft Pretence to rid themfelves of him, in order to acquire it. The Evening I fpent with *Melec*, getting all Things ready for my Journey, and on the fourth of *May* early in the Morning, having taken Leave of the *Bey*, who covered me with Civilities, *Merat* and I fet out mounted on two fine Horfes, attended by three Camels, which carried our Provifions and Baggage, and efcorted by an *Arab* of Diftinction, at the Head of twenty Cavaliers.

WE reached the *Nile* by two Day's eafy Journey. The firft Night we lay in a Village, inhabited for the moft part by *Copts* or *Egyptian* Chriftians. I walked about in the Evening attended every where by the *Arab Chief*, who treated me with a great Politenefs, but feemed to take to himfelf as much or more State than the *Bey*; I underftood afterwards that he was his elder Brother's Son. His Name was *Hamet*, his Age about 23, he was an excellent Horfeman even in Refpect to the *Arabs*, who are all of them very expert in this Art. *Hamet* had more of the *Arabian* Haughtinefs by far than his Uncle; but at the fame Time he made Ufe of a much more ceremonious Courtefy, expreffed himfelf with all the Pomp of *Eaftern* Compliment; fo that I had no fmall Trouble in conforming to all the Niceties which this illuftrious Perfon expected.

THE next Evening we came to *Ackmin*; this is far from being a confiderable Place at prefent, but in the Neighbourhood of it lye the Ruins of a very confiderable City, among which I walked for a couple of Hours, obferving with Regret the outragious Havock which had been notorioufly made of many Monuments of ancient Magnificence. There were however fome Rows of Columns, which had not only refifted the Injuries of Time, but thofe alfo of the barbarous Lords of *Egypt*, who have fo induftrioufly demolifhed what they wanted Genius to erect. Some Apartments alfo were in a manner entire, their Walls being every where embelifhed either with Sculptures or Paintings, the latter amazingly frefh; fo that the Colours feem as if they were frefh laid on. I fhould have been more exact in examining thefe venerable Remains of Antiquity, if the *Emir Hamet* had not told me, that he was ftreightened in Time, and that he expected to meet that Evening the Patron of the Veffel in which we were to fail to *Cairo.*

I was therefore obliged to return immediately, and as he faid, we found when we came back the Perfon he expected, and his Veffel. The Mafter behaved very refpectfully to the *Emir,* and affured him, that he would ufe the utmoft Care and Expedition in conveying us to *Cairo.* The next Morning all our Baggage was put on Board the Veffel, and when we came to take our Leave of the *Emir,* he appointed two of his Cavaliers to attend us. Then turning to *Morat* he embraced him, and wifh'd him a good Voyage, defiring him to go with his *Arabians* immediately on Board the Veffel. In the mean Time he took me afide, and when we had walked a little Way together, he drew a Letter out of his Bofom, and having firft touched his Forehead therewith, and afterwards kiffed it, he delivered it to me, and I opened it after the like Ceremony.

It was fealed, or rather fubfcribed by the *Bey,* and contained an Order to deliver immediately to the *Emir*

Hamet.

Hamet the Packet with four Seals. I was so surprized I knew not what to say. The *Emir* perceived it, and endeavoured to comfort me, My Friend, said he, be not afflicted, you will suffer no Injury, either from me or my Uncle, we best know what is fit to be done in our Affairs and yours. I saw Resistance was impracticable; and therefore I gave him the Packet of Jewels, and then with a heavy Heart, in Spight of all his Promises and Assurances, I went on Board the Vessel, where I found *Morat* and the two *Arabs* with four other Persons belonging to the Bark, but the Patron was gone ashore to receive the last Instructions of the *Emir*.

I look'd upon myself to be now no longer in a State of Freedom, I considered these *Arabs* as Guards, I fancied that *Morat* looked exceedingly melancholy, and on the whole, I felt greater Pain and Disquiet than I had ever known in my Life. I began to revolve in my Mind, that vast variety of Events, which tho' a young Man I had seen; I blamed my fond Credulity which had induced me to run such real Hazards on chimerical Prospects. I saw all Things now in new Lights, I wondered how I so easily quitted my own Country, I stood amazed at my having shunned the Converse of *English* Merchants; I accused myself of a thousand Follies, of which till now I had never thought myself guilty, and I made innumerable Vows of Amendment, and of returning to a settled Course of Life, in Case Providence should please to deliver me from this Gulph of Affliction. This Thought suddenly raised me, I began to conceive the State I was in, a kind of Warning from Heaven to quit this rambling sort of Life, and to

return

return to the Performance of thofe Duties incumbent
upon me, as a reafonable Creature and a Chriftian;
with this Hope I comforted myfelf, and recollecting
my Spirits as well as I could, I began to enquire of *Morat* how he did, and how long he thought it would be
before we fhould reach *Cairo*, he faid he could not tell,
but that he believed it would not be many Days, and
that the Voyage would be very pleafant; he looked too
as if he had recovered his former Chearfulnefs, and perhaps he had never loft it, except in my Imagination.
The Patron of the Veffel was extremely courteous, as
well as very careful of us; we lodged every Night on
Shore, but as I apprehended, that the *Arabs* and the
Mafter of the Veffel had a ftrict Eye over us, I walked
very little abroad, which hindered me from viewing a-
bundance of Curiofities, that otherwife in the Courfe
of this Voyage, I might have feen. I took Notice,
however, the fecond Day of our Voyage, of a Marble
Column on our Right Hand, exactly like that of *Pompey,* near *Alexandria,* though I think not quite fo
high.

WHEN our *Arabians* became a little acquainted with
us, they entertained us with the ufual Topic's, *viz.*
Romantic Relations of the Adventures of antient Heroes,
and wonderful Hiftories of Treafures buried in Mountains, Caftles erected by Art Magic, and *Talifmans*
capable of performing more ftupendous Miracles than
ever entered into any Legend. They delivered all they
faid with a Gravity, which fhewed that they believed
themfelves all that they defired others to credit, and I
who had profited much by *Haffan*'s Admonition, fuffer'd
thefe Stories to amufe my Melancholy, and to divert

the

the Paffage, which exceedingly delighted the *Arabs*, who love to be liftened too, and treated with Confidence, which notwithftanding the Stories that are told of them, I think they very rarely abufe.

I AM the rather inclined to this Opinion, becaufe that I know their *Emirs* and *Princes* chaftife with the utmoft Severity, fuch as injure any who are going to or coming from them, and have thereby put themfelves upon their Faith. It is true, that they are extremely poor, which makes them thievifh; but if you give them a Trifle, and treat them kindly, and like Friends, they will not wrong you; but on the contrary, ferve you with great Fidelity, and exert themfelves to the utmoft in your Defence. When we were fallen down the *Nile* within a Days Sail or lefs of *Cairo*, we landed at a Village called *Safi*, where we hired four Camels, and having put the Baggage upon one, the *Arab* who owned the Camels, *Morat* and myfelf, on the other two fet out by Land for *Cairo*, by the Direction of the *Arabs* whom the *Emir* had left with us; and we entered on the fame Side of the City, from whence we fet out for *Suez*.

IT is impoffible to exprefs the Joy which Mr. *Perez* and *Antonio* teftified on my Arrival. They had fent to *Suez*, and were informed, that my Curiofity had tempted me to make an Excurfion into the upper *Egypt*, where they took it for certain, that fome Misfortune had befallen me. I had not been at Home long before *Haffan* fent me a Meffage, defiring that I would repofe myfelf for a Day or two before I vifited him. This was to me quite unintelligible; however I was conftrained to be filent, as well as to bear with Patience the great Lofs that I had fuftained.

DURING

DURING this Space, Mr. *Perez* diverted me with the Recital of what had paſſed in my Abſence, and alſo preſented me with a long Letter from Dr. *Salviati*, in which among other Things there was a Query as to the Uſes that might be made in Chemiſtry of the Practice at *Cairo* of hatching Eggs in Ovens. Having conſidered this attentively, I began to apprehend, that very poſſibly the Experiments I made of Mr. *Pucci*'s Secret would have ſucceeded better if ſuch Ovens as theſe had been uſed. Upon this, I began to enquire very particularly into this Method of hatching Chickens, as alſo whether it was practicable to erect them in a private Houſe, which I was told it was not. Then I deſired to be informed if a Pot well luted might be ſuffer'd to ſtand in theſe Ovens for a certain Time, without Danger of its being opened, and being ſatisfied on this Head, I took two very foul Emeralds, and that which had been partly cleanſed before, and having properly ſecured them, ſent them to be placed in the Oven for nine Days.

THE Day after I went to wait on my Patron *Haſſan* according to his Appointment, he received me with all the Marks of Friendſhip poſſible, and before I had been with him twenty Minutes, produced to me the *Bey*'s Packet, with the Seals untouched. He told me at the ſame Time, that the Baſhaw having ſent a *Chiaux* to *Mehemed Bey* while I was at his Palace, that Lord was apprehenſive, that upon ſome Intelligence given, I might be ſeized in my Return to *Cairo*, which would have been fatal to them all ; he therefore diſpatch'd his Nephew the *Emir*, with an Anſwer to the Baſhaw's Demands, and knowing that he would not be ſuſpec-

ted

ted or searched, gave him Directions to take a certain Packet from me, and deliver it when Opportunity serv'd to *Haffan*.

WE immediately broke open the Seals, took out the Bag, and divided the Emeralds according to the written Directions of the *Bey*. *Haffan* was not a little furprized at the Choice I had made of imperfect Stones, which as he rightly obferved, were from their Size above the Purchafe of unskilful Judges, and from their Quality unfit for thofe who had Skill. I admitted what he faid to be true, and could defend myfelf only by faying, that my Money would hold out no farther. My Patron obferved, that he had forbid *Morat* to enter his Houfe, and had fent to hinder my vifiting him till fuch Time as the *Emir* was returned, left on our Meeting fuch Civilities might pafs as might poffibly beget Sufpicion, in which I confefs he acted very reafonably. Two Days afterwards he fet out for *Rofetta*, from whence in a few Weeks he tranfported himfelf and his Family to *Algiers*, having before difpofed of his Houfe and Gardens to the *Turkifh Aga*, who on that Account winked at his Departure, and fent no Advices to the Bafhaw till his Friend was out of Danger.

AT the End of the appointed Time I fent for my Pot from the Oven, and found, upon Infpection, that a thin Stone was crack'd quite thorough; another thicker one was much mended in its Colour; but as for the large Stone I bought of the Jew at *Alexandria*, and had made an unfuccefsful Attempt to rectify before, it was as fine, as clear, and as perfect as I could wifh. Having confidered this Matter attentively, and compared all the Cir-

cumftances

cumſtances together, which from Experience I knew of this Matter, I fell upon a new Method, which I executed as well as projected, and by the Means of three Lamps of different Wicks which I kept continually burning, under three Veſſels of Water, the firſt of which ſupply'd the ſecond, and the ſecond the third, with boiling Water, continually, the firſt only being fill'd up as Occaſion required with hot Water, I effected the whole Proceſs to my great Satisfaction, and, by adjuſting the Time to the Thickneſs of the Stones, came by degrees to an unhoped for Certainty, which ſoon furniſhed me with Emeralds ſuperior to moſt that had been ſeen in *Europe*.

A s theſe Things took up much Time, and required almoſt a continual Attendance, I had all the Leiſure in the World to methodize and review my Papers, to perfect my Obſervations, to raiſe new Heads of Enquiry, and to ſatisfy myſelf as to many Things about which our beſt Authors contradict each other, or elſe paſs over in Silence, becauſe they wanted either the Will or the Opportunity of being thoroughly informed about them. That I might with greater Conveniency thus employ my Time, I mentioned to Mr. *Perez* the Papers relating to *Ethiopia*, which I had brought from *Suez*, and he preſſing earneſtly to ſee 'em, I promiſed to gratify his Curioſity as ſoon as I could tranſcribe and digeſt 'em, which afforded me a fair Excuſe for being much in my own Apartment, where, at the ſame Time, I carried on this, and Buſineſs of greater Importance.

B u t as Diverſity of Studies relieve each other, ſo I thought proper to join to this Hiſtorical Treatiſe the collecting ſuch Secrets and Receipts as I had received, either from my Friends, or had tranſcribed from Books fince my Arrival in *Egypt*. I communicated alſo this Deſign to Mr. *Perez*, and received his kind Affiſtance therein, he having been no leſs aſſiduous than I in the Search of ſuch Curioſities ; for Curioſities they might properly be called, ſince they ſerved rather to amuſe, than to inſtruct, and were rather ingenious than uſeful. To theſe I added his and my own Obſervations, as to their Succeſs, want of Succeſs, their Reaſonableneſs, or Improbability ; the Cauſes of their failing, the moſt proper Remedies for thoſe Cauſes, and whatever elſe could contribute to make a Collection of this Sort ſo far beneficial as to prevent an unneceſſary Waſte of Time in fruitleſs Experiments.

WHEN theſe were finiſhed, I drew up a ſuccinct Deſcription of *Egypt*, which I thought might be beſt done upon the Spot, where all that was ſaid might fall under the Eye of competent and impartial Judges, where Errors might be eaſily rectified, Deficiencies properly ſupply'd, and all Grounds of Doubtfulneſs or Suſpicion removed. This too, by a ſteady Application, was quickly perfected, reviſed, corrected, and put into its laſt Dreſs. It happened that the Diſcourſe on the *Ethiopian* Empire, and the Deſcription of *Egypt*, were in my Hands when we left *Cairo* ; ſo that theſe I have preſerved.

BUT as to the Collection of Receipts, and five ſmall Treatiſes on the *Oriental Philoſophy*, *Alchymy*, the *Chriſtian Religion*, ſo far as its *Truth* is acknowledg'd by *Mohammedans*; the *Veracity* of *Oriental Hiſtorians*, and the true Principles of the *Religion* of the *Indians*, I had delivered them to Mr. *Perez*, who deſired to tranſcribe them, by which Means they were loſt to me. The *Hiſtorical Pieces*,

Pieces, as they have an intimate Relation to these Memoirs, follow here as in their proper Place.

A RELATION *of the* PRESENT STATE *of* ETHIOPIA. By a *French* Surgeon.

IT was not Choice, flowing from an avaricious Desire of possessing Part of those immense Riches which the *Portuguese* every where give out to abound in *Ethiopia,* that drew me thither. I had the Misfortune to be taken by a Crew of Pirates in the *West-Indies,* Part of whom, after having for seven Years committed incredible Ravages in those Parts, sailed for the *Red-Sea,* at the Persuasion of a Person who had been Servant to the Governor of *Barbadoes,* and had heard it frequently said at his Master's Table, that Privateers in those Seas might easily possess themselves of immense Wealth, an Argument of all others most prevalent with this kind of People.

THEY were very lucky on their first coming on the Coasts of *Arabia,* but they had not taken many Prizes before they were alarmed with a Story of an *Arabian* King's fitting out a great Fleet, on purpose to take them. This induced the Captain of our Ship, for there were three in all, to stand over to the *Ethiopian* Shore, where he put into the Port of *Arkiko,* and sent me, with three Men in the Boat, to desire Leave of the Governor to trade with the People.

WE were no sooner on shore than we were sent to Prison, and the Captain, the next Day, fairly sailed
away

away without us, a Thing I did not at that Time much regret, being heartily weary of living among such a wicked Race of People. I regretted it the lefs, becaufe I was immediately fet at Liberty, and left to do with myfelf what I thought fit. The three Men who came on Shore with me engaged themfelves in the *Turkifh* Service as Mariners, and I fuffered myfelf to be perfuaded by fome *Jewifh* Merchants to go with them into *Ethiopia*, on a Promife that they would carry me the next Year into *Egypt*, with a Caravan; in which they deceived me, and not contented therewith, treated me very harfhly, forcing me to exercife my Profeffion as a Surgeon, and taking to themfelves whatever Prefents the People fent.

AFTER this Manner they dragg'd me quite crofs the Empire of *Ethiopia*, from the *Red-Sea* to the Sea of *Dambea*, which is no other than a very great Lake, through which the *Nile* paffes, and lies in the Weft Part of *Ethiopia*. Here I got releafed, and was kindly entertained by many of the People who had been formerly converted by the *Portuguefe* Fathers, and do ftill retain a great Veneration for them, and on their Account for all Catholicks. I then traverfed this great Lake, and turning next to the South, entered the Kingdom of *Gojam*, where in two Days Journey I paffed from the River *Nile*, where it was large and rapid, and had run at leaft three hundred Miles, to its Source, the River forming the Figure of an *Italick O*, the Top of which is open, and reprefents the near Approach of the winding Body of the River to its Fountains after fo long a Courfe, whereby the Kingdom of *Gojam* is made a perfect Peninfula,

the

the Isthmus contained between the two Branches of the *Nile* being not above 20 Miles broad.

I RESIDED near 20 Years at *Azazo*, the Capital of this Kingdom, 'till being feized with a ftrong Paffion of returning into *Europe*, I travelled firft due Eaft, to the famous Fortrefs of *Ambafel*, and then directly North to *Axuma*, which is generally efteemed the Capital of *Ethiopia*, from whence, after three Years Stay, I found Means to get to *Suez*, where I wrote this Account, having traverfed the greateft Part of that Country, which makes fuch a Noife in *Europe*, and which is really the moft different in the World, from what it hath been reprefented.

THIS Country is by fome call'd the *Higher Ethiopia*, but I think more commonly *Abyffinia*, which Word is derived from the Name given to their own Country in their own Language, by the Inhabitants of this Empire, *viz. Habefh*; but whence that is derived, or what it fignifies, I know not; and perhaps fome who affect to deal in Etymologies, know as little as I. As to the Extent of this Empire, it was formerly much greater than it now is, and at prefent its Bounds are not eafily fettled; however, I think that in length, from South to North, it may be near five hundred Miles in Extent; and from the *Red-Sea* to the *Nile*, it may be about two hundred. As it lies from 8 to 17 Degrees of North Latitude, it is plainly in the Torrid Zone, which to me is a Demonftration that the Moderns are not much more exact than the Antients in their Sentiments as to the Effects of the Nearnefs or Diftance of the Sun, fince it is certain that *Ethiopia* is not fo hot as *Spain*, but of fuch a Temperature as in the warmeft Provinces of the Kingdom I mention

tion the People feel in Spring; on the Coaſt, indeed, it is exceſſive hot in the Summer Months, which are the ſame as with us in *Europe*; but in the inland Parts Summer and Winter are reverſed, that is to ſay, the Winter commences in the Middle of *June*, and laſts to the Middle of *September*; and the Summer commences in *December* and ends in *March*. I am well informed, that on the other Side of the *Red-Sea*, the Tables are turned again, the Winter on the Coaſt laſts from *June* to *September*; and in the inland Parts of *Arabia*, from *November* to *February*.

THE rainy Seaſons are indeed equally terrible and troubleſome; for every Day, to a Stranger, appears the laſt in which this World is to ſubſiſt, and yet from three o'Clock in the Afternoon, to Seven, includes the whole of this amazing Scene; by that Time all is over, and the next Morning breaks with a Serenity the moſt pleaſing that can be imagined; about Noon the Clouds gather, and at Three Thunder, Lightning, and Rain, ſpread a Terror and Confuſion not to be deſcribed. I have often thought from this, and from a hundred other Circumſtances, that *Abyſſinia* might be ſtiled the Land of Contradictions. At firſt Sight this Expreſſion will appear only a Flight of Thought, but it is in Truth a very weighty Obſervation, ſince it reconciles at once the oppoſite Accounts we have from different Authors.

As to the Fertility of this Country, who would not be led to admire it when he is told that there are always two, and ſometimes three Harveſts, and yet there is no Place on the Globe the Inhabitants of which are ſo often plagued with Famine. This ariſes from various Cauſes, Firſt, there are but here and there Spots of arable Land, and

and thefe are not very fertile. Secondly, the Locufts often come and deftroy every green Thing with a Fury fcarce to be conceived. Thirdly, the Emperor's Soldiers live every where at free Quarters, and confequently fpread Want and Penury wherever they come. Fourthly, the Lightnings frequently deftroy their Stores; and, laftly, the *Gallas*, and other barbarous People, harrafs the Frontier Provinces continually.

THE Fruits of this Country are very excellent, and might be had in great Plenty if their Conftitution encouraged the People to cultivate them; which it is fo far from doing, that one can fcarce conceive how they are able at all to fubfift themfelves and their Families. As to all Sorts of Herbs and Flowers that are to be found in the *Indies*, they are found here; and befides, there are alfo fome Vulneraries which I believe are peculiar to this Soil. It would require much Time, and more Knowledge than I am Mafter of, to defcribe all the Curiofities in this Country; which I am the lefs capable of doing, becaufe I had not any Conveniency of making *Memorandums* on the Spot; fo that I write entirely from Memory, with this Caution, however, that I infert nothing but what I certainly remember. In the Number of thefe Things I reckon thefe three. Firft, the Grain call'd *Teff*, the great Bread Corn of this Country, very nutritive and pleafant, and yet ten Grains of it are not larger, taken together, than a Grain of Millet. The *Hanfut* Tree, fomewhat like a *Palmetto*, its Rind fmooth, its Leaves beautifully green, and very thick. This Tree produces nothing, and yet is the moft ufeful and defirable in the Country. Its Leaves, when dry, rub into a pleafant wholefome Meal; the Tree itfelf, cut down, fliced into convenient Pieces, and boiled in Milk, taftes exactly like a Millet Pudding; and from its Root there ftarts out numberlefs young Sprigs, which quickly grow to a confiderable Size. The third Curiofity is the Herb *Azazo*, the moft noble Alexipharmic in the Univerfe; the very Smell of it is faid to benumn the moft dangerous Sort of Vipers. A little of the Powder taken inwardly, never fails to cure their Bites; and it is certain that thofe who have lately taken it pafs boldly through Places infefted by Serpents, without Fear of being bitten, the Effluvia from their Bodies making thofe Creatures fick. Oranges, Lemons, Figs and Sugar-Canes, are found in various Provinces of *Abyffinia*.

Gold, I believe there is none in the whole Empire, notwithftanding what fo many have boldly afferted; what they have comes to them from the Weft; but as for Iron and Lead, they have both in Plenty. On the Coafts of the *Red-Sea* they have a Sort of *Sal gemma*, or Rock Salt, which they cut out into Pieces like Bricks, and thefe are the current Money, or rather Meafure of Exchange throughout the Empire, but with great Variation in their Value, for on the Sea Coaft fixty of them are equal to a Sequin, whereas in other Parts a Sequin will fetch but five, nay, but three. Mountains are very frequent, and in fome Places there are Rocks fhoot up like Pillars, which ferve for Fortreffes, and are impregnable in their Nature; thefe are ftiled *Amba*'s. There are alfo Chains of Mountains running this Way and that, affording very narrow Paffages from one Province to another, and lying in fome Places fo as to oblige the Travellers to pafs over them, which cannot be performed but with great Trouble and Danger. Befides the *Nile,*

of

of which I fhall fpeak afterwards, there are many very confiderable Rivers in *Abyffinia*, fome of which as the *Maleg* fall into the *Nile*. Others, as the *Lebea*, after a long Courfe, roll into the Sea. And a third Sort again, as the *Hahobax*, little inferior to the *Nile*, after watering for many hundred Miles a barren Country, roll at laft into more barren Sands, and are there drunk up and loft.

T H E Animals in *Ethiopia* are of all Sorts, as well fuch as are found in *Europe* as in *Afia* and *Africk*, but they have efpecially Plenty of three Kinds. Firft, of excellent Horfes. Secondly, of beautiful and ferviceable Mules. Thirdly, a prodigious Quantity of black Cattle, in which the chief Riches of the People confift. As to wild Beafts, there are too many of them ; for I think there is fcarce any Species of which this Country hath not its Share. Elephants there are in vaft Numbers, fo that one fometimes meets a hundred of them in a Herd on the Road ; yet have they no Notion of taming them, or of making any other Ufe of them than that of felling their Teeth. They have likewife Lions of various Kinds, fome very ftrong and high mettled, not lefs than nine, though fome fay twelve, Feet in Length : They are very terrible to the Sight ; nor is it to be conceived with what Fright all Animals fly at the firft hearing of their Roar. There is likewife in this Country the *Giraff*, an Animal capable of ftriking with Wonder the moft incurious Spectator. It moft of all refembles a Camel in its Form, but vaftly exceeds it in Size, fince it is bigger than an Elephant, but its Limbs are very flender, and it makes a very odd Figure.

U

T H E

THE Birds of *Ethiopia* are very numerous; and befides thofe common to *Europe*, and the *Indies*, there are many peculiar to this Country, which I think needlefs to defcribe; I fhall therefore content myfelf with obferving, that their Ducks are larger, fatter, and better tafted than thofe in *Europe*; their Partridges as high tafted as ours, and of the Size of Capons. River Fifh they have, but not in very great abundance; neither have I feen any that merit a particular Defcription. I come now to fpeak of the People.

THE Inhabitants of *Abyffinia* are compofed of Chriftians, Jews, and Mohammedans; of thefe I think the two laft make a Third. The *Abyffines* themfelves are *Chriftians*; the Men and Women are generally well made, middle-fiz'd People, of a beautiful Tawney, with long curled Hair, of which they are very careful. They are without all queftion, in their own Natures, the moft harmlefs, docile People in the World, pious to Excefs, and charitable to a Fault, whatever our Miffionaries may think fit to fay. As to their Religion, it is indeed a very odd Mixture, the *Jews*, *Pagans*, *Mohammedans*, *Chriftians*, all circumcife, either from a Principle of Religion, or to avoid Reproach. It is certain, that before the *Abyffines* were converted to Chriftianity, they were *Jews*; and it is as certain that they ftill retain a Mixture of *Judaifm* in their Religious Cuftoms. As to their heretical Notions, they are chiefly fuch as flow from the *Eutychian* Herefy. Our Miffionaries magnify them exceffively, and yet they are more folicitous to introduce Submiffion to the *Papal See*, than to fet them right in any other Point; and yet a Man of any ordinary Underftanding cannot fail, on a fhort Acquaintance with thefe

People,

People, to difcover that this is the laft Point to be touched upon, as Experience hath fhewn; that continually infifting upon it, hitherto hath kept the Catholick Religion out of *Ethiopia*, and has even made it odious there, infomuch that the Bulk of the People would rather embrace *Mohammedifm*.

THE *Abyffines* worfhip God with great Devotion; and there are amongft them fuch a Multitude of Churches, that one is always within Sight of another; and there are frequently feveral within Sight of each other. The Clergy are meek innocent People; and all the Monks labour with their Hands for their Subfiftance. They faft very rigoroufly, tafting neither Meat nor Drink 'till Evening; and they give to thofe that afk them whatever they afk; and therefore it is no Wonder that *Ethiopia* is over burden'd with Beggars. In Marriage only their Morals are irregular, inafmuch as they retain the *Jewifh* Cuftom of divorcing upon the flighteft Occafions, the Man and Woman marrying again where they pleafe. On this Head it is very remarkable, that a Hufband frequently pardons Adultery, but if his Wife fcolds he divorces her without Mercy. The Miffionaries, while they were in this Country, took a great deal of Pains to rectify this Abufe; and it muft be acknowledg'd, to the Honour of the *Portuguefe* Fathers, that as many of them died Martyrs, and as all of them lived Confeffors, fo they maintain'd an Apoftolick Purity in their Conduct, and have, fince their Deaths, been reverenced as Saints, notwithftanding the Averfion the People have for the Catholick Religion, founded folely on the Apprehenfions they have of the Pope's Supremacy, which they call a bare-faced

Ufur-

Ufurpation, inconfiftent with their ecclefiaftical and civil Rights.

As to the Government of *Ethiopia*, it is as every Thing in this Country is, full of Contradictions. The Emperor ftiles himfelf *King of Kings*, boafts fometimes of numberlefs Provinces under his Subjection, afferts his fole Property in the Soil of *Abyffinia*, which is acknowledged by his Subjects, who are all Tenants at Will, and are frequently difpoffeffed. As there is no Money in his Dominions, he takes his Revenue in Kind, the tenth Cow every third Year, the tenth Piece of Cloth from every Weaver, and fo in other Things. Yet this Monarch is very far from being abfolute, for the great Men frequently prefcribe Laws to him, and the Loyalty of his Subjects hangs very loofe about them ; fo that tho' they acknowledge their Emperor for a defpotic Prince, yet it is with this Salvo, that when he does not pleafe them, he fhall be no longer their Emperor. After this Account, I need fcarce add that the People are very poor and miferable, fince it is plain a Civil War makes all People fo ; and ten Years is a long Truce in *Ethiopia*, where in Time of Peace the Nation are moft abject Slaves. When the Emperor beftows a Government, a Herald proclaims at the Door of the Tent; *His Imperial Majefty hath been pleafed to make fuch a one his Slave, Ruler over fuch a Province.* And he does the fame Thing when he takes a Lady to his Wife. The Phrafe then is; *His Majefty hath made fuch a one his Slave Emprefs.* In the *Abyffinian* Language a King is call'd *Negus*. Their Monarch they ftile *Negus Negafta*, which is as much as to fay, *King of Kings.* Formerly the *Abyffinian* Monarchs made ufe of two Minifters to tranfact all publick Affairs,

being

being themselves scarce ever seen by their Subjects. These Ministers were stiled *Betudets*, and were in fact *Mayors* of the *Palace*, or in other Words, *Kings*, while the Emperor, with all his Titles, was but a Cypher ; but within these hundred Years the Emperors have conde-scended to be Men, and, in consequence thereof, have resumed their Authority. The Prime Minister, when there is one, is stiled *Raz*, and his Office is much the same with that of the Vizir *Azem* at the *Porte*. I have read in some *Portuguese* Voyages, that the *Ethiopian* Monarchs live very meanly. This I can disprove, tho' I never saw the Emperor, because his chief Lords are very richly dressed in Velvet Jackets, and Surtouts of Brocade : But I shall readily agree that they are the only well-cloath'd People in the Empire. The Governor of a Province is stiled *Xumo*, or rather *Chumo*, for so they pronounce it. And they have abundance of other Offi-cers in the Nature of Intendants and Lieutenants for the King.

T H E R E are abundance of Princes dependent on the *Abyssinian* Empire, who, as far as outward Marks of Respect will go, confess this Dependence, and perhaps send considerable Presents ; but as for Obedience, that's not to be expected, unless some *Abyssinian* Monarch should arise of an enterprizing, and at the same time of a regular Genius, who after new modelling his own Empire, should turn his Arms upon his Neighbours ; for in this Case he would undoubtedly restore the ancient Glory of the *Abyssinian* Name, since these People are naturally good Soldiers, brave, obedient, patient of Fa-tigue, and very capable of Discipline, if they had Offi-cers who knew how to instruct them ; their Horse are

naturally

naturally very good, and might be managed so as to become the very best in the World, as they have the Speed of the *Arabian* Coursers, and the Strength and Fierceness of our Horses in *Europe*. As it is the first Shock determines a Battle, and tho' personally the *Abyssines* have as much Valour as any People in the World, yet in pitched Battles they are easily defeated ; for if their General be kill'd, if Artillery be brought to play upon them, if they are attack'd in Flank, a Pannick presently takes them, and they run all away; nor is it possible to bring them together again by Promises or Threats. The Emperor moves about with a flying Army, under the Name of Guards, and seldom, if ever, resides any where but in a Camp, which is the Reason that there are no great Towns, much less Cities, in *Ethiopia*, but Villages are thick ; in some Places they almost touch each other ; so that the whole Country is a straggling Hamlet.

THEIR Houses are no better than Cabbins, and their Furniture a low Table, a few Mats, and a Hide to sleep on. As for Plates and Dishes, none but Persons of Distinction have any, and they are a kind of black earthen Ware. The ordinary People make a Sort of broad thin Cakes, which they bake in such a Manner as to leave them very tough ; these they lay upon the Table, clap their Meat upon them, also use them to wipe their Fingers, after which their Slaves, or their Women, eat them ; and in every other Respect they are alike nice, that is, not at all so. The grand Dainty in *Abyssinia* is raw Beef, of which they lay a whole Quarter upon the Table hot, as it is cut from the Creature, with a Bladder or earthen Cup full of the Gall ; this they mix with Pepper and Salt, and dipping the Flesh into it, eat it

with

with all the Greedineſs of *Tartars*. They likewiſe make a kind of Muſtard by mixing with Salt and Pepper the Chile which they find in the Stomach of the Beaſt when it is kill'd; and this they properly enough ſtile a Rarity, becauſe a Quantity of Pepper, ſufficient to make it, is ſeldom to be had. Though it may be concluded from this Account, that the *Abyſſines* live but indifferently, yet it muſt not be imagined that Strangers are in Danger of wanting amongſt them; on the contrary, they are better provided for here than perhaps in any other Country in the World, as well in Right of the Laws, as from the charitable Diſpoſition of the People. As ſoon as a Traveller comes to any Village, he looks about for the beſt and moſt convenient Hut or Houſe therein, into which he inſtantly enters, and is there as much at his Eaſe as if it were his Brother's. The Maſter preſently ſends to his Neighbours to inform them that he has a Gueſt, whereupon they bring him whatever may contribute to the Stranger's Refreſhment, and are ſure to ſatisfy all his Demands, becauſe, if he ſhould complain, the Governor of the Province would mulct them in twice as much: However, there is rarely any Inſtance of Complaints of this Sort, the *Abyſſines* having a natural Generoſity, eſpecially towards Paſſengers.

I HAVE ſaid that this is a Country of Contradictions, and ſo it is in the Character of its Inhabitants. They are naturally honeſt, beneficent, and inclined to live peaceably, yet are they involved in continual Wars, either againſt their Neighbours, or amongſt themſelves; Treaſon and Rebellion being as natural to that Country as Rain or Sun-ſhine, and almoſt as frequent. For this, two Reaſons may be aſſigned. Firſt, the Corruption

U 4

of

of their Grandees, which is as exceſſive as in *Europe*; all the Grandees being quite another Race of People, void of that Probity, Humanity, and peaceable Diſpoſition viſible in the reſt of the Nation. To be ſure it is not the Air of the Court, or their ſeeing the Emperor daily, that ſo ſtrangely changes theſe People, I believe rather it is the Nature of the Life they lead ; for being as they are called from all Attention to their private Affairs, in order to take Care of thoſe of the Publick, they ſet no Bounds either to their Deſires, or to their Expences, at the ſame Time that they expect the Publick ſhould pay for all. Their Hopes and Fears alſo being much ſtronger, and more powerful than thoſe of meaner Men. They engage in Frauds, Conſpiracies, or Rebellions, to gratify theſe, or to ſecure themſelves from thoſe. Hence the Corruption of the Great is here as well as elſewhere, the prime Cauſe of Diſorder in the State. But Secondly, theſe Grandees, by the Conſtitution of the *Abyſſinian* Monarchy are poſſeſſed of too great an Authority, and alſo of too great an Influence over thoſe they govern. Hence it comes to paſs, that a diſcontented Governor hath it frequently in his Power to engage the People in Support of his private Intereſts, by ſpecious Pretences of Zeal for the *Publick Service*. The Clergy alſo, who are about the Court, looſe that Sanctity of Heart, and Purity of Manners, which is the Ornament of their Order, and acquiring in their ſtead a ſpiritual Pride, and a boundleſs Luſt of Power. They uſe their Characters, becauſe ſacred, to cover thoſe Crimes which are too black for publick View; whence it happens, that the *Abuna* or Patriarch of *Ethiopia* is often at the Head of a Conſpiracy, and

has

has fometimes drawn together 50 or 60,000 *Monks* to abet his perfonal Quarrel, under Colour of fupporting the *Abyffinian* Religion. Thus between the Priefts, who name every Scuffle for their private Views a Contention *pro Aris*, and the Governors, who when they are in Danger of being removed, fright the People into a Rebellion *pro Focis*, the honefteft Folks in the World yearly cut one anothers Throats for the Gratification of thofe who deferve to have their own cut according to Law.

I have been led to thefe Obfervations from the Remembrance of one and twenty Rebellions in fifteen Years, not one of which was occafioned by any ill Conduct of their Princes, but meerly through the Villainy of the Grandees, and the Ignorance of the common People. This Account explains a Maxim in the *Abyffinian* Polity, which can be explained no other Way, I mean that fcrupulous Obftinacy with which they perfift in fhutting all Strangers out of the Empire. The Grandees know from Reafon, and from Experience of former Times, when the *Portuguefe* had footing in this Country, that the *Abyffinian* Emperors would emancipate themfelves from that Bondage in which they hold them, if they could have the Affiftance of any Foreign Prince, only fo far as to fecure their Perfons, which by Reafon of the Artifices of their great Officers and their Clergy, are never in Safety while guarded by their own Subjects. This Maxim, either by falfe colouring, the great ones deceive their Sovereigns into a good Opinion of, or elfe they adhere to it in fpight of his Commands, which is eafily done in a Country where they have made it the firft Article of their political Creed with the People, in Virtue of that inveterate Defire which the Mif-

fionaries

fionaries profeſſed, of ſubjecting the *Abyſſines* to the *Pope*, a Thing they feared the more, the leſs they underſtood it. They might if they pleaſed at preſent, ſpare a great part of this Trouble, ſince I am perſuaded, that no *European* who enters *Abyſſinia* will be very deſirous of ſtaying there, or of ſending his Countrymen thither, ſince it is a Place where there is very little to be got. The richeſt Emperors ſeldom poſſeſs half a Million of Livres, and notwithſtanding all that is poſitively affirmed by our Authors, I am very confident there is no Gold in *Abyſſinia* ; all that the Emperor receives coming from Regions lying to the South or South Weſt, farther into the Heart of *Africa*. I know that the *Abyſſines* themſelves do ſometimes pretend, that there are very rich Mines of Gold in their Country, but that they conceal them for fear of the *Turks* ; yet I am perſuaded this is falſe ; for if there were Gold Mines in their Hills, there would be Gold Duſt in their Rivers, their tempeſtuous Autumns eſpecially conſidered, and yet there is not ; Iron and Lead indeed they have, but not in the Plenty that ſome have reported. Again, if there had been Gold Mines in *Ethiopia*, their ancient Emperors would have been rich ; and as the *Abyſſines* are naturally vain, they would ſurely have left us ſome Marks of their Magnificence ; whereas there is neither City nor Palace in all *Abyſſinia*. I do indeed believe, that a Thouſand Years ago there might have been Cities and Palaces both ; but then the Emperors had not only thoſe Countries I ſpoke of under their Dominion, but a great Part of *Arabia* alſo, of which they were diſpoſſeſſed a little before the Birth of *Mohammed*, as their Hiſtorians ſay. This therefore proves nothing as to the Gold of

Abyſſinia,

Abyffinia, and as to the *Afiatic Ethiopia*, or of the *interior Ethiopia* in *Africk*, I believe that it abounds in both Countries, and to them therefore the *Europeans* muft go who would fetch it, and not into *Abyffinia*.

As our Writers generally deceive us, in refpect to the Riches of this Country, fo they deceive us not lefs in what they fay of the Poverty of its Inhabitants, taking that Word in a moral Senfe; for the *Abyffines* are fo far from being ftupid or indocil, that they are in Truth a very quick witted and tractable People, excepting only in fome Points which concern their Civil and Religious Rites, wherein they conceive it to be the Intereft of all Strangers to miflead them. As to Learning, without queftion there is not much of it in *Abyffinia*, yet are its Inhabitants not abfolutely deficient in this Point. They have a good Verfion of the Scriptures of the Old and New Teftament in their own Tongue; a large Collection of the Works of the Fathers of the Primitive Church, in which it is faid there are none of the Errors of the *Eutychians*, or *Neftorians*; a Modern Body of Divinity, which is full of them; feveral Volumes of the Lives of the Saints; many Treatifes on Monaftic Life; feveral Hiftories of *Ethiopia*, of which I faw two, one that might have made ten Volumes in Folio, the other about half as big. The *Pfalter* of *David* is the Book moft common amongft them, and many of their *Monks* can repeat forty, fifty, nay a hundred Pfalms. Their Books of Hiftory are written in a flowery figurative Stile, which however is far from being inelegant or unentertaining. On the contrary, *David Gomez*, who was a kind of Engineer in the Kingdom of *Dambea*, fhewed me the beginning of

a

a History which he had translated into *Portuguez*, which would have been read with great Applause in *Europe* ; where if the *Ethiopian* Writings are disliked and disesteemed, it is because they are not properly translated; for the figurative Language of one Country ought not to be rendered into the literal, but into the figurative Language of another Country, and read with a proper Allowance for the Genius of the People from whose Tongue the Version is made. It is very true, that the *Monks* for the Generality are very unlearned ; but it is also true, that they live very inoffensively, and I am likewise certain, that some of them are well acquainted with all the Learning they have. However it must be acknowledged, that the Grandees, the great Officers at Court, and Governors of Provinces, are Men the best versed in History, a Study in which most of them very much delight, and on this Account they have always about them some who addict themselves to this kind of Literature, and compose Memoirs of what passes in their own Times, which they dedicate to their Patrons.

In common Conversation the People are very complacent and communicative, nay, what is still more extraordinary, the Inhabitants of the Kingdom of *Narea*, which lies the farthest from the *Red-Sea*, and consequently from all Correspondence with our part of the World, are by far the most polite People in *Abyssinia*; nay the very Respect paid by their King to the Emperor, is the pure Effect of Politeness, since the *Abyssinian* Monarch is in no Condition of exacting such Marks of Homage, if the King of *Narea* should refuse them. *Abyssinia* is not only vexed by very potent and cruel Neighbours,

Neighbours, differing from its Inhabitants in Religion, but there are alfo in its Bowels many Colonies of thefe their Adverfaries, who give them not a Grain the lefs Trouble for being their near Neighbours. Of thefe I fhall fpeak in their Order. Firft then, the *Moors* or *Mohammedans* are poffeffed of almoft all the *Eaft* Coaft of *Abyffinia*, for the King of *Dancali*, and the King of *Adel*, with all their Subjects, are *Mohammedans*; and on the *Weft* Side, the King of *Sennar*, and the People on the other Side of the River *Melec*, are moft of them *Mohammedans* alfo. Formerly the *Moors* from *Adel* came in like a Torrent, and conquered a great part of *Abyffinia*; but they were quickly driven out again, as indeed moft of its Conquerors have been; for as foon as the *Abyffines* perceive that they are not able to meet their Enemies in the Field, they retire to their *Ambas*, or inacceffible Mountains, and leave the Conquerors to burn and plunder as they think fit. Then as foon as it is perceived that their Martial Ardour is abated, that they are exceffively fatigued and over loaden with Prey, the *Abyffines* begin to affemble, and falling upon them from all Quarters, oblige them at leaft to quit their Country, if not to leave their Booty behind them.

SUCH of the *Moors* as are fettled in *Abyffinia*, are an induftrious harmlefs People, and feem better difpofed to cultivate the Earth, and to improve the Places where they dwell than the *Abyffines*. As for the *Jews* I am at a Lofs what to fay of them; for if we confider the feveral forts of them who live in and round *Abyffinia*, and the Cuftom of the *Abyffines* themfelves, to obferve the Sabbath ftrictly, to circumcife on the eighth Day, to ufe the Levitical Purifications, to abftain from forbidden

Meats,

Meats, to fend away their Wives on every flight Occafion with a Bill of Divorce, and to boaft as they do, that their Monarch is the *Lion* of the Tribe of *Judah*; I fay when one confiders all this, one might be tempted to fay they are all *Jews*. But to avoid giving Offence, after feperating the *Abyffines*, who are a kind of Chriftian *Jews*, the remainder may be divided into *Jews*, properly fo called, and into thofe who are *Jews* only by Defcent. Of the firft there are great Numbers in the Kingdom of *Dambea*; thefe were formerly very troublefome, pretending to live in an independent manner, without yielding either Tribute or Submiffion to the *Abyffinian* Emperors. Thefe Princes for a Time wink'd at this, till an Opportunity ferv'd for reducing them, againft which, tho' to no Purpofe, the *Jews* made a vigorous Refiftance. Since then, many of them are turned Chriftians, and incorporated with the *Abyffines*; but the remainder of them now very numerous, are the moft induftrious Mechanics and Traders in the *Abyffinian* Empire. On the very Borders of this Country, on the other Side of the *Nile*, and among the barbarous People, there are many independent Colonies of *Jews*, of whofe Government and manner of living very little Account can be given, except that they have the Scriptures of the old Teftament in *Hebrew*, fpeak themfelves that Language corruptly, and moft bitterly hate the Chriftians.

As to thofe who are *Jews* only by Defcent, they are the famous Nation of the *Gaus*, *Gallas* or *Challas*, which laft I take to be their true Name, at leaft fo themfelves pronounce it. It fignifies white Men, and yet thefe People are black. However that they were once white is plain enough, for they have moft of

them

them *Roman* Noses, thin Lips, and comely Features. They are tall, robuft, well limb'd Men, very brave, but withal very cruel, and moft abominable Thieves. It is not above an hundred Years that they have vexed the *Abyffinian* Empire, or indeed that they were ever heard of there ; but in all probability it will be at leaft another hundred Years before the *Abyffinians* get fairly rid of them, for they are now fettled up and down all the Weft Borders of the Empire. They live like the ancient Patriarchs, on the Product of their Herds and Flocks, never cultivating any Land, or Building any Thing more than Cabbins to cover them from the Weather. They worfhip one GOD, circumcife, and vehemently abhor Idolatry ; but as for any other religious Tenets, it does not appear what they hold. When their Children are young, their Fathers regard them no more than Dogs ; but when they are grown big enough to hunt, and to fight, then they treat them with all imaginable Kindnefs and Affection. Thefe People are moft juftly accounted the moft dangerous Enemies in the World ; in offenfive Wars they are generally Victorious, and when they act on the diffenfive are always fo. When they fight they either conquer or die ; when they are attacked by a fuperior Force, they drive away their Cattel, and retire fo quick, that their Purfuers are quickly involved in their inhofpitable Country, where there is neither Houfe, plow'd Field, or any Thing which can furnifh Subfiftance ; fo that there is a Neceffity of retiring *Re infecta* ; and it is well if thefe People do not incommode their Retreat. Their Armies are compofed of Horfe and Foot, the former are the more numerous, but the latter are the better Troops.

They

They are divided into feveral Tribes, fome fay feven, others nine ; but I believe that Point to be uncertain ; they are governed by a fingle Magiftrate, whom they ftile *Lufo,* he has the Authority of a limited Monarch, acting nothing but by the Confent of his Council. In Point of Promifes, Treaties, or Agreements, thefe People are the moft punctual in the World ; when they make any it is with a great deal of Pomp and Ceremony, and they are never known to break them, or to deceive thofe who truft them. Such of their Children as have been left in *Abyffinia* in their fudden Retreats, and have been bred up there, prove ftrong, induftrious, and beautiful Perfons, and when thorougly inftructed in the Chriftian Religion, are wonderfully pious, and much more conftant than the *Abyffines,* readily braving Death, rather than abjure their Faith. About the Year 1648, thefe People broke at once in fix or feven Places into *Abyffinia,* ravaging from South to North, and from Weft to Eaft, killing and deftroying without Mercy all that came in their Way, prefuming fo far, as to inveft the *Turkifh* Fortrefs over-againft the Ifle of *Suakem* ; but fome Pieces of Cannon being difcharged upon them, they retired from thence, and in about nine Months Space withdrew into their old Quarters. Since then they have made two other great Irruptions, and are continually making fmall Incurfions ; but in thefe they are content to plunder without doing any Body any Hurt, unlefs they find them with Arms in their Hands. While I wandered about in this Country, my Profeffion made me every where welcome ; and if the Inhabitants had been rich, I fhould doubtlefs have brought fomething confiderable from thence. As it was, I collected

ted in *Abyſſinia*, chiefly in the South Weſt Parts, eleven Ounces of Gold in Grains, three Topazes, one Emerald, and five greeniſh colour'd Stones tranſparent, hard, and beautiful; but what they are call'd I know not. Here ends this Relation, excepting what the Author ſays of the River of *Nile*, which I have inſerted in another Place, for the Sake of uniting my own Obſervations with his, that the Hiſtory of that noble River might not be broken or interrupted.

A Description of *EGYPT*, &c.

THE ordinary Cuſtom of Travellers in mixing their Geographical, Philoſophical, and Hiſtorical Remarks on Countries with the Thread of their Narratives, having often given me a great deal of Trouble in the peruſal of their Works, I therefore determined to eſſay another Method, which in Idea, at leaſt, ſeem'd more diſtinct and intelligible; and this gave Birth to the enſuing Picture of the Country of *Egypt*, its Produce and Inhabitants, wherein I have ſtudied to digeſt Things as naturally as I could, that their Connection might render them reciprocally clear, and the whole appear a Body of tollerable Symmetry, and not with ſuch Ricketty and unproportionable Limbs as I have ſometimes ſeen in Things of this Nature.

EGYPT then is in Scripture called either *Mizraim*, or the Land of *Cham*. The *Copti*, or natural In-

X   habitants

habitants of the Country call it *Maſr* or *Chemi*, the *Turks Miſſar*. Theſe are all in Effect one Name, and ſeem an evident Demonſtration of the Veracity of the *Moſaic* Writings. As to the Name of *Egypt*, which with ſome difference in the Orthography, is the Appellation this Country is known by in our Weſtern parts, it is derived from the Story or Fable of the *Greeks* concerning *Egyptus*. But to paſs from Names to Things.

EGYPT ſtretches itſelf from the 22 deg. to the 31 deg. of North Latitude, being bounded on the Eaſt by the *Iſthmus of Suez*, a mountainous Country, which divides it from that part of *Arabia* lying between it and *Judea*. I ſay, it is bounded on this Side by theſe Mountains, and by the *Red-Sea*, which waſhes all its Coaſt up to its Southern Boundaries, which are the frontier Kingdoms of the *Abyſſinian* Empire, *viz. Fungi* and *Sennaar*; on the Weſt it hath the great Deſarts of *Africk*, to which I chuſe to give no Name; becauſe the Names we give ſerve only to confound us. On the North it hath the *Mediterranean* Sea, and we may ſafely affirm, that there is not a Country in the Univerſe better ſituate for Defence than this.

MANY Authors affirm, that the Letter Y affords an eaſy and accurate Notion of the Form of *Egypt*. At one Point they place the City of *Roſetta*, the City of *Damietta* at the other. *Grand Cairo* at the Junction of theſe Limbs with the Body of the letter, and the Cataracts of the *Nile* at the Foot of it. To me theſe Notions ſeem trivial and puerile, and much more capable of doing Hurt than Good. I grant that this Deſcription ſuits the *Nile* well enough; but I deny that it gives any tolerable Account of *Egypt*, becauſe the City

of

of *Alexandria* lies a great Way on one Side of the *Y*, as the *Isthmus* of *Suez* does on the other. A Chain of Mountains run from South to North, on the East Side of the *Nile*, and another Chain of Mountains run from South to North, on the West. At *Cairo* these Mountains open and turn off with the two great Branches of the River; those on the East remain still high and arduous Mountains; but those on the West dwindle into sandy Hillocks, and form a kind of Downs. The Plain included between these Ridges, the middle of which is occupied by the *Nile*, is in some Places very narrow, in others as in the Province of *Fium* of considerable Breadth; but it is every where fertile, and well cultivated. The Mountains on the West are the Boundaries of *Egypt*, and have Deserts behind them, but the Mountains of the East are not so, they have behind them a Plain for the most part sandy and uninhabitable, reaching to the Coast of the *Red-Sea*.

This Description seems to have little Affinity with those magnificent ones, which are to be met with in ancient Authors; but this I cannot help, I am bound to speak Truth, yet I cannot avoid owning, that I think they spoke Truth too. For tho' it is certain that there is scarce any Proportion between the Number of People which are now in *Egypt*, and the Number reported to have dwelt there formerly, yet it is as certain, that there is as great a Disproportion between the Number of People in other Parts of the *Grand Seignior*'s Dominions, and those that are here still. For my own Part, I am fully persuaded, that a very great Proportion of that Part of *Egypt* which is now uninhabitable, was former-

ly

ly not only fprinkled with Cities, but very fruitful and pleafant.

ALL this was occafioned by the Induftry of the ancient Inhabitants, and the Wifdom of their Kings, as the prefent deplorable State of thefe Places are the Refult of the Lazinefs of the People, and the Folly of their Governors. *A pleafant Land maketh he barren for the Wickednefs of thofe who dwell therein*, faith the infpired Writer, and this is juft as true as that God made the World. In another Place it is faid, *that God gives Kings in his Wrath, and Governors in his fore Difpleafure*. Here is an exact Account of what happens to all Countries, and what muft happen to all. A religious and virtuous People, have religious and virtuous Princes, thefe contrive good Things, and execute them with Spirit ; a vicious and degenerate People have Kings given them in Wrath, and they depopulate the Country, and make War on Nature ; this makes the Difference between the ancient and modern *Egypt*, as it alfo does between *Switzerland*, and the *Campania di Roma*.

THE Air of *Egypt*, according to fome Writers, is the moft foul and unwholefome in the World, in the Judgment of others, the moft ferene and falubrious. For my own Part, I think them both in the Right, and both in the wrong, as I fhall fhew by ftating this Matter truly. *November, December*, and *January* are the Winter Months, wherein the *Franks* and the *Turks* wear Garments lined with Furs, believing the Weather to be very cold ; in fact however it is not fo, but the Difpofition of their Bodies makes them have very quick Senfation, as I eafily difcerned by myfelf. I arrived in the

the Winter, and thought the Weather very moderate; but the next Winter I felt it very cold, and yet by my Glaſs it appeared that the former Winter had been colder. To the Winter ſucceeds a Spring of about ſix Weeks, which is very pleaſant. About the *Vernal E-quinox* the South Winds begin to blow, and they blow more or leſs till the Sun reaches the Tropic of Cancer. The *Arabians* call theſe Winds *Chamſin*, i. e. of *Cam-byſes*; becauſe it was by theſe Winds that his Army periſhed in their *Ethiopian* Expedition; then it is that *Egyptian* Air is unwholeſome. Theſe Winds blow ſometimes three, four, or five Days together, and then for a Day or two there is a Breeze from the North; ſometimes they blow for nine, ten, eleven, or twelve Days, and then the Air is peſtiferous, and Multitudes die of an Hour's Sickneſs. All this however is uncertain, for ſome Years they do very little Miſchief, and in other Years again they do a great deal. This only is certain, that they begin to blow about the Equinox, and that they ceaſe blowing on the riſing of the *Nile*, viz. 17th of *June*. Immediately after this, the North and Weſt Winds blow conſtantly Night and Day, and ſo temper the Heat of the Climate, that it is far from being either intemperate or unwholeſome. This pleaſant Seaſon of the Year continues from the middle of *June* till towards the End of *September*, during which Space the Country being overflown, the Inhabitants give themſelves up wholly to Pleaſure, to which indeed they are always prone.

THAT *Egypt* on the whole is far from being unwholeſome, appears from the Temper of the Natives, from their enjoying almoſt a conſtant State of Health,

unleſs

unlefs interrupted by fome exterior Accident, or fonfe wrong Management of their own, and by their *Longævity*, there being in this Country Numbers upwards of fourfcore, fo robuft in their Conftitutions, as not only to ufe Women, but to beget Children. The Soil of *Egypt* as it lies in the fourth and fifth North Climate ought to be fertile, yet I think that properly fpeaking, it is not fo, but rather quite the contrary, as abounding with Salt and Nitre, and in fome Places mixt with Sand. But the Mud left by the *Nile* covering and mixing with thefe, produces a Soil fruitful to a Miracle. But where the *Nile* comes not thefe Advantages are wanting, and the Soil is perfectly barren, but not ufelefs, as we fhall fee hereafter. They dig various Clays, fit for different Purpofes, fome are of the Nature of Fuller's Earth, fome ferve to cleanfe, to ftrengthen, and to give a bright yellow Colour to the Ladies Hair, fome are medicinal, and in that Refpect of great Value ; but moft of them are fit for making earthern Ware, efpecially for Water Jars, which for cooling and clearing the Liquid contained in them, excell all the Earthen Ware in the World. Near the Burgh of *Chafagbut* in the upper *Egypt*, they dig a Clay of a pale Pink Colour, of which they make all forts of Veffels, and of a very high Price, on Account not only of their Beauty, but of their odoriferous Smell, which they never lofe.

As to the other Commodities refulting from the Soil of *Egypt*, we will divide them into fuch as are found thereon, fuch as grow therein, and fuch as are produced thereby. Of the firft the principal are Salt and Nitre. As to the Salt of *Egypt*, it is without all Comparifon the beft in the Univerfe, the Reafon of which I

take

take to be, that it is strictly speaking, the Manufacture of Nature. After the recess of the *Nile* it is found spread upon the Earth like a white Sheet, in such quantities, that it bears a small Price, neither do they hinder any Body from gathering what may suffice for his own Use. It is white as Snow, hard as Sand, peculiarly fine in its Taste, which is simply pungent without any bitterness. *Nitre*, which the *Arabs* call *Natron*, is not so easily had, neither is it taken out of the Earth in all Parts of *Egypt*. An *Arabian* Prince who resides at *Laux*, and who hath three hundred and sixty Hamlets or Villages under his Dominion, employs constantly fifty Camels in carrying *Nitre* to *Cairo*. It is thought that he sells annually as much as comes to 100,000 *Sequins*. There are two sorts of *Nitre*, the one of Rose Colour, very hard and weighty, this they call *Sultani*, the other White and light, and less valued, called *La Sultani*. *Sal ammoniacum*, or as we call it *Sal Armoniac*, is also made in *Egypt* with great Facility, and to the great Profit of such as deal in it.

A s to the Riches which are found in the Heart of the Soil, we must reckon among them that vast abundance of Marble which is met with in upper *Egypt*, an exact Description of the several Sorts whereof would take up a Volume; I shall content myself with saying, that there are Mines of an *Onyx* Colour, the Stones dug out of which are nearly transparent; there are others of a Honey Colour, wonderfully bright and shining; also a sort of green Marble regularly sprinkled with Blood-red Spots; *Porphyry* in abundance; and in the extreme Parts of *Egypt* towards *Ethiopia*, a hard, red, shining Stone, with golden Streaks and Spots. As to precious Stones I have

X 4   already

already faid enough concerning Emeralds ; and befides thefe there are Chryfolites, Heliotropes, Jafps, and I have been told Topazes ; but I cannot affirm it. There is alfo a blue Stone of great Beauty, which differs from the Turquoife as well as from the Saphire, being opaque like the former, but in Colour inclining to the latter, curioufly fprinkled as it were with Grains of Gold. Eagle Stones are alfo found here very commonly. Vitriol, Allom, and *Lapis Calaminaris* are found there in abundance ; all excellent in their Kind.

To fpeak of all the Plants of *Egypt*, would require more Time and Experience than any Traveller, who did not go thither for that purpofe, can beftow ; I fhall content my felf therefore with touching on a few Curiofities that feldom efcape the Knowledge and Admiration of intelligent Enquirers. There grows in *Egypt* a kind of Night-fhade call'd by the Inhabitants *Dtaturq*. The Bloffom of this Plant is fweet-fcented, and it produces a round Fruit enclofed in a prickly Shell, the Core of which Fruit is full of yellow Seeds. I do not know any Good that can be done either with the Fruit or Flowers, but with the Seeds they do a great deal of Mifchief, for grinding them when dry, they make a Powder or Meal, which without cafting Men into a Sleep, or apparent Heavinefs, diforders, or rather locks up the Senfes. Thieves mix it up in Bread, and travelling in a Caravan, find Means to flip it upon fome of their Companions, from whom, an Hour after they have eaten thereof, they take what they pleafe, the Men being fenfelefs, and make the beft of their Way. There is an Herb, call'd *Culcas* by the *Arabs*, by us *Colocafia*, mightily efteem'd by the Inhabitants who eat it raw and boiled ; it is of a windy flatu-

lent

fent Nature, but is a strong Provocative, and therefore these People exceedingly delight in it. The *Papyrus* grows in the *Nile*, having a strong Root, and many strait Stalks, very high above the Water; its Leaves are triangular, and pretty thick in the middle. This was, heretofore, the all-useful Plant, now of no Use at all. The Native call Cucumbers, *Chate*; and *Egypt* may be properly stiled their Country, for they grow there to an exceffive Bignefs, are almost transparent, but at the same time their Juices so thoroughly concocted by the Sun, that they are at once much pleasanter than our Cucumbers, and perfectly innocent; so that they are eaten in Fevers. In the Neighbourhood of *Alexandria* there grow in great Plenty a kind of Trees call'd *Dachel*, or *Dadel*, peculiar to this Country; and which though they seldom shoot high, bear a very large Fruit. There is no Part of this Tree which is not of Use; the Stock or Body of it is cut into found Timber; its Boughs are turned into all Sorts of Wooden Ware; with its Leaves they wrap up Things; of its Bark they make Packthread, and a Sort of Ropes; and its Fruit hath a wonderful rich fine Taste. As to Grain and Pulfe, they have all Sorts in great Plenty, and excellent, efpecially Wheat and wild Rice, with this peculiar Advantage, that they are never at the Trouble of plowing or of weeding; they only scatter the Seed in the Mud, then draw a wooden Harrow over it, and so let it reft till Harveft.

As to the Birds of *Egypt*, they have moft of the forts which are common in *Europe*, as well as many that we have not; Quails in fuch abundance, that the Country-People take them with their Hands, but then their Flefh is black, hard, and ill-tafted. The Merchants at *Alexandria*

andria buy them alive, feed them in Coops, and thereby remove that offensive Bitterness which they have from their wild Food. Turtles also abound here, and build about their Houses. They have also very good Pidgeons, and in great Plenty; Swallows of two Sorts, which I think very remarkable, one, which is exactly like ours, and a Bird of Passage; the other, of a darker Colour, and without any Mixture of white, which stays in *Egypt* the whole Year. Geese and Swans are frequently seen swimming in the Branches of the *Nile*. Storks and Cranes are common; and many of the great Men keep of the former tame. Hawks there are excellent in their Kind, and which formerly were sold into *Europe* at great Prices; as also Kites, which the *Arabs* and *Moors* know how to tame, and to make use of in Fowling. In the Desarts, towards *Suez*, there are Ostriches, but it is thought that they are not Natives of *Egypt*, but Inmates only from the neighbouring Countries. Our common Hens are the Fowls most eat in *Egypt*, where they have two Sorts, one of the same Size with ours, the other very little inferior to Geese in Bigness, both very cheap, and easily to be had every where. Besides these, they have a Kind of Fowl brought from *Numidia*, the Flesh of which is very fine, and well tasted; this is one of their greatest Dainties, and sold dear. As they hatch all their Eggs in Ovens, their Hens are consequently never broody; and Eggs also are very plenty, which is necessary, because they make a great Part of the Food of the common People.

THE *Nile* is very well stored with Fish, and the Fish therein are remarkably large and fat, particularly a kind of Pike, excessively voracious, and which sometimes

come

come to be so large as to weigh eighty Pounds. Eeles are here in great Plenty, and high Perfection, some as thick as a Man's Arm, but they are not wholesome at all Times; and in the Months of *April* and *May* especially they are so dangerous, that many People have been poisoned by eating them. There is a broad fat Fish in the *Nile*, which though it differs widely from ours in Form, yet all the *Europeans* here will have to be a Tench, because the Flesh tastes like that of a Tench, and is therefore very much esteemed. There are also spotted Mullets, that are much valued, and are indeed a fine firm Fish. In the *Nile* likewise are abundance of Tortoises, very large, and their Flesh very sweet and good, especially when thoroughly boiled, otherwise it is unwholesome. The Cities of *Alexandria*, *Rosetta*, and *Damietta*, are furnish'd with all Sorts of Sea-Fish in the highest Perfection, and at very low Prices. Of these I shall only mention Soles, which are of an extraordinary Size, and yet perfectly well tasted. They salt a great deal of Fish for Exportation, as also the Spawn of Fish, which is of a very high Relish, and is call'd *Botarac*. From the Fish I think it is most natural to proceed to the Insects, of which there are great Variety in *Egypt*.

T h e Ants there are excessively large, and very furious, stinging or biting such as disturb them with as much Rage as a Dog, whereby they excite a burning Anguish, which continues for a long Time, and is not easily cured. Some of them have Wings, and these are still more troublesome. Flies and Gnats sting here more than any where else, and there are such abundance of the latter, that without defending the Beds by Nets, there would be no such thing as sleeping. Studious Persons,

fons, and fuch, as are much within Doors, are forced to have Nets at their Windows, and at their Chamber-doors, to prevent thefe troublefome Guefts from entering. There are many Kinds of Spiders, large and venomous, with thefe the *Ichneumon Wafp* is continually at War; and nothing can be more entertaining than to obferve the Arts made ufe of by thefe Enemies to incline Victory to their Side. There are abundance of *Bees*, efpecially on the Banks of the *Nile*, where in hollow Trees, or in Caverns, they fix their Combs, and make both excellent Honey and Wax. There are many Scorpions in *Egypt*, but all of them either white or green; they do not ex-ceed thofe of *France* in Size, but in Venom they tran-fcend thofe and all other Creatures in the World. The white are lefs venomous than the green, that is to fay, their Poifon does not operate fo foon; but with Refpect to both, an Amputation of the bitten Limb is the fole Expedient for preventing Death in a few Hours time with incredible Torture. Yet the *Moors*, who make a Trade of catching thefe Creatures for the Ufe of Apothecaries, who make an Oil of them, which is very valuable; thefe *Moors*, I fay, lay hold of them without Fear, with their bare Hands, carry them in their Bofoms, take them out from thence, and put them into the Apothecaries Veffels, without the leaft Apprehenfion; neither hath it been known that any of thefe People have been bit; for I fuppofe if they were, they would not efcape better than the *Whites*. As to black Scorpions, or flying ones, of which fome Authors fpeak very confidently, and many People in *Egypt* are ready to affert that fuch Creatures there are, I fhall only fay that I never faw any, nor ever heard any Perfon of Credit affert that he had himfelf feen

any

any fuch. Serpents and Snakes there are of innumerable Kinds; I fhall mention only a few. Of Afps there are three Sorts. The firft of thefe is the fpitting or fpewing Afp, fo call'd from its ejecting its Poifon thro' its Teeth. The Antients call'd it *Ptyas*; and this was the Serpent *Cleopatra* made ufe of when fhe refolved to end her Misfortunes by Death. This Serpent is about three Feet long, and rather bigger than our Viper; its Bite is mortal, and generally efteemed incurable; bu this is far from being a proper Defcription of the Nature of its Venom, which is very fingular. It is thought that this Creature ejects lefs in Quantity than any other of the Kind; however that be, it is certain that the Punctures made by its Teeth are fcarce difcernable. After a Perfon has been bitten about an Hour, he finds himfelf heavy and inclined to Sleep, without any Pain or Diforder of Mind; by degrees, however, he finds his Limbs lofe their Strength, a kind of pleafing Stupidity invade his animal Faculties; and fo he dies without a Groan or a Complaint. The fecond fort of Afp, in Colour, Shape, and Length, refembles a *Pike*. The laft Sort are from fifteen to eighteen Inches long, their Bellies white, their Backs of a very deep blue; they have their Holes in the Banks of the *Nile*, from whence they fpring with a terrible and fatal Fury. Amputation is the only Cure, and where that cannot be had, the Patient dies in terrible Agonies. The Horn Serpent is a great Curiofity; the *Egyptians* call it *Tabyr*; and the Antients have abundance of odd Stories about it. After all, it is far from being uncommon, and a little Care is fufficient to remove all the Doubts that have been raifed concerning it. It is of a yellow Colour, about eighteen Inches long,

long, a round flender Body, with a broad flat Head; the Females have at the Corner of their Eyes two ftrong pointed Horns; the Male hath but one, which is towards his Nofe. They live chiefly in dry Places, and are thought to draw their Nourifhment from Nitre and Salt. They are extremely venomous, and Thofe who are bitten by them die of Thirft; which no Art can palliate. As to Serpents of great Magnitude, they are not frequently feen, but there are certainly in *Egypt* fome as thick as a Man's Thigh, and fifteen or twenty Feet long: But for Dragons and flying Serpents, I am apt to believe they rather live in the Heads of fanciful Men, than either in this or any other Country. I will conclude this Article with an Account of the moft wonderful, though the moft common Serpent in *Egypt*. This is call'd by the Inhabitants *Tobbam*, and is generally between three and fix Feet long, though fome have been feen a great deal bigger. It hath a flefhy Subftance reaching on each Side of its Neck from its Jaw to about a third Part of its Body; this it either ftiffens or contracts as it will, and thereby not only erects itfelf in a furprifing Manner, but alfo throws it felf forward as if it flew. It is ufually found in the *Catacombs*, and among ancient Ruins; but its Affection for Men, as it is very fingular, fo it is alfo unaccountable. If the Juglers only, who never fail to have many of thefe Species of Serpents, were poffeffed of the Skill of Taming them, it would be lefs wonderful; but this is fo far from being the Cafe, that all Degrees of People who delight in Animals feed and keep thefe Creatures about them. They are not only tame and innoxious, but alfo ufeful and docible, to a degree beyond our Dogs in *Europe*, infomuch that nothing

thing can be more diverting than to fee them play over
the Tricks they are taught.

Of Scaly Lizard-like Animals, there are great Variety in *Egypt*, particularly the *Cameleon*, which refembles
much an ordinary Lizard, yet is it far lefs beautiful,
neither has it almoft any of thofe Properties for which it
was celebrated by the Antients. It is fo far from living
upon Air, that it is a very voracious Animal, maintaining it felf by catching and eating of Flies. As to
changing of Colour, that too is a Miftake, unlefs its having a changeable colour'd Skin may pafs for a Wonder.
As to its Eye turning every Way, therein the Defcription is right, for it doth fo in a very odd Manner, one
Eye looking forwards, and the other frequently behind ;
and this Provifion Nature hath made that it may eafily
catch its Prey. The *Scinos*, or Land-Crocodile, is a
very exact Copy of the Water One, but very little and
harmlefs, feeding moftly upon Flowers and Herbs, efpecially fuch as are of a fweet Smell. The Crocodile it
felf delights in the *Nile*, but more in the great Lakes
formed by Channels, derived from thence. In the *Delta* there are fometimes Crocodiles feen, but fmall and
lean ; this the Inhabitants of *Egypt* afcribe to the Power
of a *Talifman* ; but the true Reafon feems to be the
Number of Boats on the River, and of Villages on its
Banks, for the Crocodiles naturally fly from and avoid
Men in Companies ; for if they are fingle, and in the
upper *Egypt*, they will venture to attack them. The
Ancients have certainly reported abundance of things
falfely of this Creature, for which there was the lefs Occafion, fince in it felf it is a wonderful Creature, as well
as moft terrible and cruel. It is believed to grow as long
as

as it lives, and it is certain that some have been seen upwards of thirty Feet long. It runs swiftly, but cannot easily turn; its great Strength lies in its Tail, which it uses very nimbly, striking its Prey therewith, and so stupifying it before it eats it. Some have spoken of tame Crocodiles, but surely with little Certainty; since at *Cairo* it is known by Experience that when a young Crocodile is taken, it will refuse Meat till it dies. The Female Crocodile lays about sixty Eggs at a time; they are not bigger than those of a Goose; the young Crocodiles are small in Proportion, but they are amazingly swift in their Growth. They are taken by various Arts; and some of the *Moors* are so hardy, that with a strong Rope they will venture into the *Nile*, and after a long Combat, drag out a Crocodile, and bring him to *Cairo*, where they first make a kind of Show of him, and then kill him.

T H E Inhabitants of *Egypt* are *Copts*, or *Cophti*; *Jews*, *Moors*, *Arabs*, *Turks* and *Franks*, or *European Christians*. Of all these in their Order. The *Copts*, or *Cophts*, are the natural Inhabitants of this Country. This Name signified originally the Inhabitants of the *Coptic Nome*, the Capital of which was the City of *Coptos*; but by degrees it hath been extended to all the *Egyptian Christians*. In like manner the *Arabians* stiled them *Kibthi*, from *Kibth*, which is the modern Name of the ancient City of *Coptos*. These poor People may be justly reckoned among the most dejected and distressed Nations in the Universe. The *Turks*, and all the *Mohammedans* in *Egypt*, treat them with the opprobrious Name of Infidels; and, on the other hand, the Christians, in Communion with the Church of *Rome*, look upon them as Heretics.

Heretics. Thus are they perfecuted and defpifed by Friends and Strangers, and lead their Lives in the moft abject Sort of Slavery that can be imagined. They were formerly very numerous, but at prefent they are much reduced, and daily decreafing. The Language they ufe is peculiar to their Nation, and feems to be a Compound of the ancient *Egyptian*, and of the *Greek* Tongue as it was fpoken by the Soldiers of *Alexander* the Great. In refpect to their religious Tenets, they have been grofly mifreprefented; and though it be true that they are not a learned or very quick-witted Nation, yet are they far from being fo ftupid or ignorant as they are generally reprefented.

It is certain that they are zealous Chriftians, and that they have very juft Notions of the Caufes and Confe-quences of C H R I S T's Coming, whom they ftile the *Meffiah*. They baptize by three Immerfions, invoking the Perfons of the Holy Trinity feparately. Namely, one at each Immerfion. They likewife ufe many Unc-tions with that Ceremony. When any of them are in-difpofed, the Prieft comes and prays by them, and not only anoints the fick Perfon, but alfo All who are prefent with him in the Room with confecrated Oil, for which they affign this Reafon, that the Difeafe may not retire from the fick Perfon to any of his Friends, which they believe to be prevented by this general Unction. The *Roman* Catholicks affect to treat this Proceeding with great Contempt; and yet an indifferent Perfon will be apt to think that it is juft as well founded as theirs. In giving the Eucharift they are very fingular, for to In-fants, immediately after Baptifm, they give only the Wine, to Men they give the Communion under both

Y   Species;

Species ; and to the Women, who offer their Devotions without the Sanctuary, they give the Bread only, having first moistened it with a drop or two of the Wine. Confeſſion to Prieſts they permit, but they do not compel it ; they faſt conſtantly on *Wedneſdays* and *Fridays*, and obſerve beſides three *Lents* in the Year ; but then they eat Fleſh on all the *Sundays* in the Year, and every *Saturday*, except the *Saturday* in the Holy Week. They are wonderfully ſincere in all their Acts of Devotion ; and though their extreme Poverty, and that exceſſive Dejection of Mind which is derived from thence makes them contemptible in the Eyes of the *Franks* in general, yet thoſe who endeavour to lay aſide theſe Prejudices cannot but receive much Edification from the Purity of their Lives, and the Humility of their Deportment.

T H E I R Clergy conſiſts of Subdeacons, Deacons, Prieſts, Biſhops, Archbiſhops, and a Patriarch, who ſits in the Chair of St. *Marc*, whoſe Succeſſor he is by an uninterrupted Chain of Prelates, which gives him a great Authority in this Part of the World. Their Biſhops are eleven in Number, their Patriarch making the twelfth. As for the laſt he is a Monk, one, of whoſe Chaſtity there is no Suſpicion, and who is generally compell'd to take upon him this high Office. He is a kind of Prince or Judge of his People, and beſides conſecrates the *Abuna*, or Patriarch of *Ethiopia*. To this Patriarch of the *Copts*, who is generally ſtiled Patriarch of *Alexandria*, there belongs a Revenue of near ſix thouſand Pounds Sterling *per Annum*, all of which he beſtows in the Relief of the Poor, or on national Occaſions, reſerving for his own Subſiſtence the Alms of good Chriſtians, which he aſks with great Humility, and lives upon them very frugally,

riding

riding up and down on an Aſs without any other Enſign of Dignity than his paſtoral Staff. The greateſt of their Errors ſeems to be that of Circumciſing, which is either the Remains of ſome *Judaical* Notion, or which is more probable, hath been introduced ſince the Conqueſt of *Egypt* by the *Mohammedans*, in Complaiſance to them. But this Practice begins to be difuſed, and ſeveral of their Patriarchs have declared againſt it. Their Monks live in Deſarts, in large Monaſteries, where they fare very hardly, labour with their Hands, and ſpend all their Time in Acts of Piety and Charity, which they exerciſe chiefly towards the *Arabs*, who travelling in theſe waſte Places, find themſelves often on the Point of periſhing for Want, from which they are delivered by the Supplies afforded them by theſe Monks. As to the Laity, they are either induſtrious Mechanics, laborious Peaſants, or Stewards to *Turkiſh* Lords, who make Choice of them for their remarkable Fidelity. With Trade they meddle not, leſt it ſhould corrupt their Manners: And ſo ſtrictly are they bound to their Religion and their Country, that no Proſpects of Preferment can ever allure them to think of quitting *Egypt*, or changing that laborious Life which they lead there for one more commodious in another Place.

T H E *Jews* are very numerous here, for which there is a very good Reaſon, *viz.* the great Conveniency they have of getting Money, for which, it is well known, that they compaſs Sea and Earth, and neglect no Methods of attaining it that their own quick Wits ſuggeſt. There are certainly forty thouſand at leaſt in *Egypt*, who All live upon the Labours of others; for, except a few Toys and childiſh Baubles, they make nothing themſelves; but by Peddling, Quacking, acting as Brokers, and

Y 2

above

above all, turning Collectors of the Revenue, Tax-ga-
therers, and Financiers, they make a Shift to amafs
Fortunes at the Expence of the People, which they feldom live to enjoy, at leaſt in Quiet, for Reaſons that
will hereafter appear. The common Opinion is, that
the Climate and Soil of this Country transform all its
Natives into perfect *Egyptians*, that is, into Men without Will to Labour, Courage to Fight, or Ambition to
diſtinguiſh themſelves any other Way, Finery excepted. The *Jews*, however, eſcape this Infection pretty
well, and ſeem to preſerve their Subtilty, Avarice, and
adulatory Addreſs, as well here as in other Parts of the
World. There is no ſort of Trade carried on without
their having not only a Share therein, but the principal
Direction thereof : So that *Chriſtians* and *Turks* are conſtrained to make Uſe of them, though the former are
always diffident of them, and the latter deſpiſe and deteſt
them. As a Proof of this, I need only obſerve, that
the *Mohammedan* Divines aſſign to the wicked *Jews* the
loweſt Parts of Hell, where they fancy they are confined
ſeparately from thoſe of their Religion, and from the
Chriſtians. Whenever they ſpeak of them, they do it
in Terms of Hatred and Contempt ; and yet their moſt
important Affairs are managed by them, of which, as
near as I can, I ſhall endeavour to point out the Reaſons.

THE *Jews*, as they are ſcattered over the Face of
the Earth, ſo they maintain amongſt themſelves a very
ſtrict and regular Correſpondence ; this gives them vaſt
Advantages, eſpecially among People who keep no Correſpondence at all ; and therefore the Need they have of
them obliges the *Turks* to employ them. Again, their

Skill

Skill in Money-Matters, their Knowledge in Trade, their Acquaintance with the Means of felling or procuring any thing that is offered or wanted, renders them a fort of Tools which are not only convenient, but which Men, like the *Turks* and *Arabs*, cannot be without. But above all, their Subtlenefs, their Fawning, their mean Condefcenfions, and their adroit Flattery, makes them the propereft Agents in the World for the *Turkifh* Officers, who are equally indolent, and proud, defirous of enjoying all Things, and who notwithftanding cannot bear the Thoughts of doing any thing. Hence from the Bafhaw of *Cairo*, down to the Aga in any garrifon'd Place, there is not one of them but hath *Jews* about him, by whofe Advice and Affiftance he pillages the People, and enriches himfelf. The *Jews*, however, here, and throughout all the *Eaft*, affect to diftinguifh themfelves from the *Jews* of the *Weft*, (who alfo come on their Occafions into thefe Parts of the World) and treat them as if they were much below them, chiefly on this Account, that they boaft of having preferved greater Privileges in the *Eaft* than their Brethren have in the *Weft* ; as alfo that their Copies of the Scripture are purer and more correct ; whereas the *Turks* ftick not to affirm, that they have corrupted the Scriptures, which is the Reafon they affign for their being punifhed more in the other World than any other Nation. Many of thefe People pretend to Skill in Phyfic, but few of them are any better than Empiricks, exceffively ignorant, and as exceffively arrogant. There are alfo abundance of them Aftrologers, Geomantifts, and Profeffors of other occult Sciences ; but miferable Profeffors they are, for if their Impudence be excepted, which is indeed fuperior to other

People's

People's in a fuperlative degree, they have feldom the common Rudiments of Knowledge even in thofe Arts in which they boaft themfelves Proficients.

In Impofture they have gone farther than any other Nation, which is the fole Reafon, as I apprehend, that the Story of the wandering *Jew* hath circulated over all the World, and is equally believed by the Vulgar in *China* and in *Great Britain.* The *Mohammedans* tell us very ferioufly that he is *Zerid,* a Defcendant from *Elias,* and that he was feen by one of their Prophet's Commanders in a certain high Mountain, where he told him that he had remained all this time alive by the Command of JESUS CHRIST, and that he was to attend his fecond Coming, of which he pretended to acquaint the *Arab* with certain Marks or Tokens, not unlike thofe, which in the *Revelations* are made coincident with the coming of Antichrift. The Chriftians again, I mean the Oriental Chriftians, have contrived a very orderly Story on this Head, from which they feldom or never vary; and the Subftance of it is this, that the Name of the wandering *Jew* is *Jofeph,* and that he was an Ufher to *Pilate,* in which Quality pufhing our Saviour out of the Palace with opprobrious Language, JESUS turned and faid, *The Son of Man goeth hence, but thou fhalt remain here until I come.* Struck with thefe Words, it is faid that he became a Convert to the Chriftian Religion, and hath fince that Time wandered up and down the World, renewing his Age after this Manner. When he attains the Age of a hundred, he falls firft into Convulfions, and then into a Swoon, or deep Sleep, from which he awakens in the full Vigour of a Man of forty-five. They pretend that his Memory remains perfect, and that he is able to give a

distinct

diſtinct Account of whatever hath come to his Knowledge throughout all the Time he has lived. Dr. *Salviati* aſſured me that ſuch a Perſon had been ſeen about the middle of the ſixteenth Century in *Germany*, where though he was very ſtrictly examined by *Jews* as well as *Chriſtians*, they were unable to detect him in any Falſehood : And I have been alſo told, that a Perſon aſſuming this Character had been ſeen in *Egypt* ſeveral Times. All the Uſe I make of this Relation is to ſhew the univerſal Prejudice of the Inhabitants of all Countries againſt this unhappy People, whoſe Diſperſion, and the Circumſtances attending it, afford ſuch convincing Proofs of the Truth both of the *Moſaic* and *Chriſtian* Revelations, as might convince any Man who would be at the Pains to conſider them attentively.

UNDER the general Name of *Moors* I comprehend all the *Mohammedans* from *Algiers*, *Tunis*, *Tripoli*, *Fez* and *Morocco*, who flying from the Poverty of their native Countries, come by Multitudes into *Egypt*, to pick up a miſerable Subſiſtance by all Sorts of ſlaviſh Employments, or by downright begging. To ſay that theſe People are treated with the utmoſt Scorn and Indignity by the *Turks*, is to give them no diſtinguiſhing Character at all, ſince they treat without Diſtinction all the Peaſants and Villagers in *Egypt* whom they ſtile *Felacs* in the ſame Way. They impoſe on them what Tasks they think fit, exact Obedience by any Means rather than fair ones, abuſe and maltreat them with their Tongues and with their Hands ; and after all this, if the poor Wretches ſhould make the leaſt Reſiſtance, Death would certainly be the End of all their Miſeries. What Wonder then that theſe hopeleſs People ſhould be timid in their Natures

tures

tures, whofe Spirits are broken from their Infancy, and in whom the Difpofition of a manly appearance would be fatal ? Hence the Word *Felac* is amongft the better fort of People of all others the moft outragious Reproach, as carrying in it an Impeachment of a Man's Under-ftanding, Morals, and Bravery, finking them at once into the Rank of Blockheads and Cowards. But to return to the *Moors*.

In a Country where there are fo many who require Service, and where no Man will labour who can fubfift in ever fo poor a manner without it, there muft be occafion fufficient for many Hands, and this is that which invites thefe poor People to *Alexandria*, *Rofetta*, *Damietta*, and other Towns in *Egypt*, where they let out Affe, work in the Gardens, ply as Porters, and perform whatever elfe is required of them for fuch daily Wages as in *England* would fcarce be offered to a Beggar at the Door. Bread, Herbs and Salt, are all their Subfiftance, and tho' they live in a Land of Plenty, yet they look like fo many Ghofts, efpecially where their Numbers very much exceed the Neceffities of their Mafters, as frequently happens, and then the Fear of their thieving or doing worfe Mifchiefs, obliges the Inhabitants of the Places to which they refort, to drive them away by Force. A few *Moors* of Quality indeed do refide in *Egypt*, and live there in Reputation and Splendor ; becaufe as I fhall hereafter fhew, this is a fort of Privileged Place, to which Men from all Countries retire to live at Eafe on that Wealth which would be fatal to them elfewhere, and which is alfo fometimes fatal to them here. All thefe *Moors* are alike zealous *Mohammedans* ; and tho' in other Refpects many of them are

ignorant

Ignorant to the laſt Degree, yet in reciting their Prayers enjoined by their Law, they ſhew a Fire and Spirit of Devotion, which would be very edifying if it did not border a little on Enthuſiaſm. The *Franks* are as great Enemies to theſe People as the *Turks*, they ſpeak of them always as if they were the Dregs of all Mankind, and alike void of Senſe and Virtue ; to make up theſe Deficiencies, they allow them Vices without Number, and yet when the Thing is candidly examined, it does not appear that theſe People are worſe than their Neighbours. Their extream Poverty tempts them to thieve, and the Severity with which they are uſed, extirpates in them that Compaſſion which uſually attends human Nature. But is this Matter of Reproach towards them, or ought it not rather to fall upon thoſe who hammer into them theſe baſe Notions by their bad Treatment?

MEN are pretty much alike in all Countries and in all Climates ; it is the different Modes of governing, and various Ways of living, which make Men in one Place ſo unlike Men in another ; and therefore in all Countries the Governors are reſponſible to reaſonable Men here, and to the God of Truth and Juſtice hereafter, for the epidemic Errors of their People. If thoſe who are entruſted with the Management of publick Affairs in *Egypt* would but think it incumbent on them to contrive proper Means for the ſupport of thoſe over whom they rule, theſe wretched *Moors* inſtead of being a Burthen and Diſgrace to this Country, as now they are, might be employed in repairing publick Works, which would not only reſtore the ancient Luſtre of *Egyptian* Magnificence, and exceedingly benefit all the Inhabitants of that vaſt Country, but alſo turn to the immenſe Profit of

of the *Grand Seignior*. This I am the rather perſuaded
of, from the Behaviour of the *Moors* in the Service of
my Patron *Haſſan*. They were moſt of them ſuch as
he pick'd up in *Egypt*, and ſet to work as much out of
Charity, as for the Sake of what they did for him.
Theſe were all diligent, faithful, laborious Creatures,
and in the Concerns I have had with any of that Nation, I have never been able to diſcover that the Prejudices againſt them were founded in any Thing but their
Misfortunes, their extream Indigence, and their as extreme ill Uſage. I do confeſs that this Opinion is ſingular, but ſingular Opinions are not always groundleſs.
Moſt Men judge by Experience, and believe themſelves
juſtified in ſo judging; and therefore in following this
Cuſtom, I rid myſelf of ſingularity, and go in the
beaten Tract again.

BEFORE I quit this Subject I cannot help taking Notice, that theſe *Moors*, who are thought to have ſcarce
common Senſe in *Egypt*, are in their own Countries
known to be as artful, and as cunning, as any People
in the Univerſe. The Chriſtian Slave of *Haſſan*, who
brought me firſt to his Maſter's Acquaintance, furniſh'd
me with a Multitude of Inſtances in ſupport of what I
have advanced, amongſt theſe I have ſelected one,
which to me is not inferior to any Stratagem mentioned
by the *Greek* and *Latin* Authors.

MOHAMMED Almadi King of *Fez*, was a
Prince who in his younger Years, either had or affected
a ſtrong Paſſion for the Study of Divinity. The Aſ-
cendancy he gained over the Minds of Men, by being
believed to have more Religion than is uſually found
in Heads covered with Crowns, enabled him to puſh
Things

Things farther than moſt of his Predeceſſors; all his Clergy were devoted to his Intereſts, his Nobility ſtood in great Fear of him, and his People really believed that in him were united the Characters of Prince and Prophet. The Inhabitants of a Country lying to the South of his Dominions, had erected a kind of *Ariſtocratical* Common-wealth, under which they lived if not happily, at leaſt much better than any of their Neighbours, and the Report of their being a rich and opulent People, vehemently ſpurred *Almadi* to attempt the bringing them under his Government.

With this View he ſet a great Army on Foot, marched into the Frontiers of his Neighbours, began to take their ſtrong Places, and to ravage all the open Country. In vain the poor People oppoſed him, his Army was victorious in ſeveral Actions, tho' not without Loſs, and he ſeemed to be on the Point of compleating his Deſign, when he was informed, that the Enemy had drawn together an Army ſuperior to his own, in order to make their laſt Effort for the Preſervation of their Country. *Almadi* upon this, directed his March towards their Camp, and in a few Days a general Battle enſued, which for many Hours was fought with great Bravery and Reſolution on both Sides. At length the Army of the King of *Fez* was conſtrained to retire, leaving many thouſand dead Bodies on the Field of Battle.

Then it was that the Soldiers for the firſt Time ſhewed a Diſlike to their Prince's Conduct. They ſaid that he had led them far from their Families to periſh in a Foreign War, meerly to gratify his Ambition; that if as he pretended, he had undertaken this Expedition by the

the Command of God, they fhould have been miraculoufly affifted, or at leaft they fhould not have been
beaten ; and therefore they determined to compel him
to retreat. *Almadi* having Intelligence of this mutinous
Difpofition, fent for a few of the Officers on whom he
could depend, and having laid before them the Reafons
he had to believe that the Enemy was in a worfe Condition than they, he fhewed them the Probability there
was of perfecting the Conqueft of this Country, if the
Courage of his Soldiers could but be reftored; and in order to this, he propofed the following Expedient. That
thefe Officers fhould in the dead of the Night go and
lay themfelves among the dead Men, from whence by
the King's Orders they were to be brought off, and interr'd in certain Tombs which were in a Village hard
by, and in which fuch Holes were made as were fufficient to furnifh them with Air.

THIS Propofition being agreed to, and carried into
Execution, *Almadi* affembled other Officers, of whofe
Fidelity he doubted, and having reproached them with
want of Loyalty, and the injurious Things they had
faid of him ; he exhorted them to go to the Tombs of
their Companions, and after recommending themfelves
to Heaven by Prayer, to enquire of the deceafed Captains, whether the Promifes he had made them of Felicity in the other World, were not accomplifhed to
the full. Thefe laft mentioned Officers, in Purfuance
of the King's Inftructions went, accompanied with a
great Company of Soldiers, where after folemn Prayer,
they were furprized to hear the following Speech pronounced by a fhrill Voice from one of the Tombs;
Fight valiantly my Brethren in the Caufe of God and
the

the King, since all who fall therein pass immediately to Paradise, and enjoy all the Bliss promised by our Prophet, let their past Life be ever so wicked.

THE Troops inspired with new Valour retired from the Tombs, and having encompaffed the Tent of their Prince, promifed him to follow him chearfully wherever he pleafed to lead them. *Almadi* thanked them in a long and pious Speech, and as foon as he had difmiffed them, went with a few Attendants to the Tombs, where he caufed all the Air Holes to be ftopped up, fuppofing that thofe who had ferved him fo faithfully when living, ought not to refufe to die for him, when that alone was capable of furthering his Service. This I think is a fufficient Proof, that if the *Moors* are as wicked as our *Europeans*, they are likewife as capable of being wicked to fome Purpofe, if the Purpofes of the Great deferve that Name.

THE *Arabs* in *Egypt* may be divided, as indeed they may be every where into two Claffes. Such as live in Towns, and who differ little from the reft of the *Egyptians*, and fuch as live altogether in the Defarts, and are properly fpeaking *Bedoui* or *Arabi*, whom we call *Bedouins* and *Arabs*. As to thofe whom the *Turks* call *Cara Arabi*, or *Black Arabs*, they are properly fpeaking no *Arabs* at all, for by this Appellation they diftinguifh all fuch as have a Dufkinefs or Darknefs in their Complexion, fuch as the Inhabitants of *Abyffinia*, *Nubia*, and the lower *Ethiopia*. Moft Travellers tell us, that the *Arabs* who inhabit Towns, are honefter and more civilized than the wild *Arabs*, as they are pleafed to call them, upon whom they beftow all the villainous Epithets that a heated Imagination can fuggeft. Yet is all

this

this the Effect of downright Ignorance ; for in Truth
these civilized *Arabs* are so corrupted by living among
the *Turks*, that it is not very safe to trust them, while
on the other Hand, the free *Arabs* are not only a generous and polite People, but are above all Things remarkable for keeping their Faith, which they readily
give to any Stranger who trusts them on his own Accord, and are never known to break it.

. The Reason why most of the *Franks* entertain such
wrong Notions of these People, is because they will not
take the Pains, or as they call it, run the Hazard of
being acquainted with them; they are pleased with the
Arabians in Cities, because they have a frankness, and
pleasantness in their Tempers, which is rarely met with
in the *Turks*; they are prejudiced against the other
Arabs, by seeing them frequently brought to *Cairo*, and
other Places for robbing on the Highway, where they
are constantly put to the most cruel Deaths, which
they endure with what appears to be a brutal Obstinacy. All Nations like all private Men have their Faults,
and as we are better acquainted with our Neighbour's
Failings than with our own, so the Inhabitants of one
Country decry another on Account of Customs they
do not understand. Instead of doing this, a wise Man
makes it his Business to enquire narrowly into those
Customs; for whatever some People may think, Surprize is always the Child of Ignorance; if we know little, we are apt to be surprised at every Thing ; but in
Proportion as our Knowledge encreases, this Disposition
wears off. In like manner young Horses are apt to
start, but when they have been compelled by the Spur
to approach the Objects of their Fear, they are cured
of

of this Vice; fo much more judicious are we in managing our Horfes than our Children. But to return from this Digreffion.

As the *Arabs* believe themfelves defcended from *Ifhmael*, they are extremely proud of their Nobility, looking down with Contempt on the *Turks*, whom they regard as a mixt People, and confequently of mean Birth, for the Purity of their Families is with them the Ground of Nobility. They are however fo modeft as to confefs that they are not able to trace their Genealogies fo high as this Father of their Race, but content themfelves with deriving their Families from fome of his Defcendants. The whole Nation is divided into Tribes, and thofe again are fubdivided into Families, each of which has a Chief. Their fole Profeffion is Arms, for they think it beneath them to exercife any manual Trades, whereas the *Sciences* they exceedingly affect, efpecially Rhetorick and Poefy. They feldom care to come into Cities, tho' fometimes they do upon the publick Faith; for the *Turks* and they live in continual Hoftilities. Thefe People, I mean the *Arabs*, look upon it as a Difgrace to die in their Beds, and this it is that makes them fo fearlefs in their Expeditions. If they are made Prifoners they fo much difdain the *Turks*, that they will not vouchfafe to fpeak; but fometimes when they come to fuffer Death, which is generally the terrible one of impaling, they converfe with each other on indifferent Things, and fo yield up their Breath with a Conftancy, of which it is impoffible to give a proper Defcription. I do not fay that this Behaviour is right or commendable, but I fay it is Heroifm, tho' built on falfe Principles; for to conferve the Abilities of the Mind in

the

the midft of Misfortunes and Pains, is the utmoft Effect of human Courage, and is always admirable, let its Caufe be what it will. For my own Part, the Courage of the *Arabs* appears more Heroic to me, than the Courage fhewn by Chriftians ; becaufe the Principles upon which Chriftians act are plain and fimple, and provided they are truly Chriftians, it is impoffible that Death fhould alarm them much ; whereas the *Arabs* are generally governed by temporal Motives, which one would think fhould render Life dearer to them than they do. But Cuftom, Example, and above all the Exhortation of their Women, who place all the Merit of a Man in his Valour, brings them into fuch a ftubborn Habit of fupporting Evil, that the Patience of an *Arab* is in Practice a great deal fuperior to the Patience of a Stoic in Theory.

As to their Perfons, the *Arabs* are generally middle fized thin Men, their Features regular, their Prefence noble and majeftic, extremely nimble in their Motions, and the compleateft Horfemen in the World. In their Tempers they are generally grave, generous, full of Ambition, amorous, prone to the occult Sciences, and fond of Poetry to excefs, Magnificent in their Habits where they have it in their Power, but frugal beyond Belief in their manner of living, extremely tender of their Children, but too fevere towards their Subjects and Slaves. I might extend this Character by digreffing into a multitude of other Particulars, but I chufe rather to paint the *Arabs* from the Life, and by relating Facts to raife an Idea nearer Truth than any Defcription I can make would ever excite. The grand Charactriftick of the Genius of the *Arabians* is a fubtile Vivacity

of

of Mind, of which the following Inftance hath fo charmed the oriental Nations, that it hath been made the Subject of two long Pòems, and indeed it is extremely well chofen, inafmuch as it unfolds exactly a Temper otherwife not eafily reprefented.

THREE *Arabs*, Brethren of a noble Family, who were travelling together for the fake of improving their Minds, were met by Accident by a *Camel Driver*, who afked them, if they had not feen a Camel which had ftrayed from him in the Night? *Was not the Camel blind of an Eye?* faid the eldeft: *Yes*, faid the Man. *It had a Tooth out before*, faid the fecond: *It is very true*, replyed the Man. *Was it not a little lame?* added the third: *Why really it was*, returned the Driver. The *Camel Driver* took it for granted that they had feen it; and therefore befought them to tell him which Way it went. *Follow us Friend*, faid they; the Man did fo. He had not gone far before he happened to fay, that the *Camel was laden with Corn. And it had*, added the *Arabians*, a *Veffel of Oil on one Side, and a Veffel of Honey on the other: It had fo*, faid the Man, *therefore let me conjure you to tell me where you met it. Met it*, replyed the eldeft of the Brothers, *Why we never faw your Camel at all.* The Man lofing Patience at this, began to load them with Reproaches, and as they were paffing through a Village raifed the People upon them, and caufed them to be apprehended. The Judge of the Village not being able to determine the Caufe, fent them to the Prince of the Country, who perceiving by their Behaviour that they were Perfons of Diftinction, fet them at Liberty, lodged them in his Palace, and treated them with all the Refpect imaginable. After

Z

fome

fome Days were over, he took an Opportunity to intreat them to clear up this Myftery, by explaining to
him how they could poffibly hit upon fo many Circumftances without ever having feen the Camel. The
young Men fmiled at the importunity of the Prince,
and after having returned him abundance of Thanks for
the Civilities they had received, the eldeft of them fpoke
thus: " *We are not either Deceivers or Necromancers,*
" *we never faw the Man's Camel, nor did we ufe any*
" *other Inftruments of Divination than our Senfes and*
" *our Reafon. I for my Part judged it was blind, be-*
" *caufe I obferved the Grafs eaten on one fide of the*
" *Road, and not on the other.* I, faid the fecond,
" *gueffed it had loft a Tooth before, becaufe where the*
" *Grafs was cropt clofeft, there was conftantly a little*
" *Tuft left behind. And I,* added the third, *conceived it*
" *was Lame, becaufe the Prints of three Feet were di-*
" *ftinct in the Road, whereas the Impreffion of the fourth*
" *was blurred; whence I concluded, that the Beaft*
" *dragged it, and did not fet it to the Ground.* All
" *this I apprehend,* faid the Prince, *but how in the Name*
" *of Providence could you difcover that Oil and Honey*
" *made a part of its loading? Why,* returned the *Ara-*
" *bians, we gueffed this, becaufe on one fide of the Road*
" *we faw little Troops of Ants ferriting the Grafs, and*
" *on the other we faw the Flies affembled here and there*
" *in Groups, infomuch that few or none were on the*
" *Wing.*" Whether this Story be true or falfe matters
not much, fince it fo exactly expreffes what it was
meant to exprefs, the quick and deep Penetration of the
Arabs.

ALL

ALL their Sayings are ſtrongly impregnated with this ſort of Spirit ; but it requires a kind of Enthuſiaſm to apprehend the force of them, for I have known *Europeans* of ſo phlegmatic a Temper, as to ſee nothing ſhining in their brighteſt Sayings. For Example, I heard a *German* Monk diſpute the Elegance of the *Arabian* Maxim, *That in* God *is the ſole Refuge from* God. By which they mean, that acquieſcing in his Will is the ſole Remedy againſt thoſe Evils, which through the Courſe of Providence fall upon us, and hurt us only by our Impatience, ſince they are always intended for our Good, either here or hereafter, which if we underſtood, they would be no Evils at all.

THEY are extremely diffident of the *Turks*, whom they look upon as the moſt perfidious People in the World, and alledge this as a juſt Cauſe why they are continually exerciſing their People in Excurſions, which very ſtrongly reſemble Robberies. During the Time I was in the upper *Egypt*, I had the following Story from the Mouth of the *Bey*, who tho' the Subject, was yet the implacable Enemy of the *Grand Seignior*. *Hamet* Prince of *Sait* was, in the beginning of the ſixteenth Century, the moſt powerful Lord in *Egypt*, and having a juſt Conception of the Maxims of the *Turkiſh* Government, ſent regularly the ſtipulated Tribute to *Cairo*, but would never be prevailed upon to go thither in Perſon, either by fair Means or foul. The Exploits he performed with great Bodies of Horſe, that were always at his Command againſt ſuch of his Neighbours as juſtly incurred his Reſentment, ſpread his Fame even as far as *Conſtantinople*, where it was reſolved, that he ſhould be taken off by ſome Means or other. The

Report

Report of the *Baſſa* of *Cairo* demonſtrated that this could not be done by Force ; and therefore it was made a ſtanding Inſtruction to all his Succeſſors, to allure *Hamet* to *Cairo*, and there to ſecure his Perſon till the *Sultan's* Pleaſure ſhould be farther known. Several Years were elapſed before this could be brought about. At laſt *Haſſan Baſſa*, a *Eunuch*, a Man of great Experience and Addreſs, by repeated Aſſurances of his Maſter's particular Reſpect and Favour towards this Prince, drew him to *Cairo*, attended by the *Baſſa's Chiaja*, to do him the greater Honour. As they entered the Suburb *Bulack*, they ſaw a fine gilded Barge in the *Nile*, on Board which were many *Chiaux* eating and drinking, who as ſoon as they ſaw the *Bey*, ſent one of their Company to invite him to partake of their Repaſt. *Hamet* alighting from his Horſe, went on Board the Barge, but he was ſcarce ſate down to Meat, before thoſe who invited him ſeized his Arms and bound him ; however before they could ſtop his Mouth, he cryed out to his People on Shore, and told them that he was betrayed. The *Arabs* were not above thirty in number, yet they plunged into the River to come to the Aſſiſtance of their Maſter. The *Turks* immediately iſſued from all the Poſts where they lay in Ambuſcade, but not Time enough to prevent the *Arabians* from delivering *Hamet*, and ſetting him on Horſeback. They made no Doubt of retaking him when he came on Shore ; but they erred even in this, for he and his Attendants charged them ſo briſkly, that tho' they were ſeven hundred in number, yet the *Arabs* broke through and eſcaped into the Deſart, having ſlain fifty *Turks* in the Action. On his Return to *Sait*, the *Baſſa* ſent

to

to compliment him, and to affure him that the Attempt was not made by his Order. *Hamet* anfwered, that he readily believed it was not, and that he had ftill fo great a Confidence in the *Baffa*, as to rely upon his Intereft for the Remiffion of a third Part of his Tribute, which from this Time forward he referved for his own Ufe, and the *Turks* were very glad he exaćted no dearer Satisfaćtion; becaufe all the *Arabs* in *Egypt* feemed inclined to refent the Affront, which if they had done, the *Bey* might have brought a hundred thoufand Horfe into the Field; but he revenged himfelf with lefs Hazard.

Horses are the great Riches, and almoft the fole Inftruments of Power which thefe *Arab* Princes poffefs. Of thefe they have Numbers in their Stables, all of them of great Value, and I was going to fay, of great Quality alfo. The *Arabians* as they pique themfelves on their own Nobility, fo they are no lefs jealous of the Defcent of their Horfes, whofe Genealogies they keep as exaćtly as their own; nor is a Horfe ever parted with without giving at the fame Time an authentick Certificate of his Pedigree. The true *Arab* Courfers are not fo beautiful to the Eye as the Horfes bred in *Egypt*, but they are ftronger, and of more Mettle. However the *Egyptian* Horfes are very ferviceable, and there need not be either for Shew or Ufe better Cavalry than the Troops in this Country, if the Men were as capable of Difcipline as the Horfes. The great Excellency of the *Arabs* lies in their Retreats, which they perform with fuch incredible Speed, and pufh their Horfes up fuch Hills, and through fuch Woods and Moraffes, as fets them quickly without the Reach of any Enemy, and

as

as they never fly through Fear, gives them an Opportunity of confidering how they fhall next attack the Enemy, or provide for their fafe Return into their own Territories. Their Horfes as well as themfelves, bear not only Fatigue but Want. alfo, with incredible Fortitude. Next to their Horfes, their Wealth confifts in Camels, which they make Ufe of to tranfport their Women, Children and Baggage, from Place to Place. Thefe Creatures too are wonderful hardy, infomuch, that they will bear five Days want of Water very well, as the Horfes will three. To enter farther into the Cuftoms and Manners of the *Arabs*, would carry me into too long a Digreffion, efpecially, as I confider them only as fettled in *Egypt* ; and therefore I fhall turn from them to the *Turks*.

In order to have a diftinct Idea of the *Turks* fettled in *Egypt*, it is neceffary to divide them into three forts. The firft confifts of fuch Perfons as having either fuffer'd Difgrace at Court, or finding themfelves without Employment on the Death of an Emperor, withdraw themfelves into this Country to live at their Eafe. Of thefe there are a confiderable Number who enjoy in this delicious Kingdom all the Pleafures which Men of their Difpofitions affect moft, fuch as rich Habits, fine Houfes, a great number of Slaves, and above all a *Serail* well filled with Women. What is moft extraordinary is the number of *Eunuchs* who are fettled here, who in all other Refpects do not only fupport the Dignity of Men once eminent in Courts, but alfo in Women, are more nice, have greater Variety of Miftreffes, and part more freely with Money for handfome Women, than any other Perfons whatfoever: For this I have heard

no

no good Reafon affigned ; and therefore I will not pretend to give any, much lefs my own Conjectures, which
have at various Times been fo different and fo unfatis-
factory, that I did not think them any way worthy of
Prefervation.

THE fecond fort of *Turks* are fuch as come hither
in fome fort of Office or other, and thefe Lord it over
all the reft of the People, with a Haughtinefs mixt
with fuch Meannefs and Avarice, as will be made fuf-
ficiently apparent when I come to fpeak of the Government of *Egypt.* Thefe fort of Folks are in general very rich; for having it in their Power to extort
what they pleafe, and in their Will not to leave an *Af-
per* untaken which can be poffibly got, having daily
Prefents from fuch as need their Favour, and feizing
too frequently on the Goods of fuch as want Intereft to
fupport them againft thefe Violences, we may eafily
conceive, that while the rich Commodities of this noble
Country bring into it immenfe Sums from all Quarters, thefe Men have a very large Share.

THE third fort of *Turks* are the Defcendants of
both the former forts, but they live in a very different
manner ; for whereas thofe I mentioned before enjoy
Wealth and Authority in abundance, thefe feldom arrive at any Share of either, but are treated with Contempt as *Felacs* or Natives, only they are allowed to
enter into the Service, where they remain private Men
to their Lives End, fo unfortunate a Thing it is to
be born in that Country, wherein, notwithftanding, the
Turks defire moft of all to live.

As to the Manners of this Nation, they are far
from being fo amiable as fome Chriftian Writers would
Z 4 reprefent

reprefent them ; Haughtinefs and Vanity are infepe-
rable from their Nature ; proud of their Dominion, they
look down with Contempt on their unhappy Subjects ;
infolent when they act from the Dictates of their Heart,
fuperciliously courteous when they have it in view to
deceive or work upon a Stranger, oftentatiously fond of
their Religion, exact in their Obedience to fuch Precepts as regard exterior Things, but feldom very cau-
tious in refpect to Actions which concern their Neighbours, either in their Perfons or their Properties; pro-
fufe in Promifes of Friendfhip, but fparing in the Performance of them; abandoned to Senfuality, and wholly
devoted to Self-Intereft. It is true, that fome by the
Help of Learning and Converfation get the better of
their evil Inclinations, and thereby maintain as well as
acquire the Character of honeft Men ; but the Character
of the Nation is taken from the many not from the
few, and therefore it is fufficient to acknowledge that in
this as well as in other general Defcriptions, we muft
fometimes allow of Exceptions.

As to the *Franks* or *European* Chriftians in *Egypt*,
they are for the moft part *Englifh*, *French*, or *Italians*.
Such as refide conftantly, are under the Protection of
their refpective Confuls; and fuch as come meerly to fatisfy their Curiofity, are not only recommended to the
Confuls, but generally alfo to fome particular Merchant, that they may be the more at their Eafe, and
have the greater leifure to purfue the Inquiries they
come to make. As to the Trade of *Egypt*, the manner in which it is at prefent carried on, the Improve-
ments of which it is capable, and efpecially the very
great one of purchafing *Eaft-India* Goods by Exchange

- for

for our own Commodities, whereas we fend Silver to the *Indies*; concerning all thefe things I have elfewhere fpoken at large; and therefore I fhall only throw together fome fcattered Thoughts on the Conduct of *Europeans*, and which could not fo properly come in, in another Place.

I have always obferved that the Subjects of the State of *Venice*, and other *Italians*, manage their Affairs more to their own Profit, and much more to their Credit, than the other Merchants who live there, though the latter have in many Refpects the Advantage of the former. Of this I conceive the chief Reafon to be that Sobriety fo natural to the Natives of *Italy*, Vigilance, Penetration and Civility; for all thefe Qualities they poffefs in a fupreme Degree. The becoming Gravity of their Behaviour fuits fo well the affected Solemnity of the *Turks*, that they look upon them as wifer than other Chriftians, and therefore advife with, and confide in them more than the reft. Their conftant Attention to the Bufinefs upon which they come, keeps their Affairs in a clearer and more certain Courfe, than can be well imagined by thofe who have not feen them. The Pains they take to examine more curioufly, the Commodities in which they deal and the Methods of Trade and Manufactures amongft the Natives, than is common with the Merchants of other Countries, gives them great Superiority of Judgment, which they never boaft of, though they neglect no Occafion of ufing it. Their Addrefs is fo courtly, and at the fame Time hath fuch an Appearance of Candour, they are fo nice in all Things which refpect good Manners, and fo punctual in all Offices of Friendfhip, that the politeft and moft fenfible of the *French* and *Englifh* converfe more with them than with

their

J

their own Countrymen. To say the Truth, we have borrowed from the *Italians* all that we know of Trade, as our Books of Account testify, and the Terms made use of by the Merchants of *England*, *Germany*, and *Holland*. It would be well if we could borrow also when we go abroad their Manners and their Virtues ; I say nothing of their Vices, because those we are apt enough to steal, and by affecting their Foibles and ill Qualities, prejudice our Countrymen against their good ones.

THE Protestants take little Pains to propagate their Religion in *Mohammedan* Countries ; and as to the Popish Missionaries, whatever they may pretend, all their Efforts produce but little Fruits ; for which I pretend not to assign the Reasons, only I think it would contribute to their Success, if their Priests did not meddle with temporal Concerns, or endeavour, as they frequently do, to promote other Interests than those of Religion : If they applied themselves more to the Learned, than they commonly do, because all who are acquainted with the Oriental Countries know that there are Philosophers there, as well as in other Parts of the World ; and that many of these far from being prejudiced against the Christian Religion, are strongly inclined in its Favour, not from any exterior Impressions, but through the Effects of their own Reading and Observation : If they insisted more on the fundamental Points of the Christian Religion, such as the Nature of CHRIST's Mission, the perfect and eternal Rectitude of the Maxims of the Christian Faith, the clear Proofs that still remain of these Points being revealed by God, the superior Purity of the Gospel-Morality to that of the *Jewish* and *Mohammedan* System, the perfect Conformity between the Doctrines of CHRIST

and

and the Dictates of right Reason ; and above all, the Peace, Comfort, and Tranquillity resulting from a Life led according to these Rules. If the less important Matters, and especially such as Difference one Christian Church from another, were never mentioned, it would not be the worse. And as to Popish Doctrines, they ought in common Prudence not to be taken notice of even by Papists, since they serve only to rivet these *Mahammedans* in their old Notions, for they will not be brought to apprehend why they should worship the Saints of other Countries, rather than their own. They think their own Fables about a middle State, as worthy of Belief as the Tales they hear about Purgatory. And as to the Authority of the *Pope*, they are frighted at the very Apprehension of it, believing his Claims to be much the same with those of their ancient *Caliphs*, on a Title far less clear. But of these Matters enough ; let me now return to the History of the *Mahammedan* Natives of this Country, their Religion, Government, and Learning, which when I have explained, I shall take my Leave of them, as having many other Subjects to consider.

IT is not to be supposed that barely travelling through Countries inhabited by *Mahammedans*, should render a Man perfectly skill'd in the Theory and Practice of their Religion ; because we see plainly that travelling through *France* and *Italy*, doth not necessarily produce any competent Knowledge of the Sects, Religious Orders, or different Opinions in Religion embraced by the Inhabitants of those Countries. I say we see that bare Travelling produces nothing like this, but when joined with Reading, Observation, and Enquiry, it may. On this Ground I presume

to

to speak of the Religion of *Mohammed*, having not only talked of it with those who professed it, but having also read the Book of its Author, and considered the Drift of his Design as impartially as I believe ever any Christian did; and on this Account it is very probable that what I shall say on this Subject, will not be altogether so reconcileable to what has been said about it already, as might be expected; but if it be not irreconcileable with Truth, differing from other Men will not give me much Concern.

We are told by *Schariftani*, a very eminent *Arabian* Writer, that the Angel *Gabriel* appeared once to *Mohammed* in the Form of an *Arabian*, and besought him to declare in few Words what the Precepts were of that Religion which he pretended to deliver to the World; to which *Mohammed* answered thus, " It consists in " confessing that there is but one God, and in owning " me for his Messenger; in fulfilling punctually the " Precepts relating to Prayer, in giving Alms, in fasting " during the Month of *Ramedan*, and, if it may be " conveniently done, going in Pilgrimage to *Mecca*." It must be acknowledged, that this is a very succinct, and at the same time a very exact Account of the Religion of *Mohammed*. The Belief of the first Proposition, and paying an exact Obedience to the other four Precepts, is all that is required to constitute a good *Mussulman*; but of these more particularly.

The sole Article of Faith required by this Religion *is believing in one* God *only, and that* Mohammed *is his Messenger*. At first Sight there seems to be two Propositions contained in this Sentence, *viz. that there is one* God, *and that* Mohammed *is his Prophet*. The Learned ed among the *Arabs*, however, will not suffer this Distinction, and therefore we muſt hear how they explain it. God, ſay they, at all times hath preſerved to himſelf a certain Number of true and faithful Servants, who have worſhipped him as he ought to be worſhipped, whilſt the reſt of Mankind walked in Darkneſs, and adored the Chimera's of their own diſtracted Imaginations. The Method by which God preſerved his Beloved in the true Faith, was by ſending them from Time to Time, Prophets to reveal to them his Will, and to expoſe ſuch Errors as might by degrees creep in amongſt them. At laſt, ſay they, he ſent *Iſa*, or JESUS, whom, as I have elſewhere ſhewn, the *Mohammedans* acknowledge to have been above all Prophets, who taught Men their Duty on Earth, and on what Terms they might hope to enter the Kingdom of Heaven ; but in Proceſs of Time the Chriſtians ſuffering themſelves to be miſled by their Doctors, and giving generally into the Belief of the Trinity, (of which by the way the *Mohammedans* have very abſurd Ideas) *Mohammed* was ſent to revive the true Faith, by teaching, that there is but *one* God, *unalterable*, and *indiviſible* in *Eſſence*, *unbegotten*, and *unbegetting*. Therefore, ſay they, believing *in one God*, and that *Mohammed* is his Meſſenger, is one and the ſame Propoſition, becauſe the *Unity* of the *Godhead* was the Meſſage given to *Mohammed*, or in other Words, the Cauſe of his Miſſion.

HEREIN lies the great Strength of this Religion, and, without Queſtion, nothing hath ſo much aſſiſted its Propagation as the great Merit which its Propagators always take to themſelves of being the ſole Aſſertors of the *Unity* of the *Godhead* ; whereas the Chriſtians, according to them, give him for *Partners* in *Power*, I uſe their
own

own Expreffion, the *Son* and the Virgin *Mary*, for this is their general Notion of the *Trinity*. It muſt be owned, that they have made a very good Uſe of their obſtinate Ignorance as to the Principles of other People's Religion. They alledge, that the *Magians* worſhip the Fire, and that the *Zabians* adore the Stars; though neither of theſe Nations do ſo, nor ever did, in the Senſe the *Mohammedans* underſtand this Poſition. But as theſe are Foils which make their own Faith ſhine the brighter, they will not ſuffer them to be taken away, but treat *Jews*, *Chriſtians*, and *Perſees*, with the common Title of *Infidel*, though they all worſhip *one God*, as well as the Diſciples of *Mohammed*.

THE Notions we have in *Europe*, that this Man was of mean Origin, void of Literature, and of groſs Underſtanding, are utterly void of Foundation. The *Arabs*, as I have elſewhere ſaid, are divided into Tribes; ſome more, ſome leſs noble, according to their Antiquity. Now *Mohammed* ſprung from the *Coraiſhites*, the moſt noble of them all. That his Circumſtances were mean is true; but thoſe who are acquainted with the *Arabian* Hiſtory know that this was not Matter of Reproach in the Times in which he lived; on the contrary, the ſupporting of Poverty was with them a Mark of Magnanimity; and the two firſt *Caliphs* lived as poorly in all Reſpects as *Mohammed* himſelf, though they commanded vaſt Armies, and were Lords of great Provinces. As to his Genius, it was indiſputable, vaſt and enterpriſing; and he was ſo far from being a rude and artleſs Perſon, that he was a Man of great Addreſs, and one of the moſt powerful Speakers of his Time. It is true, that he calls himſelf *a ſimple, or idiot Prophet*, and

that

that his Followers infift much upon this, but to what
Purpofe ? Why, that they may make his mighty Gifts
the pure Effects of Infpiration. But if this ferves their
Purpofe, and they therefore make it an Article of their
Faith, how are we obliged to believe it too ? Or why
fhould we not rather fay that *Mohammed* having great
natural and acquired Abilities, applied thefe to the framing of that Syftem which he impofed upon his lefs intelligent Countrymen for a divine Revelation ? Sure I
am, that this is a more rational Account of the Matter
than that which is ufually given, nor can I be brought
to believe that the Structure or Succefs of his Scheme is
fo very aftonifhing as we generally conceive it.

F o r firft, as to the Materials from which his Syftem
was compofed, they were eafily collected by a Perfon
who had fpent his junior Years as *Mohammed* had done,
in travelling and converfing with all Sorts and Degrees
of People. He had by this Means the beft Opportunity in
the World for enquiring without the Caufe of his Enquiry's being guefled at. Strangers are naturally inquifitive, and no-body fufpects that a Stranger will turn Prophet ; he might therefore profecute with Eafe whatever
Difcoveries he defired to make among the *Arabians*, *Perfians*, and *Greeks*, with all of whom it is known that he
had an intimate Correfpondence. But if he had not, he
might have had all he knew from the *Arabians* only ;
fince at the Time he fet himfelf up for a Prophet, fome
of the Tribes of that Nation were of the *Jewifh*, fome
of the *Chriftian* Religion, but Hereticks ; fome of the
Perfian or *Magian* Faith, and others *Gentiles*. Out of
all thefe Syftems he might and did collect the Subftance
of his own. Circumcifion was a Rite univerfally ufed
in

in *Arabia*; this therefore he retained. All the historical Part of the Old Testament, which came to his Knowledge, he digested into his own Book, and thereby declared it sacred in his Opinion: Of CHRIST he spoke respectfully, but in the Language of a *Photinian*: And as to the Ceremonies which he established, either by his Writing or Practice, they were conformable enough to those used by the *Persians*, and *Gentiles*, especially those who worshipped at *Mecca*. So much for the Matter of his Religion.

Now as to the Manner in which he published, and by which he propagated it: It was so far from being without Example, that he had a very recent one, *viz.* that of *Mazdek*, the *Persian* Impostor, who either lived in, or but a very little before his Time. This Man, by brewing together *Magiism*, *Manicheism*, and *Libertinism*, produced an excellent new Religion, the Purity of which, amongst other Things, consisted in an absolute Community of Women, and an equal Distribution of Effects. This Prophet had not only the good Luck to find a Multitude of Followers, but also to mislead the King of *Persia*, and in a few Years made greater Strides than *Mohammed* did in all his Life. This Fellow too was but a Copyist after *Manes*, the famous Heretick, and therefore why *Mohammed*, who lived under the same King who put *Mazdek* to Death, should be held so potent in Invention, for playing his Tricks over again, I profess I cannot apprehend; nor do I see any thing incredible or unaccountable in what he performed, much less in what was performed by his Successors. For if he was a Hypocrite, They were but Enthusiasts; and that such Men at the Head of many Thousands like themselves

felves fhould be too hard for other People, is no ftranger
than that Madmen fhould be too hard for Folks in their
Senfes, becaufe the latter can never fufpect to what
Lengths the former will go. Thus I am come back to the
Point from whence I fet out ; for it is certain that the
Secret of *Mohammed* lay in perfuading his Followers,
that they were the true and only Worfhippers of the
Almighty, and confequently all the reft of Mankind his
Enemies as well as theirs ; the fitteft Doctrine imagin-
able for a Man who meant to argue as he did by the
Sword, and to purchafe *Dominion* in Right of *Grace*.

Previous to my Explication of the reft of the Precepts, I muft fpeak of Wafhings, or Ablutions, which
fome call the firft of the five Points which conftitute a
Muffulman ; yet I think improperly, becaufe they were
not fuperinduced by *Mohammed*, but were practifed by
his Countrymen long before his Time. Thefe Wafhings are of three Sorts, the firft preparatory to their
Prayers, which is called *Abdeft*, which I have Reafon to
think is an old *Perfic* Word, and that the Ceremonies
they ufe on this Occafion were originally borrowed from
the *Perfees*. However, be that as it will, their Method
of performing them is this, They firft wafh their Hands
and Arms, then the Neck, the Forehead, the Crown of
the Head, the Ears, the Teeth, the Face, under the
Nofe, and their Feet ; but if either the Place or the
Weather permit not this without great Inconveniency,
then they content themfelves with making a Semblance
of doing fo. The fecond Sort of Ablution is that performed after a Man hath converfed with a Woman ; and
this is no more than Bathing, called *Gufur*. The third
kind of Ablution is called *Tabaret*, and is performed be-

fore

fore Eating and after Evacuation. In all thefe they are
very ftrict, feldom if ever neglecting them where it is
poffible for them to be performed.

As to their ftated Prayers, they are performed five
Times in twenty-four Hours. The firft Time of Pray-
ing is between Day-break and Sun-rife. The fecond at
Noon. The third at the middle Hour, between Noon
and Sun-fet. The fourth at Sun-fet. And the fifth, an
Hour and a half in the Night. They ufe abundance of
Geftures in their Devotions, and are fo very fervent in
them, that if a Fire fhould break out in the Room,
they will not break off. They are not tyed to exact
Forms of Prayer, though the Heads or Subftance of
their Prayers are fettled, and the People in general ufe
Forms. One Thing is remarkable, that in the Grand
Signior's Dominions they not only pray for his Health
and Profperity, but alfo that God would be pleafed to
fend a Spirit of Difcord and Diffenfion among his Enemies, to which they attribute all the Diffenfions and
Wars amongft the Chriftians, which it muft be allowed
are agreeable to, though to be fure they are not effected
by their Petitions. They are fo precife in this Article of
Prayer, that if by any Accident they are difturbed therein fo far as to wander in their Thoughts, they begin
again, fuppofing that the fmalleft Abfence of Mind a-
brogates all the Petitions they have made. Hence fnee-
zing, or rubbing the Hand or the Neck where a Flea has
bit, or turning the Head on a fudden Noife, vacates the
Prayers that have been faid before, and the Perfon to
whom fuch an Accident has happened is obliged to begin
again. They are no lefs exact as to the Time of praying, for wherever they are, in the Street, in the Market,

or

or on the Road, they ſtop to offer their Devotions, and omit none of the Ceremonies uſual in Praying on Account of their being in a Publick Place.

THE third Point is *Alms,* which they call *Zacab,* a Word derived from a Verb, ſignifying to purify, becauſe, according to their Notion, a Man's Subſtance is purified by giving Alms out of it to the Poor. There is nothing of which we have ſo indefinite a Notion as of the Meaſure or Proportion by which, according to their Law, the *Mohammedans* are obliged to give Alms. Some of our Writers ſpeak of a tenth, others ſay a hundredth Part. The Truth is, that they are commanded to give different Porportions of different Sorts of Goods, and are over and above charged to regard no Bounds in their Liberalities to the Poor. Hence it comes to paſs, that many give the Third of what they are worth ; many a Fourth ; ſome have given half of what they were worth, once in their Life-time ; and there have been Inſtances of Men who have given all their Fortunes to the Poor, and liv'd ever after upon Alms themſelves. To ſay the Truth, there are no People in the World among whom Poverty is ſo honourable as among the *Mohammedans,* who have a common Saying, *That the Fear of Want is a Mark of the Judgment of* GOD. They likewiſe ſay of a Perſon who makes a voluntary Profeſſion of Poverty, that as he poſſeſſes nothing, he is poſſeſſed by nothing, by which they mean to ſuggeſt, that in the midſt of his Poverty he is Maſter of the World, by reaſon of that Detachment from carnal Deſires which he enjoys by Virtue of his Profeſſion, which Deſires, in their Opinion, make all other Men Slaves.

The fourth Point is the keeping the Faſt of *Rammeldan*. This is no more than the Name of the *ninth Month* of the *Arab Year*. Anciently this always fell in Summer, but now, ſince the *Arab Year* is become perfectly lunar, it ſhifts and varies, and falls out in all Seaſons. The Rule in Faſting is this: A Believer muſt not eat, drink, or converſe with his Wife from the Time that the Sun riſes, till ſuch Time as the Stars appear, or the Lamps are hung out upon the Moſques, which is done during this Month, that the People may the better know when to take their Repaſts. Of ſuch indiſpenſible Obligation is this Command held, that if a Man ſhould openly break it, he would be puniſhed with Death; neither are Travellers, ſick or wounded Perſons, exempt therefrom; but in caſe their Neceſſities oblige them to eat within that Month, then they are obliged to faſt another entire Month in the Year to attone for it. Yet as there are among the *Mohammedans*, as well as amongſt Chriſtians, very many who deſire to avoid ſuch rigorous Reſtraints, they have found an eaſy Method of doing it without violating the Letter, and thereby expoſing themſelves to the ſecular Arm. They eat and drink plentifully in the Night, and divert themſelves therein every other Way, going to bed as the Morning draws on, and ſleeping the greateſt Part of the Day. This is a *Turkiſh* Invention, and exceedingly abhorr'd by the ſober Part of thoſe who profeſs the *Religion* of *Mohammed*.

The fifth Point, requiſite to conſtitute a true Believer, according to the Doctrine of their Prophet, is the *Pilgrimage* to *Mecca*, which every Man who is free, and hath ſufficient Ability, that is in reſpect to Riches, is commanded to undertake once in his Life. It is eaſy

enough

enough to account for this Injunction, which certainly had no other than thefe two Motives. Firft, the Love which *Mohammed* bore to the Place of his Birth. And Secondly, the Defire he had to gratify his Countrymen the *Arabians* in their extraordinary Fondnefs for the *Square Temple* at *Mecca*. This holy Place, which the *Arabs* call *Cabah*, was certainly a very antient Structure, and had ferved for the chief Place of Worfhip for all the feveral Religions, or rather Superftitions, which in a long Succeffion of Ages had been embraced by this Nation; in the Infide thereof there was a *black Stone*, and *two* Golden Images, which were prefented, as fome Writers fay, by a King of *Perfia*, and as others fay, by an *Arab* Prince. Thefe were both Objects of high Veneration, tho' I dare not fay of idolatrous Worfhip, becaufe it is with me a great Doubt, whether ever thefe *Eaftern* People were, in the proper Senfe of the Word, Idolaters; for if they worfhipp'd the heavenly Bodies, or any Telefmetick Images, as Reprefentations of the fupreme God of Heaven and Earth, then I am afraid we muft exempt them from the Imputation of *Idolatry*, or extend that Term fo as to take in fome who look upon themfelves to be the only good Chriftians.

The *Mohammedans* tell us a very notable Story concerning the Building, Confecration, and Holinefs of this fame Temple. In the firft Place, they are pofitive that *Hagar* was not the Concubine, but the Wife of *Abraham*, and dearly beloved by him: They acknowledge, however, her Flight into the *Defert*, with her Son *Ifhmael*; and they affirm, that it was in the Neighbourhood of *Mecca* they fixed themfelves after their Flight. Here

Abraham

Abraham came to vifit his Son; and that he might have an Oratory wherein to offer his Prayers to God, he counfelled him to build this Square Temple, and affifted him in the Work. It was as it ftill is, a very rude and contemptible Structure, ftanding due Eaft and Weft, And though it is called a Square, yet its Length is four and twenty Ells, and its Breadth from North to South but twenty-three. In this Temple *Abraham* placed the myfterious black Stone whereon it is faid he found *Hagar* fitting when he firft embraced her; and having eftablifhed his eldeft Son *Ifhmael* in the firm Poffeffion of *Arabia*, fixed this Place for the Worfhip of the true G o d, whence, fay they, it came to be reverenced by the Dependants of *Ifhmael*, and to be held the moft noble and valuable Part of their Poffeffions.

In Procefs of Time, however, they were deprived of it, and it paffed into the Hands of another Tribe. The *Ifhmaelites* kept up their Claim, and at laft, by Force, re-acquired the Protection of this holy Place. The Enemy, however, carried off the black Stone and Golden Images, and threw them into the Pit *Zemzem*, where they remained for a long Series of Ages, but at laft were difcovered by the Grandfather of *Mohammed*, who had for that Purpofe an exprefs Revelation from Heaven, as he very pofitively affirmed; fo that *Mohammed* was not the firft of his Family who took upon him the Character of a Prophet. The Religion of the *Arabs*, when *Mohammed* attempted to fet up himfelf for a Perfon divinely infpired was Deifm corrupted, that is, mingled with heathenifh and Pagan Rites, of which, however, the *Cabah* was the Centre. Thither the People reforted to worfhip, and there they did Worfhip
with

with great Formality, and with Abundance of Osten-
tatious Ceremonies, most of which *Mohammed* preserved, and brought into his Religion, obliging the People
who professed it not only to this Pilgrimage, but also to
turn their Faces towards it, that is, towards the Point
of the Compass regarding it, as often as they pray'd, in
what Part of the World soever they were. This Honour was by no Means of *Mohammed*'s Invention, but
taken from the Practice of the *Jews* and *Persians*, who
were wont to turn their Faces when they worshipped,
the one to the *East*, and the other to the *West*, which
Ceremony is in *Arabick* stiled, *Al. Keblah*, and is one
of the main Points of Distinction in the Religions of the
East. Thus much for the Reasons inducing *Mohammed*
to stamp such extraordinary Marks of Respect on the
City and Temple of *Mecca*.

Let us now return to the Pilgrimage, which, as an
essential Point of their Religion, is punctually comply'd
with by the *Mohammedans* of *Asia* and *Africk*. Such as
come from the middle Provinces of the Grand Signior's
Dominions, assemble at *Damascus*, the *Persian* Pilgrims
at *Babylon*; those from *Africk*, at *Caira*. They draw,
however, All into one Body, on a certain Mountain
near that City, to which they go in solemn Procession,
leaving behind them their Christian Slaves, lest they
should polute this *Holy Place*.

It may not be amiss to observe, that in this, as well
as in other Things, the wiser *Mohammedans* have Notions far enough removed from those of the People; for
Instance, though they look upon the Pilgrimage to *Mecca*
as a Point of indispensible Necessity, yet they stick not
to spiritualize it, and to affirm, their Prophet instituted

A a 4   it,

it, to put them in mind, that Life itself is but a Pilgrimage, wherein we ought always to have our immortal State in View, which they conceive to be figured by the Holy Temple at *Mecca*, and therefore they do not place the Efficacy of this Pilgrimage in barely travelling so far, in kissing as they are wont to do the black Stone, or in performing the other Ceremonies annexed to that Act of Devotion, but in performing all this with a right Mind, that is, with a penitent Heart, and a just Sense of the Contemptibleness of carnal Things, compared with those spiritual and eternal. Thus I finish my Commentary on the five Points of the Law of *Mohammed*, which I hope sufficiently demonstrates that they are not either so crude and so absurd as some Men would make them, or so politick, so refined, so perfectly of the Prophet's Invention as they are made to be by others, but of a mixt Nature, and such as a wise Man will behold without Contempt or Admiration.

I HAVE heard it often alledged, both in *England* and in *Italy*, that the *Mohammedans* were more united in their Sentiments, and more constant in the Profession of their Faith than Christians; but this I am very confident is said without the least Foundation. I cannot indeed affirm, that the Controversies among them are more in Number than amongst us; but I can truly say, that I believe it impossible to compute the Number of Controversies amongst either. In all Revealed Religion there are many things hard to be understood; and indeed there must be so, for if they were self-evident, they could not be the Subject of Divine Revelation; and these Points are alike Grounds of Debate amongst *Mohammedans* as well as *Christians*. For example, the

Questions

Queftions relating to *Predeftination* and *free Grace* have been agitated among the *Arab* Doctors, with as much Heat and Vehemence as ever they were in *Chriftendom*. If we have *Pietifts*, or Profeffors of myftical Divinity, fo have they; nor have there been wanting *Mohammedan Quakers*, who fuppofing themfelves above all Ordinances, have acted according to the Dictates of what they call the Spirit, and have been looked upon by Men of Underftanding, as a fort of *grave Infidels*.

Many of the beft *Perfian* and *Arabian* Poets have been fufpected of *Chriftianifm*, and many more of *Atheifm*; but the common Name for impious Perfons is *Zendik*, which I take it ftrictly belongs to thofe who affert the Eternity of the World, and are properly fpeaking *Materialifts* or *Naturalifts*. Such as exclude all Ideas of fpiritual Subftance, and conceive that all Beings whatfoever have an innate Power of producing what we fee them produce, without deriving it from any other. Tho' there are many who are fecretly in thefe Sentiments, yet there are a very few only, who either privately or publickly acknowledge any Thing like them. The Reafon is, becaufe the Government would fpeedily take Notice of it; for the *Turks* judge rightly, that fuch Men as are loofe in Principles of Religion, are not faft Friends or good Subjects to any Government whatever. Among the *Arabs* a fort of enthufiaftic Piety prevails, and thofe who are perfectly acquainted with their Language, are extremely edified with this Spirit and Fervour of their Devotions. But the moft rational Books of Devotion have been written by *Perfians* who have a more calm and courtly Stile, and lefs of that ecftatic Rapture which is fo productive of Obfcurity.

rity. On the whole, tho' the Religion of *Mahammed* rather declines than increases, yet it still possesses the best Part of the habitable World, under the four great Empires of the *Grand Seignior*, the *Shah* of *Persia*, the *Great Mogul*, and the Emperor of *Morocco*, besides the numberless petty Princes in *Arabia*, the *East-Indies*, and the inland Parts of *Africa*. I have now fulfilled all that I proposed to myself to say on the Head of Religion, and shall turn next to the Government of *Egypt*, especially as it stands at this Day.

I HAD some Thoughts of writing a succinct History of the successive Changes in Government which have happened in *Egypt*, from the Time it was first peopled, to the Conquest thereof by *Selim* Emperor of the *Turks*; but having never had Time enough to compare and translate the Materials necessary for such a Work, I contented myself with throwing together some Observations on the different Masters of *Alexandria*, which I have elsewhere inserted in these Memoirs, and shall here confine myself to the present State of *Egypt*, under the *Turkish* Government. Previous however to this, I will set down something concerning the *Mamalukes*; because from what I have read in our *European* Historians, I have been induced to think, that we have very confused, if not false Notions concerning this People.

THE Word *Mamlouck*, for so it ought to be spelt, signifies a *Slave*, the Plural of this is *Memalik*, or *Slaves*, and this is the proper Appellation of the People of whom we are speaking. They were truly such, but not *Christian*, or born of Christian Parents, as we have been made to believe; on the contrary, the *Tartars* were at that Time so powerful as to ravage all *Asia*, and
these

these poor Creatures were strong able bodyed *Turks*, whom they seized and sold to *Al Malek Ajoub* Sultan of *Egypt*. He made use of them at first to guard the outer Courts of his Palace, and as their Numbers, and the Reputation of their Fidelity encreased, he not only fixed them in *Cairo*, but also placed Garrisons of them in most of his Maritime Places. He dying left the Crown to his Son, who was so fortunate in War, as to take Prisoner in Battle St. *Lewis* King of *France*. Yet neither his Valour nor the many Virtues he possessed, could preserve him from being murthered by these Slaves of his, not without the Participation of a Person who ought to have protected him. This Person was his Mother, whose Name was *Schagredar*, who was also a *Turk*, and commenting an Intrigue with *Ibek* the General of this Militia, for so they were now become, consented that he should dispatch her Son, and jointly with her assume the regal Dignity, which accordingly he did, in the Year of the *Hegira* 648, according to our Account, in the Year of our Lord 1250.

He did not however long enjoy that Power which he had so basely usurped; the same ambitious Woman destroyed him too, but the Crown was preserved to his Posterity. This is the History of the first *Mamalukes*, who from their having the Custody of the Sea Ports, were stiled *Maritime*, or *Sea Mamalukes*. The Princes of this Race to secure themselves more effectually against foreign Invaders, and Domestick Treasons, instituted a new Militia, composed of young *Circassians*, bred up in the great Cities of *Egypt*, where they were taught all sorts of Exercises, and were intended to do the same Service to these *Sultans* as the *Grand Seignior* expects

from

from his Janizaries. But they copying the Behaviour of their Masters, suddenly rebelled against the Prince who had settled and disciplined them, and quickly deprived him of Life and Crown.. These were the second Race of *Mamalukes*, and called themselves by Way of Distinction *Inland Mamalukes*. These were they who were conquered by the *Turks* under the fortunate *Sultan Selim*, about the Year 1517, and were the last independent Princes in *Egypt*. That Country having been since that Time only a Province of the *Turkish* Empire.

THE supreme Governor of this great Kingdom is generally stiled the *Baffa* of *Cairo*, on Account of his Residence in that City. He is always honoured with the Title of *Vizir*, and, next that of the *Vizir Azem*, it is the first Employment in the Gift of the *Grand Seignior*. It is seldom obtained but by Bribery, a Thing so customary at the *Porte*, that it is no way scandalous. Before a Man sets out for this Government it costs him fifty, sixty, or seventy Thousand Pounds. When he arrives in *Egypt* he finds himself invested with all the Ensigns of Authority and absolute Power, which the proudest Mind can wish, but it depends entirely on his own Prudence, whether he shall enjoy any more than the outward Appearance of all this Authority, as will be hereafter seen. The *Grand Seignior's* Tribute consists annually of 600,000 *Sequins* in ready Gold, which is sent at the Expence of the *Baffa*, who likewise furnishes to the *Seraglio* Coffee, Sugar, Sherbets, and *Indian* Commodities nearly to the same Value. Besides this the *Baffa* furnishes all the Expences the *Grand Seignior* is at in sending the two Caravans of *Cairo* and

Damascus

Damafcus to *Mecca*, and he is likewife charged with the Civil and Military Appointments of all who are in the Service of the *Grand Seignior* within the Bounds of his Government. To defray all this, and to enable him to maintain Spies and Protectors in the *Serail*, he is allowed to take and receive without Account all the Revenues belonging to the *Grand Seignior*, which amount to an immenfe Sum. He is never appointed for any longer than a Year, yet is feldom removed from his Government in lefs than three, and fome have remained there longer, but every Year's Continuance cofts a hundred thoufand Crowns in Prefents, without which there is nothing to be done.

His Refidence is in the Caftle of *Cairo*, where he holds his *Divan* with greater Pomp and Splendor than the *Grand Seignior* himfelf at *Conftantinople*. He hath about his Perfon and in his Councils all the great Officers ufually attendant on a Court, fuch as a *Kiajah*, or great Steward, *Reis Effendi*, or Chancellor, *Teftadar*, or Treafurer, *&c.* Under him he has twenty-four *Beys* or *Sanjacks*, who govern fo many Provinces, tho' their Number is feldom compleat ; and to thefe People he fells their Governments, which is one Method of acquiring Money, and no inconfiderable one ; befides which they pay an annual Tribute, and keep up a Body of Militia at their own Expence. Thefe *Beys* command only the open Country, for almoft every great Village is an independent Government poffeffed by a *Chek* or *Cheik*. So much for the Civil Adminiftration. As to the Military Force, it confifts in different Bodies of Troops, all independent of each other, and which is ftill more fingular, independent of the *Baffa*. The *Azaphs* or *Afaphs*,

are

are a Body of Infantry, confifting of above five thoufand effective Men, under the Command of Officers chofen from among themfelves. They are looked upon as much inferior to the *Janizaries*, and on that Account there is an inexpreffible Enmity between them. The *Spahis* are Corps of Cavalry, confifting of three Regiments, diftinguifhed by the Titles of the Green, the Yellow, and the Red, each Regiment confifting of a thoufand effective Men. They are commanded by a *Kiajah*, and as they are independent of the other Corps, fo they mortally hate the *Afapbs*, and the *Janizaries*. The *Bachouchs* are alfo certain Corps of Infantry, deftined to various Services, confifting of three Regiments, each of five hundred Men. Laftly, the *Janizaries*, confifting of feven thoufand effective Men, and about as many more nominal only ; they are commanded in Chief by a *Kiajah*, whom they chufe when they think fit, and alfo depofe when they think fit ; he is abfolutely independent of the *Baffa*, and in fome Meafure or the *Grand Seignior*, for without the Confent of the Council of Officers, neither he nor any private *Janizary* can be put to Death, notwithftanding the *Sultan's* exprefs Order.

IT is not eafy to frame an Idea of the mighty Power of this Militia, but one may have fome Notion of it from hence, that the whole Bufinefs of the *Baffa* of *Cairo* is to contrive Ways and Means to balance the Authority of the *Janizaries* by that of the *Spahis*, and the reft of the Troops, which he is fometimes unable to do, and fo is depofed and imprifoned. The *Janizaries* are no lefs Tyrants in refpect to the People, fo that purely to efcape their Vexations, many rich Merchants inroll

inroll themſelves in their Order, for which they pay
conſiderably at their Admittance, and are ſubject to
Contributions all their Life time after, on one Pretence
or other ; beſides at their Demiſe all they have goes to
the Order, which is the Heir general of all its Members,
a Thing monſtrous, and almoſt inconceiveable. When
any Perſon who has the Reputation of being rich, and
who was not a *Janizary* dies, the Order have as fair a
Title to his Effects, for they have a falſe *Muſter-Roll*,
into which they put the Names of ſuch as they would
be glad to have of their Order, and a little hard ſwear-
ing and a Preſent to the *Baſſa*, makes this as authentick
as a Decree from the *Mufti*. If the *Beys* are at any
Time upon bad Terms with the *Baſſa*, they do not indeed
inroll themſelves *Janizaries*, but they put themſelves
under the Protection of the Order, which is the ſame
Thing, for they are effectually covered let their Crimes
have been what they will. The *Aſaphs* and *Spahis*
have likewiſe found the Sweets of this Method, ſo that
where a Man has the Will and the Power of bribing,
Juſtice muſt keep at a Diſtance from him, and the
Baſſa with all his Parade of Sovereign Authority muſt
be content to wink at him, tho' he ſhould be as noto-
rious a Criminal as himſelf. This Expreſſion muſt ſeem
very general, and to imply very little leſs, than that all
the *Turkiſh* Governors are Men given to Fraud and
Rapine ; and truly I believe that moſt People who have
reſided in that Country, will be ready to confeſs this
Character general and unguarded as it is, not very far
wide of Truth ; however I am content to reſtrain it as
much as I may, by confeſſing that there really are
Baſſas of a different Character, Men of Honour and
Generoſity,

Generofity, Lovers of Juftice, and inclined to make
the People happy ; but then this does not at all contradict what I have faid, fince their Governments are
not a Grain more advantagious to themfelves, or beneficial to the People, but on the contrary produce new
Inconveniencies to both.

PROBITY is not only rarely feen amongft the Great
at *Cairo*, but it is alfo abfolutely inconfiftent with their
Authority, nor can there poffibly be a virtuous Adminiftration in *Egypt*, Oppreffion and Tyranny runs thro'
the whole Syftem of Rule, and all Attempts to introduce Humanity, and other oppofite Virtues, are
confidered as fo many Violations of the Conftitution.
The *Beys* and the *Cheiks* live magnificently, and amafs
Fortunes by plundering the Country People, the *Janizaries*, *Spahis*, and *Azaps* live at their Eafe, by pilla-
ging thofe in Town. The *Baffa* hath vaft Demands
to fatisfy, and in order to have wherewith to fatisfy
them, it is moft evident that he muft plunder too; a
Difpofition to do this puts him upon a Par with his
Neighbours, and as many of them may want his Affiftance, they are glad to afford him theirs. Hereby a
Method is opened to him of acquiring that Authority
which he ought to receive from his Commiffion, his
Skill in balancing Parties, and preferving the cafting
Vote to himfelf, may enable him to anfwer all the
Charges of his Government, and even to gain a Fortune for himfelf; but an appearance of Honour and
Virtue, the being known to have a Difpofition of doing Juftice, immediately unites the moft inveterate Enemies, and engages them to turn all the Bitternefs which
they exercife towards each other, upon him as upon
the common Foe.

THIS

THIS is the true Sense of that Divine Adage of our Saviour's, *The Children of this World are wiser than the Children of Light.* For tho' it be true, that all just and good Men are allied to each other, that an Injury done to one, is an Injury done to them all, because it is an Injury done to that System of Rule which they support; yet they do not readily perceive this, or when they do, they are not wont to unite with Vigour, in order to redress the Grievance sustained; and so Vice and Folly gain upon them by Degrees, till at last Resistance is vain, and Redress becomes impossible. It is not so with wicked and unjust Men, their Interest here is their sole Concern, and they are wise enough to know that what prejudices one Man's worldly Interest, will also prejudice another's. Self-Interest therefore teaches them Union, and they act in a bad Cause, with a Prudence and Spirit which would do them the highest Honour if they were engaged in a good one.

But it may be enquired why the *Grand Seignior* winks at these Disorders; Disorders so dishonourable to his Sovereign Authority, and so apparently prejudicial to his Finances. The Reason of this too is easily understood, for he acts upon the same Principles with his *Janizaries* and *Baffa's*, and is so far from looking upon this State of Things as destructive to his Interest, that he considers it as the sole Support thereof. A few Words will suffice to explain this Mystery. The *Baffa* rules *Egypt* by balancing Parties which would be infinitely too strong for him if they were united, the *Grand Seignior* preserves *Egypt*, by allowing the Power of the People to balance the Authority of the *Baffa.* Union and Tranquillity amongst his Subjects is the only Thing he fears;

for

For in such a Case He apprehends that one of these two Evils would certainly follow, that his *Baffa* would become a Sovereign Prince, by throwing afide his Allegiance, or the People would expel him, and fecure their own Freedom, by chufing a Prince from among themfelves. Diffenfion, Bloodfhed, and Oppreffion, are therefore fuffered, or rather maintained by the *Sultan*, that he may fecure his Revenue, and the Dependance of *Egypt* ; they are permitted and promoted by the *Baffa's*, becaufe they are fubfervient to their Authority ; they are exercifed by the feveral Corps of Militia, becaufe they are this Way fupported without Labour.

Thus do Men out-do Wolves, for they not only prey, but prey on each other, and that without Neceffity. Here is the Thing that affrights weak Minds, when by Chance they difcover thefe Things, or learn them as Difcoveries from others ; they immediately caft the Blame upon Providence, and are on the Point of turning Infidels, becaufe they have not Senfe enough to difcern the Divine Wifdom. A Man would be laughed at, who pretended to quarrel with his Maker for not having created an Ox, an Afs, or a Horfe, a Hog. And yet this Objection is the fame Thing, for it is quarrelling with God, becaufe he has created Men, Men, and not Brutes ; becaufe he has given them Reafon as well as Senfes, and a Power of attaining intellectual Happinefs, which they could not have had if their Nature had been otherwife conftituted than It is. We do not fuppofe a Farm-houfe equal to a Palace, tho' we ftand in the yard of one, and fee the other at three or four Miles diftance ; but a vicious Man prefers the Beauty of this World to the Paradife promifed hereafter, wifely

becaufe

becaufe it is nearer; and therefore is as much a Fool in this Cafe, as he would be if he acted in the fame manner in that. But fhall we blame God for this, and not ourfelves? Shall we believe it juft for us to merit, and unjuft for him to punifh? What Equity is there in this? Or what difference is there between our talking at this Rate, and our affirming that the Author of our Reafon has lefs Reafon then we have ourfelves?

But it is now Time to come to the Learning of this People, of which I promifed to fpeak, and of which there is much to be faid, and of which I flatter myfelf I can fay fomewhat not altogether befide the Purpofe. The Learning of *Egypt* ought in my Opinion, to be divided into the Learning of the ancient *Egyptians* before they were conquered by the *Affyrians* and *Perfians*, and the Learning of the Modern *Egyptians*, which I confefs might with greater Propriety, be called the Learning of the *Arabians*. However, as both are diftinct enough from the Learning of *Europe*, it may not be altogether amifs to give a general Account of both, the rather becaufe many who have fpoken on thefe Points have done it without any tolerable Comprehenfion of what they intended to explain, and in Terms fo immethodical and obfcure, as ferved rather to confound than enlighten their Readers. After having fpoke fo freely of others, I cannot expect to efcape Cenfure myfelf, but if I deferve it, it fhall not be in the fame Way with my Predeceffors, I will at leaft have the Merit of attempting to treat this Affair in a rational Way, and not endeavour to pafs a Declamation on the Wifdom of the *Egyptians*, upon the lefs knowing Perufers, for an Account of the *Egyptian* Learning; much lefs will I at-

tempt

tempt to impose my own Conjectures for the revived
Fragments of that Science, the Veneration due to which
hath been too often diverted to such false Relicks. I
think it may be laid down as a self evident Maxim,
*That Knowledge was there first perfected where Men
were first settled.* For it is natural for the human Race
to seek first Safety, then Necessaries, next Convenien-
ces, and by Degrees Instruments of Luxury. Now as
none of these can be had without Invention, Reasoning,
and Industry, it follows that Knowledge and Learning
must encrease gradually, and must have come to Perfection first, in the first Plantation of Mankind. All
Histories Sacred and Prophane, agree that *Egypt* was
very early planted ; and therefore it is reasonable to believe, that Learning was very early established in *Egypt.*
We ought therefore to give Credit to those Accounts
we meet with in the most early Writers of the Knowledge of the *Egyptians,* tho' I do not think that those
Writers are always to be depended upon, in what they
tell us of the Learning of the *Egyptians* ; for tho' this
People might be very knowing, yet their Neighbours
might have but confused and imperfect Ideas of their
Knowledge. This I take to be very reasonable, and am
thoroughly persuaded, that it is Matter of Fact. After this
previous Admonition, I will proceed to speak, First of
the Fame of the *Egyptian* Learning, and secondly of
its Extent. We are told by *Moses,* that when *Abraham*
went down into *Egypt,* he found that Kingdom perfectly well settled, and was received there with much Civility and Politeness. It does not however appear, at
least to me, that there was any material difference between the Religion of *Abraham,* and the Religion then

profeſſed

profeſſed in Egypt. I ſay material difference, for I do not think that the Religion of Abraham and his Houſhold, was exactly the ſame with that of Egypt; becauſe if it had, there would have been no Occaſion for the Revelations made to that Patriarch, but I ſuppoſe that the Egyptians ſtill worſhipped one God, tho' it might be with a Mixture of Superſtition, which in a ſhort Time degenerated into Idolatry. Joſephus informs us, that the Father of his Nation found the Egyptians much inclined to Learning, but not excellent therein, and that he was extremely careſſed for his ſuperior Knowledge, and for the Diſcoveries he made known to them in various Sciences. All this is perfectly probable, for Abraham being by Birth a Chaldean, and Chaldea according to Moſes, being the firſt Peopled Country in the World, Learning muſt have become perfect there before it could be ſo in Egypt, and indeed there is great Authority to prove, as well as the higheſt Reaſon to believe, that the Progreſs of Learning was from Chaldea to Egypt, and from thence to the Weſtern Parts of the World. When Joſeph went down into this Country, of which we are ſpeaking, he found Things much altered, as we may well conceive they might be in the Space of two hundred Years. The Egyptian Monarch kept then a regular and magnificent Court, the Religion of the Egyptians was then quite new moulded, and the Learning of Egypt was held in very high Eſteem. We ſee too what ſort of Learning that was, what were the principal Cauſes, Inclinations, and Arts of Policy among the Great in that Kingdom. It is from this Hiſtory, I mean the Hiſtory of Joſeph as written by Moſes, that we have the beſt and plaineſt

Account

Account of the ancient State of *Egypt*, and therefore whoever would profecute the Story of this Nation at large, ought to ftudy this Part of the *Mofaic* Writings carefully, and to prefer what he difcovers there from to all that can be learned from *Herodotus, Diodorus Siculus*, or the Fragments of *Manetho*; becaufe fetting afide his Infpiration, *Mofes* according to the ftricteft Laws of Criticifm, is by far a more authentick Writer than any of thefe, as being much nearer the Times of which he wrote, and having much better Opportunities of knowing the *Egyptian* Affairs than any of thofe Writers could poffibly have. It is recorded of this great Man, I mean *Mofes*, that he was verfed in all the Learning of *Egypt*, and this was no doubt intended to fill up his Character, as a wife and knowing Man, before he received the Sanction of a prophetic Miffion, and had his Mind illuminated by divine Infpiration. All that he fays of himfelf is fo humble, and all that is faid of him by the reft of the facred Writers, is fo general, as well as concife, that it is not eafy to fpeak with any Degree of Certainty of the Sciences wherein he was inftructed while he lived in *Egypt*: However as he was educated in the Royal Family, there can be no Ground to queftion his having a thorough and perfect Idea, as well of the hidden as of the open Literature of *Egypt*, which was a Diftinction begun fo very early, that there is Reafon to believe it had commenced befcre his Time. If we were to take in, under the Notion of affured Commentaries on the facred Text, what hath been written on the Life of *Mofes* by *Jofephus* and *Philo*, then we fhould be able to fpeak very explicitly; but they write fo apparently in the *Greek* Stile, that is in the Stile of

Con-

Conjecture, that for my own Part, tho' I have a high Opinion of both their Judgments, yet I cannot bring myfelf to rely upon the Authority of either. But tho' *Moses* hath not left us any Account of the Learning of *Egypt*, we may find in his Writings a great Variety of Facts which have a Reference thereto, and from which we may conclude, that it was both folid and extenfive, as I fhall have Occafion to fhew in the Profecution of this Difcourfe.

In the Time of *Solomon*, *Egypt* was in the very Zenith of her Glory, and this it was that induced that wife and magnificent Prince to defire to ally himfelf to its Monarch, by whofe Affiftance he reduced one of the Maritime Cities of the *Philiftines*, or rather had it given him by the King of *Egypt*, when he had taken and burnt it with Fire, which fhews that the *Egyptians* were then very perfect in the Art of War. In the Reign of *Rehoboam*, *Shifhak* made a perfect Conqueft of his Kingdom, that is as perfect a Conqueft as he made of any Kingdom, for he pretended to no more than honorary Tribute, and an Acknowledgment of his being *Lord Paramount*, as we fpeak. This *Shifhak* was the *Sefoftris* of the *Greeks*, and the only great Conqueror who reigned in *Egypt*, if we except *Ofyris*, and the reft of the fabulous Heroes. The facred Hiftorians of fucceeding Reigns fpeak very frequently of the *Egyptians*, their Knowledge, Induftry, and Prowefs; and it muft be confeffed even by fuch as would difpute their divine Authority, that the Accounts we have from thefe Writers are the moft confiftent, the moft rational, and the moft ufeful that are any where to be met with.

B b 4

A s

As to the Fame of the *Egyptian* Learning among the *Greeks*, it is impoſſible to conceive any Thing greater or more illuſtrious than it was. The Founders of the States and of the Religion of *Greece* were all either *Egyptians* or Perſons who boaſted of their being verſed in the Learning of the *Egyptians*. Their greateſt Poets celebrated that Kingdom as the Region of Science: The wiſeſt of their Legiſlators acknowledged themſelves indebted for their Abilities in that ſublime Art, to the Inſtructions they had received, and the Obſervations they had made in the Country we are ſpeaking of. Their beſt Hiſtorians affected nothing ſo much as the recording the Exploits of this People, and endeavouring to ſet their Hiſtories in a clear Light, as the *Greek* Philoſophers never pretended to diſown their being indebted to the *Egyptians* for the Rudiments at leaſt of all that Knowledge which they taught their Diſciples. I might have quoted in Support of what I have been ſaying, the Writings of *Homer*, *Herodotus*, *Diodorus Siculus*, *Plutarch*, and above all *Ariſtotle* and *Plato*, with the reſt of the *Greek* Writers of Eminence, who all agree in affirming, that the *Egyptians* were a moſt learned and knowing People. Here therefore I reſt that Evidence which I think ſufficient to prove, that the Fame of the *Egyptian* Wiſdom was great and univerſal, and conſequently ſuch as deſerves Credit. But as I before remarked, tho' the Reputation of the *Egyptian* Learning may well be underſtood by the Accounts given of it by the *Greeks*, yet can we gather but a very imperfect and indifferent Idea thereof, from the Particulars they have been pleaſed to communicate.

SOME

SOME of them, such as the Poets, and miscellaneous Writers, mention it occasionally, or partially, as it suits with their Subjects. Others, as Historians and Antiquarians, insist upon it ; but then they are so concise on such Heads of the *Egyptian* Science as they understood, and so diffuse on those Points which they confessed they did not understand, that one is frequently astonished, but very seldom enlightned by what they say. Hence it is that the fabulous History of *Egypt*, as the *Greeks* have given it to us, is the most unintelligible Jumble of Absurdities that ever appeared. We are indeed told in Excuse of this, that the *Egyptian* Priests did not only do their utmost to conceal the History and Antiquities of their Nation from Strangers, but even took a Pleasure in imposing on them, and in passing on them romantic Stories, and ridiculous unintelligible Allegories, for grand Secrets, and the hidden Mysteries of their sacred and civil Institutions. To believe therefore in the Gross all that the *Greeks* have told us is irrational, and must lead us into Error, and to reject the whole would be to own an absolute Ignorance, and a Despair of being better informed. The middle Road therefore is in this, as in most other Cases the safest ; and we ought to believe that the *Egyptians* were well versed in all the Sciences, and that what is excellent and worthy of a wise People, in the Accounts given of them by the *Greeks*, ought to be esteemed just and authentick ; whereas all Things mean and trivial, that are found mixt in these Accounts, ought to be looked upon as spurious, and the Effects of the Author's Credulity or Boldness.

I AM now come to the second Head I proposed, that is, the real Extensiveness of the ancient *Egyptian* Learning ;

Learning; and in Support of this I shall offer Facts only, having already placed all Authorities on this Subject under the former Head. As to the Knowledge of the ancient *Egyptians* in Theology, I am persuaded it was very great. Nor can I bring my self to believe that any of the Fables which are attributed to the *Egyptians* were believed by them, that is, strictly and literally. On the contrary, I am convinced that they were allegoric Systems of natural Mysteries, and that we have the true Keys of very few of them. As to that Division which I heretofore mention'd of *hidden* and *open* Divinity, I will not hide my Suspicion, that as the *open* Divinity consisted in downright Idolatry, so the *hidden*, which was in very few Hands, did not fall much short of the true Religion, that is to say, it consisted in knowing that the popular Religion was made up of Types and Shadows, and that the true Worship of God consisted in acknowledging his Unity, and in doing Good to his Creatures. Neither do I conceive that this *hidden* Divinity was peculiar to the *Egyptians*, but that it was known to the Legislators of most of the heathen Nations, and that the Discoveries they sometimes made of it to their favourite Disciples gave Rise to those Suspicions of Atheism, which we find so rudely fixed upon them by Writers who were zealous, or affected to be zealous for the *Vulgar Faith*.

I should very willingly enter into the Detail of the Reasons which have not only led me to, but confirmed me in this Opinion, were this a proper Place. But inasmuch as such an Account would take up a great deal of Room, and lead me into many Digressions, I will content my self for the present with observing, that it in

the

the Sequel of this Difcourfe I fhall prove that in other Refpects the ancient *Egyptians* were a well-governed, wife, polite, and induftrious People, then it ought to be inferr'd, that the beft of them had rational and confiftent Notions in Religion, and that even the People were not fo ftupid as to believe a Religion altogether without Art or Contrivance, which would have been certainly the Cafe, if the Religion of the *Egyptians* had been really fuch a one as many of the *Greek* and *Latin* Writers reprefented. To this I will add, that the Ridicule fo freely play'd by thefe Writers upon the *Egyptian* Religion, is a ftrong Prefumption that they were not right in their Sentiments about it; for how can we believe that thofe who were the Mafters of the *Greeks* in all their Sciences, as they again were of the *Romans*, fhould fall fo miferable fhort of them in this firft and moft important of all Sciences? But to pafs from Religion to Government.

THIS feems to have been the Glory of the People of whom we are now fpeaking; and the Accounts we have of it are fo far from being obfcure, that they are fufficient to prove this Nation the wifeft of any in the World in the Settlement of its Conftitution, and the moft happy in its Effects. As to the Form of Rule which prevailed in *Egypt*, it was that of *Monarchy*. The ancient Kings of *Egypt* were ftiled *Pharaohs*; which was a Name of Dignity, and followed by the proper Name of the Prince, as *Pharaoh Hophra*, *Pharaoh Neco*. He was ftiled abfolute, and he might be abfolute if he pleafed. Yet there was a Table of Rules for the Conduct of the King, which defcended to the minuteft Points. Such as the Time of his Rifing,

his

his Meals, and the Hours of his Diversions, to which he usually submitted, not only in Conformity to his Predecessors, but because he knew that though he was above all Men during his Life, yet he should not fail to be judged after he was dead by his People. This was the sole Limitation, if it may be so called, under which an *Egyptian* Monarch lay. He was daily admonished by the Priests, but in a distant and respectful Way; and as soon as he was dead, certain Officers, appointed by the People, commenced a Suit against his Reputation, wherein, with great Freedom, they examined all his Actions; and if on a fair Trial the People condemned him, then his Corps was not interred with Funeral Solemnity, an Evil of all others most dreaded by the ancient *Egyptians*. This Custom the *Israelites* carried with them from hence, and preserved it very carefully, as appears from the several Memorandums we meet with in the *Chronicles*, concerning the Burials of the Kings of *Judah*, which are exactly conformable to this *Egyptian* Law.

As to the People, they had their Properties exactly secured to them, were all divided into certain Classes, and each Class had its Trade or Profession, in which Men were bred from Father to Son, and out of which they could not possibly be removed. By this Regulation, all Professions were alike cultivated; and though they were not alike honourable, yet were none of them esteemed base or mean. The Priests and Soldiers were particularly esteemed. The former were not only the Ministers of the Gods, but the Counsellors of their Kings, and had thereby a very great Power; whence in all Probability it came to pass that the ancient *Egyptians* were addicted rather to Peace than to War: Yet we must

must not suppose that they were then what the modern *Egyptians* are, a timid and effeminate Race of People, altogether averse to military Discipline, and incapable of Hardship ; for their Militia, on the contrary, was the very best in the World, and their Cavalry especially, capable of performing Wonders. But the Love of their Country abated their martial Ardour, and made them content to think that distinguishing themselves in defensive Wars was not only a just, but a sufficient Title to military Praise, that is, to so much of this Sort of Reputation as they desired. But the History and Polity of this People, their Power, their Wealth, and their Magnificence, are not expressly the Subjects of this Discourse, but come in occasionally, as Proofs of their Wisdom. The Constitution of *Egypt* was such, as joined to the natural Fertility and Beauty of the Country made the People both happy and satisfied, which was the Reason, that though the Love of Glory induced them to march under the Command of the great *Sesostris*, to the Conquest of all the Countries between the *Ganges* and the *Danube*, yet they affected not to retain any of the Provinces they subdued, but contented themselves with Tribute, Acknowledgments of Sovereignty, and erecting strong and lasting Monuments to perpetuate the Remembrance of their Victories.

AFTER this, they enjoyed a long and uninterrupted Peace, which they spent in adorning their Country, and in rendering habitable those Wastes and Deserts which now through Want of Care are become as inhospitable as ever. To say the Truth, the Cities, Publick Buildings, Royal Sepulchres, Pyramids, and other Monuments, are the clearest and most indisputable

Proofs

Proofs of the Knowledge, as well as the Publick Spirit
of this Nation. The Accounts we have in the ancient
Historians of the Wonders of the ancient *Thebes*, may,
for ought I know, be fabulous; but the Ruins that
are still to be seen in all Parts of *Egypt*, are apt to beget
Doubts in the Minds of Travellers whether any thing
reported of the *Egyptian* Buildings be Fable. For these
Ruins so evidently surpass any thing that is to be seen
elsewhere, except those of *Persepolis*, (which some *Arabian* Authors affirm to have been built by *Egyptian*
Workmen) that Men are apt to gather from thence, that
the Palaces and Cities of *Egypt*, when entire, were as
much superior to those in other Parts. It is true, that
this Supposition may be false; yet this is uncertain,
whereas that it is probable is a Thing of which we cannot doubt.

ALL the Ruins and Remains of Antiquity in this
Country, proclaim, if I may be allowed the Expression,
with one Voice, the exquisite Taste, as well as the
great Skill and admirable Industry of Those who erected
them. A simple Grandeur, a Magnificence arising from
Proportion, a Disposition that pleases every Beholder
from the Perspicuity of its Perfection justly surprises an
intelligent Spectator when he contemplates either the
Palaces or the Temples of *Egypt*. As to the Hieroglyphicks with which the Walls of those Buildings are
covered within-side and without, I pretend not to meddle with their Contents; for, as I cannot demonstrate
exactly the Wisdom contained in them, so I can never
bring my self to believe that they are such Marks of Folly
as the vain and puerile Interpretations of some of the
Learned have made them. I have read that the *Ethiopians*

pians and *Scythians*, made use of Figures instead of Letters in expressing their Notions. It may be, that in ancient Times this was the universal Language of the Learned throughout the East ; and I think that it may in some Measure confirm this Notion what the most learned Travellers have observed of a sacred and profane Language, as well as Character, which is still in Use in almost every Oriental Country. To this I think I may add, that the Pictures of Animals were fit to compose what might be called an *Alphabet* of *Nature*, because they would represent the same Ideas to all Beholders who were once initiated in this Character, which by this Method might be made universal ; whether it was, or was not so, is what I cannot, but it is possible some body hereafter may prove.

THE other Publick Works of the *Egyptians*, such as their Mounts, their Canals, their artificial Lakes, are at such a Distance of Time seen with vast Disadvantage. Time hath either levelled, or at least reduced to Hillocks, the first, rendered the second Ditches, or Gutters, to what they were, and converted into loathsome Morasses those glorious Repositories of the best Water in the World, which the Wisdom of the ancient Kings of *Egypt* contrived, and which their industrious and obedient People executed with incredible Labour. But if they are not what they were, they still serve to shew us where these Miracles of Art once were : And there are so many clear Proofs deducible from the Uses to which they served, as well as from the Accounts given of them in History, that we cannot doubt of their being as vast and wonderful as they are represented. By what has been said of the City of *Alexandria*, it will be most evident,

evident, that thefe were not fimple Works of Magnificence, or that any more Labour or Coft was employed about them than was neceffary to make them what it was fit and requifite they fhould be. Thus the Lake *Moeris* was to have a Capacity fufficient, if I may fo fay, to pour another *Nile* through the Defarts, between it and *Alexandria*. I am convinced, from the Veftiges that ftill remain in the Country on the other Side of the *Nile*, that the like Arts were ufed to fupply that Territory with Water. And hence, in my Opinion, arifes a double Proof of the Populoufnefs of this Country. For, if there had not been almoft an incredible Number of People, how could thefe immenfe Works have been performed; and, on the other hand, if *Egypt*, in the Condition it is now in, had been fufficient to fupply its Inhabitants with all Things neceffary, to what End was fo much Pains beftowed to render thefe Defarts habitable, which in their natural State might have ferved for Fortifications. As to the Number of the Inhabitants under its moft ancient Kings, it may well be thought an impracticable Talk to afcertain it. However, I think I can render it very probable, that under *Sefoftris* there were in this Country between twenty and twenty-fix Millions, which I think I could alfo fhew might live as well, and as comfortably in that Country in the Condition it was then in, as the *Swifs* do in their's, which I take to be the moft populous Country in *Europe*.

THUS I take my Leave of this Subject; for if the framing a Religion fo as to anfwer all the Ends of State; if the fettling a Conftitution which fubfifted fixteen hundred Years without Alteration; if the inventing a military Difcipline which enabled thofe who were trained

up

up therein to conquer the greateſt Part of the then known World ; if the making artificial Seas and Rivers, turning ſandy Deſerts into fruitful Fields, and erecting fine Cities where Nature had not afforded Materials for a Cottage : If, I ſay, all theſe Things, and many more of as ſtupendous a Nature, which, were it not to avoid Prolixity, I could eaſily reckon up, do not prove the Authors of them to have poſſeſſed ſolid and extenſive Wiſdom, then I muſt confeſs my ſelf miſtaken, and that my Partiality for the ancient *Egyptians* hath led me aſtray.

I ſHALL now ſpeak of the Learning of the modern *Egyptians*, which is no other than that of the *Arabs* ; and I ſhall the rather do it, Firſt, becauſe there is no Country in which it is better cultivated than it is in this : And ſecondly, becauſe from the Accounts I have heard of this Sort of Learning in *Europe*, I am apt to think our Notions concerning it are not either ſo juſt or ſo diſtinct as they might be. That the *Arabs*, in the Days of *Mohammed*, were a very rude and indigent People, is certainly true ; but that they had been always ſo, or that at this very Time there were none amongſt them that had the leaſt Tincture of Literature, is what I think not altogether ſo apparent as ſome would make it. The Reaſon of my Opinion is this : The *Koran*, or *Bible* of the *Mohamedans*, is written not only in a ſublime, but elegant Stile, and, as I obſerved before, its Elegance is one of the grand Arguments for the divine Inſpiration of *Mohammed*. Thus they put it. Our *Prophet*, by his own Confeſſion was an illiterate and ſimple *Man* ; his Book, however, is written in a pure and flowing Language, adorned with all the Figures of Rhetorick, and ſuperior

C c

to

to any thing that hath been written in the same Language since, therefore he wrote it by the Direction, or which is the same thing, had it delivered to him by the *Almighty*. To refel this Proposition, there is nothing more necessary than to consider the manifest Imperfections visible in the *Koran*; such as Facts false stated, Errors in Geography, and Chronology; and, which is still of greater Importance than any of these, flat Contradictions. But if the *Koran* be not divinely inspired, it is nevertheless excellently writ; and this is a Proof that the *Arabian* Stile arrived at Perfection, either in, or before the Days of *Mohammed*; whence I suppose it will follow, that those who used this Language were not utter *Barbarians*, but Men tollerably acquainted with the most useful of the Sciences, and who were accustomed to discourse of Things natural and divine.

T H E Critics admit that there are in the Book of *Job* abundance of *Arabick* Words, and it is indisputably written in the Manner of that People. This seems a strong Confirmation of what was said before; and indeed I think it can be hardly conceived, that a Nation should remain *Barbarians* in the last Degree, and yet make use of a comprehensive and a copious Language. The Truth seems to be, that a certain Kind of mixt Theology, a sort of moral Philosophy, and a jumbled Notion of Astronomy and Astrology, made up the Learning of the *Arabians*, who were Cotemporaries with *Mohammed*, or lived in the Ages before him. Those who succeeded him were barbarous indeed, for they affected Barbarism, and for several Successions made War on the Republick of Letters, as fiercely as they did on all the neighbouring Nations. It was in this unfortunate Season

when

when Enthufiafm was triumphant, and Literature in Difgrace, that *Egypt* fell into their Hands, and fuffered no lefs by their burning all the Manufcripts therein, than by their overturning and deftroying thofe Edifices which Time itfelf, and all *Barbarians* but thefe had feen with Reverence. By degrees, however, this Paffion for Ignorance wore off ; and as the *Caliphs* began to think themfelves Princes as well as Priefts, they likewife grew content to fuffer Learning to revive a little, and at laft began to cultivate and encourage it. *Abu Jaafar Almanfur* the Second *Caliph* of the *Abaffides*, was the great Reftorer of Science among the *Arabians* ; for he, not contented with the Study of their Language and Laws, which had been hitherto the utmoft Limit of any *Caliph's* Knowledge, apply'd himfelf to the Sciences, and fhew'd a great deal of Countenance, not only to the learned Men of his own Country and Religion, but to Strangers alfo. As his Reign was long and glorious, fo his Conduct gave a Sort of Rule to his Succeffors, who were no longer afraid or afhamed to acknowledge themfelves Protectors of Learning, and of its Profeffors.

THERE did not want, however, fome enthufiaftical Doctors, who thought that profane Literature might endanger their Religion ; and thefe Men having great Credit with the People, could not mifs of having fome alfo with their Sovereigns, till at lenth the *Caliph Almamun*, who was the Sixth of the Houfe before mentioned, freed himfelf from all Reftraints, engaged the Learned in all Profeffions, of all Religions, and from all Countries, to affemble in his Court, and patronized a Multitude of Tranflations, as well from the *European*, as from the Oriental Languages : By the former, I mean

the

the *Greek* and *Latin*; and by the latter, the ancient *Persian* and *India* Languages. On this Account he is regarded as the *Augustus* of the Learned; but the Bigots are not yet reconciled to his Memory; they are persuaded, that by an Affectation of Magnificence and universal Benevolence, he corrupted the Manners of the Faithful, and by introducing of foreign Philosophy, made Room for a Number of Heresies which have followed in Religion. I mention this to shew, that Men who would cover their own narrow Notions with the Veil of Religion, talk much the same Language in all Places; not that I am insensible of the Mischiefs which Religion hath suffered by the Intrigues of Men of Letters; on the contrary, I am sensible that a Heresy is seldom dangerous, but when such a Man is at the Head of it; yet I cannot think that Learning ought to be discouraged on this Account, because, if it should, I know of no Remedy that could be applyed to this very Evil. *Julian* was so sensible of this, that though he detested that Method of persecuting, which had been used by *Nero* and *Dioclesian*, yet he bethought himself of another, which would have been more fatal to the Church, that of forbidding her Children to study human Literature. Is it not strange that Bigots and Persecutors should think alike, and recommend one and the same Method with such different Views, as the extirpating and securing Religion? Or ought we not to be careful of admitting That as a Medicine, when prescribed by suspicious Friends, which our Enemies would force upon us as a Poison? The wiser Part of the *Mohammedans* have been always in this Sentiment, and especially the Princes of that Religion, who reigned in *Egypt*. These were great Encouragers

of

of Learning, and the Sun-shine of their Favour brought many Strangers of Merit to their Courts.

It is true, that the *Mamaluks* turned all Things upside down, and were as open Enemies to Letters, as to Virtue; fond of their own brutal Policy, Power was the Idol they worshipped, and a licentious Luxury the only Happiness they sought. No wonder then that all the Professors of Learning fled out of *Egypt*, nor have they returned thither but by slow degrees; however, in this last Age a Number of concurring Accidents have made the *Arabian* Literature flourish here again. What chiefly contributed thereto was, the retiring hither of many of the richest *Moors*, who were driven out of *Spain*; as also the Munificence of such *Turkish* Lords as having shelter'd themselves in *Egypt*, enjoy either under the Protection of the *Spahis*, or *Janizaries*, the Possession of large Estates, which they acquired at Court. Add to this the Temperature of the Air, and the Serenity of the Climate, which seem naturally to incline the *Egyptians* to certain Studies. But it is time to be more particular, and to enter into a direct Detail of the Sciences which are at present in Vogue amongst the politer Part of the Inhabitants of this Country. This I shall endeavour to perform as succinctly and impartially as I can. For, as on the one hand I can never subscribe to the common Opinion, that the Inhabitants of all Parts of the Earth, except *Europe*, are *Barbarians*; so I shall never be brought on the other to allow, that the *Europeans* fall short of these in true Wisdom and useful Knowledge, which some who have grown enthusiastically fond of the Oriental Learning would persuade us.

I shall

I SHALL begin with obferving, that although nothing is more common in *Europe* than to meet with Men who have no Sort of Tafte for Books, or Learning of any Kind, yet this is feldom, or rather never the Cafe in this Country, efpecially among the *Arabs*. For though there are but few comparatively fpeaking, who can read or write tollerably, yet the Knowledge of paft Events, and the Contents of Poems and Hiftories, famous amongft them, is a Sort of univerfal Paffion. Befides, for their Genealogies, and the Hiftories of their refpective Tribes, if we may call this Learning, every Man is poffeffed of it : They tranfmit it from Father to Son : They employ all their leifure Time in hearing or telling the Exploits of their Anceftors ; neither is there any thing that endears a Foreigner to them fo much as his lift'ning patiently to thofe Recitals. Poetry feems to have been in Efteem with all the Oriental Nations from the earlieft Point of Time ; and indeed if Enthufiafm, or fupernatural Tranfport be, as it is generally efteemed, the Effence of Poetry, then the Anthors of this Country ought to carry away the Prize, as well in Point of Excellence, as of Numbers. The *Arabick* is, of all Languages, except the *Greek*, the beft fuited to poetick Compofitions, for it is extremely fonorous, very copious, abounding with Epithets, and extremely capable of that Figure which the *Greeks* call *Paranomafia*, which I think I cannot exprefs better than by calling it a Method of affifting *Senfe* by *Sounds*, an Embellifhment frequently met with in the Sacred Scriptures, and which has certainly very happy Effects ; though I know it has not been held a true Beauty by our modern Critics. The *Perfian* Language is alfo extremely capable of all the

Excel-

Excellencies of Poetry, and tho' there are not fo many, yet there have been as great and as celebrated Poets of this Nation, as of any other in the *Eaſt* ; for which Reaſon all who pretend to Learning, not only throughout *Egypt*, but through the whole *Turkiſh* Empire, and the Dominions of the *Great Mogul*, apply themſelves to this Language, ſo as to acquire a Facility not only in ſpeaking and reading it, but of writing it alſo, for without this Accompliſhment, there is no acquiring the Character of Politeneſs in any of the Courts of *Aſia*. The *Turkiſh*, which is in Fact a mixture of various Tongues, *viz.* the *Arabick*, *Sclavonick*, and modern *Greek*, is yet capable of Compoſitions very muſical and pleaſant ; but there are not many Poems of great Fame in this Language unleſs tranſlated, the politer *Turks* content themſelves with Madrigals, Sonnets, and a ſort of Elegiac Poems, which yet would not be held deſpicable in any other Language.

Next to Poetry, we may reckon their Paſſion for Moral Philoſophy, the Precepts of which are generally delivered in a mixt kind of Works, that is, partly Proſe and partly Verſe. There are of theſe in all the Oriental Languages, and they are alike read and eſteemed in all. They conſiſt of certain Maxims or Aphoriſms, illuſtrated by ſhort Diſcourſes, Compariſons, Allegorics, Apologues, Paſſages from Hiſtory, Quotations from Poets, and ſometimes Prologues and Epilogues in Verſe, by the Authors themſelves. This kind of Books are uſually recommended to young People, in reſpect as well to their pleaſantneſs, as to the Tendency they have to correct their Manners. They likewiſe make a part of the Entertainment of ſtudious and ſedentary People, and

C c 4   are

are sometimes read in select Companies of Friends, who assemble for the Sake of promoting Knowledge. The ordinary sort of *Turks* content themselves with reading, or hearing read to them certain Romances, full of strange incredible Adventures, but connected by such a strong Spirit of Enthusiasm, and so diversified by the Fecundity of the Oriental Genius, that to those who have heard and understand them, the Pleasure the *Turks* take in them is not at all stupendious, much less ridiculous, as some of our Authors would represent it.

I remember amongst others, to have heard once the following Story read in a pretty large Company : One of the *Caliphs* finding himself in Danger, from the Ambition, Wealth, and Power of one of his Ministers, conceived that the safest Way of delivering himself was to sacrifice this Man to the People ; and therefore having ordered him to be put to Death, he at the same Time by Proclamation, bestowed his House and all his Wealth on the Populace. There wanted nothing more than this Royal Permission to set the Mob to work, who instantly tore the House in Pieces, every one taking what came first to hand. The Author of this History digresses on this Occasion, into a large Account of the Minister's Luxury, which as he informs us, was such, that there were in his Kitchen constantly a certain number of Dishes ready to be set on the Table. Amongst the Mob there was one *Kohak*, a poor miserable Fellow, who subsisted by selling Greens ; this Man stumbled by Chance on a Bag with two thousand Pieces of Gold, a great good Fortune in outward Appearance, but the Business was how to secure it ; *Kohak* carried it as well as he could into the Kitchen, and seeing there an earthern

them Pot half full of Rice and Mutton, he threw his Bag into it, and then setting the Pot upon his Head, marched off in Triumph. The Crowd made Way for him as he passed, shouting and jeering him for making Prize of a little Victuals, *Well, well,* said *Kobak, you who have Riches may covet Riches, to me it is something that I have got a Dinner.* The People were so well pleased with the Modesty of this Answer, that they commended the Man, and suffered him to go peaceably to his Hut, where he quickly discovered to his Family that he had brought them Rice and Mutton for their Life-time. The *Turks* laughed immoderately at this Relation, which so provoked a *German* who was present, that he could not avoid asking *Osman Effendi,* who brought him, where the Wit or Sense of that Story lay. *Why,* Friend answered the *Turk* gravely, *Art thou one of the Mob, that amongst the Rice and Mutton loose Sight of the Gold, and think your own Ignorance Wisdom.*

NOT to carry Things farther than they naturally go, I think I may affirm, that as the Oriental Imagination is wonderfully sharp, amazingly rapid, and yet always pleasant and amusing ; so there is a Profundity in Judgment, especially observable in the *Moors* and *Arabs,* who have applyed themselves to Learning, which can never be described. When one of these Stories hath been read, the Book is generally laid by. Then somebody starts a Question, another replies, and as the Conversation grows warm, a Multitude of shining sublime Things are said, which would appear altogether incredible if repeated. The publick Accademies, or as we call them in *Europe* Universities, are very numerous in the Countries possessed by *Mohammedan* Princes, and there are a pro-

digious

digious number of Scholars educated in each of them. It is not therefore a real Want of Learning, which makes thefe People appear fo ignorant to our *European* Travellers, but their valuing that Learning moft which we value leaft, and in which, few of our Travellers have any Skill at all. Befides it requires a great deal of Time and Application to acquire any Degree of Knowledge in the *Arabian* and *Perfian* Tongues, and a much longer Space to relifh the Hiftories, Poems, and Effays, that are wrote in them. However if no other Good refulted from it, this alone would juftify a Man in taking fuch Pains, that he hath thereby an Opportunity of reading many *Greek* and *Latin* Authors entire, of which we have only mutilated Copies. For inftance, there is certainly a compleat *Arabick* Tranflation of *T. Livius*, and I have been informed, that there is a compleat Verfion of *Curtius* in *Perfian*. To condemn therefore in the grofs all thefe People efteem, is abfurd ; becaufe we at the fame Time include what we ftudy and admire ourfelves. But of this enough.

WE are in *Europe* ftrongly prejudiced againft Oriental Hiftories, but this Prejudice is derived rather from their Manner than their Matter, and fometimes for want of diftinguifhing Romances from Hiftory. It is many Ages ago that *Xenophon* borrow'd from the *Perfians* the Plan of the Inftitution of *Cyrus*, a Work not written ftrictly according to Facts, and yet not fill'd up with Falfehoods, but with the Appearances of Truth, fitted to amufe and to inftruct, not to deceive or to delude the Reader ; for it is well known throughout the *Eaft*, and was no Doubt as well underftood by the *Greeks*, that thefe Pieces were not ftrict Hiftory, but
that

that they had what the skilful in Muſick call a *Ground of Fact*, the reaſoning and Decorations flowing from the Genius of the Author. But beſides theſe hiſtorical Romances, which are indeed very numerous, there are in the *Eaſt* a great abundance of original and well wrote Hiſtories.

Some of them contain general Tranſactions in all Nations, from the beginning of the World, to ſome certain Period ; ſome the particular of certain Nations ; ſome containing the *Dynaſties* of the ancient Kings before the Time of *Mohammed* ; ſome recording the Hiſtory of the Princes of that Faith, who have ruled in all the Nations that have embraced it. Moſt of theſe are in *Perſian* or *Arabick*, ſome in the *Turkiſh* Language, and a great many tranſlated into it. There are no leſs than thirteen Hiſtories of the Houſe of *Othoman*, written by ſeveral Authors, ſome in Proſe, and ſome in Verſe. Beſides, there is hardly a great City in all the *Eaſt* of which there is not one, or more Hiſtories. The Lives of *Caliphs*, *Sultans*, famous *Generals*, *Stateſmen*, *Hiſtorians*, *Poets*, and *Holy Men* are written apart ; and there are likewiſe numberleſs Accounts of Earthquakes, Famines, Plagues, Rebellions, Revolutions, and other remarkable Events, penn'd in the Way of Chronicle, with excellent Remarks, and curious Obſervations. Some great Men have compiled large Collections in the Eſſay kind, long before that kind of Writing was heard of in *Europe*, and the *French* Ambaſſador at *Conſtantinople* ſent his Maſter about the Year 1670, ſeveral Volumes written in this Way four hundred Years ago, by a *Vizir* of the *Sultan* of *Khoraſſan*.

A 3

As to Annals, they have Works in that Form of great Accuracy, and of vaſt Extent. Thoſe of *Perſia* make two hundred Volumes, and I am well aſſured, that the Annals of *China* are of the ſame Bulk; but then they are an Abridgment only, for thoſe called the Royal Annals of *China* make five hundred Volumes. And there is a general Hiſtory of the *Tartars*, which is ſaid to have been examined by a hundred learned Men, divided into five Parts, each containing twenty Volumes. It muſt however be allowed, that the want of Printing, and the exceſſive Price of Manuſcripts, render Libraries very thin in *Mohammedan* Countries, that is in Compariſon of ours; yet their Libraries are more comprehenſive then they ſeem, ſince they contain no variety of Editions, much leſs Duplicates of the ſame Book. However in Royal Libraries, and thoſe collected by Men in high Station, and of great Fortune, there are noble Collections. The Royal Library at *Fez*, contains thirty thouſand Volumes, of which many noble *Moors* have Catalogues. I need ſay the leſs on this Matter, becauſe I underſtand there is a learned Man in *Europe*, who is about to publiſh a Treatiſe expreſly on this Subject, which will be very curious and entertaining.

As to Chronology and Geography, thoſe neceſſary Lights to Hiſtory, our *Weſtern* Authors have ſo habituated themſelves to ſpeak with the utmoſt Contempt of the Abilities of *Eaſtern* Writers in reſpect to them, that it may be dangerous to endeavour the Removal of ſo old and ſo univerſal an Error. But as it is an Error, I will venture to remove it, by affirming, that there are as exact Geographical Deſcriptions in the *Arabick* Tongue as in any other whatſoever; and why ſhould
there

there not? Did we not recover *Ptolemy* from thence? For want of ftudying thefe Geographers, we are miferably deceived, and while we laugh at the Ignorance of the Oriental Nations, it is only their Ignorance of our Ignorance, that hinders them from deriding us. For that they have better Accounts of their own Countries than we have, that the Defcription and Hiftory of every little Kingdom fwallowed up long ago in the *Eaft*, ftill fubfifts in their Libraries, is a Fact that cannot be queftioned. And as to Chronology, there are *Arabian* and *Perfian* Authors, who have written very learnedly on all the Æras that have been in Ufe among the Nations of the *Eaft*. Nay, I have feen a *Perfian* Chronicle, in which the Reigns of the Princes before *Mohammed*, or rather before *Omar*, are computed by Days, and a Method propofed for reducing the Æra of the *Hegira*, to that of *Ifdegerd*.

But that I may not feem to be as much prejudiced in Favour of the Oriental Nations, as fome are againft them, I will admit that many of the *Turkifh* Men of the Law are very ignorant, and fo are moft of the *Grandees*; the Profeffors of Aftrology and the occult Sciences are alfo meer Blockheads; but then, have thefe fort of People no Brethren elfewhere? Are all Men of the *Robe* in *Europe Solomons?* All Men of Quality Men of Letters? All Figure-Cafters Men of Parts and Probity? If not, what does the Ignorance of thefe fort of Men in the *Eaft* prove? Surely, nothing againft the Learning of others, which is what I fpeak of.

As to Numbers, we ought in Confcience to allow the *Arabians* a competent Knowledge in them; becaufe we have borrowed our very Figures from them. But
befides

befides the common Doctrine of Arithmetic, they are
extremely well acquainted with that moft curious Science, which we call *Algebra*, tho' I think not very properly; becaufe this is pure *Arabick*, and the *Arabians*
never call that Science fo, but conftantly ufe this Form
of Expreffion, *Al Gebr ou Al Mocabelah*, i. e. *Computation by Comparifon* ; for *Mocabelah* fignifies Oppofition, or comparing, and every Body knows that this is
the moft effential part of that Science.   When this
Science was firft known in *Europe*, or to fpeak more
accurately, was recovered by the *Europeans*; the common Opinion was, that this Method of computing had for
its Author *Geber*, whom the *Arabians* call *Giafar*, and
thence came our Appellation.   But as this Notion was
abfolutely without Foundation, as the very Compofition
of our own Word fhews to a Perfon moderately skill'd
in *Arabick*, fo 'tis but reafonable that this Error fhould
be removed, and tho' I do not plead for changing the
Name of this Science, yet I cannot help wifhing that
this Appellation fhould be univerfally underftood.   The
Perfians have been remarkably careful in the Cultivation
of this Branch of Knowledge, there being in their Language as well as in the *Arabick*, both in Profe and in
Verfe, a vaft Variety of Works relating to analitical
Computation.   I cannot however deny, that the *Eaftern* Sages entertain fome grofs Miftakes about this Science, and that they have mifapplyed it ftrangely.   For
Example, they attribute the Invention of this Art to
Ariftotle, whofe Fame is very great in the *Eaft*, and
of whofe Works they have a far better Collection than
we.   Yet in this they fpeak without Foundation, for
Algebra was certainly devifed by *Diophantus* of *Alexandria*

dria, who lived in the second Century, and whose Works both the *Arabians* and *Persians* have in their own Language. As to the wrong Use they make of this Science, it is the same which they make of all Sciences, that is, they would fain convert it into a sort of Divination. The very Piece they ascribe to *Aristotle* is written in this Stile, and bears the Form of a Letter to his Disciple, acquainting him with the Method of Divining by Numbers, which Army would be victorious in Battle. A miserable Fall this! and altogether unworthy of that great Genius on whom they would Father it. But perhaps I have been already too long upon so dry a Matter, for which I have no other Excuse, than that Men generally fancy they may be allowed to talk much on a Subject which they have studied much. Let me now speak of the present State of Physic in *Egypt*, and so conclude this Discourse.

I have before spoken in general of the ancient and present State of Professors of Physick in *Egypt*, I have also expatiated on the Seasons and different Temperaments of Air in this Country, but as my Intention is to treat this Subject more strictly here, I will resume a few Particulars with respect to the latter, and also add not a few to what I have said of the former. The Air of *Egypt* considered Physically, is hot, dry, unequal, and in some Months nitrous and chilly. In the extreme Heats of Summer, the Inhabitants have recourse to variety of Inventions, for the procuring cool Air, in which they are wonderfully successful; tho' sometimes to their Prejudice. The North Winds which blow, as I have elsewhere shewn, suddenly and incertainly in the hottest Seasons, are received with too great Avidity,

and

and with too little Precaution, by a People half burnt
by the raging Heat of the Seafon. As there is a prodigious mixture of Nations in this Country, it follows
from thence, that their Habit, Temper, and manner of
living, cannot be a Phyfical Senfe, be very exactly defcribed. For Inftance, in *Cairo* one may eafily reckon
up between twenty and thirty different Nations, fuch as
*Egyptians, Arabs, Abyffines, Ethiopians, Indians, Per-
fians, Affyrians, Greeks, Turks, Tartars, Hungarians,
Scluvonians, Ruffians, Moors,* &c. We may however
make a new Divifion of the Inhabitants of this Country, fo as to ferve our Purpofe tollerably well. In the
firft Place let us reckon thofe who inhabit Cities and
great Towns; thefe lead indolent, eafy, and luxurious
Lives, affect a moift cooling Diet, drink cool Liquors
in abundance, and bath often, hence they are generally
speaking, extremely fat, fome monftroufly fo; have
weak, cold Stomachs, are fubject to Ruptures, Drop-
fies, and Fluxes, and are feldom without Rheums,
Defluxions on the Breaft and Lungs, and other fuch like
Diftempers, which are exceedingly increafed by the exceffive Ufe of Women. The fecond fort are the *Arabs,*
who by keeping ftrictly to the Cuftoms of their own
Country and Nation, efcape many, if not moft of thefe
Difeafes, and are of a quite different Temperament,
that is have fpare and hectic Conftitutions. The third
fort are the Villagers or Peafants, a Race of laborious,
hardy People, who endure all Seafons, and all Weathers,
eat little, work much, are of a dark Sun-burnt Complexion, and are fo feldom the Objects of a Phyfician's
Care, that it is hard to fay what their Conftitutions are,
farther than as they are reprefented by the foregoing
Defcription.

THIS

THIS Account will ferve well enough to fhew how People come to be fick, unhealthy, and fhort lived; but as many of the *Egyptians* efcape all thefe Evils, and attain extreme old Age, it is neceffary that this alfo fhould be accounted for, at leaft as far as it may be. All the ancient Hiftorians, and not a few modern Travellers affure us, that the *Egyptians* live long, and indeed the Fact is indubitable, but then we muft admit of proper Diftinctions. The native *Egyptians*, the *Arabs*, and the Peafants are long lived, together with fuch as are pretty careful of their Health, of which there are feveral Caufes, (amongft which however the Air muft never be reckoned,) but the principal Caufe is Temperance. In *Egypt* few People eat much Flefh, and the Flefh they do eat, is either Veal, Mutton, or Fowls; they are likewife no Drinkers of ftrong Liquors, and are extremely careful in preferving a calm and quiet State of Mind. This may feem not very confiftent with what I faid of their Luxury, but that is not my Fault, the general Intemperance of the Northern and Weftern Parts of *Europe* give the Inhabitants of thofe Countries a falfe Idea of Luxury, which is found in many Things befides eating and drinking, fuch as in Habit, Attendance, Baths for Pleafure, Perfumes, and a thoufand other Things difcoverable by human Invention, when turn'd to fo unworthy a Purfuit. With refpect to thefe Things the *Egyptians* are luxurious, nor are they altogether free from it in Point of Diet; for they are careful in gratifying their Taftes, but not immoderate in the ufe of what they like.

OUR Accounts of *Egypt* always fpeak of the Plague as a Difeafe common in *Egypt*, and fo indeed it is, for

it

it vifits the Inhabitants once a Year punctually, and fometimes commits great Havock ; of which more particularly hereafter. But befides the Plague, the Inhabitants are vifited by peftilential Fevers, which are mortal in twenty-four Hours; young People efpecially at *Cairo* and *Alexandria*, are in Danger every Summer from a malignant kind of Small-Pox which rages exceffively. The Leprofy is alfo a common Diftemper, efpecially among the meaner fort of People, occafioned by their Meat and Drink. They have in this Country a fort of fat, falt, half rotten Cheefe, which both on Account of its cheapnefs and of its Relifh, is much eaten by the ordinary Peafants, who likewife take up with Greens, Roots, and Pulfe, as well as with Flefh not in Perfection, and in the Summer Months when the *Nile* is low, are conftrained to ufe other Water, which is not only unwholefome by Comparifon with the *Nile*, but perhaps the moft unwholefome in the World. In the Neighbourhood of *Cairo*, and even in the City itfelf, Numbers are afflicted with a kind of Leprofy, which is properly an *Elephantiafis*, whereby from their Hips downwards they are fwell'd in fuch a manner, as to lofe the Form of their Limbs, as well as the Ufe of them, and inftead of Legs and Feet, they are fupported by fhapelefs Pillars, like the Legs of Elephants; yet is this extraordinary Swelling without Pain. All kinds of Ruptures, and fome of them equally hideous and painful, are very frequent, and fo is the Gout, the Gravel, and the Stone, obftructions, and Inflammations in the Bowels, and all the Difeafes of which the Head and Eyes are capable. But of thefe I forbear to fpeak particularly, becaufe I do not know that they differ much

from

from the fame fort of Difeafes in *Europe*; and becaufe
I am willing to fpeak diffufely of the Plague, which
I have faid, conftantly vifits *Egypt*, and of which, tho'
our Authors fpeak much, yet I think little hath hitherto been faid accurately about it.

THIS grievous and deftructive Malady, tho' it be
much ftrengthened and encreafed by the Heat of the
Air in *Egypt*, is feldom or never bred there; fo that
tho' it may be ftiled *endemial* and *epidemic* in *Egypt*,
yet it cannot be called *indigenous*, fince it is certainly
derived either from *Greece* or *Syria*, on the one Side, or from
Barbary or *Libya* on the other; and thefe Plagues are
very different. The Plague when it comes from *Greece*
feizes many, but its Symptoms are mild, and there are but
a few to whom it proves mortal; the Plague from *Syria*
is more fatal, for tho' few are feized thereby, yet more
die than in the former Cafe; but when the Plague comes
from *Barbary*, or *Libya*, it lays all *Cairo* wafte, preying
on all Degrees of People with grievous and prodigious
Symptoms, which moftly terminate in Death, fo that few
who are ftruck therewith, preferve either Hope or Reafon. When the Plague comes early in the Year, that
is in the Months of *September* or *October*, it does moft
Mifchief, and continues longeft; but when it is late in
the Seafon before it vifits *Cairo*, it does not fpread fo
exceffively, or do fo much Mifchief. But whenever it
comes, or of whatfoever fort it be, the rifing of the
Nile delivers the People at once, not only from the
Difeafe, but from all Apprehenfions of it. Seven Months
therefore is the Circle of its Reign, in which if we
may believe what the Inhabitants of *Cairo* unanimoufly
affert, it hath fometimes carried off half a Million of

Perfons;

Persons; but this is very rare, and if seventy thousand die in a Year of that Distemper, it is held to be a very great Mortality.

T w o Things there are which I think not easily, if they are at all to be accounted for, and that is, the coming and the going of the Plague, both of which are Facts so thoroughly asserted, that no Man in his right Senses pretends to doubt of them. That the Plague is propagated in, and transferr'd from Place to Place by the Air, seems to be a Thing out of Dispute, but how it is generated therein, I must confess I cannot say. Those who have lived at *Constantinople* affirm, that it is always more or less in that City, and the common Opinion in *Egypt* is, that the Plague is always in some Part or other of *Barbary*; which if true, one might with some Colour of Reason suggest, that the Wind blowing long from either of these Quarters, might bring along with it the infected Air, which once suck'd in, might give a beginning to the Disease in *Egypt*, where it must be kept up and continued by the stifling Heat of the Summer Months, which tho' not sufficient to produce, may be very capable of circulating and spreading the Disease, and of heightening the Degree of the Infection. The stopping of the Plague, or rather the entire Cessation thereof, is a Thing still more perplexed, because it happens suddenly, on the first rising of the Waters of the *Nile*, and when the North Winds do but begin to blow, However I will offer something on this Head too, which if it be not perfectly reasonable, yet may provoke some more knowing Man to confute it, and establish something better in its Room. Experience hath justified what Men at first, perhaps from Fancy rather than Reason, fon, took for certain, that Plenty of running Water renders Places wholefome, the Reafon of this I conceive to be the frequent Change of Air that muft necefſarily happen in fuch a Place, for the one Fluid fuftaining the other, they both move at once; and therefore I apprehend, that running Water fupplies in fome Meafure the Place of Wind in purifying the Air. Now it is certain, that while the Plague continues in *Egypt*, the *Nile* runs very flowly, and at laft fcarce runs at all. But when its Waters begin to fwell, which happens by the Supplies they receive from *Ethiopia*, I conceive they bring down with them frefh Air, which is difperfed through the Country at the fame Time that the former infectious Air is brufhed off by the blowing of the North Wind. I might offer in Support of this Opinion, that wonderful Change that then happens with refpect to the Cloaths, Goods, and Domeftick Utenfils of Perfons infected, which are inftantly made Ufe of without any ill Confequences following thereupon, which I think can have no other Caufe then the entire Alteration of the Air, now render'd incapable of fpreading Infection.

By this Remark I have been put in Mind of a Circumftance of very great Importance, and that is, the Means made Ufe of by the *Mohammedan* Inhabitants of *Egypt*, to fpread, to propagate, and fupport the Plague, if I may fo term their Obftinacy in fhewing a Zeal without Knowledge for their Law. This they do not only by converfing freely with fuch as have Plague Sores upon them, but by putting on their Garments as foon as they are expired, and even felling thefe together with their Moveables publickly, and thereby circulating the

In-

Infection throughout the whole Place, all which flows from an Opinion, that God having pre-determined the Time of a Man's Death, all Precautions are alike fruitless and ridiculous, from which Notion, the bulk of the People are not to be wearied either by Reason or Experience. From the Diseases let us now pass to the Physicians. —

THERE are in *Egypt* many Professors of the different Branches of Physic, of both Sexes; many Occulists, Men who make it their Business to bleed and scarify, and indeed all these are very dextrous in their Way; but for a regular Physician, one who has made the whole Body of the healing Science his Study, and fortified his Reading by compleat Observation, there are none such in *Egypt*, if we except those who come thither from *Europe*. The *Egyptians* are great Takers of Medicines, as well in good Health as when they are sick, some Things they chew for a sweet Breath ; they use Electuaries for curing Crudities in the Stomach ; they have Syrups and Confections, which answer divers Ends, but above all, they are great Takers of Opium, and other Drugs of that sort, in Order to promote an exhilerating Sensation, in which some *Europeans* have imitated them, but with little Reason, and not much to their Satisfaction ; for they have found at last the Necessity of abandoning Opium, from the Accidents which follow from their not having it by them at the accustomed Time of their taking it, which tho' it rarely happens, yet by being mislaid, or by twenty other Accidents, it may happen to any Man, and then his Life is immediately in Danger, he is surpriz'd with Fits, with Convulsions, Vomiting, and such a mighty Depression of the

Spirits,

Spirits, that nothing can be more frightful, or more alarming, than to see a Person in such a Condition. But it may be enquired, how since such Symptoms follow the Neglect of it in a single Dose, Men ever find the Method of leaving it entirely? To which I answer, that this is not to be done but with Circumspection; for first of all the accustomed Dose is abated, which that it may give the less Pain, is in some Measure supplyed to the Patient, by adding to the reduced Dose a Glass of generous Wine. The Quantity of Wine is encreased as the Quantity of Opium is diminished, till at length the Person is brought to drink at his accustomed Time pure Wine, without any Inconvenience. Afterwards the Wine is decreased in Quantity, so that in six Months it may be left off as well as the Opium, and Nature left to perform what was before the Effect of Art; for what a Man does who has taken Opium, is like what a Puppet may be made to do by Clock-work, it astonishes the ignorant, but Men of Sense have no Opinion of it.

THE *Egyptian* Physicians bleed very copiously almost for all Diseases, frequently without any Disease at all, and this they do without distinction of Age or Sex, which certainly produces a great deal of Mischief, and I make no Question that it heightens to a dangerous Degree, many of the Disorders which it is made Use of to abate. The Practice in this Case is not more destructive than the Principle on which it is grounded is ridiculous; for these Dealers in Medicine having as I said before, no comprehensive Knowledge of the Art they profess, assign such Causes for Diseases as will best satisfy the People. They pretend therefore, that all the Water of

the

the *Nile*, which a Man receives into his Body, becomes
Blood ; and this they fay hath been the Cafe ever fince
Mofes changed the Water of that River into Blood. But
tho' they may bleed too much, and certainly do it often
without any true Reafon, yet it muft be owned, that
they do it more dexteroufly, and to better Purpofe than
we do in *Europe*. For inftance, they open more Veins
than we do. Where there is an intenfe Head-ach, they
bleed in the Forehead, and in the Nofe, and thereby
frequently cure the Patient upon the Spot. They bleed
likewife on the Wrift, behind the Ears, in the Neck,
&c. But their great Skill lies in opening of Arteries,
which they do frequently, and very fuccefsfully, in all
Parts of the Body, and without any of thofe Symptoms
which attend the accidental pricking thefe Veffels in our
Northern Climates. They likewife cup and fcarify very
dexteroufly ; fo that I am apt to think, that as they
have certainly forgot and loft the Theory of the Antients,
they yet as certainly preferve the Methods in Ufe
in thofe Days, which ought to give us higher Ideas of
the practical Skill of the old Phyficians than we are apt
to entertain ; which whether it arifes from Envy towards them, or Vanity in our felves, I pretend not to
determine.

I must not omit, now I am fpeaking of the fingular
Operations performed by the *Egyptian* Surgeons, if I
may fo call them, an odd Way of extracting Stones out
of the Bladder, which, as I never heard of in *Europe*, fo
I have Reafon to think it has never been practifed there.
This is a Bufinefs by it felf, and thofe who are fkillful
therein get a great deal of Money, for the Stone is a
common Diftemper, not only amongft the *Jews* and
Chriftians,

Christians, but amongst the *Turks* and native *Egyptians* ; and it is easy to conceive, that those who are troubled therewith are content to purchase Ease almost at any Price, especially where there is no cutting in the Operation. This the *Egyptian* Artist performs thus. He brings two or three small Tubes of different Sizes, which fit one in another like the Pieces in a Hautboy. They are composed of a cartilaginous Substance, which is extremely capable of Extension. One of these, which is the largest, he introduces through the urinary Passage to the Neck of the Bladder, then passing the Finger of his Left Hand into the *Anus*, he pushes the Stone towards the Neck of the Bladder ; when this is done, he takes the other End of the Pipe in his Mouth, and by blowing with all his Force wonderfully dilates the Passage, 'till finding the Stone at the Mouth of the Tube, he draws up his Breath at once, and having receiv'd it into his Pipe, he slips down his Hand, and secures it thereby from returning into the Bladder ; then fitting another of his Pipes to the End of that which he had before used, he draws the Stone through the *Penis*, 'till he is able to extract it either with his Finger or an Instrument. How incredible soever this may seem, and I know it will appear incredible to those who believe themselves best Judges in these Matters, yet the Fact is certain, and I could relate much more concerning it, but that I think this sufficient to those who will believe it, and to those who will not, adding any thing more would only serve to excite farther Contempt.

In the Dropsy they cut very boldly, and often ease the Patient, nay, and sometimes cure him ; but then it must likewise be owned, that Instances are not infrequent

where

where Gangreens have followed upon this Operation, in part owing perhaps to the Unskillfulness of the Operator, and in part to the Obstinacy of the Patient: For as in *Spain* no sick Person will be restrained from high season'd Hashes, so in *Egypt* Men will rather bear any thing than be interdicted cool Liquors.

THIS Humour of theirs, which seems at first sight so effeminate, is in truth the Source of their bearing with wonderful Patience such Operations as would terrify People almost out of their Wits in any other Place. For instance, in the Gout, and other Diseases, nothing is more common in *Egypt* than to suffer the Part afflicted to be burnt, not by any Potential, but by an actual Cautery; which Operation is performed after the following Manner. The Patient being in Bed, the Person who undertakes the Cure rolls up a Piece of Cotton Cloth in the Form of a Pyramid, leaving a spiracle or Air-hole in the middle; this Piece of Cloth, thus rolled up, being set on fire, is placed on the Member affected, and there it is suffer'd to remain till it is consumed to Ashes. By this Means a running Wound or Ulcer is formed, which is kept open as long as may be, and by this means the Patient is very frequently cured, when all other Methods have failed. This they frequently practise for almost all Diseases. For the Head-ach they burn the Temples, and behind the Ears. The *Lumbago* they cure by burning on the Loins. The Dropsy, by raising an Ulcer on the Belly. The Sciatica, by burning on the Hip; and the Gout, by burning above and below the Joint on which it fixes. It is not necessary for me to enquire whether the Cures that certainly follow this uncouth Manner of Proceeding ought to be attributed to

the

the drying up of the Humours by the Operation it felf, or to the draining them off by keeping the Ulcer open; perhaps it is ferviceable both Ways. However, it muft be owned, that in fome Chronical Diftempers, where the Patients have been quite worn out, and the Wits of our Phyficians abfolutely at a Stand, this *Egyptian* Remedy hath been try'd with wonderful and unexpected Succefs. But then it is worthy of Remark, that this, and the reft of their Operations, always fucceed beft under the Direction of fome *Italian* or *French* Phyfician, which I conceive to be owing not fo much to their Skill in Phyfick, as to their Knowledge in Anatomy, wherein moft of the *Egyptian* Operators are very indifferently verfed, though one would think quite the contrary, from their finding and opening the fmalleft Veins with incomparable Eafe and Dexterity: But this Knowledge they have by Tradition, and their Adroitnefs comes by Practice; fo that what I have advanced cannot be looked upon as incredible or improbable.

I MIGHT add to this Difcourfe Accounts of the *Egyptian* Preparations for ftimulating Luft, for appeafing Care, and for delighting the Mind by pleafant Dreams; but I think the mentioning of them fufficient to fhew that they do not deferve to be particularly treated of, and therefore I fhall fay no more of them, or of thofe who contrive and exhibit them. What I have faid is fufficient to give a general Idea of the prefent State of Learning in this Country, which is all I propofe to give, and therefore my Tafk being ended, I willingly lay down my Pen.

It is now Time to return to my own Affairs, and to the Reafons which led us to a precipitate Return into

Europe,

Europe, after having render'd a Country not very agreeable to Strangers, almoſt as eaſy to us as to its natural Inhabitants. In the Month of *Auguſt*, we received a Letter from Mr. *Fetherſtone*, full of very good News, but with an Intimation, that our Preſence at *Legborn* might be as uſeful to us, or rather more ſo, than a longer Reſidence in *Africk*. In a private Letter to me, Mr. *Fetherſtone* informed me that *Johnſon* had ſold in *France* a little Collection which I had ſent him of valuable Stones, for two thouſand five hundred Crowns, which was a fifth Part more than I expected ; and he likewiſe hinted, that if I could bring more of theſe Stones into *Europe*, they would be more beneficial than Curioſities, on account of various Royal Marriages which were then talked of. Theſe Letters did not determine either Mr. *Perez*, or my ſelf, to be very haſty in our Motions ; on the contrary, we reſolved to make a very large Collection before our Return to *Italy*, eſpecially of Medals, which we purchaſed very cheap, and of Manuſcripts, and figured Gems, which we knew to be much valued in *Europe*, by the Perſons ſent from *France* and *Italy* to collect them, of whoſe Errands we had very particular Accounts ; though, for many Reaſons, we cautiouſly avoided any perſonal Correſpondence with them. In three Weeks after the Receipt of Mr. *Fetherſtone*'s Letter, I had a Meſſage from the *Venetian* Conſul, directing me to attend him the next Morning, and, to my Surprize and Concern, was informed that he had two large Boxes which were directed to be put into my Hands by his Correſpondent at *Roſetta*, together with a Letter, which notified the Death of my good Friend Dr. *Salviati*, who left me his Papers, ſome Curioſities he had collected

in

in *Egypt*, and several other Things of Value. I thank-ed the Consul for his Care and Goodness on this as well as on many other Occasions. He received my Compliments with the utmost Civility, and told me, that he was well acquainted with the sincere Esteem I had always shewn for the Deceased, who was his particular Friend; and that when I inclined to return into *Europe*, he would charge me with a private Commission relating to his own Affairs. I told him, that I had already Thoughts of returning into *Italy*, and was actually disposing my Affairs so as to be able to depart very soon. He said his Business did not require any great Dispatch, and that he should be glad I would give him a Week or ten Day's Notice.

ON my Return home, I found another Packet from Mr. *Fetherstone*, the Contents of which were not very material, with respect to me; but there came inclosed a Letter to Mr. *Perez*, which made a very great Impression upon him, and engaged him to be more expeditious than he intended in his Return to *Europe*. As in respect to his own Concerns he was a Man of a reserved Temper, I could never be perfectly informed of the Contents of this Letter, the utmost I could learn by putting together broken Expressions and distant Discourses was this, that his Uncle, who had been imprisoned by the Inquisition, had, by dint of Interest, escaped; and the Court finding it necessary to intrust him with Remittances into *Flanders*, he was left more at Liberty than Men usually are who have been once under the Displeasure of the Holy Office. He did not fail to make a proper Use of this Indulgence, for having by large Sums given to Convents, Fraternities, and other Catholick Institutions,

Inftitutions, confirmed the Priefthood in a good Opinion of him, he at laft found Means to retire to *Bayonne*, after remitting into *France*, *Holland*, and the *French Flanders*, an immenfe Sum of Money, of which he was poffeffed when he was firft feized, and which he had found Means to fecret in fpite of all the Vigilence of the Inquifitors. This Event made a great Alteration in the Affairs of Mr. *Perez*, not only on account of his near Relation to this Perfon, but by reafon of his having a confiderable Part of his Fortune in his Hands, which he was now in a Condition to reftore. What this Proportion was, either of Mr. *Perez's*, or of his Uncle's Subftance, I never knew; but I have Reafon to think, that it was very confiderable from Mr. *Perez's* Conduct. His Refervednefs was not on Account of himfelf, but of his Relations, of whom he had many in *Spain* and *Portugal*, whofe Safety depended entirely on his Taciturnity. After meditating a Day or two upon this Letter, he told me that he was determined to go immediately to *France*, when an Opportunity fhould offer; that as to his Effects, he would leave them to my Care, and that on my fettling a general Account with Mr. *Fatherftone*, he would let me know his Sentiments farther. In the mean time he became very grave and thoughtful, fpoke little, affected to be alone, and feem'd to be uneafy at our longer Stay in *Egypt*.

This induced me to make all the Hafte I could in fettling Things for our Return; which having at laft performed, I went to wait upon the *Venetian* Conful, and to receive his Commands. They related to the Sale of fome Jewels which he had already fent to *Venice*, and about which an Agent from a great *Italian* Prince had

had given himself a good deal of Trouble. The Conful had fome Sufpicions which he communicated to me, directed me how I fhould be fatisfied, and at the fame time put into my Hands an Order to his Correfpondent to follow in this Affair the Directions he fhould receive from me. As I look'd upon my felf to be extremely honoured by this Mark of the Conful's Favour and Confidence, fo I was no lefs obliged to him for a Prefent he made me of a Cabinet of Curiofities at my Departure, and the Pains he took in recommending me to the Captain of the Ship in which I returned to *Italy*. But of thefe Things hereafter. At our leaving *Cairo*, *Antonio*, who had ferved us long and faithfully, engaged himfelf fo far in an amorous Intrigue as to make it his Choice to ftay behind, and to enter into the Service of the *French* Conful. Mr. *Perez* exprefled fome Surprize at this, having been extremely kind to him, and intending him much greater Favours. At firft we could not penetrate his Reafons, but before we left *Rofetta*, we learned that he had married a *Greek* Wench; fo that in all Conditions of Life it feems Love hath for a Time a ftronger Influence than Intereft.

We arrived at *Rofetta* in the Beginning of *November*, and the firft Place I went to was the Patron's of my Friend *Salviati*, to return them Thanks perfonally, as I had already done by Letter, for their Care and Exactnefs in fulfilling that good Man's Will. They told me, that though he had had confiderable Opportunities of getting Money, yet he did not die worth above four hundred Sequins, which he had left to them to be diftributed in Charity; and which they put into the Hands of the Fathers of Mercy, to be employ'd in the Redemption,

demption of Chriſtian Captives, adding a hundred Sequins of their own. I cannot, on this Occaſion, avoid
ſetting down what I have often obſerved, that there is
in eminent Merchants a greater Fund of Juſtice, Honour
and Beneficence, than there is in almoſt any other kind
of People; at the ſame time that of all others they ſpeak
leaſt of theſe Things, but content themſelves with
that Satisfaction which is the Reſult of doing worthy
Actions, and which is infinitely more grateful, as well
as leſs diſturbing to a wiſe Man, than the Acclamations
of a Multitude. After three Weeks Stay at *Roſetta*,
Mr. *Perez* found an Opportunity of going directly to
Marſeilles, which he eagerly embraced, promiſing, that
on his Arrival he would write to Mr. *Fetherſtone*, and
acquaint him either with the Time of his returning to
Leghorn, or of any other Meaſures he ſhould find it neceſſary to take. He took his Leave of me with all
imaginable Teſtimonies of the moſt ſincere Friendſhip,
preſenting me with a very fine Ruby ſet with Diamonds;
in return I gave him a gold Tobacco Box, which was
very curiouſly wrought, and which had been intended
for the *Baſhaw* of *Cairo*, as a Preſent by a *French* Merchant; who dying ſuddenly, I bought it of his Nephew.

I w a s under a Neceſſity of remaining a Fortnight
longer at this Place, during which Time, an *Armenian*
Merchant, whom I had firſt ſeen at *Leghorn*, and whoſe
Name was *Ephraim Sadi*, had well nigh perſuaded me
to think of going to the *Indies*. He had been there
twice, and was immenſely rich; yet neither the Fatigues
he had endured, the Perils he had run through, or the
Wealth he had acquired, could cure him of that Itch of
Travelling which ſo unaccountably poſſeſſes the Mind

of a Man, and urges him to wander for the meer Sake of Wandering, and to fly that Quiet, to procure which is the sole reasonable Cause for Travel. This Signior *Ephraim* was a Man of wonderful Genius ; he spoke nine Languages perfectly, among which were *English* and *Low Dutch*. He had the most extensive Idea of Traffick of any Man I ever conversed with, and a Generosity in dealing, which, wherever he came, secured him a Preference in every Thing. He was perfectly skill'd in Jewels, and in all the Trades relating to them ; he understood the cutting and setting them to the utmost Nicety, and had so many Secrets for helping their Defects, and heightning their Lustre, that tho' I had been now for many Years conversant in these Things, yet I found my self, in respect to him, Mr. *Pucci*'s Secret excepted, a perfect Novice. He was affable, communicative, sincere, beneficent, and the most amiable Man in the World, if he could ever have thought of staying in a Place. He was now going to *Leghorn* ; he proposed travelling from thence by Land into *France* ; then, after visiting *Amsterdam* and *Bruffels*, he thought of going to *London* ; from thence by Sea to *Portugal* ; whence he was to sail to *Goa*, as soon as an Opportunity should offer : And all this he proposed to do in the Compass of three Years, being then about fifty-one, and having, as he assured me, never felt any Sickness, except now and then some wandering Pains in the Stomach and Bowels, which he cured by bathing, and anointing with warm Oils.

I could not forbear sometimes opposing a little his favourite Humour of Travelling, by hinting, that it took off all Love for our native Country ; that it seem'd

repugnant

repugnant to the Nature of Man, that it kept the Spirits in a continual Flutter, and that above all things it exposed Men to the Danger of immature and unprovided Deaths. He was always mightily pleased to have an Opportunity of displaying his Eloquence on this Subject. He laughed at the Love of one's Country, as an idle and narrow Notion. One God, said he, created us all; we come the same Way into the World; we have the same Business in the World, and when we go out of it we are to account before the same Judge: All Men therefore are Brethren, and the World only is every Man's Country. For my part, said he, I have seven People constantly in my Family; my Physician, who is a *Spanish Jew*; my Steward, a *Greek*; my Secretary, an *Italian*; my two Footmen, *Swiss*; my Cook, a *Frenchman*; and my Groom, a Native of *Lorrain*. We live all together very happily, and we account our selves all Countrymen. As to the Nature of Man, said he, there can be no Repugnancy to it in Travelling, any more than in any other Action; besides, there is nothing more various than the Nature of Man, and therefore every Man has a Right to do what is agreeable to him, provided it be innocent to others. As to the Hurry of Spirits, it is, continued he, a Distemper of the Mind, and wherever it seizes a Man, it seizes him in some Place or other; therefore the changing of Place, or remaining in the same Place, hath nothing to do with this, for the Mind may be kept easy and unmoved when the Body is in Motion, as well as when it is at rest; nay, I am apt to believe, that Travelling contributes to Quiet as Motion does to Ease; Change of Objects, soothing the Soul, as the Heat resulting from Motion, assuages Pain.

Pain. But in all thefe Cafes the various Tempers and Conftitutions of Men are chiefly to be regarded. Immature and unprovided Death, added he, we ought all to fear ; neither can we either by Travelling, or making long Voyages by Sea, efcape from it ; but this being fo, it is plain we may as well die in one Country as another, or to fpeak more like a Chriftian, we ought not to confider fo much where or how we may die, as in what Frame of Mind Death fhall find us. This depends upon ourfelves ; and if we take but Care to be good Men, evil Accidents, and even a fudden Death, will not much terrify or afflict us. Human Life is a checquer'd Tablet, which retains its Mixture of black and white, whether moved or left ftanding.

These were the Arguments he ufed to juftify his Love to Roving ; and tho' it muft be acknowledg'd that they are of fuch a Nature as Reafon is forced to dictate when the Imagination is too ftrong for her, yet I confefs they made fome Impreffion upon me, or, to fpeak the Truth, I was charmed with his Magnificence, and princely Way of Living, and fuffered my Mind to fwell with the vain Ambition, of imitating what I ought to have pitied. But as a waking Dream led me wrong, fo a Vifion of the Night fet me right. It happened one Evening, after having fate late with my Friend *Ephraim*, for we lodged in the fame Houfe, when I retired to my own Apartment, I found my felf little inclined to fleep, and as little inclined to read. I walked up and down for fome Time without thinking, if it be poffible, of any thing, till I found my felf weary on the fudden, and fcarce able to keep my Eyes open, when throwing off my Clothes, I got as foon as I could into Bed. I

E e 2

had

had scarce closed my Eyes, before I fancy'd my Man *Johnson* was in the Room, and that I was conversing with him as I was wont about my Affairs; to which, methought, he made me little Answer, but seem'd rather to be uneasy that I continued this Discourse. Upon this I press'd him, with much Warmth, to speak his Sentiments, assuring him, that I had a great Deference for his Advice, and that I would take nothing ill he should think fit to say to me. Upon this I thought he began to look more pleasant, and at length addressed me thus. I am always, Sir, exceedingly concerned when I differ from you in Opinion, and when my Affection for your Person obliges me to cross your Inclinations; however, give me Leave to say, that you have hitherto been guided a little too much by hasty Notions and Opinions, not quite so well digested as might have been expected from a Man of your Parts. Do not you remember, Sir, the Sentiments you had, and the Resolutions you framed in your Voyage down the *Nile?* Can you imagine, Sir, that Providence will always extricate you out of those Difficulties into which you willfully plunge your self? You left *England* because you was not safe; you left *Europe* because you had a small Fortune; you have nothing now to fear or to wish; why then would you go to the *Indies?* This *Armenian* hath no Country, and therefore he does well to look upon every one as his own; but it is not so with you; you ought to know this, and to make a right Use of it. While I fancied I was meditating on what *Johnson* had said, I awaked, but so confused and disturbed, that I much doubted whether I retained my Senses. I got up, addressed my self to those Means which never fail

to

to calm the Spirits of Men who truft in God, and by Morning compofed my felf to a fettled Refolution of returning, if it was practicable, into *England*, and there leading a quiet and retired Life.

A FEW Days after this, I received a Packet from the *Venetian* Conful, acquainting me, that a Veffel would fhortly arrive at *Rofetta* from the *Arches*, and that upon his Letter to the Captain, which was inclofed, I might find a fafe and commodious Paffage to *Leghorn*. This accordingly took effect, the Veffel arrived the fame Week, and failed a few Days after, having no Paffengers on board except Signior *Ephraim*, his Family, and my felf. There happen'd nothing fingular in our Paffage, except the Illnefs of the *Jew* Phyfician, who was fo extremely diforder'd with Sea-Sicknefs, that if we had not made the Port as we did, he would in all Likelihood have died. I affifted him the beft I could; but inafmuch as he would take no Broths of our making, I knew not what to do with him till I thought of Chicken-broth, fome of which, on feeing the *French* Cook cut off the Head of the Creature, and drain it thoroughly of its Blood, he, with fome Difficulty, confented to take which kept up his Spirits, and faved his Life. He was a very honeft Man, but moft inordinately fuperftitious, having with the *Jewifh* Obftinacy all the Punctilio of a *Spaniard*. Signior *Ephraim* depended much upon him in all Things, and with Reafon, for he was certainly a Man of Skill in his Profeffion, and of great Probity, for which the *Spanifh* Jews, perhaps, as *Spaniards*, are eminently diftinguifhed.

ON my Arrival at *Leghorn*, Mr. *Fetherftone* hardly knew me, on Account of my having loft much Flefh,

and

and my Complexion altogether. *Johnson* was gone to *Florence* to fell a large Cabinet of Medals, which I afterwards underftood was bought by a *French* Gentleman for the Chancellor of *France*. I would not fuffer Mr. *Fetherftone* to write to him of my Arrival, that I might have the Pleafure of furprifing him at his Return to *Leghorn*. In this I certainly acted very foolifhly; for tho' Mr. *Fetherftone* was fome time before he knew me, yet *Johnson* difcover'd me at firft Sight, and was fo much amazed at this unexpected Interview, that he fwoon'd, and was with Difficulty recovered. Thus, for the Gratification of an idle Humour, the meaneft Pleafure in the World, I put the Life of one of the honefteft Men in it to the Hazard, an Act for which I cannot eafily forgive my felf.

It was not long after my Return to *Leghorn*, before, in a Converfation with Signior *Ephraim*, the Price of Jewels at that Time happen'd to become the Subject of Difcourfe, he thereupon afk'd me whether I had ever feen any that were truly excellent, and of a very large Size, adding, that he had lately fent into *France* fome of the beft colour'd Stones that ever were brought into *Europe*; of which, at my Requeft, he fhew'd me the Models. Among thefe were fome Saphires, blue, and white, of a very extraordinary Size, and according to his Defcription, of uncommon Beauty; but as for the Emeralds he fent, I judged them to be far inferior to mine; and fo I told him. Upon this he defired to fee them. I fhew'd him feven, referving the four largeft I had for another Time. He faid very ingenuoufly, they were the fineft he had ever feen, that is, they had the feweft Imperfections, moft or all of which might be
taken

taken away by their being judiciously set. To cut the Matter short, he told me that he had at that time such a Commission as would enable him to give more for these Stones than I could reasonably expect, or than I could possibly get for them, especially if I sold them all together. He then named a Price, which he affirmed was the utmost he would give, and indeed it was such a one as in Prudence I could not refuse; so the Bargain was presently concluded, and I had the Pleasure of seeing this Point of a settled Fortune, which I had been so long pursuing, compleated in a few Hours. After this Signior *Ephraim* spoke to me of Diamonds, and of Rubies, but I told him that I had none worth shewing him, but that I had an Authority to dispose of some that were excellent at *Venice*, if a Person who had bid Money for them did not come up to the Price, which by the next Post I should set upon them. He smiled, and asked me if the Jewels were not in the Hands of such a Person, and if such a Man had not offered Money for them. I was amazed at this, supposing that the *Venetian* Consul at *Cairo* had spoke to him upon this Subject, but I was mistaken, the Person at *Venice* was Signior *Ephraim*'s Agent; he told me so frankly, and offered to send a Person who should pay the Money at *Venice*, provided I sent an Order for the delivering the Jewels. I accordingly consented, and Mr. *Johnson*, notwithstanding the Fatigue he had lately undergone, readily agreed to go with Signior *Redi*, the *Armenian*'s Secretary, in order to put an End to this Business which was of very great Concern.

I was afterwards informed, that Signior *Ephraim* collected all these Jewels for a *French* Merchant who had

been

been in the *Indies*, and having fold all the Stones he brought from thence, took this Method of recruiting, and by dint of his Character, got a large Profit for himfelf, tho' he gave very high Prices, yet he would deal in nothing that was not perfect in its kind. All this was nothing to me, the quick Negotiation of fuch important Affairs effectually fatisfying all my Defires, and making me richer than I thought I had any Title to be ; fo that I fometimes doubted how I came by fuch Sums of Money, and was amazed at the Kindnefs of Providence, knowing that I had not deferved fuch Things ; perhaps they were given me that I might deferve them. While Mr. *Johnfon* was gone to *Paris*, Mr. *Fetherftone* and I employed our Time in fettling a general Account, Mr. *Perez* having written him a Letter fome time before my coming to *Leghorn*, defiring it might be done as fpeedily as poffible, and fuch a Valuation made of the Effects remaining, as Mr. *Fetherftone* and I fhould agree upon and this being done, he defired the Account might be tranfmitted to Mr. *Abraham Lopez*, a Merchant at *Marfeilles*. Upon adjufting all Matters, it appear'd that there was a Balance due to him of three thoufand Piftoles, half of which Sum we remitted with the Account, and offered him the Remainder when he fhould be pleafed to draw for it ; but inftead of doing this, Mr. *Perez* wrote us a moft obliging Letter, wherein, after defiring me to take out of the Effects whatever Curiofities I might efteem, he gave all the reft to Mr. *Fetherftone*, concluding his Letter with thefe Words. *God hath now reftored to me fo ample an Eftate, that not to make my faithful Friends participate with me, would be an Ingratitude capable of drawing upon me another Reverfe of Fortune.*

AFTER

AFTER this we heard no more of Mr. *Perez*, and we had Reason to believe he did not long furvive his good Fortune, a Friend of his at *Genoa* having received a Letter by the fame Poft that we did, without ever having a fecond, and we both writ in vain to *Marfeilles* feveral Times. I neglected nothing during the Abfence of Mr. *Johnfon* that might contribute to the drawing my Affairs within a very narrow Compafs. As for Mr. *Fetherftone* his Affairs were now very eafy, and he feemed to wifh as I did for an Opportunity of returning to *England*. However we both referr'd all Thoughts of thefe Matters, till we fhou'd have difpofed of all the Curiofities we had by us, and amongft thofe there were upwards of 700 Medals of Gold, Silver, &c. We difpofed them in feveral Cabinets, together with Gems, Bafs Reliefs, and other Antiquities, with Defcriptions in *French* and *Italian*, in preparing of which we had the Affiftance of the Virtuofi. Thus employ'd, and all along with a View of returning to *England*, it fell out that one Morning after I had been awake and reflected on feveral Things, I fell faft afleep, and dreamt exactly the fame Dream I had at *Venice*, that is to fay, I faw myfelf in a large Meadow bounded by a River on the other Side, of which I faw *Lucia* walking, but whereas before I was at a vaft Diftance from the Bridge, I faw myfelf now very near it, and *Lucia* on her Side feem'd advancing to me. When I awaked and confidered this, I rofe with as much Alacrity and Satisfaction as if fome great good Luck had befallen me, and I had all that Day fuch an unufual flow of Spirits, that every Body took Notice of it. How frail a Thing is Man? a Dream alters his Conduct, and at the Diftance of thirty Years, he has a fecret Pleafure in owning his Folly.

ON

ON the Return of *Johnson* to *Leghorn*, after the first Ceremonies were over, and Mr. *Fetherstone* was withdrawn, he gave me an Account of the Success of his Journey, the Delivery of the Jewels, and presented me with a Letter from the *Venetian* Consul, which contained a short Compliment, and a Draught on a Merchant at *Leghorn*, for the Value of 300 *Sequins*, as a Compensation for the Trouble and Expence I had been at in negotiating this Affair, which I gave Mr. *Johnson* as a Gratification for many fatiguing Journies he had taken in my Service, tho' his Modesty was so great, that it was with some Difficulty I prevailed upon him to accept it. These Things adjusted, I was upon the Point of calling Mr. *Fetherstone*, when *Johnson* stopt me, stay Sir, said he, I have Business now of another Nature with you. I call'd on Mr. *Hales* to know whether he had had any farther Account of your Affairs, there with some Difficulty this Letter was found, which had been transmitted to *Geneva*, and returned from thence; so that to be sure it is of an old Date, I had several Times a Mind to open it, but having considered better of it I desisted. This Letter was from *Lucia*, it contained an Account of her Brother's carrying her into *England* a kind of Prisoner, under Pretence of her eloping from her Husband. On her coming to *London*, he would not suffer her to stir abroad, but on Condition of marrying the Gentleman lately returned from the *Indies*, which she absolutely refused, upon which he hurried her down into *Leicestershire*, to an Aunt of this Gentleman's, where she was not less strictly guarded, till at last she took a bold Resolution of Writing to a Justice of Peace a little before the Assizes, and enclosing a Letter

to

to the Judge, which throwing out of her Window into the *London* Road was taken up, and delivered as directed. Upon this she was immediately set at Liberty, and retiring to her Father's House in *Lincolnshire*, found him still living, but so childish, that he hardly knew her. Her Brother-in-Law and Sister not a little incensed against her by the Arts of her Brother, which afflicted her so much, that she resolved to come to *London* and live privately there. These Transactions took up seven Months, and the Letter being transmitted to *Venice*, was sent from thence to *Geneva*, where my Landlord being dead, it was according to a Direction sent with it returned to *Venice*, where it lay till it fell thus into my Hands.

I instantly wrote an Answer according to a Direction at the Foot of this Letter, beseeching *Lucia* to afford me a farther Account of her Affairs as soon as possible. In the mean Time I redoubled my Preparations for returning into *England* at all Events, tho' by the Way, this was a very mad Proceeding, considering that I stood out-lawed, and the *English* Court did not shew any great Inclination to treat Persons in my Condition with Lenity. However Mr. *Fetherstone* and *Johnson* having as strong a Passion as I for seeing once again their native Land, did not oppose me therein, relying upon my Prudence in taking Care of my own Safety. When the Time was elapsed, in which I might reasonably have expected a Return from *London*, I grew very impatient, and at length melancholy. A thousand Inventions occurr'd for gaining Intelligence from *England*, and were thrown aside again as impracticable.

At length a Letter from *Lucia* arrived, which deliver'd me from this Perplexity that had wasted my Spirits more than

than all the fatiguing Journies I had taken, and all the Difficulties I had run through. This Letter informed me, that her Father being dead, she was gone down to Leicestershire to settle her Affairs when my Letter came, and that it had been kept for her till her Return; that her Circumstances were now very easy, tho' the barbarous unkindness of her Relations had for two Years and a half, made her suffer the greatest Difficulties; that she had some Interest with the *Temple Family*, with Sir *Leoline Jenkins*, Secretary of State, and the Lord *Daventry*, lately created Lord High Chancellor, so that she made no Question of procuring my Outlawry to be reversed, if I was really determined to come to *England*. I mentioned something of this to Mr. *Fetherstone*, but he immediately suggested another Method, which was addressing myself to the Duke of *Bucks*, tho' he was at that Time on bad Terms with the Court; but he advised that the other Interest also should be kept and made Use of. His Reasons were these, he said, that the discontented Party in *England* were very numerous and powerful, and that if I applied myself to the Ministry, they would not fail to cause such Representations to be made, as might possibly prevent the Outlawry from being reversed; but that if I applied to the others, they would recommend the Thing to the Duke of *Monmouth*; upon which it would in all Probability be referred to the Lawyers, and then my Interest with the *Chancellor* and the *Secretary*, would stand me in great stead. But above all he pressed me to get as strong Recommendations as I cou'd to Sir *William Temple*, who was then in *Holland*, for as he was a Gentleman agreeable to both Parties, and had at that Time a very

great

great Intereſt, there was Reaſon to believe his eſpouſing
my Cauſe would effectually ſecure it Succeſs. To this
I anſwered, that I had no manner of Intereſt with the
Duke of *Buckingham*, that except what I learned from
him, I ſcarce knew any Thing of the State of my own
Country, but that however I was very anxious to ſee it
again. You do not at preſent, Sir, ſaid Mr. *Fetherſtone*,
want Money, and he that hath that, hath an Intereſt, or
the Means of creating an Intereſt in all Courts, and in
that of *England* particularly. I told him, that having
been never over fond of Money, I ſhou'd not be un-
reaſonably tenacious of it at this Time. He ſmil'd, and
made me Anſwer, he wou'd make it his Buſineſs to
conſider how it might be employ'd for my Advantage.
In a Day or two *Johnſon*, he, and I, being together, I
asked him whether he had conſidered as he promiſed me
of a Method for facilitating what we all ſo much wiſh'd,
a ſafe and ſpeedy Return into our own Country. Mr.
Fetherſtone anſwered he had, and that he wou'd be accountable for its Succeſs. *Johnſon* ſeemed to be no leſs
pleaſed at this than I, for as he told me, he was not a
little diffident on this Head, tho' he ſaid nothing for Fear
of diſcouraging me. We then deſired Mr. *Fetherſtone*
to explain himſelf upon this Point. There wants, ſaid
he, but very little Explanation. You know Sir, continued
he, addreſſing himſelf to me, how I procured the Favour of his Grace of *Buckingham* once before; we are
now better provided, I will carry over a Cargo of Curioſities, ſome Jewels, and a little Money, and in a
Month or two be aſſured that you may follow me,
provided you furniſh me with Inſtructions how to cultivate that Intereſt which you ſay you have yourſelf at

that

that Court. All this appeared as feasible to us as it did to him, and therefore that no Time might be lost in the Execution of our Project, I wrote that very Night to *Lucia*, to acquaint her therewith, and we resolved that Mr. *Fetherstone* shou'd depart the very Moment we received her Answer. But our Measures received an unexpected Change in a few Days, by Means of a Letter that I received from *Lucia*; she advised me, that two Persons in the same Circumstances with myself, had been pardoned at the Intercession of the Duke of *Monmouth*, and that as she was related to Mr. *Draycot*, who was his Grace's Gentleman of the Horse, she look'd upon it as a Thing certain, that if I thought it proper, she cou'd secure an Interest there. Upon maturely deliberating this Proposition, *Johnson* offered it as his Opinion, that Mr. *Fetherstone* shou'd without more ado, embark on Board a Ship ready to sail for *England*, in order to co-operate with this Lady in so important an Affair. Mr. *Fetherstone* readily came into this Motion, and the third Day after sail'd for *England*, of which I also advertised *Lucia* by Letter. It must be owned, that tho' Mr. *Fetherstone*'s Care and Diligence conducted this Matter to a happy issue, yet our Measures were very precipitate, in as much as they exposed Mr. *Fetherstone* to some Hazard, and drove this Business very hard, which rather shou'd have been conducted with leisure. However as it was attended with no Loss but that of Money, I had no Occasion to repine, neither did I, but I cou'd not help seeing that I had acted wrong, and therefore I note it, for tho' *Luck* may cure *Blunders*, yet it ought never to hide them.

DURING

During Mr. *Fetherstone*'s Absence I had Recourse to my old Method of diverting myself by digesting my Papers, and by putting into Writing such Observations as occurred to me on several Subjects. I likewise made a choice Collection of *Italian* Books, and of such *Greek* and *Latin* Authors as had been printed at *Rome* and at *Venice*. I likewise consulted the *Virtuosi* on some of the many Oriental Manuscripts I had brought over, and by these Arts of withdrawing from myself passed my Days with tolerable Ease, which otherwise I believe I shou'd not have done. One Morning when I was hard at my Studies I was informed that a strange Gentleman desired to speak with me; they call'd him strange, because they saw he was just arrived. He proved to be a *French* Jeweller, sent on purpose to know if I had or cou'd procure one Emerald more of the Size of them I had sold to Seignior *Ephraim*. I told the Gentleman I could not, at which he seemed very much concerned, adding, that if I cou'd, he wou'd have given a great Price for it. I told him I had an Emerald by me which was larger than any of those. Ay, Sir said he, but then it must be foul, I told him it was not, and upon my producing it, he was so amazed, that he cou'd hardly speak. He was himself a very good Judge of Stones, yet we had some Difficulty in settling the Point whether it was or was not an Emerald, in respect to which he insisted on his shewing it to the Jeweller of the Grand Duke, to which I wou'd by no means consent; however I told him, if he wou'd buy it, he might then shew it to whom he wou'd, and that he shou'd deposite the Money in a Person's Hands whom I wou'd name, who shou'd restore it to him if he was not contented in three

Days

Days Time. To this he wou'd have affented, but he had not the Money ready, not expecting to be afked above half the Sum I infifted upon for this Stone. This Difficulty I prefently removed, for I confented to take a third Part of the Money down, and two Parts in Bills, which being depofited in the Hands of an *Englifh* Merchant I named, the Stone fhou'd be produced to the Jeweller of the Grand Duke. In three Days the whole Affair was adjufted to every Bodies Satisfaction, the Grand Duke's Jeweller offering a hundred Crowns to my Chapman to quit his Bargain, which he refufed to do, and fo I received the third Part in Money, and Bills for the other two thirds immediately. Another Piece of unexpected good Fortune, for which I ftood accountable to Providence.

BEFORE I received any News from Mr. *Fetherftone* I had another Letter from *Lucia*, purporting that my worthy Coufins having Notice of fome Applications made for reverfing my Outlawry, were come up to Town in order to folicite againft it, to prevent my filing a Bill for the Principal and Intereft of the Mortgage on my Uncle's Eftate. The Paffion of going Home was fo ftrong upon me, that I immediately executed a general Releafe before a Notary Publick, and tranfmitted it to *London*, where Mr. *Fetherftone* delivered it to my Coufins, who upon this became my very good Friends, and joined heartily in doing me all the Service they cou'd, the rather I fuppofe, becaufe they apprehended that I was returning Home very rich. However when all came to all, and much Time and Money had been fpent in procuring a Warrant for the Reverfe of my Outlawry, it appeared that I had never been Out-

outlawed at all. My Name was in a Lift for that Purpofe, and part of that Lift were outlawed, and the Remainder were ordered to be outlawed at the next County Court, but by the Death of the Sheriff, and the removing the Under Sheriff this Order flept, and there was no Record of the Outlawry, and confequently no poffibility of reverfing it. On this Head I had no body to blame but myfelf; I had been advifed of the Outlawry by my Uncle, I acquainted Mr. *Fetherftone* with it, and my Coufins affured him, that the Thing was fo. When it came out, as it did, the younger of my Coufins afked Mr. *Fetherftone* what he intended to do. I intend anfwered he, to write to him to come Home. Not fo, faid my Coufin, he hath been very generous to us, and we will be juft to him; thefe Courtiers have had his Money, why fhould he not have a general Pardon? This was well put in, for otherwife I had affuredly come Home, and when the *Swearing Harveft* came on, I had certainly ftood a Chance of being put into a *Popifh* or a *Proteftant* Plot, if not both. In confequence then of this juft Obfervation a Warrant for a Pardon was obtained, of which I had Advice given me, it being fuppofed that I might with Security enough now return Home.

I received this Letter in the Month of *March*, and refolved immediately to embark for *England*. On this Occafion *Johnfon* interpofed, he faid he apprehended it wou'd be better if I did not go to *England* till the Pardon was actually fealed, that it was not impoffible but new Difficulties might be ftarted, and that it would be very difficult to get over any of them if I was in *England* at the Time. I was however not to be moved,

F f

which

which when *Johnson* faw, he made another Propofition; it was this, that he fhould embark with my Effects on Board a Veffel then in the Port, and that I fhould go by Land to *Paris*. This was fo reafonable that I could not but approve it. Accordingly three Days after *Johnfon* had embarked I fet out for *France*, and travelling very leifurely, arrived at *Paris* the 21ft of *April*.

I wrote that very Night to *London*, and by the Return of the Poft was acquainted of *Johnfon's* fafe Arrival with my Effects, and that my Pardon was fealed but the Day before; fo that *Johnfon's* Forefight came in Time, and I reaped that Benefit, for which few Men are thankful, the Bleffing of having a Servant wifer than myfelf. All Obftacles being now removed, I fet out from *Paris* with the Secretary of M. *Courtin* the *French* Ambaffador for *Calais*, and the Day after we arrived there, croffed to *Dover* by Noon, and the next Day being *May* the 9th 1676 arrived in *London*, where I found all my Friends at Mr. *Fetherftone's* Lodgings in *Aldermanbury*, having been fixteen Years out of the Kingdom, and returning now almoft as great a Stranger to it as if I had not been born therein.

F I N I S.

I N D E X.

A

His

INDEX.

INDEX.

I N D E X.

His

INDEX.

INDEX.

F

INDEX.

F

G

INDEX.

J

INDEX.

I

Account

INDEX.

INDEX.

INDEX.

The

I N D E X.

INDEX.

F I N I S.

CPSIA information can be obtained
at www.ICGtesting.com
Printed in the USA
BVHW080546270819
556819BV00010B/1780/P